The Audubon Society Master Guide to Birding

**A Chanticleer
Press Edition**

Consultants
Davis W. Finch
Paul Lehman
J. V. Remsen, Jr.

Authors
Henry T. Armistead
Stephen F. Bailey
Larry R. Ballard
Louis R. Bevier
Clait E. Braun
Peter F. Cannell
Sadie Coats
Charles T. Collins
Thomas H. Davis
Susan Roney Drennan
Kim R. Eckert
John Farrand, Jr.
Davis W. Finch
Eric D. Forsman
Philip K. Gaddis
Kimball L. Garrett
Daniel D. Gibson
Helen Hays
Kenn Kaufman
Wesley E. Lanyon
Paul Lehman
Dennis J. Martin
Guy McCaskie
Ron Naveen
Wayne R. Petersen
J. V. Remsen, Jr.
Lester L. Short
Arnold Small

David Stirling
Paul W. Sykes, Jr.
Scott B. Terrill
Theodore G. Tobish Jr.
James A. Tucker
Peter D. Vickery
Terence Wahl
Richard Webster
D. H. S. Wehle
Claudia Wilds

The Audubon Society Master Guide to Birding

2 Gulls to Dippers

John Farrand, Jr.,
Editor

 Alfred A. Knopf, New York

This is a Borzoi Book
Published by Alfred A. Knopf, Inc.

Prepared and produced by
Chanticleer Press, Inc., New York.

Color reproductions by Nievergelt Repro AG, Zurich, Switzerland.
Type set in Century Expanded by Dix Type Inc., Syracuse,
New York. Printed and bound by Dai Nippon Printing Co., Ltd.,
Tokyo, Japan.

First Printing
Library of Congress Catalog Number: 83-47945
ISBN: 0-394-53384-4

Contents

Acknowledgments

This book was written not only for the birders of North America but by them. While preparing these guides even my non-birding associates at Chanticleer Press became converts. I was gratified when an enthusiastic group turned out recently in the early morning for a staff bird walk in Central Park. I wish to celebrate the spirit of my colleagues and to thank them for their good will and their professional help.

I am deeply grateful to the authors of the species accounts, both for their expert prose and for suggestions on what photographs and artwork were necessary to accompany their text, and for numerous suggestions and advice. Without their enthusiastic and industrious cooperation, this book would not have been possible. I am equally thankful to the authors of the special text sections, whose contributions have expanded the scope of the book.

Davis W. Finch, Paul Lehman, and J. V. Remsen served as consultants and read all or some of the species accounts. Their careful perusal of the text resulted in many improvements, and the authors and editors are indebted to them.

In addition to the authors and consultants, thanks are due to many other birders and ornithologists for suggestions, advice, encouragement, and additional tangible assistance in the preparation of this series. I would like to make special mention of John Bull of the American Museum of Natural History for his frequent advice on nomenclature and distribution. Others who have assisted the authors and editors are Dennis J. Abbott, Paul Adamus, C. Wesley Biggs, Paul A. Buckley, William S. Clark, Elaine Cook, Betty Darling Cotrille, Robert H. Day, Joseph DiCostanzo, Matthew P. Drennan, Jon Dunn, R. Michael Erwin, Norm Famous, Frank B. Gill, Sharon Goldwasser, Delphine Haley, John P. Hubbard, George L. Hunt, Jr., Ned K. Johnson, Lars Jonsson, Ivy Kuspit, Mary LeCroy, Lori Leonardi, Trevor Lloyd-Evans, Fred E. Lohrer, Frederick C. Mish, Burt L. Monroe, Jr., Gale Monson, Joe Morlan, J. P. Myers, John P. O'Neill, Dennis R. Paulson, Roger Tory Peterson, William C. Russell, Lawrence A. Ryel, Gary D. Schnell, Fred C. Sibley, Kenneth K. Tate, Michael H. Tove, Guy A. Tudor, Barbara Vickery, Peter Warshall, Bret Whitney, Janet Witzeman, and Alan Wormington.

I am deeply indebted to Arnold Small, Kenneth Fink, Herbert Clarke, and the 203 other photographers whose work forms the bulk of the color illustrations in these volumes. I would like to thank Thomas H. Davis, who helped to identify the difficult plumages of gulls, and Stephen A. Bailey for his assistance in selecting photographs of western *Empidonax* flycatchers. I appreciate the help of Robert Cardillo, Martine Culbertson, Alec Forbes-Watson, and Mark Robbins of VIREO, the growing library of bird photographs at the Academy of Natural Sciences in Philadelphia, for their hospitality and willingness to make their files available to me; to Charles Walcott and David Blanton of the Laboratory of Ornithology at Cornell University for permitting us to use their photograph collection for this project; and to Helen Kittinger of the Alabama Ornithological Society for generously sharing the photograph collections of that organization.

Of the many fine bird artists whose work so enhances this book, I am especially indebted to art editor Al Gilbert, who took on the task of assigning the paintings and drawings, coordinated the efforts of the team of artists he assembled, and executed many fine paintings himself, and to art consultant Guy A. Tudor, whose valuable advice was frequently sought and generously given. The other artists who have contributed their work to this book are James E. Coe, Michael DiGiorgio, Georges Dremeaux, Robert

Gillmor, H. Jon Janosik, Michel Kleinbaum, Lawrence B. McQueen, John P. O'Neill, John C. Yrizarry, and Dale A. Zimmerman. All of these artists have been inspired by the late George M. Sutton, and many have benefited from his direct tutelage in the art of bird painting. "Doc" Sutton would surely have been proud of the illustrations herein—of their lifelike quality and the careful attention to proper habitat. The artists would like to dedicate their work in these volumes to the memory of George M. Sutton—ornithologist, teacher, friend, and one of America's greatest painters of bird life.

Special thanks are due to the authorities of several museums for making specimens available to the artists and authors: Lester L. Short and his staff at the American Museum of Natural History; Ralph W. Schreiber and Kimball L. Garrett of the Los Angeles County Museum of Natural History; J. V. Remsen and John P. O'Neill of the Louisiana State University Museum of Zoology; and Stephen M. Russell of the Department of Ecology and Evolutionary Biology at the University of Arizona.

To Les Line, Editor-in-Chief of Audubon magazine, I am indebted for his early endorsement of the idea of this work, and for his constant encouragement during its preparation.

I am very grateful to Massimo Vignelli, who translated the concept of the book into an effective and workable design.

At Chanticleer Press, I owe a debt of gratitude to Paul Steiner for his energetic and wholehearted enthusiasm for the project since its earliest stages; to Gudrun Buettner for the original conception of the book and for her spirited assistance in solving editorial and graphic problems during the preparation of the series; to Susan Costello, whose encouragement and problem-solving abilities have done much to make this book what it is; to Ann Whitman for her assistance in editing and coordinating the manuscript in its various stages and her seemingly tireless attention to editorial details; to Mary Beth Brewer for her invaluable help in editing the special essays and organizing the material to enable us to meet our deadlines; to Carol Nehring, for the knowledge and expertise she brought to bear on the layouts, and her assistants Laurie Baker, Ayn Svoboda, and Karen Wollman; to Helga Lose and Amy Roche, for their expert efforts in ensuring the accuracy of color reproductions and shepherding the project through its intricate production stages; to Edward Douglas for his assistance in gathering and selecting the tens of thousands of photographs that were reviewed during the preparation of this book; and to Karel Birnbaum, Katherine Booz, Lori Renn, and Susan Van Pelt for their assistance in editorial matters.

At Alfred A. Knopf, Inc., I wish to extend my appreciation to Robert Gottlieb and Anthony M. Schulte, whose sponsorship of the project and confidence in it made this ambitious work possible; to Charles Elliott for his unwavering support and help in shaping the editorial content of the work; to Angus Cameron for his far-ranging knowledge of natural history; and to Barbara Bristol, who should be commended for her competent stewardship of the guides.

John Farrand, Jr.

The Audubon Society

The National Audubon Society is among the oldest and largest private conservation organizations in the world. With over 500,000 members and more than 480 local chapters across the country, the Society works in behalf of our natural heritage through environmental education and conservation action. It protects wildlife in more than 70 sanctuaries from coast to coast. It also operates outdoor education centers and ecology workshops and publishes the prizewinning *Audubon* magazine, *American Birds* magazine, newsletters, films, and other educational materials. For further information regarding membership in the Society, write to the National Audubon Society, 950 Third Avenue, New York, New York 10022.

Preface

For years the birding community has been waiting for an advanced
field guide, one that would include the increasingly sophisticated and
subtle clues to bird identification discovered in recent decades.
These have been brought to light by birders whose expertise may lie
with a particular group of birds, the birds of a specific habitat or
region, or a single species. The new information resulting from these
field studies has validated our assumption that it is impossible for an
individual birder to know everything about all the species on our
continent.

For this reason we have tried to prepare the most complete, up-to-
date, and useful field identification guide ever devised. We began by
assembling a distinguished panel of expert authors from all parts of
the continent, from Florida to Alaska and California to Maine. The
61 authors contributed 835 species accounts in their areas of
concentration or wrote special essays; consultants with a special
understanding of both the eastern and the western regions reviewed
the text. In addition, we asked the authors to advise us on
photographs required to illustrate each species. In some instances a
single photograph was sufficient; in others up to six pictures were
required. We invited the most accomplished bird photographers to
submit their work. From the tens of thousands of transparencies
that we reviewed, we selected those that best show the diagnostic
field marks of each bird. To illustrate those rare or elusive species
that are infrequently photographed, we commissioned nine well-
known artists to paint portraits of the birds in their habitats. Artists
also provided the hundreds of black-and-white drawings, many of
them flight diagrams, to supplement the field marks shown in the
color photographs and paintings.

While these guides have been designed to satisfy the demands of
advanced birders, we have also supplied beginners with what they
need to know to start an absorbing hobby that can last a lifetime. To
provide the vital information required during the few seconds a bird
may be visible, we list key field marks for each color illustration.
For further clarification, those features that can be easily seen are
shown with arrows and numbers on the illustration. Maps that
illustrate the range descriptions are also given. Of interest to
birders of all levels are the special essays that expand the scope of
the guide. They explain how to find and identify birds, how to report
the finding of a rare bird, what rare bird alerts are and who to call to
find out what rare birds are currently in your area, and what birding
equipment you will find useful in the field.

Rather than present all of this material in a single massive volume,
we decided to divide it into three volumes, each of which may be
conveniently carried into the field. We have arranged the species
according to the latest classification of North American birds
adopted by the American Ornithologists' Union in 1982. Accidental
species are placed in an appendix of the volume that covers birds
related to it.

We hope these guides, with their contributions from many experts,
will be what they are intended to be: a master guide to birding.

Part One

Introduction

Bird identification has today almost become a science. Using color, pattern, shape, size, voice, habitat, and behavior, birders are continually finding new ways to distinguish similar species. The journals *American Birds* and *Birding* frequently publish articles on field identification, while at the annual meetings of the American Birding Association, birders attend seminars on how to identify such puzzling groups as storm-petrels, immature gulls, the small sandpipers known as "peeps," and diurnal birds of prey. Birders have spent long hours in the field working out subtle but useful distinctions, such as the differences in the head shapes of gulls, in the wing- and tail-flicking of *Empidonax* flycatchers, and the flight characteristics of storm-petrels. There are now specialists in the identification of shorebirds, gulls, storm-petrels, shearwaters, and hawks. Clues are being found that allow us to differentiate birds that have long been considered indistinguishable.

Birding has come a long way during its history, and the term "birder" itself, in the evolution of its meaning, reflects the change in our attitude toward birds. For centuries a birder was someone who killed birds, usually for sport or for food; Shakespeare used the term in this sense. The modern meaning of the term arose in the 1940s, as birding became an increasingly popular pastime. Today's birders, armed with binoculars, telescopes, and cameras, and aided by the great collections made by the bird students of the 19th century, are vastly more sophisticated than their counterparts of decades ago.

Ludlow Griscom

Born in New York City in 1890, Ludlow Griscom may justly be called the father of modern field identification. He began attending meetings of the Linnaean Society of New York at an early age. Entirely on his own, he set out to learn the birds of the northeastern United States. Later in his life he wrote:

"At a meeting of the Linnaean Society of New York when a school boy, I reported having seen Bicknell's Thrush [a form of the Gray-cheeked Thrush], my identification being based on the erroneous supposition that its call-note was diagnostic. The resultant storm of criticism rendered me practically speechless. Then and there I planned to become a reliable observer and to investigate the scientific possibilities of sight identification."

The results of this determination were not long in coming. Although his prowess in field identification was doubted by many of his colleagues, Griscom developed an ability to identify birds in the field better than anyone else in his time. To prove his point, he finally took one of his friends, a doubting Thomas, into the field. When Griscom identified a small bird high in the trees overhead as a female Cape May Warbler, his friend was skeptical but prepared. Having brought along his shotgun, he collected the bird. When the specimen was retrieved from the ground, they found it was, as Griscom had said, a female Cape May Warbler. After a few more incidents of this kind, the idea that birds were identifiable while still alive and in the field began to gain ground.

The 19th Century

The practice of shooting birds rather than just looking at them was standard among serious ornithologists in North America before Griscom's time. The main method of study for men like Alexander Wilson, John James Audubon, and Thomas Nuttall was to shoot the birds they encountered and then identify them in the hand.

Most birders were men of leisure or professional collectors, and their attention was devoted to discovering new species of birds and documenting, with specimens, the ranges of these species. Although

these pioneering ornithologists learned much about the habits of
birds, as an examination of Wilson's nine-volume *American
Ornithology* or Audubon's five-volume *Ornithological Biography* will
attest, there was only one way to enter the field of ornithology—
armed with a shotgun.

Gaining a knowledge of birds in the first half of the 19th century was
a long and arduous task, the work of a lifetime. North American
birds were still poorly understood; many species had not yet been
discovered, and males and females of a single bird were sometimes
considered separate species. Throughout much of the 19th century,
for instance, there were thought to be three species of
waterthrushes, rather than two. Moreover, the differences between
species that had been discovered were sometimes unappreciated; it
was not until 1811, for example, that Alexander Wilson established
that the Common Nighthawk and the Whip-poor-will, two abundant
eastern birds, are two separate species. A student of birds during
this period faced enormous difficulties; communication between
ornithologists was poor, and there was no reliable book on the bird
life of North America until 1808, when the first volume of Wilson's
American Ornithology appeared.

A major ornithological work in its day was Elliott Coues' two-
volume *Key to North American Birds*, published in 1872 and still in
print in the early 20th century. This monumental book began with a
58-page section entitled "Field Ornithology: being a manual for the
collecting, preparing, and preserving of birds." In counseling
beginning ornithologists, Coues stated: "The Double-barrelled Shot
Gun is your main reliance."

The only bird records that were accepted were those accompanied
by a specimen. This attitude is succinctly stated in an expression
common among ornithologists of the day: "What's hit is history;
what's missed is mystery." Private collectors assembled large
cabinets of bird specimens, just as entomologists do today. These
specimens eventually found their way into public institutions and
now form the core of the collections of many museums.

Toward the end of the 19th century, the shotgun began to give way
to binoculars and telescopes. By then nearly all North American
bird species had been discovered and their ranges established with
collected specimens; the sequence of their molts and plumages was
generally understood. This gradual change came about partly
because ornithologists were turning their attention to the study of
living birds in the field and partly, perhaps, because of the growing
public distaste for killing birds that were not game birds or species
thought to be harmful to crops and livestock. Books began to appear
in which field identification was stressed. Foremost among these
were Frank M. Chapman's *Handbook of Birds of Eastern North
America*, published in 1895, and Florence Merriam Bailey's
Handbook of Birds of Western North America, which appeared in
1902. Both of these books were less cumbersome than earlier bird
books had been, and had briefer descriptions. But even Chapman's
book included complicated "keys" intended for identification in the
hand, and Chapman considered a shotgun an important piece of
equipment in bird study.

Birding Today

The development of field identification techniques was gradual. As
late as 1922 Ludlow Griscom himself had certain reservations that
seem amusing today. He wrote, for example, that it was "practically
impossible" to distinguish immature Forster's, Arctic, and Common
terns, the two species of scaups, male Cooper's and female Sharp-
shinned hawks, and immature Blackpoll and Bay-breasted warblers.
He considered it "very difficult" to tell apart adult Great and
Double-crested cormorants, female Common and Red-breasted
mergansers, Snowy Egrets and immature Little Blue Herons,

Greater and Lesser yellowlegs, and Herring and Ring-billed gulls. Yet through the efforts of Griscom and the younger men he influenced, among them Allan D. Cruickshank, Joseph J. Hickey, and Roger Tory Peterson, field identification became respectable. At the same time on the West Coast, Ralph Hoffmann was writing *Birds of the Pacific States;* this ground-breaking book appeared in 1927 and was the first to use the term "field mark"—a term familiar to all birders today. Hoffmann italicized his field marks, just as present-day field guides do, and his descriptions were brief, concentrating on the points of distinction between species.

It was Roger Tory Peterson, a disciple of Griscom but like him largely self-taught, who put field identification on firm footing. His *Field Guide to the Birds* was published in 1934 and his *Field Guide to Western Birds* in 1941, and both have appeared in several editions. These were the first truly compact field guides, and with Peterson's own paintings, they resolved the distinctions between the "impossible" or "very difficult" species that Griscom had listed just a few years earlier. The guides gave field marks for all the species then known to occur regularly in North America. Bird identification was now within the reach of anyone willing to learn about it. No mention was made of shotguns; binoculars and telescopes were standard equipment for birders.

Today only a small number of museum ornithologists still require a specimen to verify an unusual sighting, and specimens have become very difficult to obtain. Federal and state permits are usually issued only to professional ornithologists and stipulate which species and how many specimens may be collected. Moreover, rarities usually turn up in parks, wildlife refuges, and bird sanctuaries—places where collecting is impossible. Birders today often document rarities with a camera and recognize them by using the many new field marks that have been found since Ludlow Griscom first made field identification an exacting and respected pursuit. Griscom once said that the secret to identifying birds in the field was to have as clear a mental image as possible of each species. The mental images of the modern birder are growing clearer every year.

John Farrand, Jr.

Head
1. *Malar streak/*
   Mustache
2. *Throat*
3. *Chin*
4. *Lower mandible*
5. *Upper mandible*
6. *Lores*
7. *Forehead*
8. *Median crown stripe*
9. *Crown*
10. *Eyebrow*
11. *Eye-ring*
12. *Nape*
13. *Ear coverts*

Body
1. *Breast*
2. *Lesser wing coverts/*
   Shoulder
3. *Median wing coverts*
4. *Greater wing coverts*
5. *Belly*
6. *Flanks*
7. *Back*
8. *Scapulars*
9. *Wing bars*
10. *Tertials*
11. *Rump*
12. *Secondaries*
13. *Uppertail coverts*
14. *Outer tail feathers*
15. *Undertail coverts*
16. *Primaries*
17. *Leg/Tarsus*

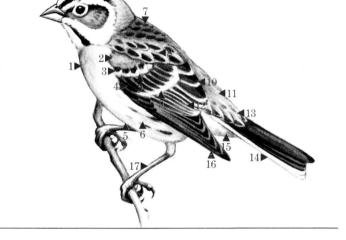

Upperwing Surface
1. *Primaries*
2. *Primary coverts*
3. *Alula*
4. *Wrist*
5. *Lesser wing coverts*
6. *Median wing coverts*
7. *Scapulars*
8. *Greater wing coverts*
9. *Tertials*
10. *Secondaries*

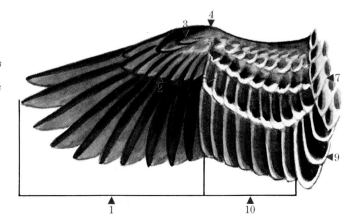

How to Use This Guide

Experienced birders will already know how to use this guide. In each volume the families and species are arranged according to the latest classification of the American Ornithologists' Union, adopted in 1982; this new sequence is followed by professional ornithologists. In all, the three volumes treat 68 families and 835 species. All but the rarest birds—116 accidental or casual species that have been recorded in North America only a few times—are treated in full; these rare birds are discussed in an appendix of the volume that contains their close relatives. If you are familiar with the new A.O.U. sequence, you can quickly refer to the proper volume and page. You can also locate a particular species by consulting the index; each volume has an index to its contents, and Volume III has a comprehensive index to all three volumes.

If you are a beginning birder, take some time to familiarize yourself with the birds covered in these guides. Examine the color plates, and note the kinds of field marks that are useful in identifying a species and in distinguishing it from similar species. Read the family descriptions, which summarize the general appearance of the birds in each family. Note that many species occur in more than one plumage, depending on the season or on the age, sex, or geographical origin of the bird. Take a moment to see how a range map illustrates the range statement for each species; the map should tell you at a glance which species are likely to occur in your area.

Illustrations

In this guide, the color illustrations and text face each other for speedy reference. Each species may have from one to six color illustrations, arranged in an order that facilitates comparison with similar plumages of other species. Next to each color illustration is a small "plate key," that is, a black-and-white reproduction of the color plate. Superimposed on this plate key are numbered red arrows, corresponding to a numbered list of field marks. Beneath this list of numbered features, other field marks such as size, shape, behavior, voice, and habitat are given. Numerous black-and-white drawings, often bearing numbered arrows as well, supplement the color plates. These drawings generally depict the same plumage as that shown in the color plates; a drawing that illustrates a different plumage is accompanied by a label.

Each family of birds begins with a general description of the family and a list of all of the members of the family found in North America. Accidental species, which are treated in an appendix, appear in light-face type in this list.

Each text entry begins with the English and scientific names of the species. A typical species account goes on to discuss the bird's habitat, its behavioral characteristics, and other useful identification information, followed by the following sections:

Description

The description begins with the approximate length of the bird both in inches and in centimeters. The bird's shape, color, and pattern are described, and where necessary, several different plumages are discussed, along with other features that vary in importance, depending on the bird. (For example, bill color may clinch identification of one species, but be of only very minor interest in another.) Geographical forms that were once considered distinct species are included; many of these forms have widely used English names of their own; where these names are mentioned, they are given in quotation marks.

Voice

The voice is described for all species in which it is useful for identification. In general, only diagnostic songs and calls are given.

Similar Species
This section refers the reader to those species with which the bird is most likely to be confused; in many cases, a brief comparative description gives the most important differences between the two. In a few instances, a bird is so distinctive that no section on similar species is included. Accidental species are indicated by an asterisk.

Range

Breeding range

Winter range

Permanent range

The breeding range of a species is generally given first, followed by the winter range. Where only one range is outlined, it may be assumed that the bird is sedentary. A brief indication of the ranges of birds outside of North America is also given. Range maps accompany the range statements. The breeding range is indicated on the map by diagonal hatching. Where there is overlap between the breeding and winter ranges, or wherever a species occurs year-round, both ranges are superimposed. For consistency, the ranges are cut off at the Mexican border, even though the ranges of many species extend into Mexico or beyond. In the case of very rare species that occur in North America infrequently as well as those that have a very limited distribution, no range map is provided.

Other Features
This guide includes a number of features of interest to both beginning and advanced birders. In the front of each book, the orders of birds covered in that volume are described briefly. Drawings have been provided to show the parts of a bird, and special essays on How to Identify Birds and How to Find Birds have also been included. In the back of each volume, a glossary defines technical terms used in the text. Also in the back of each volume is a section that discusses the accidental species that fall within the scope of that volume. The section on accidentals includes brief descriptions and an indication of where these very rare species have occurred. While the guide follows the A.O.U. sequence and nomenclature, the accidentals included are those recognized in the *A.B.A. Checklist: Birds of Continental United States and Canada,* second edition, published in 1982 by the American Birding Association.

Special essays discuss how to report the finding of a rare bird, what rare bird alerts are, and the telephone numbers to call to find out which rare species are currently in your area. Finally, an essay describes what birding equipment you will find useful in the field.

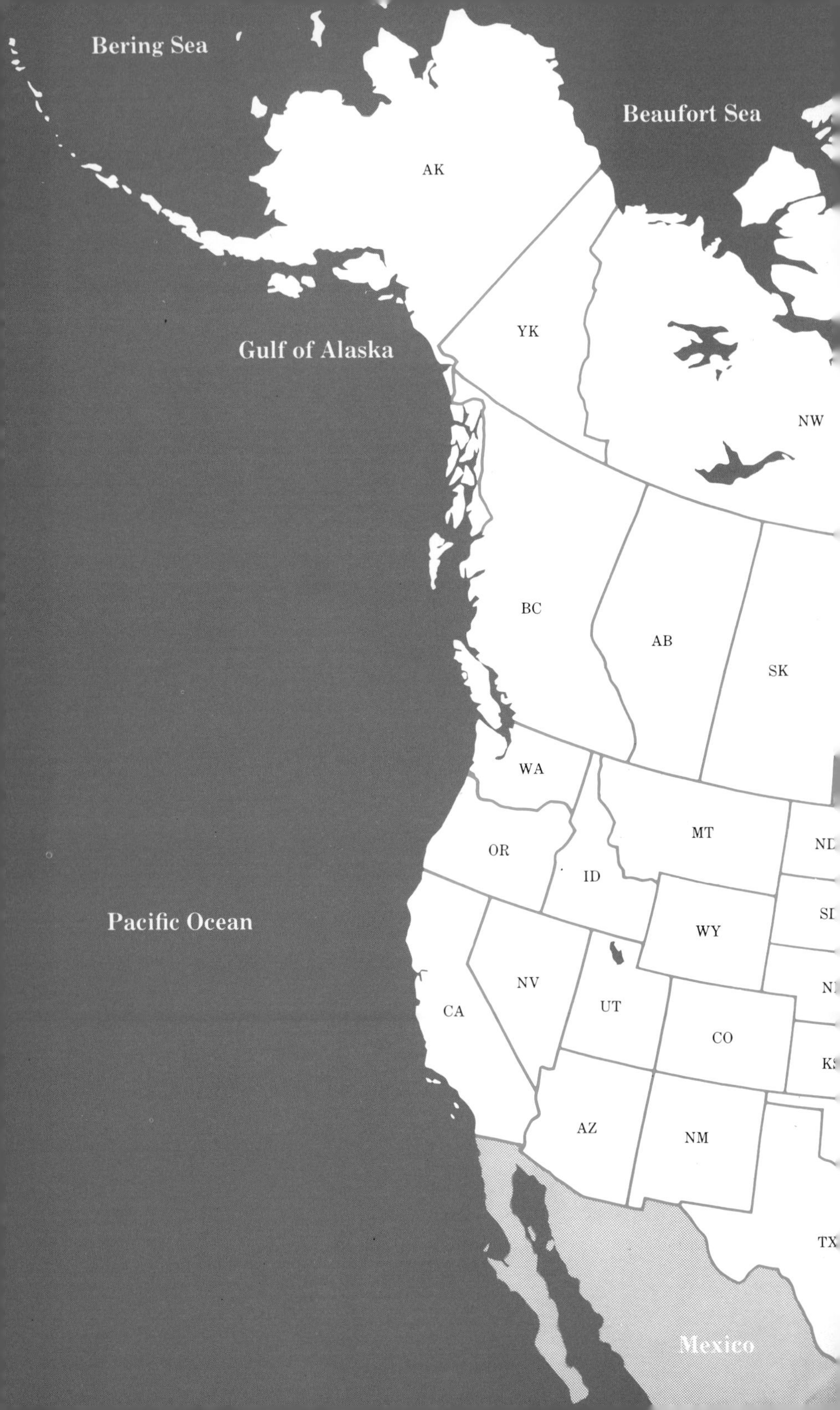
Bering Sea
Beaufort Sea
AK
YK
Gulf of Alaska
NW
BC
AB
SK
WA
MT
OR
ID
Pacific Ocean
WY
NV
UT
CA
CO
AZ
NM
Mexico

How to Identify Birds

Beginning birders usually identify species by comparing birds they see with illustrations or descriptions. To identify birds correctly, novices normally must examine them slowly in detail under favorable conditions. Experts, on the other hand, do not have to look so carefully; they have a mental picture that is far more detailed than any illustration. Their identifications are based on a variety of clues, considered singly or in combination. Here are some of the most important ones.

Size

The size of a bird, although it may be difficult to determine when the bird is far away or by itself, is a useful clue in identifying it. As you learn to recognize birds, you will quickly become familiar with their size relative to other species. Select a series of common and widespread birds of different sizes, such as the House Sparrow, American Robin, Rock Dove, American Crow, Canada Goose, and Great Blue Heron, and use these to gauge the size of other birds you see. You will soon be able to judge whether an unfamiliar bird is smaller than a House Sparrow, about the size of an American Robin, or somewhat larger than a Rock Dove. Very often in a flock of shorebirds or waterfowl, a single bird will stand out because it is larger or smaller than the others. If you already know that the other members of the flock are Sanderlings, for example, you will have a head start in identifying the single, unfamiliar bird. In cases where you cannot judge the size of a bird, its shape is the next feature to consider.

Shape

Shape is one of the most readily observed characteristics of a bird and one of the most important in identification. Your impression of a bird's shape will be influenced by several features. The body may be compact and stocky, like that of a European Starling or a member of the auk family, or it may be slender, like a Yellow-billed Cuckoo's or Red-breasted Merganser's. The neck may be very long, as in herons and the Anhinga, or very short, as in many small sandpipers. The legs, too, may be very long, as in most herons, or very short, as in terns. The bill may be conical, like that of a House Sparrow; slender and pointed, like that of a warbler or kinglet; heavy and pointed, like that of a Belted Kingfisher or a heron; decurved, like that of a curlew or Long-billed Thrasher; or hooked, like the bill of the American Kestrel and Red-tailed Hawk. The wings may be long and pointed, like those of terns, swifts, and swallows, or distinctly rounded, like those of quails. Tails vary greatly in shape. Some birds, like European Starlings and nuthatches, have short tails, while others, like gnatcatchers, thrashers, and wagtails, have very long tails. A bird's tail may be squared at the tip, like a Cliff Swallow's; notched, like that of a House Finch or Tropical Kingbird; deeply forked, like the tail of a Common Tern or Barn Swallow; rounded, like a Blue Jay's; or pointed, like a Mourning Dove's. Posture is often an important aspect of a bird's shape. Plovers tend to stand in a more upright position, with the head held higher, than sandpipers of similar size. Flycatchers usually perch with the body held almost vertically, rather than in the horizontal posture of warblers, vireos, and kinglets. Even among closely related species, there may be differences in posture: Yellow-crowned Night-Herons often stand in a more upright posture than do Black-crowned Night-Herons, and Rough-legged Hawks often perch in a more horizontal posture than Red-tailed Hawks.

Many species can be identified by shape alone. For example, virtually all North American ducks have a distinctive head shape; when seen in profile, they can often be identified by this feature.

Stocky build

Slender build

Long legs

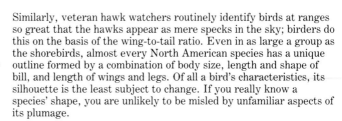

Similarly, veteran hawk watchers routinely identify birds at ranges so great that the hawks appear as mere specks in the sky; birders do this on the basis of the wing-to-tail ratio. Even in as large a group as the shorebirds, almost every North American species has a unique outline formed by a combination of body size, length and shape of bill, and length of wings and legs. Of all a bird's characteristics, its silhouette is the least subject to change. If you really know a species' shape, you are unlikely to be misled by unfamiliar aspects of its plumage.

Black-and-white wing pattern

Color and Pattern

Color and pattern are important, too. The brilliant red of a male Northern Cardinal is often one's first clue to the identity of this bird, visible before its conical bill can be seen and before one is familiar with its distinctive, tail-pumping flight. The solid blue of male Indigo Buntings and Mountain Bluebirds at once sets these birds apart from all others. In much of the continent, a flash of bright orange and black in the treetops can instantly be called a Northern Oriole. Before a beginning birder learns the distinctive shape and manner of flight of an American Kestrel, its colors—bluish-gray and rufous in the male, rufous-brown in the female—enable him to identify this small falcon. If you note that a distant goose is white with black wing tips, you have narrowed the possibilities to only two species, the Snow Goose and Ross' Goose. Among the spotted thrushes, a bird in which only the tail is rust-colored is a Hermit Thrush; one with rust on the head and back is a Wood Thrush; a bird whose upperparts are wholly tawny is a Veery; while a bird with no rust or tawny in the upperparts is either a Gray-cheeked or Swainson's thrush.

White outer tail feathers

Carefully noting the color and pattern of a bird is essential in identifying it. Watch for wing bars; vireos, for example, can be sorted into two groups, those with wing bars and those without. Other wing patterns can be helpful, too, especially if the bird is in flight. The black-and-white wing pattern of a flying Willet is diagnostic, as are the red shoulders of Red-winged and Tricolored blackbirds, and the flashes of white in the wings of White-winged Doves, Red-headed Woodpeckers, Northern Mockingbirds, shrikes, and male Phainopeplas. Watch for rump and tail patterns. A departing Northern Flicker can be identified at a glance by its white rump; the pale buff rump of a Cliff Swallow or Cave Swallow quickly eliminates all other swallows. A yellowish or greenish warbler with large yellow tail patches must be a Yellow Warbler, while one with large white tail patches and a yellow rump is likely to be a Magnolia. White outer tail feathers mark the juncos and a variety of open-country birds: meadowlarks, pipits, Horned Larks, and Vesper Sparrows. A large flycatcher with a white tail tip must be an Eastern Kingbird, while in the West, a kingbird with white outer tail feathers must be a Western.

Look carefully at the pattern of the head. Watch for eyebrows, eye-rings, eyelines, mustaches, or throat patches; note the color of the crown, ear coverts, and lores. Take special note of any unusual color pattern: the red head and yellow body of a male Western Tanager, the golden-buff nape of a male Bobolink, the white sides on the rump of a Violet-green Swallow, and the rufous rump of the gray Lucy's Warbler are all diagnostic. The pattern of many species makes them easy to identify. Flying waterfowl and many warblers usually can be recognized by pattern alone. When other features are all but invisible, particularly in poor light or at great distances, a bird's distinctive pattern can often be discerned.

White wing patches

Behavior

Many birds walk, swim, or fly in so characteristic a manner that behavior by itself can permit identification. Given an unlabeled specimen of a Water Pipit, most birders are not likely to recognize it at once, yet they can identify the living bird from hundreds of yards away by its bounding, stuttering flight or its habit of emphatically pumping its tail when on the ground. Some behavioral clues are obvious, like the big, splashy dives of Northern Gannets and Ospreys, the constant nodding of a yellowlegs, the head-bobbing motion of a swimming coot, the zigzag flight of a Common Snipe when it is flushed from a wet meadow, or the mothlike flight of a Common Poorwill. Others are subtle, such as the flight mannerisms of kittiwakes and the wing- and tail-flicks of flycatchers. Behavioral clues are almost unfailingly reliable and can help in identifying birds under a variety of circumstances. The differing flight styles of hawks, for example, or the various feeding postures of shorebirds can be used to identify them almost at the limit of visibility.

Conical bill

Vocal Clues
In many situations, it is easier to hear birds than to see them. Whether you are in the rain forest of the Northwest, the warbler-filled woods of New England, or the cypress swamps of the Carolinas, you are certain to hear many more birds than you see. The vocalizations of birds may be divided into two rough categories: songs and calls. Songs are usually given by adult males on territory during the nesting season, but may also be heard during migration and, in some species, during the winter as well. In certain species, such as the Rose-breasted Grosbeak and Northern Mockingbird, females as well as males may produce songs. Many songs are rather complex, like those of the Winter Wren and most wood warblers, but some are very simple, like the short, metallic *tslit* of Henslow's Sparrow. Calls, or call notes, are generally more simple, and are often given throughout the year under a variety of situations to express alarm, to maintain contact with other members of a flock, or during interactions with a mate or young.

Slender, pointed bill

Knowing the songs and calls of a region's birds will enable you to identify a far higher percentage than you could with binoculars alone. Identification by voice is almost always reliable. The shorebirds, for example, have flight calls, given at all times of the year, that are absolutely distinctive. Every shorebird native to North America, as well as vagrant species from the Old World, can be identified by these notes alone. Thus, if you are familiar with shorebird voices, you can identify the birds with certainty anywhere at any time of year, whether they are breeding in the Arctic, migrating through our latitudes, or wintering in South America. You can identify them even in darkness, and up to the limits of audibility. All North American songbirds, as well, have distinctive voices; in many cases, even their minor calls—lisps or chips—are recognizable. For example, of the large New World subfamily of wood warblers, about 50 fairly closely related species breed in North America. All have songs that can be learned readily; in fact, their songs differ more markedly than their plumages. Each song can be distinguished and mentally catalogued according to a variety of characteristics: pitch, cadence, duration, loudness, frequency of utterance, and quality. Although the song structure of a species may vary slightly from region to region, the quality of the song will almost always remain recognizable.

Heavy, pointed bill

Habitat and Range
Most people know that ducks and gulls are water birds and that thrushes are birds of the forest, but few beginning birders are aware of how specific most species are in their habitat requirements. Although these requirements may vary somewhat according to region and season, they are still quite rigid; experienced bird watchers expect to see certain birds in certain habitats. Warblers are as selective as any group: Tennessees breed in tamarack,

Ceruleans in tall hardwoods, Blackpolls in stunted spruce, Prairies in mangroves and red-cedar pastures, Palms in bogs, and Mournings in raspberry thickets. These are hard-and-fast rules during the breeding season, but migrants are less selective and may appear anywhere. Other species are specific in their choice of habitat even as transients. In the Northeast, two uncommon fall migrants are remarkable in this respect; Orange-crowned Warblers frequent the tops of old goldenrod blooms along the coast, and Connecticut Warblers prefer damp meadow edges and hardwood swamps that have an open understory of plants such as clethra and silky dogwood, with jewelweed underfoot.

Pointed tail

Knowing habitat preferences greatly increases the chances of finding particular birds; it can also limit what we expect to find. In many cases, habitat by itself helps us to identify species. For example, even if they can barely be seen or heard, blackbirds in northern bogs are almost certain to be Rusties. Finally, the range of most birds is determined in large part by the availability of a specific habitat. Although the ranges of most species are continuously expanding or contracting, they can nonetheless be geographically defined or mapped. Knowledge of range enters into virtually every identification, usually as a subconscious first consideration. So too does an awareness of the average arrival and departure dates of migratory species.

Becoming an Expert

Notched tail

To the uninitiated, the identifications made by experienced birders often seem to approach wizardry. Experts, rather than comparing the bird they have seen with illustrations in a field guide, weigh a number of attributes that together give the species a distinctive personality. The better you know a species, the more ways you have to identify it. Many North American birds have three or even more identifiable plumages, which can be bewildering at first, until one realizes how many factors are invariable: shape, voice, behavior, and range.

Looking at Birds

There is no secret to becoming skilled in identifying birds: Just look and listen. Observation may seem simple at first, but you will progress faster if you look attentively and repeatedly, even at common species. For many beginners, examination stops and binoculars come down the moment the bird is identified. In fact, this is the time to start looking. Make the effort. Imagine, for example, that this is the last Downy Woodpecker you will see for a long time, or that you will soon be asked to describe or even draw it. If you have difficulty getting a firm grasp on a bird's appearance, first look

Forked tail

at its eye, and to force yourself to look closely, try to ascertain the color of the iris. Then study the size and shape of the bill and its length in relation to the distance separating its base from the center of the eye. Next, extend your study of the bird's proportions to the length of its legs and to the position of the folded wing tips in relation to the tip of the tail. From these observations, proceed to an examination of the bird's coloring and patterns. This deliberate approach might seem tedious, but birds lend themselves to careful observation, and you will almost certainly find it engrossing and rewarding. You will soon discover that you can memorize birds in much the same way you memorize human faces. It is possible to acquire a permanent familiarity with a seemingly limitless number of bird species, but to do so you must look carefully. Most expert bird watchers spend much time simply studying the appearance of birds, even familiar ones. This enjoyable exercise results in a far more detailed acquaintance than is required for simple identification, but it also makes one aware of the differences between species that superficially appear to be similar. Bear in mind that you can know what a bird looks like only by *looking* at it. This sort of bird study demands fairly close-range and leisurely observation, but do not pass up a chance to watch a distant bird—you may be surprised at how much you can see. With good light and good binoculars, you can identify distinctively patterned birds as small as warblers, in flight, even overhead, at a great distance, but you will not know this until you try it.

Looking at museum specimens or, better yet, at live birds trapped at a banding station, can also be extremely helpful. Side-by-side comparison of similar species can reveal differences that may help you in field identification. Juxtaposing and comparing eight or ten species of warblers, for example, will demonstrate as no field guide can the diversity that exists within this group. You will discover how much these species vary in size, bill shape, wing length, rictal bristles, or any number of small details. Studying specimens or captive birds will also help you to learn about the arrangement of feathers: which ones are involved in the wing bars, for instance, and how the tail feathers are shingled, with the central pair, or "deck feathers," on top and the outermost underneath. These insights will help you to understand what you see in the field.

Rounded wings

Listening to Birds

Learning bird songs may seem difficult at first, but we learn them much as we learn melodies, by attentive and repeated listening. You can be more or less energetic in acquiring this familiarity with bird voices, but you will progress faster if you make it a rule to track down every unfamiliar call. This may initially seem overwhelming, but your ear will soon become remarkably good at resolving a tangle of noise into recognizable voices, and a dawn chorus of bird song will become a delightful exercise in auditory discrimination. Try to attach a set of associations to each bird vocalization by describing it to yourself or comparing it with other sounds you know; make your mental description of sounds as detailed as possible. If you can whistle, try to copy the sound you are learning; to imitate it acceptably you will have to listen closely to the model. The more characteristic sounds of most North American birds are available on commercially produced recordings. Although listening to records or tapes removes the learning process one step from direct experience, it will at the very least make you sensitive to aspects of bird song that make the voices of each species distinctive and recognizable. Even the least expensive recording equipment can be helpful, too, since listening to your own tapes allows a comparative or analytical approach to the study of bird song. Moreover, playback of a reasonably good field recording will often attract the singing bird and enable you to observe it more closely.

Long, pointed wings

Conclusion

Bird watching has attracted an ever increasing number of devotees in North America. The science—some would say the art—of bird identification has been considerably advanced and refined in recent years. Field problems have been clarified or resolved, vocalizations studied, behavioral clues detected, and distinguishing characteristics isolated. As a result, bird watchers of today are immeasurably more sophisticated than those of only a few decades ago. Bird identification is now a field in which one can quickly achieve a high degree of competence, with all its attendant satisfactions. And bird watching—need it be said?—is a pursuit with many, many rewards.   *Davis W. Finch*

How to Find Birds

To become a successful birder, you may have to change the habits of a lifetime. The best birders rise before dawn, put on drab clothing, go out in all weathers, and learn to move carefully and quietly, keeping their ears open and their voices soft.

Clothing

Unless you have always been an outdoor person, you will find your wardrobe gradually transformed and your conversation increasingly filled with discussions of boots, rain gear, and long underwear. The most important rule is: Wear dull colors, preferably the natural ones, muted greens, browns, and grays. Steer clear of apparel that squeaks, rustles, or gets snagged easily. In the desert, birders need footgear that is thornproof; elsewhere, choose comfortable shoes that dry quickly or waterproof boots. Boots with rubber feet and leather tops are a widespread favorite, but as you track birds across mud flats and marshes you may want knee or hip boots as well. Since birding often requires standing around in sharp winds and icy temperatures, layers of protection against the cold are essential. However, soundproof ear coverings should be avoided, except perhaps on winter boat trips, one of the coldest of all birding situations.

The Clock

Songbirds are easiest to see during the three hours after dawn, when they feed most actively. The two hours before sunset can also be productive. During the rest of the day, most small birds are relatively sluggish and silent, especially on a warm afternoon. On the other hand, most kinds of water birds are easy to find throughout the day. Vultures, hawks, and eagles are most likely to be seen well after sunup; they hunt when visibility is best and soar on the thermal currents formed by sun-warmed air.

Dusk is the best time to scan winter fields and marshes for Short-eared Owls, cruise back roads for nightjars and displaying Woodcock, and visit summer marshes for spectacular flights of herons and ibis and glimpses of most of the rails. Birders usually search for rails and owls at night and arm themselves with tape recordings of owl calls and strong flashlights. During spring migration and early in the nesting season, birders in the field at first light are treated to the auditory excitement of the dawn chorus; woodland species in particular join in a crescendo that gradually dies away after sunrise.

Regional Resources

Many states, provinces, and regions now have annotated checklists or bird-finding guides that indicate the time of year that each species is present and most common, as well as the locations and habitats where each might be found. Such a list or guide should be one of your first purchases. If your region has not yet produced this kind of guide, buy one for the area nearest you.

Local bird clubs schedule field trips to visit areas at the times of year that birds are most plentiful there or when seasonal specialties are present. If you cannot join a group expedition, try to visit the site within a week or two of a scheduled outing. Club newsletters or calendars often list other events of interest, like pelagic trips organized especially for viewing seabirds and marine mammals.

In many areas throughout the United States and Canada, recorded telephone messages are available to birders. Updated once or twice a week, they supply information about unusual sightings in the area as well as news of migration, birding sites, and field trips. Call the local Aubudon Society chapter for the telephone number, or ask birders you meet in the field for it. These messages often provide

directions to spots where rare birds have been found; these spots
are often fruitful places for a visiting birder to look for common local
species as well.

Weather

Every birder yearns to go afield on a beautiful spring or autumn
day, but wind, rain, and extremes of temperature may keep you
inside when some birds are most visible.

Although strong winds keep small birds out of sight, many water
birds huddle close to the windward shore, in the lee of protecting
banks, dunes, or vegetation. In autumn especially, a day or two
after a cold front has passed through, northerly winds bring the best
conditions for watching raptors migrating down mountain ridges or
along the coasts. Onshore gales accompanying major coastal storms
provide the best opportunities for observing seabirds of all kinds
from land, and the first day after a hurricane many birders rush to
the coast or to bays, rivers, and major lakes within a hundred miles
or so of the sea.

Although bird-watching is virtually impossible in heavy rain, there
is a lot of activity immediately after the rain stops. If you can keep
your binoculars dry, a low ceiling and light drizzle can produce the
best possible conditions for seeing migrating passerines. Songbirds
are often forced down by nasty weather aloft; since they may occupy
whatever cover they can find, you are likely to see a hedgerow, a
clump of trees, or a brushy ravine alive with birds.

The hottest days of summer coincide with the peak migration time
for southbound shorebirds. During the heat shimmer of late morning
and early afternoon, go for a swim or hide in air-conditioned shelter,
but take advantage of the long hours before and after the worst heat
of the day.

Cold winter weather is good for birding snugly from your car,
searching open country for raptors and visiting seedeaters such as
longspurs and Snow Buntings. You may want to comb through
stands of conifers for wintering owls, seek out patches of open water
where waterfowl crowd together, or scan landfills, harbors, and
beaches for rare gulls. If you notice a feeding station, check to see
what species are visiting it.

Effective Behavior

The fundamental skills of birding are looking, listening, moving
carefully, and concentrating on one bird at a time.

On foot, a birder is likely to cover less than one mile an hour. The
point is to hear every chip note or rustle in the foliage and to spot
every movement. Once you have heard a sound or seen a movement,
your goal is to locate, identify, and observe the bird without
frightening it away.

Although sharp eyes are partly a gift, the ability to pick up motion
improves with practice. Always locate and relocate the bird first
without binoculars. Keep your eyes on the motion while you move
your binoculars in front of them. When you acquire a telescope,
study the bird's surroundings through binoculars before you narrow
your field of vision a second time by looking through the more
powerful optical instrument.

Study an unfamiliar bird thoroughly before you turn to a field guide.
If you cannot bear to take notes on its appearance and behavior
before you try to identify it, at least tell yourself exactly what
features you are seeing and hearing before you turn to a guide; if the
bird flies away when your eyes are not on it, you will still have
several features to check. If there are two of you, you can describe
it to each other; one person can keep track of the bird while the
other does the first round of research.

Looking for land birds requires a minimum of conversation and a
maximum of attention to sounds. Speak only when you must, and

then in a soft voice or whisper. Learning to recognize songs takes most of us much longer than visual identification, and learning all the chips, calls, and alarm notes is the task of a lifetime. Begin by tracking down and identifying every invisible singing bird you can. Try to verbalize the pattern you hear, and commit it to memory. Avoid abrupt movements: Shift position only if you have to, and then do so slowly and gently. Learn to refrain from pointing, or to point with your finger only, keeping your hand against your body. Better yet, practice describing where a bird is as economically as possible.

As you stalk a bird, learn to recognize its signs of alarm: a freeze in posture, a cocked head, a half-raising of the wings, and so on. If these clues tell you that you are getting too close, back off a little, or at least stop moving until the bird shows that it is used to your presence.

Try not to loom over a bird. Stay off the skyline if you can; on high ground, crouch or sit. The less conspicuous you are, the more birds you are likely to see.

Imitations of the Eastern Screech-Owl's call in the East or of the Northern Pygmy-Owl's in the West are enormously effective for attracting small birds. If you cannot master the screech-owl's tricky call, use a taped version; it works even better. Anybody can learn to "spish," that is, to make the sound "spshsh, spshsh, spshsh," which can draw quite a crowd of songbirds if you keep at it long enough. One responsive chickadee can pull in dozens of other birds if you keep it fussing at you. Most important, remember that overuse of these techniques quickly turns into harassment, and there is no excuse for seriously upsetting a bird, especially one that may be nesting.   *Claudia Wilds*

Orders

In zoological classification all birds are placed in the class Aves. Classes are divided into orders, which are in turn divided into from one to several families. Discussed below are the orders of birds covered in this volume.

Charadriiformes

Lari and Alcae, two suborders of the diverse order Charadriiformes, contain the gulls and terns and their allies (Lari), and the diving birds, which are variously called auks, murres, puffins, auklets, and murrelets (Alcae). The Lari are nearly worldwide in distribution; the Alcae are restricted to Arctic and northern temperate oceans and coasts. The Lari are mainly coastal and marine, the Alcae are exclusively so.

The suborder Lari contains only the family Laridae. In addition to the familiar gulls (subfamily Larinae) and terns (subfamily Sterninae), this family is now considered to include two groups formerly placed in families by themselves: the jaegers and skuas (subfamily Stercorariinae) and the skimmers (subfamily Rynchopinae).

All Lari are long-winged, web-footed, and aquatic, at least in the nonbreeding season; some species are highly pelagic as nonbreeders. They nest on islands, coasts, and tundra, and on freshwater marshes or other inland habitats. Most species have a complex array of subadult plumages; a knowledge of these is important for species identification.

Gulls employ a variety of foraging techniques; many species feed largely by scavenging. Most terns plunge-dive for food. Jaegers and skuas are terrestrial scavengers or rodent hunters during the breeding season, but feed primarily by pirating food from other seabirds during the nonbreeding season. Skimmers feed, as their name suggests, by skimming the water's surface with their uniquely adapted, knifelike bills.

The suborder Alcae contains only the family Alcidae—small to medium-size seabirds with stubby bodies, small, narrow wings, webbed feet, and variously shaped bills. A variety of bill and head ornaments develop during the breeding season. Head pattern and bill shape are often the best identifying characteristics for members of this group.

Columbiformes

The familiar pigeons and doves of the family Columbidae are the only North American representatives of the order Columbiformes. Other families in this order are the sandgrouse of the Old World family Pteroclididae, which are thought by some to be closer to the Charadriiformes and to the extinct dodos and their relatives.

North American pigeons and doves are seed and fruit eaters. Most species forage on the ground, although some pigeons are arboreal. In most species, the sexes look alike and immatures closely resemble adults. The cooing vocalizations of most species are quite distinctive.

Psittaciformes

The parrots and parakeets and their relatives of the large family Psittacidae are contained in the order Psittaciformes; the lories and cockatoos of Australasia are sometimes placed in separate families. The family Psittacidae is only marginal in North America; the only species that was ever widespread, the Carolina Parakeet, is now extinct. The family is found throughout the world's tropics and subtropics, but is most diverse in the Neotropics and in Australasia.

Parrots and parakeets are brightly colored birds that are predominantly green. They have strong, hooked beaks and four toes, two extending forward and two backward. They are highly

arboreal, blending in well with foliage, and are often best seen as they commute to and from feeding areas. Favored as cage birds, parrots and parakeets frequently escape, and many species have established feral populations in the warmer parts of North America.

Cuculiformes

The cuckoos and their allies make up the order Cuculiformes. Only the cuckoos of the family Cuculidae occur in North America; also in this order are the Old World turacos and plaintain-eaters of the family Musophagidae. The tropical South American Hoatzin of the family Opisthocomidae is also usually considered a member of this order.

Except for the Greater Roadrunner, North American Cuculiformes are short-legged. All have four toes, two extending forward and two backward. Most species have long, somewhat graduated tails and slightly decurved bills.

Cuckoos are found in temperate zones and in greater numbers in tropical areas throughout the world. North American species are not colorful; they are represented by the woodland-dwelling cuckoos, the arid-country, ground-dwelling roadrunner, and the subtropical-brushland anis.

Strigiformes

The order Strigiformes contains the familiar, although often elusive, birds of prey, the owls. The two families, the barn-owls (family Tytonidae) and the typical owls (family Strigidae), are similar in general appearance. Most owls are nocturnal. Both families are nearly worldwide in distribution.

Owls have large, forward-directed eyes that are usually set in a feathered facial disk. They have strong, hooked beaks and strongly clawed feet. All are marked variously in brown, gray, black, and white.

As in the diurnal raptors of the order Falconiformes, members of the order Strigiformes are often dimorphic in size, with females larger than males. Habitat, overall size and shape, and, especially, vocalizations are useful clues in distinguishing species.

Caprimulgiformes

The uniform order Caprimulgiformes contains the nightjars of the family Caprimulgidae, to which the North American species of the order belong, plus four additional small, tropical families. All members of the order are characterized by nocturnal or crepuscular habits. Their plumage is soft mottled brown or gray, and they have small, weak legs and feet and a small bill with an exceedingly wide gape. The North American species are long-winged insect hawkers that fly primarily at dawn and dusk. With the exception of the high-flying nighthawks, most species are far more often heard than seen. Consequently, for nearly all species, vocalizations provide the easiest means of identification. The family Caprimulgidae is nearly worldwide in distribution; most North American species are highly migratory.

Apodiformes

The order Apodiformes contains two distinct groups of small, long-winged birds that have excellent powers of flight. These are the swifts (of which the typical swifts of the family Apodidae are represented in North America) and the hummingbirds (family Trochilidae). The wide-ranging swifts are found over much of the world, whereas the hummingbirds are restricted to the New World; the latter are most diverse in the Neotropics.

Both swifts and hummingbirds have pointed wings and short legs with small feet. The primaries are long, and there are relatively few secondaries; the bend of the wing therefore lies close to the body. The short bill and wide gape of the swifts are quite unlike the needle-shaped bill of hummingbirds. Swifts are rapid and agile fliers and may remain airborne throughout the day; hummingbirds beat their wings rapidly, which enables them to hover at food sources, primarily flowers. Many swifts and hummingbirds are highly migratory; both groups contain species that may undergo torpor. Among swifts, the sexes and age groups are generally similar; most are gray, brown, or black. Male hummingbirds are usually highly iridescent and more brightly colored than females.

Trogoniformes

The small tropical order Trogoniformes contains only one family, the Trogonidae. Trogons are colorful, stout-billed, long-tailed forest birds of tropical and subtropical Asia, Africa, and Middle and South America. They generally feed on insects and on fruits gathered during short, hovering flights. Males are brighter in color than females; in the North American species, the males have bright red bellies and green or blue-green breasts and upperparts. The complex black-and-white tail patterns are often species specific. Only two species reach our borders, and only one does so regularly.

Coraciiformes

The diverse order Coraciiformes contains several families confined to the Old World, including the hornbills, bee-eaters, and rollers. The West Indian todies and the tropical motmots are found only in the New World. The largest and most widespread family in the order is the Alcedinidae, or kingfishers. Except for the accidental Hoopoe of the family Upupidae, the Alcedinidae are the only family represented in North America.

The coraciform birds are highly diverse in shape and coloration; many are quite brightly colored. In most families, there is some degree of fusion to the toes, which distinguishes birds of this order from birds of other orders. Kingfishers show this fusion strongly. In addition, most coraciiform birds have long, strong bills that are variously adapted for obtaining insect and vertebrate prey.

The kingfishers are diverse in the Old World tropics but poorly represented in North America. Of our three species, only one is widely distributed north of the Mexican border.

Piciformes

Although the order Piciformes contains several families found exclusively in the tropics, such as the toucans, barbets, puffbirds, jacamars, and honeyguides, the best-known group in the order is the woodpeckers (family Picidae). Woodpeckers are the only family in this order represented in North America. Although they occur in wooded areas nearly worldwide, they are not found in Australasia or on oceanic islands.

The woodpeckers are a rather uniform group of birds that have adapted to climbing on trees and excavating into wood for food and for nest cavities. North American woodpeckers have stiff tails, a zygodactylous toe arrangement (two toes extending forward and two toes or, rarely, one extending backward), and chisel-shaped beaks. In most North American species, the sexes are roughly similar, although adult males typically have more extensive red markings on the head than adult females. In females of many species the red may be altogether absent.

Passeriformes

Considerably more than half of the world's bird species belong to the diverse order of perching birds, the Passeriformes. Found worldwide, they constitute the great bulk of species in most terrestrial bird communities. Their tremendous variety of feeding adaptations makes it difficult to generalize about the Passeriformes, but all show a "perching foot," consisting of three toes extending forward, and one toe extending backward on the same level. In

North America, passeriform birds (often called passerines) range in size from that of a wren or a kinglet to that of a raven.

The largest passerine family discussed in this volume is the Tyrannidae, or tyrant-flycatchers. They are part of a large evolutionary radiation of New World passerines of the suborder Tyranni, which also includes the Neotropical antbirds, ovenbirds, woodcreepers, manakins, and cotingas. Although the family Tyrannidae contains a variety of adaptive types, the North American species feed primarily by sallying for insects. Most of our tyrant-flycatchers are highly migratory.

The other passerine families noted in this volume are either widespread in distribution or found mainly in the Old World. An exception is the primarily New World family Troglodytidae, which contains the wrens. Consult the individual family accounts for further characteristics of the passerine families. The remaining families in this large order are covered in the third volume of this set.   *Kimball L. Garrett*

Skuas, Gulls, Terns, and Skimmers

(Family Laridae)
Members of this family are graceful, adept fliers with long pointed
wings. They have webbed feet, and are usually found near water.
The family is divided into 4 distinct groups of birds. Jaegers and
skuas are aggressive, streamlined birds that live at sea except when
breeding in the Arctic or Antarctic. Their swift, agile flight enables
them to steal food from other birds, especially gulls and terns. At a
distance, jaegers can often be recognized by the twists and turns
they make as they pursue their victims. Adult jaegers have
elongated central tail feathers. Because of the great variation in
color (there are light-phase, dark-phase, and intermediate birds),
jaegers of all ages can be difficult or even nearly impossible to
identify. One clue is their size, which can sometimes be judged in
comparison to the birds they are chasing. Skuas are larger, heavier
birds with thick necks and often a hump-backed appearance in flight;
they show a conspicuous flash of white in the primaries. Gulls are
less powerful and agile in flight than jaegers and skuas, but are still
strong, direct, and dextrous fliers. They are found not only along
coasts and in some cases far at sea, but also on interior wetlands.
Adults of most species are white with gray or blackish upperparts;
some have black heads in breeding plumage. With few exceptions,
young gulls are darker than adults of the same species. Smaller
species take 1 or 2 years to reach maturity; larger ones take longer.
Immature plumages can be difficult to identify. Knowing the age of
the bird is helpful, and the amount of molt and feather wear, the
shape of the head, bill, and body, and the color of the legs and bill
are also important. Terns are slender, buoyant fliers with long and
very pointed wings and often relatively long and forked tails. Terns
typically dive into the water for food. Most terns are white or
whitish, with dark caps that become reduced in size outside the
breeding season. Calls, bill color, wing pattern, and the relative
length of the tail are important clues in distinguishing members of
the genus *Sterna*. The fourth group is the skimmers, with only 1
North American species. Its bill is largely red, and the lower
mandible is longer than the upper; this feature distinguishes it from
all other members of the family. (World: 96 species. North America:
49 species.)   *Scott B. Terrill and Ron Naveen*

Pomarine Jaeger
Parasitic Jaeger
Long-tailed Jaeger
Great Skua
South Polar Skua
Laughing Gull
Franklin's Gull
Little Gull
Common Black-headed Gull
Bonaparte's Gull
Heermann's Gull
Black-tailed Gull
Mew Gull
Ring-billed Gull
California Gull
Herring Gull
Thayer's Gull
Iceland Gull
Lesser Black-backed Gull
Slaty-backed Gull
Yellow-footed Gull
Western Gull
Glaucous-winged Gull
Glaucous Gull
Great Black-backed Gull
Black-legged Kittiwake
Red-legged Kittiwake
Ross' Gull
Sabine's Gull
Ivory Gull
Gull-billed Tern
Caspian Tern
Royal Tern
Elegant Tern
Sandwich Tern
Roseate Tern
Common Tern
Arctic Tern
Aleutian Tern
Forster's Tern
Least Tern
Bridled Tern
Sooty Tern
Large-billed Tern
White-winged Tern
Black Tern
Brown Noddy
Black Noddy
Black Skimmer

Pomarine Jaeger

Stercorarius pomarinus

Jaegers and skuas are the raptors of the ocean. Superficially resembling gulls, they are skilled pirates, and are often seen harassing other seabirds, particularly terns. Ideally, adult jaegers of different species could be distinguished by the shape and length of their central tail feathers (rectrices); however, these feathers are often broken or missing. Dark-phase adults, juveniles, and subadults are very troublesome to identify, having inconsistent and variable plumage characteristics. There are very few clear criteria for distinguishing these birds; the observer must rely on subtleties such as wingbeat rhythm, breadth of wing, and bulk. These very subjective matters require much field experience, and many jaegers —especially in the fall—cannot be identified. As yet, our understanding of tail-feather growth on all jaegers is incomplete, but in time this feature may prove to be species-distinctive. The Pomarine is the bulkiest jaeger and is most often found far offshore, but can be seen somewhat regularly from shore along the Pacific Coast. Full adults have long, twisted central rectrices.

Description
20″ (51 cm). The Pomarine Jaeger is about the size of a Ring-billed Gull and smaller than a Herring Gull; it appears large-headed and large-billed. The Pomarine's normal flight is powerful, steady, purposeful, and slow, with relatively shallow wingbeats. This species' wings are very broad at the base; the bird does not seem to rise and fall with each wingbeat. Light-phase adults have a broad breastband and dark vent, a light belly, and barring on the flanks. They often have a capped appearance, a yellow wash to the cheeks, and a white throat. The upperparts and upperwings are dark, with obvious white flashes on the primaries; the spoon-tipped central rectrices are longer than the other tail feathers. Dark-phase adults may retain some of the capped appearance, but are best recognized by the central rectrices (if present). The flight and the large-headed, large-billed, bulky appearance are also diagnostic. Juveniles are brown and heavily barred below; they lack the distinctive central rectrices. Identification of dark-phase juveniles is extremely difficult and subjective, and must rely on their large size, broad-based wings, and strong, slow wingbeats. Subadults resemble adults, but do not show the spoon-tipped central rectrices and may show barred underparts that encircle a white belly patch.

Similar Species
See Parasitic and Long-tailed jaegers; Parasitic usually seen closer to shore. Great and South Polar skuas larger and bulkier, with broader wings.

Range
Breeds from Alaska to north-central Canada and Greenland. Common migrant along both coasts; very rare migrant to Great Lakes. Uncommon in winter along Pacific; rare along Atlantic Coast. Casual inland in migration. Also in northern Eurasia.
Ron Naveen

Light-phase adult
1. *Dark cap.*
2. *Broad breastband.*
3. *White belly.*
4. *Blunt, spoon-tipped central tail feathers.*

Immature in flight
1. *Broad-based wings.*

   Steady, slow flight, with shallow wingbeats.

Light-phase adult in flight
1. *Broad breastband.*
2. *White belly.*
3. *Blunt central tail feathers.*

Parasitic Jaeger

Stercorarius parasiticus
The Parasitic Jaeger's flight is more buoyant than the Pomarine's;
its body seems to rise on each downstroke. Its narrower wings
appear more angled, and are not as broad at the base. The Parasitic
is very adept at pirating the prey of other seabirds and appears to
move with falconlike ease. Of the 3 jaegers, the Parasitic is the one
most regularly seen from shore—often harassing terns—
particularly along the Pacific Coast in migration.

Description
18″ (45.5 cm). In all adult Parasitic Jaegers, the elongated central
rectrices are sharply pointed rather than spoon-tipped, and they are
shorter than the Long-tailed's (although the latter species' tail
feathers may be broken). Light-phase adults show a dark cap with
some white on the forehead, a less pronounced white wing flash and
thinner bill than the Pomarine, and a diffuse wash or dark blotching
on the breast (in contrast to the Pomarine's complete breastband).
The undertail coverts are dark gray and meet the white belly at a
point corresponding with the trailing edge of the wing. Dark-phase
adults are brown all over, often with a discernible dark cap; they
display the white wing flash and buoyant flight of all jaegers.
Juveniles and subadults show much variation and are best
distinguished by flight characteristics and shape.

Similar Species
See Pomarine and Long-tailed jaegers.

Range
Breeds from Alaska to north-central Canada and Greenland.
Common migrant and rare winter visitor along both coasts. Rare
but regular migrant on Great Lakes; casual elsewhere inland. Also
in northern Eurasia.   *Ron Naveen*

Long-tailed Jaeger

Stercorarius longicaudus
The adult Long-tailed Jaeger, with its extremely long central
rectrices, is unmistakable. This bird flies in a ternlike fashion; it is
the most pelagic of the jaegers, and very rarely seen from shore.

Description
12–14″ (30.5–35.5 cm) without the long central rectrices; 20–22″ (51–
56 cm), including these feathers. This is the slimmest of the jaegers
and a very buoyant flyer, perhaps even more so than the Parasitic.
Most birds are light-phase individuals, with small heads and a small
black cap; this cap is accentuated by a collar on the back of the neck
formed by the white chest and cheeks. There is no breastband, and
the mantle appears grayer than those of other jaegers, with a dark
trailing edge to the wings. When present, the very long central
rectrices are diagnostic, but these may be missing or broken. The
white on the outer primaries is restricted and less obvious than the
white wing patches shown by Pomarines and Parasitics. The
undertail coverts are dark and extend to the midbelly between the

Juvenile in flight
1. *Narrow-based wings.*

Wings appear more angled than in Pomarine Jaeger; flight more buoyant.

Light-phase adult in flight
1. *Incomplete breastband.*
2. *White belly.*
3. *Spike-tipped central tail feathers.*

Adult in flight
1. *Small, dark cap.*
2. *Very long, pointed central tail feathers.*

Slender build. Small-headed look. Graceful flight.

leading and trailing edges of the wings. In flight, adults show pale
gray coverts on the upper wings and back, contrasting sharply with
the very dark bar formed by the secondaries. Subadults are best
distinguished by flight characteristics and shape, although
distinguishing them from young Parasitics may be quite difficult.
Juveniles pose a similar difficulty, although some show distinctly
pale heads. Under some conditions, the immature Long-tailed can be
recognized by its overall gray color, its narrow wings, and rather
even mottling on the underwing.

Similar Species
See Pomarine and Parasitic jaegers.

Range
Breeds from Alaska to north-central Canada and Greenland. Rare
spring and fall transient off both coasts. Not recorded during
migration as often as Pomarines and Parasitics, partly because of its
highly pelagic migration and difficulty of separating juvenile and
subadult Long-taileds and Parasitics. Casual inland in migration.
Ron Naveen

Great Skua

Catharacta skua
The Great Skua, an inquisitive and aggressive bird, is highly pelagic
except when breeding.

Description
23″ (58.5 cm). Similar in size to Herring Gull but bulkier and darker,
with prominent white flashes across bases of primaries. Wings
broad; posture hunched. Warm brown or reddish-brown color and
streaked look above are best marks, but only visible in good light at
fairly close range.

Similar Species
South Polar Skua basically gray, lacks streaked or mottled look;
light phase has obvious pale area on nape, looks 2-toned.
Intermediate phase shows uniformly pale but less prominent area on
nape. Dark phase uniformly dark, including nape.

Range
Breeds in far northeastern Atlantic; regular winter visitor south to
Maryland waters.   *Ron Naveen*

South Polar Skua

Catharacta maccormicki
In summer, virtually all skuas seen in our range are South Polar
Skuas; in winter, it is the Great Skua that finds its way to our area.

Description
21″ (53.5 cm). In good light, appears uniformly gray with no streaks
or mottling. Light-phase birds have very pale nape (can be nearly
white) that creates 2-toned look. Intermediate phase has less pale
nape; dark phase has dark nape. All phases show gray tones in good
light. Immature dark blackish-gray; may look black in poor light;
2-toned bill visible only at close range.

Similar Species
See Great Skua.

Range
Uncommon in late spring, casual in summer, rare fall transient off
southern California; occasionally farther north. Rare off North
Carolina and Maryland, May to July.   *Ron Naveen*

Nonbreeding adult in flight
1. Small head with dark cap.
2. Grayish upperparts.

   More slender and graceful than other jaegers.

Adult in flight
1. Warm mottled or streaked brown plumage.
2. Broad wings with much white at base of primaries.

   Large size. Hunched appearance.

Adult in flight
1. Uniformly gray plumage.
2. Broad wings with much white at base of primaries.

   Large size. Hunched appearance.

Laughing Gull

Larus atricilla

A slim, long-winged gull that breeds along the Atlantic and Caribbean coasts, the Laughing Gull is locally common during summer in the northern part of its range. It is an abundant year-round resident of southern beaches and salt marshes, where it nests in large colonies and feeds on small crabs, surface fish, and shrimp, as well as a seasonal banquet of horseshoe crab eggs. At plowing time and after heavy rains, it ventures a few miles inland to pluck earthworms from wet pastures and freshly turned earth. It also hawks for flying insects, and is sometimes seen near human habitation, patrolling for refuse. Laughing Gulls are notorious beggars around beach picnickers and fishermen, and are noisy followers of coastal ferries and trawlers.

Description

16–17" (40.5–43 cm). The adult Laughing Gull has a lead-gray mantle and black wing tips. The 2 outermost primaries are entirely black; the rest are narrowly tipped with white like the secondaries and form a white trailing edge to the wing. The tail and underparts are entirely white. In breeding plumage, adults and some subadults have black heads; the legs and the rather long, drooping bill are dark red on most birds, much brighter on a few. Breeding adults briefly acquire a rosy bloom on the underparts. Adults in winter and immatures year-round have a mottled gray head and a black bill and legs. First-year birds have a gray breast and flanks; the brown secondary coverts are much more black on the outer wing and include dark inner primaries that do not contrast with the outer primaries and the subterminal bar on the secondaries. There is a white rump, and a wide, black subterminal tail band extending to the outermost tail feathers. The juvenal plumage, rarely seen after October, is characterized by a mostly brown head and a scaly brown mantle. Like most hooded gulls, the Laughing Gull has white eye crescents.

Winter

Voice

Typically, a high *ca-ha*, sometimes extended to a frenetic *ha-ha-ha-ha-haah-haah-haah*.

Similar Species

See Franklin's Gull. Juvenile Herring Gull much larger and heavier than juvenile Laughing Gull; has brown underparts, rump, and base of tail, and pale inner primaries.

Range

Nests from Maine to Yucatán. Regular summer and fall visitor to Salton Sea, California; casual along California coast. Accidental in Washington. Winters from North Carolina (sometimes a few birds farther north) to Brazil, and from Mexico to northern Peru. Casual visitor inland throughout United States, primarily from Great Lakes south and east.   *Claudia Wilds*

Juvenile
1. *Mostly brown head.*
2. *Scaly brown mantle.*
3. *White rump and broad black tail band.*

Slender, long-winged build.

First-winter bird
1. *Gray breast and flanks.*
2. *Dark wing tips.*

Adults in winter have mottled gray heads.

Breeding adult
1. *Black head.*
2. *Dark gray mantle.*
3. *Black wing tips.*
4. *White trailing edge to wing.*

Laughing call.

Franklin's Gull

Larus pipixcan
Franklin's Gulls are compact little gulls that breed on the northern
prairies. Huge swirling flocks of these birds migrate in steady,
buoyant flight, pausing to roost at night on lakes and reservoirs.
They establish nesting colonies in lush reedbeds and along marshy
lake shores, moving them unpredictably from one year to the next.
Franklin's Gulls hawk sociably over fields, pastures, and prairies on
the breeding grounds and in migration, consuming grasshoppers and
other cropland pests. This species is also somewhat pelagic, with
small numbers of birds recorded several miles offshore.

Description
13–15″ (33–38 cm). The white eye crescents of Franklin's Gull are
joined behind the eye and appear conspicuously thick—almost
gogglelike—in all plumages. The adult or subadult in flight is best
identified by the white bar that separates the black in the wing tip
from the gray mantle. The size of this bar varies greatly; it may be
incomplete, or the wing tip may have only a small patch of black
entirely surrounded by white. The large white primary tips are
prominent in adults at rest (except in autumn, when they are in molt
and no spots are visible). The center of the tail is gray. Breeding
birds have rosy breasts and black heads; nonbreeders of all ages
have pure white underparts and clear-cut, blackish half-hoods. On
first-year birds the tail has an incomplete blackish subterminal band;
the outer pair of feathers is white. The wing pattern is similar to an
immature Laughing Gull's, but the inner primaries are grayish,
contrasting with the dark outer primaries and dark subterminal bar
on the secondaries.

4

Voice
Varied calls include *weeh-a weeh-a weeh-a*, soft *krrruk*, and (only on
breeding grounds) *po-lee, po-lee.*

Similar Species
Laughing Gull larger, less chunky, with relatively longer wings, bill,
and legs. Adult lacks white bar across wing tip and gray in tail;
white primary tips much less prominent on folded wing, and outer
wing much more extensively black below. Nonbreeding head pale,
with indistinct markings; eye crescents not joined at rear and less
conspicuous. First-year's tail band complete; breast and flanks gray;
inner primaries dark. Bonaparte's Gull smaller, with paler mantle;
adults have white wedge on primaries; immatures have strongly
patterned mantle and inconspicuous eye crescents.

Winter adult

Range
Breeds from Saskatchewan and Manitoba south to Utah and east to
Iowa. Migrates mainly over Great Plains. Regular visitor to Great
Lakes; rare on Atlantic and Pacific coasts and in interior Southwest.
Casual in winter in Gulf of Mexico; in small numbers to Guatemala;
winters regularly offshore from Peru to Chile.   *Claudia Wilds*

2

Juvenile
1. Clear-cut blackish half-hood.
2. Bold white eye crescents.
3. Incomplete blackish subterminal tail band with white outer tail feathers.

First-winter bird
1. Bold white eye crescents.
2. Clear-cut blackish half-hood.
3. Dark wing tips.
4. Broad black tail band.

Winter adult has blackish half-hood.

Breeding adult
1. Black head with bold white eye crescents.
2. White bar across wing tip.

Smaller and chunkier than Laughing Gull.

Little Gull

Larus minutus
Smallest of all the gulls, the Little Gull is an Old World species
known to have nested in North America only since 1962. On the
breeding grounds it is usually found in grassy marshes among
colonies of Black or Forster's terns, which are often its companions
in migration as well, when it hawks for insects over marshy ponds or
flooded fields. In winter the Little Gull is likely to be found singly or
in very small numbers among flocks of Bonaparte's Gulls, picking
food from the water's surface along tidal channels and rips or at
sewage outlets and treatment plants.

*Breeding
adults*

Description
11″ (28 cm). The adult Little Gull has rounded wings that are pale
gray above and black below; the tips and trailing edges have a broad
white border. The white tail is square. Apart from the distinctive,
fork-tailed Sabine's Gull, the Little is the only black-hooded gull that
lacks white eye crescents. In breeding plumage, the black head is
set off by a rosy wash on the nape and underparts; the fine bill is
reddish-brown, and the legs are bright red. In winter, the white
head is marked by blackish eye crescents, a blackish ear spot, and a
gray cap; the bill is black and the legs dull red. First-year birds have
more pointed wings; these are marked on the upper surface by a
strong W pattern that is formed by blackish outer primaries and
primary coverts and a dark bar across the inner wing from the wrist
to the tertials. The underwing is white except for dark tips on the
outer primaries and a dark outer web on the outermost ones. The
first-year's white tail has a narrow black band, wider in the center
and not always extending to the outer feathers. The crown is
blackish, and very young birds (juveniles) have a dark collar that
extends down the back and dark brown upperparts with pale feathe
edgings. Subadults often retain some black near the upperwing tips,
the wing linings are pale, and the undersurface of the primaries and
secondaries is dusky.

First-winter

Voice
Usually silent in migration and winter. A harsh *ka-ka-ka;* also *tick-
ka-tick-ka-tick-ka.* Alarm note a *kvee-oo.*

Similar Species
Bonaparte's and Common Black-headed gulls larger; have larger
bills and white wedge on outer primaries, white eye crescents.
Adult Bonaparte's has white underwing with neat black primary
tips; immature has well-defined black trailing edge to wing,
narrowly tipped with white, and lacks blackish cap. Common Black-
headed Gull has dusky inner primaries on underwing; immature has
outer primaries mostly white above, wing with broad blackish
trailing edge, and pale bill with black tip.

Second-winter

Range
Nests locally in southern Ontario, northern Wisconsin, and
Michigan. Winters on Great Lakes, mainly Ontario and Erie, and
along Atlantic Coast, mainly Massachusetts to Virginia. Casual
throughout rest of United States and southern Canada. Breeds
across Eurasia from Netherlands to Mongolia; winters west to
Iceland, east to Japan, south to North Africa and central Asia.
Claudia Wilds

Winter adult
1. *Gray cap and blackish ear spot.*
2. *Black bill.*
3. *Gray mantle.*

Very small size. In flight shows blackish underwing. Breeding adult has black head.

First-winter bird
1. *Blackish crown.*
2. *Strong, dark W pattern on mantle.*
3. *Black tail band.*

White underwing. Second-winter birds have dark underwings.

Juvenile
1. *Blackish crown.*
2. *Dark collar.*
3. *Dark brown upperparts with pale feather edgings.*

Common Black-headed Gull

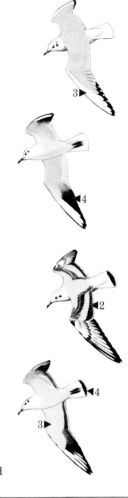

Larus ridibundus
The Common Black-headed Gull is the Old World counterpart of the
very similar Bonaparte's Gull. In western Alaska small flocks may
appear in spring, and there are fair numbers of birds at certain
places in the Northeast. Elsewhere, it is most apt to be seen singly
or in pairs among winter flocks of Bonaparte's or Ring-billed gulls,
or hunting alone along the shore and over harbors and estuaries.

Description
15″ (38 cm). Adult almost identical above to Bonaparte's Gull, but
has slightly paler mantle. Underwing shows outer 3 or 4 primaries
white with black tips; rest are dark gray. Breeding adult has
chocolate-brown head, darker at rear edge and looking black from a
distance. In winter, all ages have white head with blackish eye
crescent and ear spot; bill on adults often bright red (like legs) and
may have black tip. First-winter birds have upper surface of wing
marked by black-edged white outer primaries and white outer
primary coverts; inner wing has dark double bar from wrist to
scapulars; heavy black bar along trailing edge. On underwing,
duskiness of primaries extends across secondaries. Black tail band
like Bonaparte's. Bill usually yellowish or flesh-colored with black
tip; legs also pale. *L.r. sibiricus*, Alaska race, shows several minor
differences, including black bill in adults.

Voice
Usually silent away from breeding grounds.

Similar Species
Bonaparte's Gull obviously smaller; has white underwing narrowly
bordered with black (only primaries on adults; entire trailing edge
on immatures). Bill smaller, all or mostly black. Breeding adult's
head black with more prominent white eye crescents. Immature's
upperwing has black-edged outer primary coverts, a narrow, neat,
black trailing edge with most primaries and secondaries showing
white tips when new. See Little Gull.

Range
In North America, rare spring and summer visitor to western
Alaska; annual on Pacific Coast; uncommon winter visitor to Great
Lakes and Atlantic Coast. Recorded south to Gulf Coast. Has nested
in Newfoundland. Widespread in Old World.   *Claudia Wilds*

Bonaparte's Gull

Larus philadelphia
Small and graceful, Bonaparte's Gull is familiar as a transient and
winter visitor along the coasts of North America and as a migrant on
the inland waterways. In the warmer months, it may be seen
chasing insects over ponds, wet meadows, and flooded fields, often
in the company of Franklin's Gulls or marsh terns. In winter,
feeding flocks frequent tidal rips, snatching small fish from the
water's surface, or visit sewage outlets, bays, and inlets; they can
also be found loafing on mudflats or rough coastal waters.
Surprisingly, the breeding habitat of Bonaparte's Gull is the
northern coniferous forest, where these birds nest 10 to 20 feet high
in spruce, fir, and tamarack.

Description
12–14″ (30.5–35.5 cm). Bonaparte's is a trim little gull with neat
pointed wings and a square tail. The adult has a light gray mantle
with a long wedge of white along the outer wing. The outer
primaries have well-defined black tips forming a narrow black

Winter adult
1. *Long red bill.*
2. *Blackish eye crescent and ear spot.*
3. *Long wedge of white on outer wing.*
4. *Dark underside to inner primaries.*
5. *Red legs.*

First-winter bird
1. *Yellowish bill with black tip.*
2. *Dark bars on upperwing.*
3. *Dusky undersides on all flight feathers of wing.*
4. *Black tail band.*

First-winter bird
1. *Blackish bill with reddish base.*
2. *Blackish ear spot.*
3. *Black trailing edge to wing with narrow white border.*
4. *Narrow subterminal tail band.*

border conspicuous from above and below. Otherwise, the
underwing is white and the primaries translucent. In breeding
plumage, the head is black with contrasting white eye crescents; the
underparts are flushed with pink. In winter, the head is white with a
gray hindcrown and often a gray nape and a blackish eye spot
and ear spot; the underparts are white. First-year birds have a
narrow black tail band and a distinctive wing pattern: the entire
trailing edge, above and below, has a narrow black border, edged by
the small white tips to the secondaries and all but the outer 2
primaries. The upper surface of the wings has heavily black-edged
outer primaries and primary coverts that break up the pale outer
wing; a heavy dark bar crosses the inner wing from wrist to tertials.
At all ages, the fine, pointed bill is black, sometimes with a pale or
reddish base. The adult's legs are orange-red; those of first-year
birds are flesh-colored.

Voice
Sparrowlike conversational notes; also a distinctive nasal *reeer* from
feeding birds.

Similar Species
See Common Black-headed Gull, Little Gull, and Franklin's Gull.

Range
Breeds from western Alaska east to James Bay; nonbreeding birds
summer along northwest and northeast coasts and Great Lakes.
Winters on Pacific Coast from Washington to Mexico, from Great
Lakes along Mississippi Valley to Gulf of Mexico, and from New
England to Greater Antilles. Uncommon transient and rare in
winter throughout interior West.   *Claudia Wilds*

Heermann's Gull

Larus heermanni
This distinctive gull is a common post-breeding visitor from its
Mexican breeding grounds to the West Coast. In North America, it
is easily distinguished by its unique combination of a red bill and
uniformly dark body plumage. It is found along the immediate
Pacific Coast and adjacent offshore waters, often in the company of
other subtropical waterbirds such as Brown Pelicans and Elegant
Terns.

Description
16½–18½″ (42–47 cm). Adult Heermann's Gulls are unmistakable,
with gray plumage that is darker above, a white-tipped black tail,
and a red bill. The head of breeding-plumage adults is pure white,
but in winter birds it shows much gray or dusky color. A very small
percentage of adults shows conspicuous white patches on the
upperside of the wings at the wrist (greater primary coverts). First-
year birds are uniformly dark chocolate-brown; light feather tips
form a scaly pattern on the mantle of juveniles. Very young

Winter adult
1. *Small black bill.*
2. *White head with grayish hindcrown and blackish ear spot.*
3. *Long wedge of white on outer wing.*

Breeding adult
1. *Small black bill.*
2. *Black head.*
3. *White eye crescent.*
4. *Red legs.*

Breeding adult
1. *Red bill.*
2. *White head.*
3. *Gray body.*
4. *Black tail.*

Heermann's have a black-tipped, orange to flesh-colored bill. Older immatures are uniformly dark slate-gray with a reddish-orange bill.

Voice
Typical calls nasal and whiny.

Similar Species
Dark first-year immatures of California and other gulls much more mottled on mantle and underparts.

Range
Summer and fall visitor along Pacific Coast as far north as southern British Columbia; remains through winter along southern Pacific Coast. Casual inland in southwestern states. Accidental in Ohio. Breeds on islands off coast of western Mexico.
Kimball L. Garrett

Mew Gull

Larus canus
The Mew Gull, suggesting a dainty, diminutive Herring Gull or California Gull, is distinguished by its fine, ploverlike bill. It is abundant along our northwestern coasts and river valleys, breeding on marshy lakes and ponds of coastal and interior wooded areas. Winter flocks frequently occur around harbors, dumps, sewage outfalls, fields, and shorelines.

Description
15–16″ (38–40.5 cm). Adults have a gray mantle, darker than the mantles of Ring-billed or Herring gulls, but similar to that of the California Gull. They show extensive white mirrors on the black wing tips; the head, tail, and underparts are white; the legs are greenish. The small, fine bill is an unmarked yellow or greenish-yellow in the breeding season, smudged with dusky-greenish in winter. Winter adults show much gray-brown mottling on the head and neck. First-winter birds are softly mottled with gray-brown above and below and show a variable amount of pure medium-gray on the back; there is often a dark smudge in front of the eye. The tail of first-winter birds is mottled pale gray and has an indistinct grayish-brown terminal band; European birds, which occur casually on the East Coast, may show a darker, more distinct tail band. The legs of first-winter birds are pinkish-gray; the bill is pinkish-gray at the base and dusky at the tip. Second-winter birds resemble adults but have a broken dark subterminal tail band, extensive dusky-black in the primaries, and much dark coloring on the bill tip. The base of the bill is grayer.

Similar Species
Fine bill and small size distinctive in all plumages. First-winter Ring-Billed Gull similar, but underparts whiter and more heavily spotted; wing and tail patterns more distinct; bill stouter (note that European Mew Gulls, occurring casually on East Coast, have slightly larger, stouter bills and thus more closely resemble Ring-bills). Second-winter and adult Ring-billed Gulls have paler gray mantle, pale eye, and distinct black band on pale bill. California Gull and Herring Gull much larger, with longer, heavier bills. Immature Thayer's Gull larger with paler wing tips; first-winter Thayer's have bill entirely black.

First-year bird
1. *Dark-tipped flesh-colored bill.*
2. *Dark chocolate-brown plumage.*

First-winter bird
1. *Small bill.*
2. *Soft gray-brown mottling above and below.*
3. *Pinkish-gray legs.*

Second-winter bird
1. *Mottling on head.*
2. *Gray mantle.*
3. *Dark-tipped bill.*

Range
Breeds from central and southern Alaska and northwestern Canada
south to southern British Columbia and east to northwestern
Saskatchewan. Winters along coast from southeastern Alaska south
to southern California, and in small numbers to Baja California.
Vagrant inland in Southwest. Casual around Great Lakes, interior
eastern Canada. Very rare in winter on Atlantic Coast, primarily
New England. Also across Eurasia.   *Kimball L. Garrett*

Ring-billed Gull

Larus delawarensis
The Ring-billed is a common, medium-size, dove-headed gull that
can be found at various seasons over much of the United States and
southern portions of Canada. Its buoyant flight, rapid wingbeats,
and swirling flight maneuvers set it apart from larger and similar
congeners, even at a great distance. In addition, the Ring-billed's
larger white primary spots and the more extensively black
undersurfaces of the primaries help distinguish it from the Herring
Gull. This species forages by fluttering and dipping to the water, or
by walking, often briskly, over mud flats, along beaches, or on wet
fields. Although Ring-billeds are less frequent at garbage dumps
than certain of the larger gulls, they are commonly found far inland
at urban duck ponds and parking lots of fast-food restaurants.

Description
18–20″ (45.5–51 cm). Adult Ring-billed Gulls resemble adult Herring
Gulls but are smaller and more delicate, with less angular heads.
The clear-cut black band on the yellow bill and the bright yellow or
yellow-green legs are diagnostic. The wing tips are black with
prominent white spots. The eyes are pale yellow. In winter,
Ring-billeds are far less streaked on the neck than Herring Gulls.
Second-year birds have predominantly gray mantles that contrast
with the extensively black primaries; there is often only a single
white spot on the primaries. The tail is variably marked with dusky
subterminal marks that form a partial or interrupted tail band. The
hindneck and underparts are lightly marked with scattered dusky
spots. The eyes become pale by the second year; the legs and bill are
similar to those of adults but are often slightly green. Juveniles and
first-winter birds are paler overall than Herring Gulls at a similar
age, especially on the head and underparts; these areas are white
with varying amounts of black spotting on the hindneck and
crescentlike markings on the breast, sides, and flanks. By
September, the back is gray and the upperwings show an indistinct
brown carpal bar and a darker secondary bar. The juvenile's outer
primaries are very dark above and below. The tail, which is one of
the best points of distinction, is white with a mottled base and a
rather narrow, speckled or broken subterminal band—very
different from the wide black band of the Herring Gull. The legs are
pink; the bill has a pink base and dark tip. The eyes are brown.

Adult
1. *Unmarked yellow bill.*
2. *Gray mantle.*
3. *Extensive white mirrors on black wing tips.*
4. *Pinkish legs.*

Adult
1. *Yellow bill with clear-cut black ring.*
2. *Pale gray mantle.*
3. *Yellow legs.*

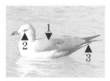

Second-winter bird
1. *Gray mantle.*
2. *Pale eyes.*
3. *Dusky subterminal marks on tail.*

Voice
Common call a *kree, kree, kree* when squabbling over food. Calls
higher-pitched than Herring Gull's.

Similar Species
Mew Gull has much finer bill; first-winter birds have darker, less
heavily spotted underparts; wing and tail patterns less distinct;
second-winter and adult birds have darker gray mantle, dark eye;
adult has unmarked bill. See California and immature Herring gulls.
Also compare second-year with adult Black-legged Kittiwake.

Range
Breeds in West from central Oregon and Washington east to
Alberta, central Saskatchewan, and south-central Manitoba, south
to northeastern California, southeastern Wyoming, and
northeastern North Dakota. In East from southern Quebec and
northeastern Newfoundland south to northern Michigan, southern
Ontario, northern New York, and (recently) northern New England.
Population increasing. Winters from southwestern British Columbia
(local) to Washington, lower Great Lakes, and Maine south into
Mexico and Cuba.   *Wayne R. Petersen*

California Gull

Larus californicus
This abundant western gull breeds in colonies on the islands and
shores of interior lakes, and winters in large flocks along the Pacific
Coast. Foraging birds range widely from coastal and interior valleys
to urban centers, seacoasts, and offshore waters. The species
suggests a small, dark Herring Gull, but adult Californias have
greenish-yellow legs and both red and black spots on the bill.

Description
18–20″ (45.5–51 cm). Adult California Gulls have a medium-gray
mantle that is darker than the mantles of Ring-billed Gulls or North
American Herring Gulls. They show contrasting black wing tips
with white mirrors; the remainder of the plumage is white. Winter
adults show some dusky mottling on the head and neck. The legs of
breeding adults are a bright yellow-green, becoming duller in
winter. The yellow bill shows black and red subterminal spots; the
black spot may be absent during the breeding season. The adult's
eyes are dark. First-winter birds are mottled gray-brown above and
somewhat lighter below, with dark, dusky primaries; they have dull
pinkish legs. In flight, first-years show dark primaries and a dusky
band across the secondaries that contrasts with the lighter, mottled
gray-brown forewing. The tail is dusky-brown with no distinct band;
the rump is barred brown-and-white. Juveniles are very dark
overall with light mottling to the upperparts. They might be
confused with first-winter Heermann's Gulls, but young California
Gulls have pale undertail coverts and pink legs. The bill of the
juvenile is black, but becomes dull gray-pink on the basal two-thirds
early in the first winter. Second- and third-winter birds have
progressively more gray on the mantle and white on the underparts,
and have gray-green legs; they may show a blackish ring on the bill.

Similar Species
Ring-billed Gull slightly smaller, shorter-billed. Adult Ring-billed
paler gray on mantle, with white eyes, black bill ring. First-winter
Ring-billed whiter below than same age California; shows pale gray
on back and tail with thinner, dark subterminal band. Third-winter
California Gulls may show distinct black ring on bill, but have
darker mantles than Ring-bills and never have pale eyes. Herring
Gull larger with stouter bill; adult paler on mantle, with pink legs,
light eye. Mew Gull much smaller, with shorter, slimmer bill. First-

First-winter bird
1. *Gray back.*
2. *Indistinct carpal bar.*
3. *Dark, contrasting primaries.*
4. *Pale underparts.*
5. *Narrow tail band.*
6. *Dark-tipped bill.*
7. *Pink legs.*

First-winter bird
1. *Gray-pink base to bill.*
2. *Mottled upperparts.*
3. *Pale mottling on underparts.*
4. *Pinkish legs.*

Second-winter bird
1. *Extensive gray on mantle.*
2. *White underparts.*
3. *Gray-green legs.*

winter Heermann's Gull similar to juvenile California Gull, but has dark undertail coverts and black legs.

Range
Breeds in western interior from Canadian prairie provinces south to east-central California, northern Utah, central Montana, and central North Dakota. Winters along Pacific Coast and adjacent lowlands from Washington to western Mexico; also locally inland in West. Vagrant east to Atlantic and Gulf coasts.   *Kimball L. Garrett*

Herring Gull

Larus argentatus
The familiar Herring Gull is the most widespread and abundant gull in North America, breeding along both coasts (although much less commonly in the West), as well as on large inland lakes and rivers. These omnivorous scavengers gather at dumps and fish wharves, around offshore fishing operations, and even in plowed fields. Early in the morning and during stormy weather, many fly inland to feed or bathe in freshwater lakes; later, they may be seen flying coastward in fixed formation toward their communal evening roosts. In sunny or windy weather, their normally steady flapping is frequently interrupted by extended periods of hawklike soaring.

Winter

Description
23–26″ (58.5–66 cm). Adult Herring Gulls are large, with pale gray mantles and extensive black wing tips with conspicuous white spots in the outer 2 primaries. The bill is yellow with an orange spot near the gonys; the eyes are pale yellow with a yellow eye-ring, and the legs are flesh-colored. In winter, the crown, nape, hindneck, and sides of the upper breast are extensively streaked with dusky coloring. Second-year birds may exhibit considerable variation, but usually have much pale gray on the back as well as a scattering of gray feathers among the otherwise mottled brown wing coverts. There is a prominent dark brown bar on the secondaries; the outer primaries are mainly black, contrasting with 4 clear gray inner primaries that produce a pale, translucent patch that is obvious in birds overhead. The head and underparts may exhibit varying amounts of dusky streaking; the tail is white with an extensive, broad, black, and variably complete subterminal band. In the second year, the bill is flesh-colored or dull yellow with a dusky subterminal band and sometimes some red near the gonys. The eye may be brown or pale. Juveniles and first-winter birds are grayish-brown, streaked below and scaly above; the dorsal pattern becomes more barred and less uniform in appearance with age. As in second-year birds, there is a pale zone between the dark brown outer primaries and the pale inner primaries, visible from above and below. The white rump and upper tail are streaked and barred with dusky coloring, with a broad, dark brown subterminal band that generally shows much lower contrast than that of similar species. The bill is black with a diffuse pale base; the eyes are dark brown, and the legs

4

Adult
1. *Yellow bill with black and red spots.*
2. *Medium-gray mantle.*
3. *Yellow-green legs.*

Breeding adult
1. *Yellow bill with orange spot.*
2. *Yellow eye and eye-ring.*
3. *Pale gray mantle.*
4. *Black wing tips with 2 white mirrors.*
5. *Flesh-colored legs.*

Dark streaks on head in winter.

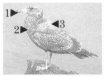

Juvenile
1. *Black bill with diffuse pale base.*
2. *Head and underparts dusky, streaked with gray-brown.*
3. *Scaly upperparts.*
4. *Wide subterminal black tail band.*

are a dull flesh-color. Wear and abrasion may cause individual first-summer birds to become very pale and blond-looking by midsummer, with the primaries appearing buff-white in some cases. In the West, many first-year birds are distinctly pale-headed.

Voice
Common calls include trumpeting *keeyow, kyow-kyow-kyow;* flushing note *eeeyou;* low *ha-ha-ha* given near nest.

Similar Species
See Ring-billed, California, Thayer's, and immature Lesser and Great Black-backed gulls.

Range
Breeds from Alaska and northern Mackenzie and east to Labrador and Newfoundland, south to southern British Columbia, southern Mackenzie, western Saskatchewan, eastern Montana, central Wisconsin, northern Ohio, northern New York; along Atlantic to North Carolina. Winters south to Panama and the West Indies. Also breeds in Old World.   *Wayne R. Petersen*

Thayer's Gull

Larus thayeri
Probably conspecific with the Iceland Gull and formerly considered a subspecies of the Herring Gull, Thayer's is often difficult to distinguish in the field. The darker first-winter Thayer's closely resembles the Herring Gull, while the paler adult and immature Thayer's may be impossible to distinguish from the Iceland. Although it breeds only in northern Canada, Thayer's can turn up anywhere, even in southern or inland areas of the United States during migration and winter.

Description
22½–25″ (57–63.5 cm). The typical adult Thayer's Gull is similar to the adult Herring Gull, except that it has a brown iris and normally little or no black on the undersurface of its wing tips. Paler adult Thayer's also occur, with larger areas of gray or white and less black on the upper surface of the wing tips; their eyes may be paler brown or dark yellow. Winter adults and third-year birds are heavily mottled with gray-brown on the head and neck; this mottling may be extensive enough to give the birds a hooded look. Typical first-winter immatures are similar to first-winter Herring Gulls. In first-winter Thayer's, the brown outer primaries are the same shade or slightly darker than the rest of the upper wing surface. The folded primaries often show pale feather edges on the tips, and the undersides of the wing tips are whitish. Some first-winter birds are paler, appearing whitish with buff or brownish-gray mottling overall; they have a solid brown or gray subterminal tail band that is sometimes difficult to see. The outer primaries and secondaries, although pale, are still nearly the same color as the upper wing coverts; they are a shade darker than the whiter inner primaries, giving the flight feathers a dark-light-dark pattern. When judging wing tip color, it is important to note that the primaries of Herring, Thayer's, and Iceland gulls often appear darker when folded at rest and paler when spread in flight. Second-winter Thayer's Gull resembles a pale, washed-out second-winter Herring Gull with a gray or grayish-brown tail band and wing tips. Thayer's Gulls often appear smaller overall than the Herring Gull, especially the bill and head, and may have a rounder head profile. All ages of Thayer's Gulls have a smallish bill with a gently curving culmen and no thickening toward the tip; this can be a very helpful field mark.

Second-winter bird
1. *Gray back.*
2. *Mottled gray and brown wings.*
3. *Pale zone between dark outer and light inner primaries.*
4. *Black tail band.*
5. *Pink or yellow bill with dark tip.*

Darker first-winter bird
1. *Smaller head and bill than Herring Gull's.*
2. *Outer primaries same shade or darker than rest of upperwing.*

Paler first-winter bird
1. *Pale gray-brown plumage.*
2. *Whitish inner primaries.*
3. *Solid gray subterminal tail band.*

Similar Species
Adult Herring Gull has yellow eyes, black on underside of wing tips.
First-winter Herring has blackish wing tips above, darker than rest
of wing; underside of wing tips usually has some black. Second-
winter Herring has black wing tips and tail band. Darker adult
Iceland Gulls not always separable from pale adult Thayer's, usually
not as dark on wing tips, mantle often paler, eye color possibly
darker brown. First-winter Iceland sometimes not distinguishable
from pale first-winter Thayer's; lacks solid tail band, although tail
mottling may suggest vague, ill-defined band: has uniform whitish
flight feathers paler than upper wing coverts. Also see Glaucous-
winged Gull.

Range
Breeds on northern Baffin Island and other islands north of
mainland Canada. Winters mainly along Pacific Coast from British
Columbia to Mexico; rare but regular in interior West, on Great
Lakes, and on northern Atlantic Coast; casual on southern Atlantic
and Gulf coasts and in inland western United States.
Kim R. Eckert

Iceland Gull

Larus glaucoides
Iceland Gulls present an identification problem because the typical
adults differ from the Glaucous Gull only in size. In addition, first-
winter Icelands and adults with dusky primaries can be nearly
identical to the paler Thayer's Gull. Some authorities consider the
Iceland and Thayer's gulls to be forms of a single species.

Description
23–26″ (58.5–66 cm). The typical adult Iceland Gull, nearly identical
in plumage to the Glaucous Gull, is nearly the size of a Herring Gull;
it has a pale gray mantle, white flight feathers, a yellow bill with a
red spot near the tip of the lower mandible, pink legs, and yellow
eyes. Darker adult Iceland Gulls also occur; these differ in having
various amounts and shades of gray on the tips of the upper surface
of the outer primaries, with some individuals having even blackish
markings; the eyes of these darker birds often appear brown. First-
winter Iceland Gulls are whitish overall with buff or grayish
mottling everywhere except on the pale flight feathers (these
feathers are the palest part of the plumage). The bill is all or mostly
dark; first-winter birds lack an obvious tail band, although there
may be mottling on the tail that suggests an ill-defined band.
Second-winter Iceland Gulls are whiter with less mottling than first-
winter birds, and have a distinct pale base to the bill. Third-winter
birds basically resemble adults.

Similar Species
First-winter Glaucous Gull has pink bill with sharply defined black
tip. Glaucous at other ages distinguished by larger size; this often
difficult to determine since smaller Glaucous overlaps larger Herring
Gull in overall size, and larger Iceland overlaps smaller Herring;
size best judged in bulk of bill, head, and neck. Wing tips of Glaucous at
rest can extend beyond tail a distance no greater than bill length;
Iceland's wing tips extend beyond tail a distance greater than bill
length. Glaucous sometimes has flatter, rather than rounded, head
profile. Paler adult Thayer's, not always separable from darker adult
Iceland, usually has more black in upperwing tips; mantle sometimes
darker; eyes possibly lighter brown or dark yellow. Paler first-
winter Thayer's, sometimes not distinguishable from first-winter
Iceland, has more obvious solid gray or brown subterminal tail band,
and dark-light-dark pattern to flight feathers, with inner primaries

Breeding adult
1. *Brown eyes.*
2. *Little or no black on underwing tips.*

Head and bill appear smaller than Herring Gull's.

Typical adult
1. *Yellow eyes.*
2. *Whitish primaries.*

Head, bill, and neck smaller than in Glaucous Gull.

Darker adult
1. *Gray markings on whitish primaries.*
2. *Brown eyes.*

palest part of upperwing surface. (Note that folded wing tips may
appear darker than when spread in flight.) Glaucous-winged Gull, a
Pacific Coast species, is similar, but has a stouter bill.

Range
Breeds on eastern Baffin Island and coastal Greenland. Winters
along Atlantic Coast from Newfoundland to Virginia, rarely on
eastern Great Lakes; casual on western Great Lakes.
Kim R. Eckert

Lesser Black-backed Gull

Larus fuscus
The Lesser Black-backed Gull, a rare European visitor, has been
seen in North America with increasing regularity, especially among
flocks of migrating and wintering gulls that gather around beaches,
harbors, and landfills of the Great Lakes and East Coast.

Description
21–22″ (53.5–56 cm). The subspecies of Lesser Black-backed Gull
that accounts for virtually all North American records is *L. f.
graellsii;* it has a dark gray mantle that is easy to distinguish from
the light gray of Herring and Ring-billed gulls and the dull black of
Great Black-backed Gull. This bird looks distinctively long-winged
at rest and has a bill typically thinner than a Herring Gull's, without
any marked expansion at the tip. The adult has pale yellow to bright
orange-yellow legs and a yellow bill with a large red spot. The black
wing tips, with 1 or 2 white spots on the outermost primaries,
contrast with the dark gray mantle. In winter, the white head
acquires heavy streaking and a dark smudge around the pale
yellowish-gray eyes. First-year birds and most second-winter birds
can be safely distinguished from Herring Gulls of the same age only
in flight; the primaries and secondaries form a continuous blackish
bar along the trailing edge of the underwing. On first-year birds, the
upperwing surface is marked by an all-dark outer wing and 2 dark
bars on the inner wing formed by the secondaries and greater
secondary coverts. The Lesser Black-backed's smaller size and
elongated silhouette are often shared by first-year Herring Gulls,
and are thus not reliable field marks until the second winter. The
juvenile's pink legs and black bill may be retained for 2 years, but
most second-year birds have bills with a pale base and tip. Most
immature birds acquire dark gray backs by early in their second
spring; from this point on, they increasingly resemble adults,
though some subadults still have pink legs and a dark smudge on
the bill. The Scandinavian subspecies, *L. f. fuscus,* still accidental in
our range, is much darker in all plumages. The adult's mantle is as
black as that of a Great Black-backed Gull, often with a brownish
cast. Birds in winter plumage have little or no streaking on the
head.

Similar Species
Herring Gull larger, with pink legs, shorter-winged appearance at

First-winter bird
1. *Pale gray-brown plumage.*
2. *Whitish flight feathers.*
3. *Tail without band.*
4. *Dark bill.*

First-winter bird
1. *Entirely dark flight feathers.*
2. *Dark greater secondary coverts.*

Second-spring bird
1. *Gray back.*

rest. Adult and subadult Herring Gulls have light gray mantle;
immatures have pale inner primaries and greater secondary coverts.
Great Black-backed Gull much larger, has pink legs, black mantle;
head unstreaked in winter. Dark subspecies of Western Gull has
pink legs, amber-yellow eyes; it and Yellow-footed Gull (with lemon-
yellow eyes) have larger bodies, unstreaked heads in winter; longer
and much stouter bill has tip bulbous above and sharply angled
below.

*Breeding
adult*

Range
Most North American records from Atlantic coastal plain but
reports increasing in Midwest and Gulf States. Recorded in
Northwest Territories, Manitoba, California, and Colorado. Also in
British Isles, northern Europe, and Iceland; winters south to
southern Africa and east to Iran.   *Claudia Wilds*

*Breeding
adult*

Slaty-backed Gull

Larus schistisagus
This large gull of the Bering Sea occurs in winter along leads and
edges of the pack ice, sometimes in flocks of more than 30.

Description
27″ (68.5 cm). Mantle is color of wet slate; often appears black at a
distance. Contrast between dark gray mantle and white spotted
black wing tips visible at close range. Primaries white-tipped;
outermost have large subterminal or terminal white spot, and
penultimate have much smaller white spot. Legs and feet pink; eye
cream-colored with pale pink eye-ring. Immature plumages
apparently parallel those of Great Black-backed Gull.

Similar Species
See Herring and Western gulls.

Range
Rare visitor in spring, summer, and fall along Bering Sea coast of
Alaska, east rarely to Kodiak Island Archipelago; more numerous in
winter. Native to Ne. Eurasia.   *Daniel D. Gibson*

Yellow-footed Gull

Larus livens
Formerly considered a subspecies of the Western Gull, the Yellow-
footed Gull breeds in the Gulf of California and regularly wanders
north to the Salton Sea in southern California. While very similar to
the Western Gull, it differs not only in leg color but in its deeper
bill, somewhat deeper call, and its apparently quicker advance to
adult plumage, as well as in some aspects of its breeding biology.
The molt sequence of this species is 2 or 3 months ahead of that of
most other gulls. At the Salton Sea the Yellow-footed Gull is seen in
small numbers, generally along the immediate shoreline.

Bill

Description
21–23″ (53.5–58.5 cm). The adult Yellow-footed Gull is very similar
to the adult Western but shows bright yellow legs and feet, a
slightly darker mantle, and a slightly deeper bill. Juveniles (seen
into August) are dark slaty-brown, with pale edges to the mantle
feathers and a strongly contrasting whitish belly and undertail
coverts; they also have more white on the rump than the Western

Winter adult
1. *Dark gray mantle.*
2. *Yellow legs.*
3. *Pale yellow-gray eyes.*
4. *Heavily streaked head.*
5. *Slim bill, not expanded at tip.*

Adult
1. *Dark gray mantle contrasting with black wing tips.*
2. *Cream-colored eye with pale pink eyering.*

Large size.
North Pacific only.

Adult
1. *Deep, yellow bill.*
2. *Dark gray mantle.*
3. *Yellow legs.*

Gull. Juveniles and first-winter birds have pinkish legs like Western
Gulls. First-winter birds have a paler head and are largely pale
below; they have some dark gray mixed in on the mantle, brown
wings, and show a black tail that contrasts with an extensively
white rump. One-year-old individuals have a dark gray mantle with
some brown mottling remaining in the wings; they have yellow legs
and a black tail. Second-winter birds resemble third-winter
Westerns in being white below and dark slate-gray on the entire
mantle, but differ in having yellow legs and a broader, more
complete black band on the tail. By the third winter, Yellow-footed
Gulls have essentially adult plumage.

Voice
Somewhat deeper than corresponding calls of Western Gull.

Similar Species
Western Gull has pink legs and feet, usually has paler mantle; bill
less deep. First-winter Westerns darker and more uniform gray-
brown below, without the strongly contrasting whitish belly of the
juvenile Yellow-footed Gull. Third-winter birds resemble second-
winter Yellow-footed but have pink legs. Other than Western Gull,
no large, dark mantled gulls normally occur in range of Yellow-
footed. See Lesser Black-backed Gull.

Range
Visitor to Salton Sea in southern California, primarily in summer
and fall. Resident in Gulf of California. Casual on Pacific Coast in
San Diego area.   *Kimball L. Garrett*

Western Gull

Larus occidentalis
The Western Gull is a large, abundant gull found in marine habitats
along the Pacific Coast south of the range of the paler but closely
related Glaucous-winged Gull. The Western is the only widespread,
large, dark-mantled gull on the West Coast. It breeds on offshore
islands and protected islets along the coast, rarely venturing very
far inland.

Description
20–23″ (51–58.5 cm). The adult Western Gull is immaculate white
with a dark gray mantle that merges into black wing tips; there are
white spots near the tips of the primaries and a white trailing edge
to the wing. Southern birds have a very dark slate-gray mantle, but
north of central California the mantle lightens to a medium gray,
slightly darker than the mantle of a California Gull. In flight, the
underside of the wing shows a pronounced dark shadow along the
secondaries. In winter, the heads of more northerly birds are lightly
marked with dusky coloring. The thick, bulbous bill of the adult is

Second-winter bird
1. *Dark gray mantle.*
2. *White underparts.*
3. *Black band on tail.*
4. *Yellow legs.*

First-winter bird
1. *Deeper bill than Western Gull's.*
2. *White underparts.*
3. *Some dark gray feathers on mantle.*
4. *Pinkish legs.*

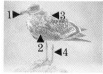

First-winter bird
1. *Thick bill.*
2. *Mottled gray-brown underparts.*
3. *Mottled gray-brown upperparts.*
4. *Pink legs.*

yellow with a red spot on the lower mandible. The legs are pink in
all age groups. First-winter birds are mottled dark gray-brown,
with much dusky black on the primaries and some white mottling on
the rump. The heavy bill is black in the first winter. Second-winter
birds are whiter below; they have some of the adult's mantle color
on the back but retain brown mottling on the wing coverts. The bill
lightens at the base in the second winter. Third-winter birds
resemble adults but have solid blackish primaries, some dark
mottling on the head and chest, and some black near the bill tip.
They retain a black tail band. By the fourth winter, most birds are
essentially in adult plumage.

Similar Species
Glaucous-winged Gull similar in all plumages but paler than even
northern Westerns; wing tips never blackish; adults show more
mottling on head, neck, and chest in winter. Intergrades between
Western and Glaucous-winged numerous in Pacific Northwest.
Adult Herring has more contrast between mantle and black wing
tips, less bulbous bill, pale yellow eye; immature Herrings paler-
winged, slimmer-billed. Yellow-footed Gull has bright yellow legs
and feet, darker mantle, deeper bill; first-years whiter below;
second-winter birds similar to third-winter Western but with yellow
legs, black tail band. See Great Black-backed Gull. Slaty-backed
Gull accidental in British Columbia; is larger, with darker mantle.

Range
Resident on Pacific Coast from central Washington south to Baja
California; a few winter north to southern British Columbia.
Vagrant inland in West.   *Kimball L. Garrett*

Glaucous-winged Gull

Larus glaucescens
This large, heavy-billed gull is a paler northern relative of the
Western Gull, with which it frequently hybridizes; some authorities
believe the 2 are conspecific. It is common in marine habitats in the
Pacific Northwest, occurring in areas similar to those preferred by
the Western Gull. The Glaucous-winged regularly wanders only a
short distance inland, except in the broad river valleys of the
Northwest, where it may occur some distance from the coast.

Description
21–24" (53.5–61 cm). The adult Glaucous-winged Gull is similar to
the adult Western but has a paler gray mantle and very pale gray
primaries showing varying amounts of darker gray near the tips.
Winter adults have much gray-brown mottling on the head, neck,
and chest; this mottling is more extensive than in the Western Gull.
Immature plumages are similar to corresponding plumages of the
Western Gull but are much paler. When the bird is at rest, the
primaries appear to be the same color as or slightly paler than the

Adult
1. *Thick yellow bill.*
2. *Dark gray mantle.*
3. *Black wing tips.*
4. *Pink legs.*

Third-winter bird
1. *Black near tip of bill.*
2. *Dark mottling on head and chest.*

   Shows black tail band in flight.

First-winter bird
1. *Black bill.*
2. *Paler mottling than in Western Gull.*
3. *Pink legs.*

remainder of the wing. Birds in worn plumage at the end of the first
and second winters may be very whitish. The gray mantle color of
the adult begins to appear in the second winter; in second-winter
plumage, the wing coverts, head, breast, and tail are mottled
grayish-buff. Third-winter birds resemble adults but retain a gray
band on the tail and are more mottled on the head and chest. In
adults, the heavy bill is yellow with a red spot on the lower
mandible; in first-winter birds, it is entirely black. Older immatures
have an irregular dark tip to the bill that is not sharply separated
from the pale base. The legs are pink in all plumages, brightest in
breeding adults. Eye color varies from yellow to brown.

3►

Similar Species
See Western Gull. Frequent intergrades in Northwest may be
superficially similar to Herring Gull, but Herring has thinner bill,
pale yellow eye, and sharply contrasting black wing tips. Thayer's
Gull usually smaller, with smaller, thinner bill and slightly darker
wing tips; however, Glaucous-winged intergrades have darker
primaries like Thayer's. Immature Glaucous-winged smudgier
looking overall than Thayer's; at rest, primaries same color as or
slightly paler than rest of wing, not slightly darker as in Thayer's.
Glaucous Gull heavier than Glaucous-winged, has whiter primaries;
immature Glaucous has black bill tip sharply cut off from pinkish to
flesh-colored basal two-thirds of bill. Western Gull has darker
mantle and primaries.

Range
Resident from Aleutian Islands and western and southern coasts of
Alaska south to northwestern Washington. South along Pacific
Coast to Baja California in winter. Vagrant inland in West.
Kimball L. Garrett

Glaucous Gull

Larus hyperboreus
This very large, heavy-bodied gull of the far North is characterized
by its largely white plumage. It nests primarily along Arctic coasts
and winters along seacoasts and larger inland lakes. In most of
North America, it occurs singly or in small numbers at harbors,
garbage dumps, and other sites that attract concentrations of large
gulls.

◄3

Description
21–26″ (53.5–66 cm). In all age groups, the Glaucous Gull is large
and heavy-bodied with a long, heavy bill and pink legs. The adults
are pale gray on the mantle but otherwise white, including the
primaries. The adult's bill is yellow with a red spot on the lower
mandible; the iris is yellowish-white. Winter adults show some
brownish streaking on the head and chest. First-winter birds are
mottled and barred with pale gray-buff; the primaries are very pale
gray-buff, becoming whitish at the tips. The bill in the first winter is
flesh-pink on the basal two-thirds, with a sharply demarcated black

Breeding adult
1. *Pure white head.*
2. *Pale gray mantle.*
3. *Darker gray at tips of primaries.*
4. *Pink legs.*

Third-winter bird
1. *Irregular dark tip to bill.*
2. *Paler mantle than in Western Gull of same age.*
3. *Pink legs.*

Breeding adult
1. *Long, heavy bill.*
2. *Pale gray mantle.*
3. *White primaries.*
4. *Pink legs.*

*Large size.
Heavy body.*

tip. Second-winter birds are paler and more buff-colored, with less
black in the bill tip. By January, most second-winter birds begin to
show pale gray feathers on the back (which may be difficult to see)
and a pale eye. (Many faded first-year birds have been misidentified
as second-year birds.) Third-winter birds resemble adults but show
some buff-brown mottling on the body and pale gray in the
primaries; they also retain a black subterminal spot on the bill.
Alaska and West Coast Glaucous Gulls are slightly smaller than
birds farther east.

Similar Species
Iceland Gull similar but has much smaller bill and often more gray
markings in primaries. Iceland smaller, but this difference
sometimes difficult to determine; size best judged in bulk of bill,
head, and neck. First-winter Iceland has bill all or mostly dark.
Adult Glaucous-winged Gull has extensive gray in primaries,
somewhat shorter and more bulbous bill; immatures may be very
pale (particularly in worn plumage at end of first and second
winters) but bill entirely black, or extensively and irregularly tipped
black. Albinos of other large, pink-legged gulls (for example
Herring, Western) are occasionally noted; they lack regular gray-
buff marbling of young Glaucous and do not show Glaucous' bill
pattern. Other gulls in worn summer plumage may be mistaken for
Glaucous.

Range
Breeds on Arctic coasts of northern Alaska and Canada. Winters
south to northern United States, primarily on coasts and Great
Lakes; rarely south to southern states (very rare in interior
Southwest). Also across northern Eurasia.   *Kimball L. Garrett*

Great Black-backed Gull

Larus marinus
The Great Black-backed is the largest gull in North America and the
only common species of the Atlantic Coast with a black mantle. Its
large size and aggressiveness make it the dominant species in mixed
gull breeding colonies as well as in competitive feeding situations.
The Great Black-backed Gull is gradually colonizing the Great Lakes
and the mid-Atlantic coast; it is abundant in winter on offshore
Atlantic fishing banks.

Description
28–31″ (71–78.5 cm). Adults are black or blackish-slate above with a
white head, tail, and underparts. In flight, the very broad wings
show a prominent white border on the trailing edge, and there are
white spots at the tips of the outer 2 primaries; this gives the wings
a diagnostic white tip. The heavy yellow bill has an orange spot near
the gonys. The eye is cream-colored with a vermilion eye-ring, and
the legs are a dull flesh color. Second-year birds are recognizable by
their large size and 2-toned upperparts; the back often shows a

Faded first-winter bird
1. *Plumage nearly pure white.*
2. *Flesh-pink bill with dark tip.*

Large size.

First-winter bird
1. *Flesh-pink bill with dark tip.*
2. *Plumage mottled and barred with pale gray-buff.*
3. *Pink legs.*

Large size.
Heavy build.

First-winter bird
1. *Heavy black bill.*
2. *Whitish head and upper breast.*
3. *Checkered mantle.*

Large size.

black-saddled effect in contrast to the wings, which have variably
mottled brown and gray-brown coverts and blackish-brown outer
primaries. The tail has a dark subterminal band of varying extent.
The head and underparts are white with variable amounts of coarse,
dusky-colored streaking on the lower hindneck, breast, sides, and
flanks. The bill of second-year birds is usually pale-based with a dark
subterminal area. Birds in juvenal and first-winter plumage are
much whiter on the head, neck, and underparts than Herring Gulls
of the same age and have heavy black bills that contrast sharply
with the white of the head and upper breast. This feature is unique
among similar East Coast gulls in corresponding plumage. The
underparts and head are coarsely streaked with dusky coloring, and
there is a conspicuous dark crescent in front of the eye. The
upperparts of juveniles are strongly checkered and barred, an effect
produced by the broad white edges on the otherwise dark feathers.
Juvenile Great Black-backeds give an overall impression of being
paler than the Lesser Black-backed and less scaly than the Herring.
The base of the immature's tail is white, and the dark subterminal
band is wide but broken and diffuse; this band is much less
continuous and complete than in either juvenile Herring or Lesser
Black-backed gull. The eyes are dark brown, and the legs are a dull
flesh color as in the adult.

Voice
Common call, a hollow *cowwp, cowwp;* also deep *err-ul.*

Similar Species
See immature Herring Gull and Lesser Black-backed Gull.

Range
Breeds along East Coast of North America from Labrador south to
North Carolina and recently inland to Great Lakes. Winters south to
Carolinas and sparingly to Florida and Gulf Coast. Also breeds in
Old World.   *Wayne R. Petersen*

Black-legged Kittiwake

Rissa tridactyla
The Black-legged Kittiwake is a medium-size gull that is common
over pelagic waters of the cool northern oceans during its
nonbreeding season. Foraging birds range widely, diving to the
surface for food and on occasion submerging briefly. Flocks scavenge
at fishing vessels, readily following moving ships while searching the
wake. Quick, short wingbeats give kittiwakes a buoyant, distinctive
flight that allows experienced observers to identify them from a
distance. Kittiwakes bank and glide more easily in strong winds
than other gulls; they are like fulmars and other "tubenoses" in this
foul-weather adaptation.

Description
17″ (43 cm). The adult is relatively slim, long-winged, and cleanly
marked, with a gray mantle and white body. The underwing is white
and sharply defined; the wing tips are solid contrasting black and cut
straight across both the upper and lower wings. An indistinct,
lighter gray upperwing area immediately inside the black wing tip

First-winter bird
1. *Checkered mantle.*
2. *Diffuse subterminal band on tail.*

Large size.

Adult
1. *Black mantle.*
2. *Heavy yellow bill with orange spot near tip.*
3. *Flesh-colored legs.*

Large size.

Breeding adult from above
1. *Gray mantle.*
2. *Distinctly marked black wing tips.*
3. *Unmarked yellow bill.*

further enhances this contrast. The white tail is squared or very
slightly notched. The unmarked yellowish bill is somewhat similar to
the Mew Gull's in length and shape; the upper mandible is gracefully
curved and the lower has a shallow angle, or "break," to the lower
mandible. In flight, the black legs are often concealed by the
undertail coverts. Winter adults have a gray suffusion across the
back of the head and nape. First-year birds are much more boldly
marked, with a strong, dark M mark across the back and
upperwings, a dark spot behind the eye, a dark bar across the nape,
and a narrow dark band across the end of the tail. The triangle
formed on the trailing edge of the wing by the dark bar across the
upperwing is whiter than the rest of the mantle. The first-year's bill
is dark. Second-year birds have a less distinct upperwing pattern
and a yellow bill.

Voice
A nasal *kittiwake*, usually heard from flocks; in chorus, a curious
barking sound; other gull-like calls occasionally heard away from
colonies.

Similar Species
Red-legged Kittiwake smaller, more compact, with rounder head,
shorter bill, darker mantle; black on wing tips more extensive and
less sharply defined; dark wing linings have window; feet and legs
bright vermilion. Adult Mew Gull similar in size and mantle shade,
but black on wing tip more extensive, irregularly shaped, and with
white spot; summer Kittiwakes with unmarked head may appear
similar to Mew when 2 species float on water. Immature Sabine's
Gull more cleanly marked.

Range
Breeds on cliffs along northern Gulf of Alaska, Aleutians, north in
Bering Sea, and in Canadian Arctic, Newfoundland, and Cape
Breton, Nova Scotia. Winters at sea south to latitude of southern
California in Pacific, and to edge of Gulf Stream waters in Atlantic.
Occurs occasionally in many inland localities, including Great Lakes.
Numbers vary from year to year at peripheral areas of range. Often
absent from pelagic range during breeding season, when even
nonbreeding birds concentrate coastally, but many 1-year-olds
encountered in Atlantic.   *Terence Wahl*

Red-legged Kittiwake

Rissa brevirostris
A small gull, similar to the much more common and widespread
Black-legged Kittiwake, this species is also relatively pelagic during
the nonbreeding season. In its habits and flight style it is similar to
the Black-legged, but flies with a slightly faster wingbeat. Like its
scavenging relative, the Red-legged often follows vessels, searching
for items in the wake. Nonbreeding birds are seen over deep waters
farther from shore than adults and most Black-legged Kittiwakes.

Description
15″ (38 cm). The adult is slightly smaller and more compact than the
Black-legged Kittiwake, with a rounder head, shorter bill,
noticeably darker mantle, and less sharply defined black wing tips.
The wings appear shorter and broader than the Black-legged's; the
dark wing linings (similar to those of a Western Gull) and the
extensively dark wing tips make distinction between the 2
kittiwakes possible at a considerable distance. The greater contrast
between the dark mantle and the white trailing edge of the flight

**Breeding adult
from below**
1. *White head and
   underparts.*
2. *Distinctly marked
   black wing tips.*
3. *Unmarked yellow
   bill.*
4. *Black legs.*

First-year bird
1. *Dark bill.*
2. *Dark bar across
   nape.*
3. *Dark M across back
   and upperwings.*
4. *Dark band across
   end of tail.*

Adult
1. *Dark mantle with
   black wing tips.*
2. *Bold white trailing
   edge to wings.*
3. *Dark underwing.*
4. *Unmarked yellow
   bill.*

*Has vermilion legs
and feet.*

feathers further accentuates the darker-winged appearance of this
species. Often the brilliant vermilion feet are not seen on flying birds
until long after other marks clinch identification. The immature lacks
both the bar across the upperwing surface and the dark terminal
band on the tail shown by the Black-legged. Immatures do show a
very prominent ragged white triangle on the upperwing surfaces
that may suggest an immature Sabine's Gull at first glance; the
rather indistinct bar across the nape can add to the confusion.

Similar Species
See Black-legged Kittiwake. Sabine's Gull has more sharply marked
white triangle on wing, black triangle on primaries, browner mantle.

Range
Breeds locally in Aleutians (Buldir and Bogoslof islands) and Pribilof
and Commander islands. Disperses in winter apparently in pelagic
waters of Bering Sea and around Aleutians, though recorded south
to Oregon. One record each in Yukon and Nevada.   *Terence Wahl*

Ross' Gull

Rhodostethia rosea

Ross' Gull, the "pink gull," is a small, pale Siberian species that
breeds on river deltas of northeastern Asia and frequents the
moving pack ice of the Arctic Ocean at other seasons. In late fall, it
occurs along the northwestern Alaska coast by the hundreds or
sometimes by the thousands, depending on movements of ice. When
conditions are suitable, these birds feed by the dozens or hundreds
along beaches, dipping for plankton in the surf. In the late Arctic
autumn, when the sun is at a low angle, these small pink and gray
gulls are easily lost among the pastel pinks, blues, and grays of the
shifting ice.

Description
12½–14″ (32–35.5 cm). Unique. Summer adults have bright peach-
pink underparts, a fine black collar, and a prominently wedge-
shaped white tail; the immaculate pale gray mantle is accented by
the black outer vane of the outermost primary. The wing linings are
medium-gray. The bill is black and very short, the legs are bright
red. In winter, adults retain the pale gray mantle, but the collar
becomes white; the pink cast of the body diminishes and may
disappear. The juvenile Ross' Gull is very similar to the juvenile
Sabine's, but slightly smaller, with a wedge-shaped, rather than
forked, tail. First-winter plumage resembles that of the Black-
legged Kittiwake in pattern, but has no dark bar on the nape. The
second-year bird resembles the adult; it has pink underparts, a black
collar, and a white tail, but retains the dark flattened M pattern on
the wings.

Range
In North America, common only as late fall migrant on Chukchi Sea
coast of northern Alaska. Rare in Bering Sea and Canadian Arctic
Archipelago. Has bred recently at Churchill, Manitoba, and north of
Bathurst Island. Accidental in British Columbia, Great Lakes, and
south on Atlantic Coast to Massachusetts. Breeds in northeastern
Siberia. Winter range unknown.   *Daniel D. Gibson*

Immature
1. *Ragged white triangle on upperwing.*
2. *Indistinct bar across nape.*

Winter adult
1. *Very short black bill.*
2. *Pale gray mantle.*
3. *Wedge-shaped white tail.*
4. *Red legs.*

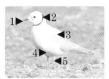

Breeding adult
1. *Very short black bill.*
2. *Fine black collar.*
3. *Pale gray mantle.*
4. *Peach-pink tinge on underparts.*
5. *Red legs.*

Sabine's Gull

Xema sabini
Larger than a Little Gull and smaller than a Black-legged
Kittiwake, the highly distinctive Sabine's Gull can be identified by
the bold wedge of black on its outer wing. This bird flies on deep
strokes in a delicate, erratic fashion, often close to the water.

Immature

Description
13″ (33 cm). In breeding plumage, Sabine's Gull is characterized by a
dark hood, a yellow-tipped black bill, and a forked tail. The black
outer primaries form a narrowly triangular black patch on the
leading edge of the wing; the black patch contrasts noticeably with
the dark mantle and the white triangular patch on the inner
primaries and secondaries. At all ages, the tricolored, triangular-
patched wing pattern is diagnostic. Adults retain much of their
summer plumage into the fall. In winter, the head lightens and
appears splotched or mottled on the nape, but the triangular wing
pattern is retained. Immatures are browner on the back and
upperwing coverts; the feathers have a fine, pale edging. The tail
has a dark tip.

Similar Species
Bonaparte's and Common Black-headed gulls have white triangular
patch on wing tips. Juvenile Black-legged Kittiwake shows narrow
M on back and mantle; lacks juvenile Sabine's considerable gray-
brown coloring on head and sides of breast; has dark bar from wrist
to tertials, does not have triangular, patched wing pattern.

Range
Breeds in High Arctic; highly pelagic in migration. Offshore, fairly
common spring and uncommon fall transient; casual spring and fall
transient in western North Atlantic. Very rare transient inland in
fall; casual inland in spring, with most records in Southwest.
Ron Naveen

Ivory Gull

Pagophila eburnea
A white, somewhat pigeonlike gull of the far North, the Ivory Gull
breeds on High Arctic islands and frequents the Bering Sea pack ice
during the nonbreeding season. It utters peculiar ternlike calls that
can be helpful in distinguishing it from other gulls before details of
its plumage can be discerned.

Description
15–17″ (38–43 cm). The unmistakable adult Ivory Gull is about the
same size as a Ring-billed Gull; it is all-white with dark eyes, black
legs, and a yellow-tipped, dark bill. Immature birds are similar to
adults but have a dark face and bill. The primaries, secondaries, and
primary coverts are black-tipped on immature birds, creating black
spotting on the mantle and the trailing edge of the wing. The tail
feathers are also black-tipped.

Voice
A harsh, ternlike *keeer*.

Breeding adult

1. *Black triangle on outer wing.*
2. *White triangle on inner primaries and secondaries.*
3. *Slight fork in tail.*

   Immature has more brown on upperparts, dark tail tip.

Breeding adult

1. *Black bill with yellow tip.*
2. *Dark hood.*

Adult

1. *Dark bill with yellow tip.*
2. *Entirely white plumage.*
3. *Black legs.*

Similar Species
Very pale Iceland Gull similar at a distance but much larger.

Range
In North America, breeds locally in Canadian Arctic Archipelago. In fall, winter, and spring, fairly common pelagic visitor within and at edge of Bering Sea pack ice. Accidental south as far as Washington coast. Rare but regular off Canadian Maritimes south as far as Newfoundland. Casual near Great Lakes, in interior Northeast, and on Atlantic Coast as far south as Long Island. Circumpolar at very high latitudes.   *Daniel D. Gibson*

Gull-billed Tern

Sterna nilotica
The Gull-billed Tern is a stocky, medium-size white tern with a short, notched tail. Its flight is more gull-like and less buoyant than that of most other terns. It hawks for large insects and only occasionally dives for small fish and marine invertebrates. This cosmopolitan species inhabits beaches, estuaries, coastal bays, salt marshes, dry and flooded fields, and some inland lakes. It is strictly a coastal species, except in southern California and peninsular Florida. In North America, this bird is uncommon but widely distributed; it was formerly more abundant along the Atlantic Coast. The Gull-billed Tern often associates with other colonial nesting seabirds.

Description
13–15″ (33–38 cm). This species is the whitest of our terns. Its bill is short, deep, black, and gull-like (but does not widen near the tip in true gull fashion); the legs and feet are black and the wings are broad and unmarked white. The adult in breeding plumage has a black cap. Adults in winter plumage and immatures have a white head with a dark smudge through the eye, and faint grayish or brownish vermiculations on the crown and nape. They appear long-legged. The combination of white plumage, stocky appearance, short, notched tail, and heavy black bill make this bird unique among North American terns.

Voice
A nasal or rasping *za-za-za* and *kay-weck, kay-weck*, or *katy-did, katy-did*. Immatures give a soft, whistled *peep*.

Immature

Range
Breeds locally at Salton Sea, California, in coastal Texas, Louisiana, and Alabama, and along both coasts and inland in Florida; north along Atlantic Coast to southern New Jersey (rarely to Long Island). Casual to Maritime Provinces. Winters from northern Gulf Coast and Florida southward. Also breeds south through West Indies and Panama, along Atlantic Coast of South America south to northern Argentina, and in Old World.   *Paul W. Sykes, Jr.*

Immature
1. *Dark face and bill.*
2. *Black spots on mantle.*
3. *Black legs and feet.*

   Ternlike **keeer** *call.*

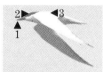

Breeding adult in flight
1. *Short, stout black bill.*
2. *Black cap.*
3. *Whitish upperparts.*

Breeding adult
1. *Short, stout black bill.*
2. *Black cap.*

   Immature has white head with dark smudge through eye.

Caspian Tern

Sterna caspia
The cosmopolitan Caspian Tern is the largest tern in North America
and is rather common inland as well as along the coasts. It is found
along river systems, canals, large lakes, coastal waters, bays, and
beaches. This bird's broad wings give it a somewhat gull-like flight,
less buoyant than that of other terns. It feeds mainly on small fish,
which it often pirates from smaller seabirds.

Description
19–23″ (48.5–58.5 cm). This bird has a large head, thick neck, and
heavy body. The mantle is pearl-gray; most of the underparts and
the notched tail are white. The underside of the primaries is black,
and there is a trace of a black crest on the back of the head. The
summer adult has a black cap; adults in winter plumage and
immatures have black caps streaked with white. At rest, the wing
tips extend beyond the tail. The stout bill is red to orange-red and
usually has a black tip. The feet are black; in many fall immatures
they are red.

Voice
A loud, harsh, deep *kraa, karr,* or *kraa-uh,* and repeated *kaks;* also
a 3-syllable *ka-ka-kraaaa;* a high squeal, *wee-ou,* from young birds
flying with adults.

Similar Species
Royal Tern smaller, slimmer; has narrower wings, more slender,
yellow-orange to orange bill, and prominent crest on back of head;
tail more deeply forked; flight more buoyant. Underside of Royal's
primaries white to gray with narrow black border; forehead white
except at onset of breeding season.

Winter

Range
Breeds locally from Washington and Oregon to Utah and Wyoming,
south through California into Baja California, and from central
Mackenzie and Manitoba southeast to Great Lakes, northeast to
Newfoundland. Also south along Atlantic from Virginia to Central
Florida, west to coastal Texas, and south into Mexico. Nonbreeding
birds disperse widely in North America. Winters from southern
California, northern Gulf of Mexico, Florida, and Atlantic Coast
from North Carolina south through Mexico and West Indies. Also
throughout Old World.   *Paul W. Sykes, Jr.*

Royal Tern

Sterna maxima
The Royal Tern is a large, common white tern with a forked tail and
a prominent, bushy crest on the back of the head. It is strictly
limited to saltwater habitats, and feeds almost exclusively by diving
for fish. It usually nests in association with other colonial water
birds on small islands with sandy beaches.

Description
18–21″ (45.5–53.5 cm). The Royal Tern's mantle is pearly gray and
the remainder of the body white. For a short period at the beginning
of the breeding season, the adult has an entirely black cap, but even
at this time it shows some white feathering on the forehead. At all
other times, the adult's forehead is white like the immature's; in
western adults, the white is somewhat more extensive, and the eye
is usually in the light part of the head. This species has a distinct
black crest; the bill is large and varies from orange to yellow-orange.
At rest, the tip of the wings may or may not reach the tip of the tail.
The feet are usually black, but in a few individuals they are orange.

Breeding plumage
1. *Large, heavy red or orange-red bill.*
2. *Black cap with slight crest.*
3. *Pale gray upperparts.*

   Large size.
   Heavy build.

Breeding adult in flight
1. *Large, heavy red or orange-red bill.*
2. *Dark underside of primaries.*

   Large size.
   Streaked cap in nonbreeding plumage.

Nonbreeding adult in flight
1. *Large orange-yellow bill.*
2. *White forehead and black crest on nape.*
3. *Light underside of primaries.*
4. *Forked tail.*

   Large size.

Voice
A *chirrup*, *keer* or *kee-er*, and *kaak;* higher-pitched than in Caspian.

Similar Species
See Caspian Tern. Elegant Tern of southern California smaller, has longer, slimmer, slightly downcurved orange-yellow to yellow bill, and longer, more shaggy black crest on back of head; bill in immatures yellowish; at rest, wing tips extend to or beyond tip of tail. White forehead of nonbreeding adults does not extend to eye.

Range
Breeds locally around northern Gulf of Mexico from Texas to northern Florida, and on Alantic Coast from Maryland south to central Florida. Formerly bred more widely in Florida. Post-breeding wanderers north to central California, across northern Gulf Coast, and throughout Florida; north to Massachusetts (casual farther north). Winters in southern California, throughout northern Gulf Coast, Florida, and north to Virginia. Also in South America and on coast of West Africa.   *Paul W. Sykes, Jr.*

Elegant Tern

Sterna elegans
This subtropical tern is the Pacific Coast counterpart of the Sandwich Tern. Flocks of these medium-size, orange-billed, shaggy-crested terns frequent estuaries and beaches along the California coast in summer and fall after dispersing northward from their breeding grounds near and below the Mexican border.

Description
15½″–17″ (39.5–43 cm). The Elegant Tern resembles the Royal Tern but is smaller and more slender, with a much thinner, proportionately longer, slightly decurved orange or orange-yellow bill. Breeding adults have a solid black crown that is elongated in the rear to form a shaggy black crest, and there is a variable suffusion of pink on the white underparts. Nonbreeding birds have white foreheads and white streaks on the black crown, but the black crest is always noticeable and black feathering extends forward through the eye. The tail is moderately forked and the mantle is pale gray, darkening somewhat on the outer primaries. The legs vary from dusky-colored to black, but are occasionally reddish. Young birds have yellowish bills and more extensive dusky coloring on the flight feathers.

Voice
A loud *keeer-rrick* or *kar-rreek*, more grating than notes of Royal Tern.

Similar Species
Royal Tern larger with stouter bill much thicker at base and deeper orange; nonbreeding Royals on West Coast have eyes surrounded by white and much shorter black crest. Sandwich Tern (accidental on West Coast) has black bill with yellow tip.

Range
Breeds near San Diego, California, and locally along west coast of Baja California and on islands in Gulf of California. Postbreeding birds occur commonly north to central California coast from midsummer through fall. Winters along coast of western South America, casually north to southern California.
Kimball L. Garrett

Breeding adult
1. *Large orange-yellow bill.*
2. *Black cap with crest on nape.*

Large size.

Breeding adult in flight
1. *Slender yellow or orange-yellow bill.*
2. *Black cap.*
3. *Forked tail.*

Large size.

Breeding adult
1. *Slender yellow or orange-yellow bill.*
2. *Black cap with shaggy crest.*

Large size.

Sandwich Tern

Sterna sandvicensis
The Sandwich Tern is a fairly large, uncommon white tern native to
both the New and Old worlds. Like the Royal Tern, with which it
frequently associates and nests, this species is restricted to
saltwater areas. Most frequently found along beaches, inlets,
estuaries, and bays, it may also forage far offshore. Its flight is
strong and swift. It feeds primarily on small fish, which it captures
by diving.

Description
16–18″ (40.5–45.5 cm). Adults at the beginning of the breeding
season have a black cap with a shaggy crest on the back of the head.
During the nesting season, the adults acquire a white forehead. The
mantle is pearl-gray and the remainder of the plumage is white; the
tail is forked. The long, slender bill is black with a yellow tip, and
the feet are black. The immature has a white forehead and
underparts, a mottled brown and gray mantle, and a dark tail. This
species is intermediate in size between the Forster's and Royal
terns; it is the only tern with a black, yellow-tipped bill.

Voice
Loud grating *kirr-ick*.

Similar Species
Gull-billed Tern has shorter, deeper bill.

Range
Breeds locally from Virginia south to southern Florida and
Bahamas, west across Gulf Coast to southern Texas and south into
Mexico and South America. Accidental in southern California and
very rare visitor north to Massachusetts; almost annual on Long
Island. Winters across northern Gulf Coast and Florida southward.
Also in Eurasia.   *Paul W. Sykes, Jr.*

Immature

Roseate Tern

Winter

Sterna dougallii
This tern is found in small and declining numbers along the Atlantic
Coast of North America. It nests on islands and protected sand
spits, usually in colonies of Common or Arctic terns; like these
species, it is often seen diving in shallows for small fish. A maritime
bird, it is rarely seen in migration away from breeding colonies.
Roseate Terns have short wings and fly with snappy wingbeats;
Roseates in flight can often be recognized by this field mark alone.
Although it is paler-backed and longer-tailed than Common or Arctic
terns, it is most easily identified by its distinctive calls.

Description
14–16″ (35.5–41 cm). The Roseate Tern is very pale above and
below. It has a very long, notably slender bill, short wings, and long
white tail feathers that extend well beyond the ends of the wings
when the bird is sitting. The wings are pale, with a narrow
blackness to the leading edge on the outermost primary (the black
and white on the feather meets along a straight line, rather than in a

Breeding adult in flight
1. *Slender black bill with yellow tip.*
2. *Black cap.*

Breeding adult
1. *Slender black bill with yellow tip.*
2. *Black cap with crest on nape.*
3. *Forked tail.*
4. *White forehead in immature.*
5. *Dark tail in immature.*

Breeding adult
1. *Black bill.*
2. *Black cap.*
3. *Upperparts paler than Common or Arctic tern's.*
4. *Tail extends beyond folded wing.*

    Churee-che *call.*

barring and edgings above; are scalier looking than young of any other *Sterna*.

Upperwing

Voice
Two calls frequently given: a distinctive chirpy call of 2–3 syllables, *churee-che-che, churee-che, churree-che-che;* also a very low *anh* call, similar to that of Common Tern, but deeper.

Similar Species
Upon arrival in spring, proximal half of Common Tern's bill red earlier; back darker and outer tail feathers short and black-edged; voice also distinctive. In winter plumage, these species nearly indistinguishable, can best be identified by call. Lighter back of Roseate, when seen in good light and in direct comparison with Common, may aid in identifying winter birds.

Underwing

Range
Breeds along Atlantic Coast from Nova Scotia to New York. Absent from North America in winter. Small colonies reported in Virgin Islands and Dry Tortugas. Also breeds in Europe and British Isles, in Southern Hemisphere on islands in Pacific, and along coastal Australia, India, and Africa.　　*Helen Hays*

Common Tern

Sterna hirundo
Groups of Common Terns may be seen diving for small fish along the coasts of North America from May to September. Like other terns, Common Terns defend their colonies vigorously. During migration, they can be seen many miles offshore.

Winter adult

Description
13–16″ (33–40.5 cm). Adults in breeding plumage have black cap, gray back, and red legs and feet; washed with gray below (usually darker than Roseate or Forster's). Tail feathers black along outer edge; do not reach beyond ends of folded wings. Upperwings have dark wedge on primaries; broad, dark trailing edge visible from below. Little or no translucence to wings. In spring, bill red on basal half; may become entirely red. Winter adults lose black cap, retain dark nape; have dark bar at bend of wing; legs, feet, and bill black. Juveniles have some mottling above, but soon become gray-backed and similar to adults. *S. h. longipennis*, occurs in Aleutians; has all-dark bill and brown or black legs and feet.

Upperwing

Underwing

Voice
Most distinctive call a drawn-out *kee-ar*, harsher and less distinctly 2-syllabled than Arctic Tern's *kee-ya*. Also a high, staccato *kip* and a lower, more nasal *aanh*. Birds carrying fish may be heard to give a series of nasal 2-syllabled calls, *aa-unh, aa-unh, aa-unh*.

Similar Species
See Arctic and Roseate terns. Forster's Tern has silvery-white surface on upper primaries, paler gray mantle, gray tail, and underparts always white; breeding adult has orange legs, orange, black-tipped bill; winter adult has gray to blackish nape, pale hind crown; immature has no dark bar across inner wing.

Range
Common transient on Pacific Coast; rare to uncommon transient in interior West. Inland populations in Alberta, Manitoba, Ontario, and Gulf of St. Lawrence. Breeds along Atlantic Coast from Nova Scotia to Virginia. Rare in winter along coasts of southernmost states; casual farther north; most winter in South America. (Most winter birds in our range probably immatures that linger only until December or so before departing.) Also in Old World.
Helen Hays

Breeding adult in flight
1. *Black bill.*
2. *Black cap.*
3. *Very pale upperparts.*
4. *Very long, forked tail.*

Churee-che *call.*

Breeding adult in flight
1. *Dark wedge on inner primaries.*
2. *Black outer edge on outermost tail feathers.*

Drawn-out kee-ar *call.*

Breeding adult
1. *Red in bill.*
2. *Black cap.*
3. *Upperparts darker gray than Roseate Tern's.*
4. *Tail does not extend beyond folded wing.*

Staccato kip *call.*

Arctic Tern

Upperwing

Sterna paradisaea
Breeding at high latitudes throughout the Northern Hemisphere, the Arctic Tern is the "common" tern of the far North. It nests in solitary pairs, small groups, or large colonies on lakes, ponds, river bars, and seacoasts throughout its range. A highly pelagic migrant, it winters at sea at high latitudes in the Southern Hemisphere and is rarely seen from shore south of its breeding grounds.

Underwing

Description
14–17″ (35.5–43 cm). Neck short; bill short and deep; head profile very rounded. In flight, can appear almost neckless, with head barely projecting beyond wing tips; this feature distinguishes Arctic from other very similar terns (Common, Roseate, and Forster's). Upperwings plain, unmarked gray; from below, translucent area on flight feathers visible; this area and well-defined dark trailing edge of primaries are good field marks. Gray below, darker than other similar terns. Undertail coverts and long tail streamers white. Breeding adults have black cap with pale streak just below it; bill, feet, and legs blood-red. Winter adults, 1-year-olds, and immatures have white forehead, black nape, dark bill, white underparts, and short tail; somewhat resemble Aleutian Tern.

Voice
A harsh, high-pitched *kee-ya*, with falling inflection, more disyllabic than Common Tern's; also a repeated *keer, keer*, or *kee-kee-kee-kee*.

Similar Species
Common Tern more heavily built, longer-legged, with stouter bill; has dark wedge in outer primaries and broader, less crisply defined trailing edge on primaries; only inner primaries, not all flight feathers, are translucent. Immature Common usually has some orange at base of bill. Forster's has no translucence in flight feathers, lacks dark trailing edge; bill larger and orange; has paler gray nape and different shape overall.

Range
Breeds from Arctic coasts south to Aleutian Islands, southeastern Alaska (has bred in Washington), north-central Canada, and Massachusetts. Migrates at sea. Casual inland south of breeding range. Also in Old World.　*Daniel D. Gibson*

Aleutian Tern

Sterna aleutica
Like various pantropical terns in appearance, this bird of the North Pacific is rarely seen away from its breeding grounds. Its surface-feeding behavior and unique calls often identify it.

Description
15″ (38 cm). Forehead clean white; bill and legs black; body and wings very gray, contrasting with white tail and tail coverts. From below, dark bar with white edge visible along secondaries.

Voice
Calls a mellow, ploverlike whistle, *whee-hee-hee*, and loud chirping from flocks (like House Sparrow's calls). Calls diagnostic; gives no nasal *keearr* notes like notes of black-capped terns.

Range
Southern Chukchi and Bering Sea coasts and islands of Alaska and Siberia; also Sakhalin Island; on Pacific Coast as far east as Yakutat and Ice Bay areas.　*Daniel D. Gibson*

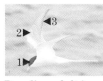

Breeding adult in flight
1. *Rounded head and "neckless" look.*
2. *Plain gray upperwings.*
3. *Thin dark trailing edge on primaries.*

Harsh keeya *call.*

Breeding adult
1. *Red bill.*
2. *Black cap.*
3. *Underparts grayer than other terns.*
4. *Tail does not extend beyond folded wing.*
5. *Short legs.*

Harsh keeya *call.*

Breeding adult
1. *Black bill.*
2. *White forehead and black cap.*
3. *Gray upperparts.*
4. *White tail.*

Chirping call.

Forster's Tern

Sterna forsteri
Inland populations of Forster's Tern breed in the lakes and marshes of the North and West; coastal populations breed on small, marshy islands. Forster's flight is swallowlike and graceful, but there is a distinctive snap to the shallow, rather rapid wingbeat.

Winter

Description
14–16½″ (35.5–42 cm). In breeding plumage, Forster's Tern has a diagnostic silvery white upper surface of the primaries, paler than the light gray of the inner wing and back. The underwing tip has an ill-defined dark wedge like that of the Common Tern. The outer web of the outermost tail feather is white; the rest of the tail is gray, most obviously so around the inner edge of the fork. Although there is white on the rump, there is little contrast between mantle and tail. The underparts are always pure white. The legs and black-tipped bill are orange, not red; the bill is longer and stouter than the Common's. The winter adult has a whitish head with a thick black mask through and behind the eye to the nape; this is often a good field mark. The nape varies from pale gray to blackish and can be a source of misidentification. The blackish bill has a rusty base. The juvenile has the same black facial mask and brownish upperparts; it has no dark bar across the inner wing. The bill is mostly brownish-black, the legs rather yellow. Older immatures often have dark upper primaries and dark bills.

Breeding

Voice
A grating, low-pitched *tzaap;* a high, short *keer.*

◄4

Similar Species
Roseate has long, deeply forked white tail, dark or basally scarlet bill, coral-red legs. Voices diagnostic. Gull-billed Tern has heavy black bill, shallowly forked tail. See Common and Arctic terns.

Underwing

Range
Breeds locally from inland British Columbia east to Manitoba, south to southern California, Colorado, Iowa; also isolated populations around Salton Sea in California and Great Lakes. Along Atlantic Coast from New York to North Carolina, Gulf Coast from Alabama to Tamaulipas, Mexico. Small numbers disperse north as far as Massachusetts after breeding. Winters on coasts from central California and Virginia south to Mexico.   *Claudia Wilds*

Least Tern

Sterna antillarum
The tiny, elegant, and lively Least Tern is a familiar summer resident along the sandy beaches of most of the coastal United States and up several of its major rivers. With its preference for shell-strewn expanses, it competes annually with people, beach vehicles, high tides, and predators in its valiant attempts to nest. These days the Least Tern is often most successful when it colonizes fresh and unvegetated dredge-spoil islands or enterprisingly takes over flat rooftops, frequently in urban areas. Its slender body and wings, uniquely rapid wingbeats, and high, urgent calls are distinctive features that make it readily identifiable as it feeds close to the ocean beach or in protected bays and ponds, hovering high above the surface and plunging after the smallest fish, or skimming low over the water. Immature Least Terns, like the immatures of other tern species, usually remain on the wintering grounds for the summer, but a few individuals do return to the breeding areas with the adults. These so-called "portlandica" terns (a name applied to summer immatures of all tern species) look essentially like winter

Breeding

Winter

Winter plumage
1. *White crown and black mask through eye.*
2. *Pale gray back.*

Breeding plumage
1. *Black-tipped orange bill.*
2. *Black cap.*
3. *Long orange legs.*
4. *Silvery primaries paler than inner wing.*

Grating tzaap *call.*

Breeding plumage
1. *Yellow bill with black tip.*
2. *White forehead.*
3. *Black cap.*
4. *Pearl-gray upperparts.*
5. *Yellow legs.*

Small size.
Shrill zreeep *call.*

adults with very worn primaries, although older "portlandicas" may
have the bright bill and legs and the complete head pattern of a
summer adult. These summer immatures are conspicuously shabby
when compared to breeding adults, which have fresh, trim wing
patterns.

Description
8½–9½" (21.5–24 cm). In breeding plumage, the Least Tern has a
broad white forehead framed by a black crown and a black line
running from the crown through the eye to the base of the bill. The
mantle and the short but strongly forked tail are pearl-gray. A long,
thin wedge of black up the leading edge of the outer wing, formed
by the 2 outermost primaries and primary coverts, is conspicuous
and diagnostic in flight. The narrowly black-tipped bill and the feet
are yellow. Winter adults have the black head pattern blurred by a
mixture of white and black feathers; the bill is brown. Juveniles
have largely white heads except for a blackish line through the eye
and a blackish nape. The entire leading edge of the wing is dark.
The bill is black and the legs brownish.

Voice
A shrill *zreeep* and a harsh *kip, kip kip;* very noisy when feeding.

Range
Breeds on Pacific Coast from northern California to Mexico; along
Cimarron, Niobara, Missouri, Platte, Mississippi, and Ohio rivers;
along Gulf Coast at least to United States-Mexico border; and on
Atlantic Coast from southern Maine to Florida Keys. Casual in
Washington, Oregon, and interior Southwest. Also Bermuda,
Bahamas, West Indies, Belize, and Honduras. Winters on South
American coast at least from Venezuela to Brazil.
Claudia Wilds

Bridled Tern

Sterna anaethetus
This highly pelagic species is common off the southeastern coast of
the United States; it flies gracefully with slow, shallow wingbeats.

Description
15" (38 cm). Bill, cap, and eyeline black; forehead and eyebrow
white. Underparts and outer tail feathers also white, as are wing
linings; collar whitish. Back, rump, and central part of tail gray
(may look brownish-gray); upperwing blackish with distinct gray
tone. Immature has white head, nape, and underparts; crown
streaked with black; blackish above, with brown feather edgings.

Similar Species
See Sooty and Black terns.

Range
Common offshore in warm months from Cape Hatteras to Florida
Keys; a few in Gulf of Mexico. Breeds in West Indies.
Paul W. Sykes, Jr.

Juvenile
1. *Black bill.*
2. *Whitish head with blackish eyeline and nape.*
3. *Dark forewing.*

Adult in flight
1. *Yellow bill.*
2. *White forehead.*
3. *Pearl-gray upperparts.*
4. *Narrow black wedge on outer edge of wing.*

Adult in flight
1. *White forehead and black cap.*
2. *Whitish collar.*
3. *Grayish upperparts.*

   Deeply forked tail with white outer tail feathers.

Sooty Tern

Sterna fuscata
The Sooty Tern is a medium-size pantropical species that is highly pelagic and ranges widely during the nonbreeding season. It is our only tern that is totally black above; it flies gracefully with deep, strong wingbeats, and often soars in circles. It eats small fish that it picks from the surface of the water; unlike most terns, it does not dive. The Sooty seldom alights on the water but will perch on floating debris at sea and generally nests on oceanic islands or small islands off the coast of a large landmass. This is perhaps one of the most abundant birds in the world.

Description
15–17″ (38–43 cm). The adult is completely black above with a white forehead; the white does not extend past the eye. The underparts are also white, and the deeply forked black tail has white outer feathers. The immature is brownish-black above and below with fine white spots on the mantle, whitish undertail coverts, and a notched tail.

Voice
A nasal *wide-a-wake* or *wacky-wack;* usually silent away from breeding colonies.

Similar Species
Bridled Tern paler above, with complete white collar; white eyebrow extends rearward; outer tail feathers white, central part of tail gray. Immature has white head, nape, and underparts. Bridled's flight slightly faster, with shallower wingbeat.

Range
Breeds commonly at Dry Tortugas, Florida, and has bred along Texas and Louisiana coasts. Seen in small numbers offshore in Gulf of Mexico and in Atlantic from Cape Hatteras to Florida Keys during summer months. Individuals often blown north inshore anywhere along Atlantic Coast during hurricanes.
Paul W. Sykes, Jr.

White-winged Tern

Chlidonias leucopterus
The White-winged Tern, a very rare visitor from eastern Europe, is usually found in May, or in early July among the flocks of Black Terns making their leisurely way southward. It is then in full breeding plumage or nearly so, a striking black-and-white bird hawking for insects low over freshwater marshes and brackish impoundments. Several of the birds seen in recent years have lingered to late August or September, molting rapidly into winter plumage, but they departed with their fellow travelers before the last traces of summer feathering had disappeared.

Description
9″ (23 cm). The White-winged Tern in breeding plumage has a black head, body, and wing linings (the lower back fading to dark gray), contrasting sharply with white upperwing coverts, rump, tail, vent, and undertail coverts, and pearl-gray primaries and secondaries. The bill is much shorter than the head; both it and the legs are red. In winter plumage, the head is white except for black ear coverts

Adult in flight
1. *White forehead.*
2. *Black cap and upperparts, with no whitish collar.*
3. *White outer tail feathers.*

Immature
1. *Brownish-black plumage.*
2. *White spots on mantle.*

Winter adult
1. *Shorter bill than Black Tern's.*
2. *White head with dark hindcrown and black ear coverts.*
3. *White underparts.*
4. *White rump.*

and the dark hindcrown. The remainder of the upper surface is uniformly gray, aside from the white lesser wing coverts and the white rump that is retained until November. The undersurface is entirely white; the bill is black and the legs reddish-brown. The juvenile, not reported from North America, has more black on the crown and a dark back sharply set off from the pale neck and rump.

Voice
Harsher than Black Tern's: *keck, krreck*, or a short *kick*.

Similar Species
See Black Tern.

Range
Most North American sightings along East Coast from New Brunswick to Georgia, with single records from Alaska, Wisconsin, and Indiana. Breeds from eastern Europe and Turkey to southeastern Siberia. Winters in Africa, southern Asia, Indonesia, Australia, and New Zealand.   *Claudia Wilds*

Black Tern

Chlidonias niger
The small, dark, notch-tailed Black Tern is a familiar summer visitor across most of the continent, wherever there are marshes, wet meadows, and insect-rich ponds. It skims swallowlike, low over the surface, hovering and snatching insects from air and water. In its protracted southbound migration, much of the population shifts to both coasts, and Black Terns may be seen well out to sea, where they feed on small marine creatures.

Description
9–10½" (23–26.5 cm). In breeding plumage, the Black Tern's head and body are black, the back fading to gray on the rump, and the vent and undertail coverts clear white. The upper surface of the wings and tail are uniformly gray, aside from white lesser wing coverts that form a small white shoulder on the bird at rest. The wing linings are pale gray. In winter plumage, the back becomes the same gray as the wings and tail, and the entire underparts are white except for a diagnostic small dark patch on each side of the breast. The white head is marked by a blackish cap joining black ear coverts. The juvenile is similar but has a darker back and wing coverts barred and scalloped brown. The black bill, with a trace of dark red at the gape, is nearly as long as the head. The feet are dark red.

Voice
Call note a shrill, metallic *krik*.

Similar Species
White-winged Tern has shorter bill; in breeding plumage has white wings, white tail, black wing linings, and red bill and legs. In fall, has much less black on head, white rump, and no breast patches. Larger terns in winter plumage much less uniform above, have clearly forked tails. Bridled Tern much larger with long, deeply forked tail.

Juvenile

Range
Breeds from British Columbia south to central California and east as far as New Brunswick south to New York. Winters in northern and western South America, casual in winter in southern California. Widespread in Eurasia and Africa.   *Claudia Wilds*

Breeding adult
1. Red bill.
2. Black head and underparts.
3. White upperwing coverts.
4. Black wing linings.
5. White rump and tail.

Breeding adult
1. Black bill.
2. Black head and underparts.
3. White upperwing coverts.
4. Pale gray wing linings.
5. Grayish tail.

Winter adult
1. Longer bill than White-winged Tern's.
2. Blackish cap.
3. Uniform gray mantle.
4. Dark breast patches.
5. White underparts.

Brown Noddy

Anous stolidus
The pantropical, medium-size Brown Noddy has a plumage pattern
that is the opposite of that of other members of its subfamily—a
white cap and a dark body. Its tail is wedge-shaped rather than
forked. This highly pelagic species often perches on floating debris
at sea, and nests on small oceanic islands. It feeds on fish caught as
it flies low over the water's surface; it does not dive or generally
alight on the water. Its flight is strong and erratic, with rather deep
strokes.

Description
15–16″ (38–40.5 cm). The adult has a dark brown body with a white
cap that blends into the brown on the nape. There is a small white
mark below the eye. The wedge-shaped tail has a slight, central
notch; the long, slender bill and the feet are black. The immature is
similar to the adult but is paler and has white only on the forehead.

Voice
A soft, low-pitched *k-a-a-a*, harsh *eye-ak*, and ripping *carrrrk* or
arrowk.

Similar Species
Black Noddy smaller, has more slender bill, blacker plumage
throughout (visible only in good light), and more sharply defined
white cap.

Range
Breeds in our area only at Dry Tortugas, Florida. Also breeds from
Bahamas southward. A few seen well offshore on east coast of
Florida in summer; hurricane-driven birds may be found inshore
north along Atlantic and Gulf coasts. Winters at sea near breeding
areas. Also in Old World.   *Paul W. Sykes, Jr.*

Black Noddy

Anous minutus
Almost every year since 1960, 1 or 2 of these medium-size,
pantropical terns have reached our area at Dry Tortugas, Florida.
The Black Noddy is similar in appearance, flight, and habits to the
Brown Noddy, but is smaller and more pelagic.

Description
14″ (35.5 cm). Adult very dark brown, appearing almost black in
most light, with slim body; bill black, slender; white cap sharply
defined against the dark head. Immature is similar but paler.

Similar Species
See Brown Noddy.

Range
Rare but regular visitor to Dry Tortugas during spring and summer;
has not been found nesting. Breeds worldwide in tropics.
Paul W. Sykes, Jr.

Adult
1. *Sharply defined white cap.*
2. *Dark brown body.*

Adult in flight
1. *White cap.*
2. *Dark brown body.*
3. *Wedge-shaped tail.*

Adult in flight
1. *Slender bill.*
2. *White cap more extensive than Brown Noddy's.*
3. *Black body.*
4. *Wedge-shaped tail.*

   Smaller and slenderer than Brown Noddy.

Black Skimmer

Rynchops niger
The unmistakable Black Skimmer is a fairly common bird of coastal areas. It is found on bays, tidal estuaries, large rivers and lakes, canals, ocean beaches, and inlets; it favors salt water, but is occasionally found on inland fresh water, particularly in Florida. This close relative of the gulls and terns has a slim body, long, pointed wings, short legs, and webbed feet. Males are larger than females; this discrepancy is noticeable in flocks. The bill is scissorlike and flattened laterally; the lower mandible is considerably longer than the upper mandible. This species feeds by flying on a steady course low to the water, skimming the surface for small fish and crustaceans with the long lower mandible. The bill and manner of feeding are diagnostic. The Skimmer's flight is very swift, agile, and graceful; the bird appears to float along with little effort. It usually nests in association with other colonial seabirds on sand spits and barrier beaches, and in recent years has used dredge-spoil islands.

Description
16–20″ (40.5–51 cm). The adult is black above and white below, with a white forehead, cheek, outer tail feathers, and trailing edge of the wings. The tail is short and slightly notched. Most of the bill is red, but the outermost third is black. The immature is similar to the adult but has mottled brown upperparts.

Voice
Soft, short barking notes; also a low-pitched *auw*, and *kaup, kaup.*

Range
Breeds locally in southern California and along Atlantic and Gulf coasts from Massachusetts south to Florida and Texas, and on Pacific and Atlantic coasts of Mexico south to southern South America. Casual wanderer north to Maritime Provinces and northern California. Winters in southern coastal California and from Virginia south to Florida and across northern Gulf of Mexico into South America.   *Paul W. Sykes, Jr.*

Adult in flight
1. *Red and black bill; lower mandible longer.*
2. *Black upperparts.*
3. *White trailing edge of wing.*
4. *White underparts.*

   Swift, graceful flight.

Immature
1. *Mottled brown upperparts.*

Auks

(Family Alcidae)
The alcids are small to medium-size, stout, chunky seabirds. They
are primarily dark above and light below. The tail, legs, and neck
are short and stocky, and the head is comparatively large. The legs
sit far back on the body, allowing for very efficient swimming and
creating an extremely upright posture when the birds are on land.
All alcids have short, narrow wings seemingly better adapted for
diving than for flying; indeed, alcids "fly" underwater, using their
wings to propel themselves through the water. The flight is direct
on very rapid, weak wingbeats. The bills vary considerably among
species and according to season, and range from small, narrow, and
pointed to huge and laterally compressed. Most species have
distinctive seasonal plumages. Many alcids are found in large
breeding colonies on offshore islands or on coastal cliffs. Several
species are nocturnal at the colony, but also feed at sea during the
day. This generally pelagic family is confined to oceans of the north
and temperate zones. (World: 23 species. North America: 20 species.)
Scott B. Terrill

Dovekie

Alle alle
The Dovekie is an absurdly small alcid that nests on cliffs and talus
slopes in the North Atlantic, primarily within the Arctic Circle.
Considered by some authorities to be one of the world's most
abundant species, these chunky little birds are a staple summer food
for many Inuit communities. Dovekies usually winter far out to sea
in the North Atlantic. Most bird watchers encounter them in late fall
and winter, when easterly storms blow these weak fliers close to
shore. Occasionally, severe gales "wreck" Dovekies inland, where a
great many perish from exhaustion and starvation. In recent years,
small numbers of these "Little Auks" have been found summering in
the Bering Straits off the Alaska mainland.

Description
8" (20.5 cm). Dovekies are Starling-size birds with short, thick necks
and stubby little bills. In winter plumage, they are black above and
white below. The black crown extends below the eye, and a black
collar wraps around the side of the neck. The white of the chin,
throat, and cheek curves up onto the ear. The scapulars and
secondaries have white edges. Dovekies molt into breeding plumage
in February and March, acquiring an entirely black head and neck.
In flight, the Dovekie is a small, stocky, neckless-looking black-and-
white bird that buzzes its wings furiously.

Voice
In winter, a squeaky *queep-quew*. High-pitched chatter on breeding
grounds.

Similar Species
In summer, may be confused with juvenile Razorbills and Thick-
billed Murres that have left nesting ledges and are on the water.
Dovekies always distinguishable by short, stubby bill. In Alaska, no
other small alcid is so sharply black-and-white with a completely
black head and neck.

Range
Breeds in eastern Arctic Canada and probably in small numbers on
islands in Bering Sea. Winters offshore to New England, Long
Island, and less frequently south to Virginia, rarely Florida and
Cuba. Occasionally blown inland. Also in Old World.
Peter D. Vickery

Breeding plumage
1. *Stubby bill.*
2. *Black head.*
3. *Black upperparts.*
4. *White underparts.*

Small size.
Thick neck.

Winter plumage
1. *Black crown.*
2. *White cheeks.*
3. *Black upperparts.*
4. *White underparts.*

Common Murre

Uria aalge
The Common Murre is abundant on the Pacific Coast, breeding from Alaska south to central California. Its distribution is more restricted on the Atlantic Ocean, though it is by no means rare—some half a million pairs were estimated from a single colony on Funk Island, Newfoundland. Both Common and Thick-billed murres nest in extraordinarily high concentrations along the narrow ledges of steep cliff faces. These nesting sites barely provide space for the adult pairs and their single, pear-shaped egg. Because of its pyriform shape, a murre's egg is less likely to roll off a ledge than a round one; nevertheless, annual egg losses remain considerable. At the nest, the adults always stand facing the cliff, protecting and warming the egg.

Description
16–17″ (40.5–43 cm). Common Murres have long, slender, pointed bills that give them a refined, attenuated appearance different from Thick-billed Murres. The upperparts, especially the head and back, are dark brown year-round; they are visibly paler than the starkly black plumage of the Thick-billed Murre. Common Murres in breeding plumage have dark heads and a white breast that, unlike the pronounced peak of the Thick-billed Murre, forms an obtuse, almost flat angle on the black neck (but this characteristic is somewhat variable and should be used with caution). The "Ringed" Murre, a form restricted to the Atlantic, has a white eye-ring and postocular line in breeding plumage. In winter plumage, Common Murres have a white throat and chin and extensively white face. There is a dark, curved postocular line that is only apparent at close range. In flight, the long, thin bill and slightly longer neck give the Common Murre an elongated profile; the head is held slightly lower than the body. The upperparts are often noticeably browner than those of Razorbills or Thick-billed Murres.

Voice
Very low, purring *murrrr*, evoking the bird's name; also croaks and growls on breeding grounds.

Similar Species
Razorbill blacker above, with heavier head and bill; tail often cocked. Thick-billed Murre has shorter, thicker bill with evenly decurved culmen; upperparts blacker and head shape less attenuated; face darker with white restricted to the lower cheek in winter plumage.

Range
Breeds from islands in the Bering Sea off Alaska south to central California. In East in Quebec, Labrador, Newfoundland, southern New Brunswick (recently), and northern Nova Scotia. Winters to southern California, and on Atlantic to Maine, Massachusetts, and, rarely, Long Island south. In northern Europe, breeds in central Portugal, Norway, Iceland, and southern Greenland. Also in eastern Asia.   *Peter D. Vickery*

Breeding plumage
1. *Long, slim bill.*
2. *Dark brown head and neck.*
3. *White underparts come to blunt point on foreneck.*

Nests in colonies on ledges of sea cliffs.

"Ringed" morph
1. *White eye-ring and line behind eye.*

Restricted to Atlantic Ocean.

Winter plumage
1. *Extensive white on face, with dark line behind eye.*
2. *Dark upperparts.*

Thick-billed Murre

Uria lomvia

One of the most abundant seabirds in the Northern Hemisphere, the
Thick-billed Murre generally has a more northerly distribution than
the Common Murre. Some Atlantic populations occur north of the
Arctic Circle; a major colony breeds on Ellesmere Island. The
slightly larger Pacific race is particularly numerous in the Bering
Sea, where millions of birds nest on the Pribiloff Islands. Pacific
Thick-billed Murres usually remain north in winter and are
especially abundant off the Aleutian Islands. The population from
the western Atlantic overshoots the more sedentary Common
Murre, occurring south regularly to Massachusetts.

Description
17–19″ (43–48.5 cm). Thick-billed Murres are slightly larger than
Common Murres, and their bills are shorter and thicker with an
evenly decurved culmen. In breeding plumage, the Thick-billed has
a starkly black back and head and a white mark on the gape of the
upper mandible that is visible only at very close range. The white
breast angles sharply into the dark neck, forming an inverted V. In
winter plumage, the Thick-billed appears dark-headed. The black
crown extends below the eye and along the nape; only the lower
cheek is white. In flight, Thick-billeds are black above with a
moderately thick-necked profile.

Voice
Similar to Common Murre's.

Similar Species
See Common Murre. Razorbill has bulky head with more massive,
blunt bill, cocked tail; white ear crescent in winter plumage.

Range
Breeds on Pacific from northern Alaska, Bering Sea, Aleutian
Islands, and Kodiak Island; on Atlantic from Ellesmere Island,
Greenland, northern Hudson Bay, Labrador, northern Quebec,
Newfoundland to Gulf of St. Lawrence. Winters on Pacific from
Bering Sea south to southeastern Alaska; casually from British
Columbia to central California; in East from Greenland south to
Massachusetts, Long Island, infrequently New Jersey, Delaware,
and Maryland; rarely farther south. Accidental to Michigan,
Iowa, and Indiana. Also in Old World.   *Peter D. Vickery*

Razorbill

Alca torda

The Razorbill is one of the most elegant birds found in the large
seabird colonies of the northern Atlantic. The sharply black-and-
white plumage, dark eyes, and thick black bill with its neat white
stripe give the bird a dignified, tuxedoed look. In swift, low flight on
rapidly beating wings, Razorbills often tilt from side to side.

Description
17″ (43 cm). The Razorbill is starkly black and white with a thick
neck, a heavy head, and a notably long, blunt, laterally compressed
bill; in adults, the bill is blazed with a vertical white stripe. The tail,
longer than that of other alcids, is frequently cocked. Adults in
breeding plumage have black heads with a barely discernible brown
hue. A thin white stripe extends from the eye to the base of the bill;
this stripe is absent in winter. Adults in winter plumage are very
black above. The white of the throat, chin, and cheek extends
behind and above the eye in a white crescent; the black crown
covers the eye. Immature birds resemble adults, but have much

Winter plumage
1. *Dark head, with white on cheek and throat only.*
2. *Dark upperparts.*

Breeding plumage
1. *Thick bill, with white line at base.*
2. *Black head and neck.*
3. *Black upperparts.*
4. *White underparts come to sharp point on foreneck.*

   Nests in colonies.

Breeding plumage
1. *Blunt, bladelike bill with white band and line on lores.*
2. *Black head and upperparts.*
3. *White underparts.*

smaller, unmarked bills and might possibly be confused with Thick-billed Murres; partly grown juveniles just off the nest resemble murres and Dovekies. In flight, Razorbills appear shorter and thicker-bodied than murres and have a distinctive, heavy-necked, bulky-headed profile. The back appears more arched than in murres, and the loose white undertail coverts often overlap the outer tail feathers, giving the appearance of white outer rectrices.

Voice
Hoarse, guttural croaks and growls.

Similar Species
See Thick-billed and Common murres.

Range
Breeds from Baffin Island, Labrador, eastern Newfoundland, and Canadian Maritimes to central coastal Maine. Winter range on western Atlantic primarily off New England, especially Georges Bank. Occurs south to Long Island, rarely from North Carolina south. Accidental inland in Ontario and Quebec. Also in Old World.
Peter D. Vickery

Black Guillemot

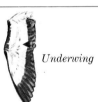

Underwing

Cepphus grylle
The graceful Black Guillemot, or "Sea Pigeon," is a familiar sight along the rugged coasts of Maine and the Canadian Maritimes. Unlike the other alcids of the Atlantic, this hardy species is nonmigratory and is unique in its preference for the shallower waters of the immediate coastline rather than the deeper marine environment of the open ocean. Black Guillemots and their close look-alikes, Pigeon Guillemots, are allopatric: Black Guillemots occur primarily on the northern Atlantic Ocean east to Scandinavia and the U.S.S.R., while Pigeon Guillemots are restricted to the northern Pacific Ocean. Their ranges overlap only in the Bering Straits off Alaska.

Description
13″ (33 cm). With their thin necks, rounded heads, and long, pointed bills, all guillemots share a distinctive profile. Black Guillemots in breeding plumage are starkly black with a prominent, unmarked white wing patch on the secondary coverts. The white wing patch is somewhat less conspicuous on sitting birds, but in flight it contrasts strikingly with the black flight feathers. The white wing linings are also an obvious and diagnostic feature. The feet and the mouth lining are bright orange-red year-round. Winter-plumage adults are mottled gray and white. Immature birds are duskier gray above, especially about the head. The white wing patch is reduced in size; the median coverts have dark tips that form an indistinct bar similar to that of the Pigeon Guillemot.

Voice
A high-pitched *squeeee;* also whistles.

Similar Species
Adult Pigeon Guillemot has distinctive dark wedge intruding into white wing patch; wing linings are silver-gray or even blackish.

Range
Breeds from Arctic Canada, Labrador, and Canadian Maritimes to southern Maine. Also northern Alaska to Bering Straits. Winters uncommonly south to Cape Cod and Rhode Island; rarely south to Long Island. Also in Old World; breeds from northern U.S.S.R. and Scandinavia to British Isles.   *Peter D. Vickery*

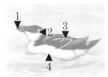

Winter plumage
1. *Blunt, bladelike bill.*
2. *Dark head with white ear crescent.*
3. *Dark upperparts.*
4. *White underparts.*

Winter plumage
1. *Slender bill.*
2. *Largely white head.*
3. *Gray-and-white back.*
4. *White wing patch.*
5. *White wing linings.*

   Bright red feet.

Breeding plumage
1. *Slender bill.*
2. *Black plumage.*
3. *White wing patch.*

   Orange-red feet.

Pigeon Guillemot

Cepphus columba

A common coastal seabird of the North Pacific, the Pigeon Guillemot is a medium-size black alcid with white wing patches, brilliant red legs and feet, and a black, pigeonlike bill. It is commonly seen sitting on rocks in the intertidal zone, above which it nests in natural cavities under beach boulders, piles of driftwood, and low cliff faces. Primarily a bird of inshore waters, the Pigeon Guillemot feeds on fish at or near the bottom, seldom venturing more than a few hundred meters from shore during the summer.

Description

12–14″ (30.5–35.5 cm). This species has the distinctive guillemot profile, characterized by a rounded head, long, pointed bill, and thin neck. In all plumages, the Pigeon Guillemot has light brown wing linings and a white wing patch on the secondary coverts that is penetrated by 1 or sometimes 2 black wedges. The feet and mouth lining are a bright orange-red year-round. Breeding birds are starkly black; in winter, the plumage becomes mottled gray and white. Immatures are duskier gray above and have smaller white wing patches; the median coverts are dark-tipped and form an indistinct bar.

Underwing

◀4

Voice

A whistled *peeeee.*

Similar Species

Winter murrelets much smaller and shorter-billed; have darker heads and backs and whiter underparts. See Black Guillemot.

Range

Breeds from northwestern Alaska south along coast to southern California. Winter range poorly known; a few annually inshore to southern limit of breeding range. Also on northern coast of Asia.
D. H. S. Wehle

Marbled Murrelet

Brachyramphus marmoratus

The Marbled Murrelet is a small, dark brown, boldly mottled alcid of protected bays and other near-shore waters of the North Pacific. Its breeding habits are poorly known, but it is nocturnal and apparently noncolonial. It may regularly breed up to 20 miles or more inland and nest on the limbs of evergreen trees or, in treeless areas, on the ground. It is a strong, fast flier, tending to rise directly off the water without first running across the surface. It will often flush at a considerable distance when approached by a boat.

Description

9½″ (24 cm). The dark brown upperparts of the Marbled Murrelet are boldly mottled red or gray; they rarely appear barred. The scapulars are often, but not always, white. The white underparts are finely mottled with brown; there may be a dark brown band across the upper breast. The wing linings are light brown or gray. The bill is long, shallow, and dark. In winter, the upperparts are sooty-gray, and a white scapular stripe is always evident; the

Breeding plumage
1. *Slender bill.*
2. *Black plumage.*
3. *White wing patch with 1 or 2 black wedges.*

Bright red feet.

Winter plumage
1. *Slender bill.*
2. *Largely white head.*
3. *White wing patch with 1 or 2 black wedges.*
4. *Dark wing linings.*

Winter plumage
1. *Long, dark bill.*
2. *Dark crown extends below eye.*
3. *Dark upperparts with white scapular patch.*
4. *White underparts.*

underparts are all-white with the edges of some feathers lightly tinged brown. The young are similar to winter-plumage adults.

Voice
A high, twittering call.

Similar Species
Kittlitz's Murrelet lighter brown, much more finely mottled over entire body; has much shorter bill. In winter, white face of Kittlitz's extends to above eye. Ancient Murrelet lacks white scapulars, has distinct contrast between blackish cap and grayer back. See Xantus' Murrelet.

Range
Breeds from central Aleutian Islands east to northern Gulf of Alaska and south along coast to central California. Small numbers winter in inshore and offshore waters of breeding range; prime wintering area unknown. Accidental east of breeding areas. Also on northern coast of Asia.   *D. H. S. Wehle*

Kittlitz's Murrelet

Brachyramphus brevirostris
Kittlitz's Murrelet is a small, brown-and-white speckled alcid of Alaska. It is locally common in summer in protected waters, particularly near tidewater glaciers. Like the Marbled Murrelet, it is nocturnal, noncolonial, and flies in a strong, swift manner. It nests on the ground, both far inland in rocky alpine habitat and on steep slopes near the sea.

Description
9″ (23 cm). Kittlitz's Murrelet is finely speckled with brown and white all over. The head and upper breast may appear darker and the belly lighter than the rest of the body. The scapulars are sometimes white but are less noticeable than in the Marbled Murrelet. The outer half of each tail feather is whitish, unlike the all-dark tail of the Marbled Murrelet; this is a good identifying characteristic as birds of both species fan their tails when taking off from the water. The bill is dark and very short. In winter, Kittlitz's is similar to the Marbled Murrelet, except that the Kittlitz's face is white to above the eye and there is a nearly complete, sooty-gray necklace.

Similar Species
See Marbled Murrelet. In winter, Ancient Murrelet lacks white scapular stripe and has longer bill; distinct contrast between blackish cap and grayer back.

Range
Breeds from northwestern Alaska south along coast, including Aleutians, to northern Gulf of Alaska and northern regions of southeastern Alaska. A few winter inshore and offshore in southern portions of North American breeding range. Also breeds and winters on northern coast of Asia.   *D. H. S. Wehle*

Breeding plumage
1. Long, dark bill.
2. Dark brown plumage mottled with red or gray.

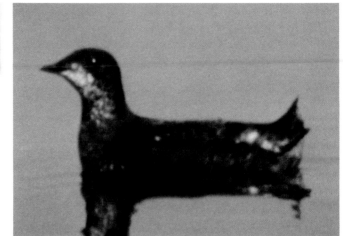

Breeding plumage
1. Short, dark bill.
2. Light brown plumage speckled with white.

Winter plumage
1. Dark crown.
2. White on face extends to above eye.
3. Dark upperparts with white scapular patch.
4. White underparts with dark necklace.

Xantus' Murrelet

Synthliboramphus hypoleucus
This small, striking, black-and-white alcid with a thin, pointed bill
nests in crevices among rocks or in other sheltered places on islands
off southern California, south to central Baja California; it spends
the rest of its life on the open Pacific. On the ocean, Xantus' are
normally encountered in pairs, or rarely in small groups of up to half
a dozen. They ride low in the water with their necks stretched
upward as if constantly on the alert. In flight they remain close to
the water's surface, moving in a straight line with rapid wingbeats.

hypoleuca

Description
8–8½″ (20.5–21.5 cm). Xantus' Murrelet is uniformly slate-black
above and pure white below, with the white of the underparts
extending from the undertail coverts to the chin. In the more
frequently encountered northern race, *scrippsi*, the white
underparts and black upperparts meet in a clean, straight line that
runs through the face just below the eye. In the more southern race,
hypoleucus, the underparts and upperparts meet in an irregular
line, the white extending upward to surround the eye in part, and
normally most prominent ahead of the eye. In both races, the white
lower cheek contrasts sharply with the black of the top of the head
and upper cheek. The wing linings are white, giving the impression
when the bird is viewed in flight that the entire underwing is white.
The thin, pointed bill is black. There is no seasonal variation.

scrippsi

Similar Species
See Craveri's Murrelet. Winter-plumage Marbled Murrelet shows
conspicuous white scapular stripes, has white of throat area
extending back to near back of neck, nearly forming a collar.
Ancient Murrelet has gray back contrasting with black on top of
head and hindneck and a short stubby bill. Cassin's Auklet shows no
white on chin and throat, never appears strikingly black-and-white.

Range
Breeds only on islands off southern California south to San Benitos
Islands off central Baja California. In late summer and fall many
move northward, occurring regularly to Monterey Bay, with
stragglers recorded as far north as Oregon, Washington, and British
Columbia. Winters on open ocean off southern California and Baja
California, normally far from shore.   *Guy McCaskie*

Craveri's Murrelet

Synthliboramphus craveri
Craveri's Murrelet is almost indistinguishable from Xantus'
Murrelet. It nests on islands within the Gulf of California and along
the Pacific coast of southern Baja California, ranging farther south
than any other member of this family.

Description
8–8½″ (20.5–21.5 cm). Craveri's is very similar to the more northern
race of Xantus' Murrelet, having a clean, straight line through the
face where the black upperparts meet the white underparts.
However, on Craveri's Murrelet the black extends slightly lower on
the face, terminating in the area of the chin, rather than at the gape
as on Xantus' Murrelet. The wing linings of Craveri's contain much
dusky coloration, and the underside of the wing appears dark when
the bird is viewed in flight. Unfortunately, these birds fly close to
the water, making it difficult to assess the color of the underwing.
The upperparts appear darker than those of Xantus' under favorable
lighting conditions, and the black on the back extends onto the sides

Adult on water
1. *Slate-black upperparts.*
2. *Dark color on head extends to gape.*
3. *White underparts.*

   Small size. Holds neck stretched upward when swimming.

Adult in flight
1. *White wing linings.*

Adult in flight
1. *Dark wing linings.*

of the breast, appearing as an inverted triangle ahead of the wing when Craveri's is viewed in flight; this mark is not prominent on a swimming bird. The bill of Craveri's is longer and thinner than that of Xantus'.

Similar Species
See Xantus', Marbled, Kittlitz's, and Ancient murrelets.

Range
Breeds on islands within Gulf of California and along Pacific Coast of Baja California from San Benitos Islands southward. In late summer and fall, many move northward, occurring regularly to the waters off extreme southern California (San Diego), irregularly to Monterey Bay, and accidentally to Oregon. Winters in Mexican waters.   *Guy McCaskie*

Ancient Murrelet

Synthliboramphus antiquus
The Ancient Murrelet is a small alcid of the temperate North Pacific. It has dark upperparts and white underparts, and its head appears very large for its small body. Its flight is swift and close to the water and lacks the rocking movement of the flight of other murrelets. Nocturnal at the breeding colony, it nests in both burrows and natural cavities under rocks and tree roots. When only 2 days old, downy young are escorted to the sea by adults. Adults typically forage in offshore waters throughout the year. There are numerous records of inland sightings, especially in autumn after periods of high westerly winds.

Description
10″ (25.5 cm). The Ancient Murrelet has a black head and a bluish-gray back; the chin, throat patch, sides, flanks, and flight feathers are sooty-brown. A white belly and breast extend upward to include the sides of the neck. A single stripe of white plumes extends from above and behind each eye, nearly joining at the back of the head. Narrow white plumes occur sparsely on the shoulders. In winter, the chin is dark, the throat is white, and the white facial stripe and shoulder plumes are absent. The bill remains cream-colored throughout the year. The contrast between the black cap and the gray back is a good field mark all year long.

Similar Species
See Marbled, Kittlitz's, Xantus', and Craveri's murrelets.

Range
Breeds from Aleutian Islands and Gulf of Alaska south along coast to British Columbia; rarely to northern Washington. Winters offshore from breeding range south to Baja California; rare in southern part of winter range. Also on northern coast of Asia.
D. H. S. Wehle

Adult on water
1. *Black upperparts.*
2. *Dark color on head extends to chin.*
3. *White underparts.*

   Small size.
   Holds neck stretched upward when swimming.

Winter plumage
1. *Black face and crown.*
2. *Gray back.*
3. *White underparts.*

Breeding plumage
1. *Black face and crown.*
2. *White eyebrow.*
3. *Gray back.*
4. *White underparts.*

Cassin's Auklet

Ptychoramphus aleuticus
Cassin's Auklet is a small, dark, white-bellied alcid that is widely
but locally distributed along the eastern North Pacific coast. It is
strictly nocturnal at its breeding colony, where it nests in a wide
variety of habitats ranging from bare, flat ground to marine terraces
and sea slopes with heavy vegetation. It feeds in offshore waters
throughout the year, but also may be locally abundant in inshore
waters during the summer.

Description
7½–8½″ (19–21.5 cm). Cassin's Auklet is sooty-gray above with a
white belly and light to dark gray throat, breast, sides, and flanks.
In summer, the worn edges of the flight feathers may appear light
brown. A small white crescent over the eye and a pale area at the
base of the lower mandible are distinctive at close range. Birds in
winter plumage and juveniles are similar to breeding adults, all
having dark upperparts, a white belly, and a dark bill.

Voice
Cricketlike chirps.

Similar Species
Parakeet Auklet has white underparts extending higher into lower
breast, sides, and flanks. All other auklets in breeding plumage,
including Parakeet, have brightly colored bill and white facial
stripes. Young Crested and Whiskered auklets have dark bellies.

Range
Breeds in Aleutian Islands and southern coasts of Gulf of Alaska,
south to Baja California. Winters in offshore waters to southern
limit of breeding range.   *D. H. S. Wehle*

Parakeet Auklet

Cyclorrhynchus psittacula
The Parakeet Auklet is a small alcid of the Bering Sea and western
Gulf of Alaska. It has dark upperparts and conspicuous white
underparts. It nests in single pairs or small, scattered groups, and
occasionally in large colonies among *Aethia* auklets. Parakeet
Auklets typically nest in rock crevices in cliff faces, talus slopes, or
under beach boulders; in some areas, abandoned puffin burrows are
used. During the breeding season, the Parakeet Auklet is very vocal
and spends much of the day in inshore waters close to its breeding
site. It probably feeds nocturnally in offshore waters.

Description
10″ (25.5 cm). The largest of the true auklets, the Parakeet Auklet is
brownish, sooty-gray above with a dark throat; the breast, sides,
and flanks are white, mottled with brown, and the belly is white. A
narrow stripe of short, white plumes runs backward and downward
from the eye. The reddish-orange bill is short, deep, and stubby; the
lower mandible curves strongly upward. In winter, the underparts,

In flight
1. Sooty-gray head and upperparts.
2. White belly.

Adult
1. Dark upperparts.
2. Dark bill with pale base of lower mandible.
3. White crescent over eye.

Breeding plumage
1. Short, deep, reddish bill.
2. Single white stripe behind eye.
3. Mottled breast.
4. Sooty-gray upperparts.
5. White underparts.

including the throat, are white; the facial stripe may or may not be
present, and the bill is dark. The immature is similar to the winter-
plumage adult, but usually has darker upperparts.

Voice
A single, often repeated, rasping note.

Similar Species
Cassin's Auklet smaller with darker bill, no white in breast, sides,
or flanks. Breeding Rhinoceros Auklet much larger, with 2 white
plumes on face and longer, slimmer bill with pale knob on upper
mandible.

Range
Breeds from Bering Strait south along coast to Aleutian Islands and
western Gulf of Alaska. Winters in offshore waters from southern
portions of breeding range casually south to California. Also on
northern coast of Asia.   *D. H. S. Wehle*

Least Auklet

Aethia pusilla
The sparrow-size Least Auklet is perhaps the most abundant
breeding seabird on the Aleutian and Bering Sea islands. It is
extremely gregarious, with some colonies numbering more than a
million birds. It nests in the rock crevices of talus slopes and on
grass-covered lava flows, often in the company of other *Aethia* and
Parakeet auklets. Like Crested Auklets, Least Auklets return to
their colony en masse at dusk from offshore foraging areas and
usually remain quite vocal until dark.

Description
6″ (15 cm). The Least Auklet is brownish, sooty-gray above with a
pure white throat. The remaining underparts are white with brown
mottling; the extent of mottling varies greatly, with some birds
appearing all-white and others very dark below. There is a narrow
stripe of white plumes running back from the base of the eye and a
scattering of white plumes on the forehead and lores. The bill is red
and extremely short. A white scapular stripe is present in winter
and in some birds during the summer; the stripe, along with all-
white underparts, is characteristic of all winter-plumage birds.
Immatures have black upperparts and sooty-gray underparts.

Voice
High, chattering notes.

Similar Species
Whiskered Auklet much grayer; has crest on forehead. See Cassin's
Auklet.

Range
Breeds on Bering Sea and Aleutian islands, sparingly in extreme
western Gulf of Alaska. Winters offshore in ice-free waters of
breeding range. Also on northern coast of Asia.   *D. H. S. Wehle*

Breeding plumage in flight
1. *Short, deep, reddish bill.*
2. *Single white stripe behind eye.*
3. *Sooty-gray upperparts.*

Has white throat in winter.

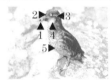

Breeding plumage
1. *Stubby red bill.*
2. *White plumes on forehead and lores.*
3. *Single white stripe behind eye.*
4. *White throat.*
5. *Mottled underparts.*

Very small size.

Winter plumage
1. *White scapular stripe.*
2. *White underparts.*

Very small size.

Whiskered Auklet

Aethia pygmaea
The Whiskered Auklet, a locally rare to abundant alcid of the
Aleutian Islands, is notable for its strikingly ornate head. A small,
gray bird, it nests under beach boulders and in the rock crevices of
talus slopes and cliffs, often in the company of other auklets. At the
breeding colony, it is crepuscular in its habits, usually arriving after
other auklet species and leaving before them. It also differs from
other auklets in foraging close to shore during the summer,
particularly in tide rips.

Description
7″ (18 cm). The Whiskered Auklet has a sooty-gray head adorned
with 3 white stripes on each side and a dark crest projecting from
the forehead. One facial stripe runs backward and downward from
behind the eye. The other 2 join at the lores; 1 runs backward below
the eye and the other extends upward in front of the eye to project
above the forehead. The remainder of the body is slate-gray except
for the lower belly and undertail coverts, which are light gray to
nearly white. The short bill is red with a pale tip. Juveniles have no
crest and have only weak facial stripes.

Voice
A kittenlike *me-ow.*

Similar Species
See Cassin's Auklet and Least Auklet. Crested Auklet larger, with
single facial stripe and larger, orange bill; crest usually fuller.

Range
Breeds only in central Aleutian Islands and Kurile Islands. Winters
in inshore and offshore waters of breeding range.
D. H. S. Wehle

Crested Auklet

Aethia cristatella
At dusk, these common seabirds of Alaska islands return to the
colony in beelike swarms, performing spectacular aerial displays.

Description
10″ (25.5 cm). Sooty-gray above and bluish-gray below with stripe of
white plumes running back and down from middle of eye. Crest
thick, dark; curves from forehead over stubby orange bill. Mouth
has orange plate at each corner. In winter, crest sparse, bill plates
absent, bill brown.

Voice
A hollow, chattering *hor-aah.*

Similar Species
See Cassin's and Whiskered auklets.

Range
Bering Sea and Aleutian Islands. Winters offshore from southern
Bering Sea to northern Gulf of Alaska.   *D. H. S. Wehle*

Juvenile
1. *Short bill without plates.*
2. *Weak facial stripes.*
3. *Slate-gray plumage.*

Breeding plumage
1. *Short red bill.*
2. *Thin, dark crest on forehead.*
3. *Three white stripes on face.*
4. *Gray body contrasting with darker head.*

Small size.

Breeding plumage
1. *Stubby orange bill.*
2. *Thick, dark crest on forehead.*
3. *Single white stripe on face.*
4. *Uniformly dark plumage.*

Rhinoceros Auklet

Cerorhinca monocerata
Actually a misnamed puffin, the Rhinoceros Auklet is a large, sooty-brown alcid of the north Pacific Coast. Its nocturnal habits at most colonies make this bird difficult to see on land. It nests in earthen burrows on sea slopes and cliff tops that are often heavily vegetated. An hour or so before sunset, large flocks usually raft close to a colony; within an hour after sunset, inshore flocks disperse, and the birds make several passing flights over the colony before landing at the nest site. Rhinoceros Auklets forage in inshore waters during the day.

Description
15″ (38 cm). The Rhinoceros Auklet is sooty-brown above with a grayish-brown throat, breast, sides, and flanks. Its white belly is usually not visible when the bird is swimming. Two stripes of white plumes run backward across the face, 1 from the base of the bill below the eye and the other from just above and behind the eye. Compared with the bills of other puffins, this bird's reddish-orange bill appears longer, narrower, and, except for a pale knob projecting from the base of the upper mandible, much shallower. In winter, the facial stripes and the knob on the bill are absent. The immature is similar to the winter-plumage adult but darker, with a smaller, darker bill.

Voice
A low growling *errrrr;* sometimes 4–7 in series.

Similar Series
Immature Tufted Puffin darker, has deeper bill, shows broad gray stripe behind eye; may occur farther offshore.

Range
Breeds sparingly on Aleutian Islands and more abundantly from Alaska Peninsula south along coast to central California, where its populations are increasing. Probably winters in inshore and offshore waters from breeding colonies south to southern California. Also on northern coast of Asia.   *D. H. S. Wehle*

Tufted Puffin

Fratercula cirrhata
The Tufted Puffin, a large, black-bodied alcid of the North Pacific Ocean, has a white face and long yellowish tufts behind the eyes. On the open sea it is usually seen swimming alone; it occurs in large flocks in coastal waters adjacent to its breeding sites and on land. It nests primarily on islands in burrows along cliff tops or on steep sea slopes, occasionally in rock crevices of talus slopes and under beach boulders. Its short, stubby wings make its flight appear laborious, and it often runs across the water for a considerable distance before taking off. When approached by a boat, the Tufted Puffin is less likely to dive than the Horned Puffin or murres.

Description
15–16″ (38–40.5 cm). The Tufted Puffin is unmistakable in breeding plumage. It has a white face, a large, laterally compressed orange-and-green bill, and long, yellow tufts behind the eyes. The body is black with brown flight feathers, and the legs and feet are orange. In winter, the tufts behind the eyes are replaced by short gray

Breeding plumage
1. *Long reddish bill with pale knob at base.*
2. *Two white stripes on face.*
3. *Brownish upperparts.*
4. *White belly.*

Winter plumage
1. *Long reddish bill.*
2. *Brownish upperparts.*

Large size.

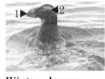

Winter plumage
1. *Bill constricted at base, orange only at tip.*
2. *Short tufts behind eyes.*

feathers, and the face and underparts become brownish-gray. The
bill is constricted at the base and is orange only at the tip. Subadults
have a mottled face; immatures have a yellowish bill. Juveniles have
an all-black bill with the underparts of the body varying in color
from dark gray to white.

Voice
A growling *errr*, sometimes repeated: *er errr*, or sirenlike *er-errr
errr errr errr*, syllables alternating between high and low pitches.

Similar Species
See Rhinoceros Auklet. Winter-plumage and immature Horned
Puffins have dusky face and white underparts.

Range
Breeds from northwestern Alaska south along coast to northern
California. Winters at sea throughout North Pacific. Also on
northern coast of Asia.   *D. H. S. Wehle*

Atlantic Puffin

Fratercula arctica
The plump little Atlantic Puffin, with its bright, multicolored bill, is
appropriately described in Bent's *Life Histories* as "a curious
mixture of the solemn and the comical." Primarily a fish eater, this
puffin is able to carry more than a dozen fish in its bill at once.
Formerly abundant in the North Atlantic, these burrow-nesters are
particularly vulnerable to predation and their numbers have
declined with the arrival of modern man. However, large colonies on
remote islands continue to flourish, and as many as 500,000 are
netted annually by local inhabitants in Iceland and the Faeroes. The
species has recently become re-established on islands where it
formerly nested.

Description
12–13″ (30.5–33 cm). The Atlantic Puffin is a stocky, medium-size
alcid. Its short, thick neck, large head, laterally compressed bill, and
notably short tail give the species a stubby, big-fronted look. Adults
in breeding plumage are distinctive with magnificent red, steel-blue,
and yellow bills; their prominent white faces can be seen at
considerable distances. Both the colorful outer sheath of the bill and
the horny eye plate are shed each fall and renewed in the spring. A
puffin's age can be estimated fairly accurately by counting the
number of vertical grooves on the bill; these increase as the bird
grows older. Winter adults have grayer faces and less obvious,
yellow-tipped bills. Immatures have dusky-gray faces and small,
dark bills; they may possibly be confused with Razorbills. In flight,
Atlantic Puffins are chunky and heavy-headed. Their unmarked,
rounded wings are quite unlike the pointed wings of the larger
alcids. Puffins lack the white secondary tips present in some other
species. Atlantic Puffins also show no white on the dorsal surface or
on the sides of the rump.

Voice
A single growl and low purrs.

Similar Species
Razorbills and murres have elongated flight profile, have puffy white
area on sides of rump. Immature Razorbill larger, not so stubby in
appearance, with elongated head and entirely white cheek and
throat.

Breeding plumage
1. *Large orange-and-green bill.*
2. *White face with long yellow tufts behind eyes.*
3. *Black body.*
4. *Orange legs.*

Large size.

Winter adult in flight
1. *Stout, dark bill.*
2. *Gray face.*
3. *White underparts.*
4. *Rounded wings.*

Chunky build.

Winter plumage
1. *Stout, dark bill.*
2. *Gray face.*
3. *White underparts with dark collar.*
4. *Dark upperparts.*

Range
Breeds from southeastern Quebec, eastern Newfoundland,
Labrador, Nova Scotia, southern New Brunswick, and central
coastal Maine. Winters offshore near breeding grounds; moves south
to Massachusetts, rarely, Long Island south. Accidental inland in
Ontario, Quebec, and Maine. Also in western Sweden, Iceland,
southern Greenland, northern British Isles, Brittany, and Portugal.
Peter D. Vickery

Horned Puffin

Fratercula corniculata
Similar in appearance to the Atlantic Puffin, the Horned Puffin is a
common resident of the northern North Pacific Ocean. During the
breeding season, birds tend to raft in large flocks in inshore waters
close to their colonies; in winter, they are widely dispersed at sea.
The Horned Puffin nests under boulders and in the rock crevices of
talus slopes and cliff faces; on some islands, however, it uses earthen
burrows almost exclusively. The Horned Puffin has the same
laborious flight as other puffins; it often dives underwater when
approached by boats.

Description
14–15″ (35.5–38 cm). In breeding plumage, the Horned Puffin is the
only North Pacific alcid with a white face and white underparts
separated by a broad, black collar. The large, triangular bill is
creamy yellow at the base and red-and-black at the tip. At close
range, a black, fleshy protuberance can be seen above each eye. In
winter, the face is dusky-colored and the bill is smaller with a dark
base and red tip. In immatures and juveniles the face is even darker;
the immature has an orange-and-brown bill, the juvenile a smaller,
all-dark bill.

Voice
A growling *errr, er, errr,* or *er, errr er er er er er,* decreasing in
intensity after second syllable.

Similar Species
See Tufted Puffin.

Range
Breeds from northwestern Alaska south along coast to Alaska-
British Columbia border. Winters far at sea south to waters off
California. Irregular spring records from Washington, Oregon, and
California. Also on northern coast of Asia.
D. H. S. Wehle

Breeding plumage
1. *Triangular bill with dark base.*
2. *Whitish face.*
3. *Black upperparts and collar.*
4. *White underparts.*

Chunky build with large-headed look.

Breeding plumage
1. *Triangular bill with yellow base.*
2. *White face.*
3. *Black upperparts and collar.*
4. *White underparts.*

Chunky build with large-headed look.

Winter plumage
1. *Bill dark at base, red only at tip.*
2. *Dusky-colored face.*

Pigeons and Doves

(Family Columbidae)
Pigeons and doves are small to medium-size rotund birds with stout
necks and rather small, rounded heads. An arbitrary distinction
classes doves as small and slender with long, often more graduated
tails; pigeons are considered to be larger and stockier with fuller
tails. In both groups, the flight is generally rapid and direct on full,
rather pointed wings. North American Columbidae are usually
rather drably colored, and each species has a characteristic tail
pattern. On the ground these birds walk with short, rapidly moving
legs, constantly bobbing the head back and forth. Females are
similar to males but are usually somewhat duller. Pigeons and doves
have unique bills with a fleshy, often bulbous swelling at the base
and another smaller, horny swelling toward the tip. Each species
has a characteristic hollow, mellow call. Unlike most other birds,
pigeons and doves can drink without raising their heads.
(World: 303 species. North America: 16 species.)   *Scott B. Terrill*

Rock Dove

Columba livia
The introduced, semidomesticated Rock Dove or "Pigeon" is a
common bird in cities, towns, and on farms throughout most of the
settled regions of North America. Its habit of associating with man,
gathering in groups, and nesting on buildings, together with its
wing-clapping display flight and the presence of many different color
forms in a single flock make the Rock Dove easy to identify. Other
pigeons of similar size usually avoid areas of human habitation.
Some small populations have reverted to their original habitat of
rocky cliffs.

Description
12–13″ (30.5–33 cm). Birds of the ancestral, wild type are gray,
darkest on the head and neck, with 2 black bars on the secondaries,
a white rump, a dark tail tip, and some iridescence on the sides of
the neck. There are numerous color variants in semidomesticated
flocks, ranging from birds that resemble the wild type in every
respect but the white rump to birds that are entirely black or white,
or largely reddish-brown. These color variants sometimes retain
some of the pattern of the wild type; the 2 bars on the secondaries
can often be seen in birds that otherwise show little resemblance to
the ancestral Rock Dove.

Voice
A muffled *coo-crooo* or *coo-took-crooo*.

Similar Species
White-crowned Pigeon all dark with white crown. Band-tailed
Pigeon has pale gray tail tip, dark wing linings. Red-billed Pigeon all
dark with red-and-white bill. White-winged Dove has bold, white
patches on wings and tail. Other town-dwelling doves smaller and
browner or paler, with narrower or more pointed tails.

Range
In New World, introduced and resident from southern Alaska and
southern Canada south through Central and much of South America;
also in West Indies. Native to Old World.   *John Farrand, Jr.*

Wild type
1. *Gray body.*
2. *Two black bars on secondaries.*
3. *Dark tail tip.*

Often shows white rump.
Common in towns.

Color variants
1. *Blackish variant.*
2. *Reddish variant.*

White-crowned Pigeon

Columba leucocephala
This Caribbean species is an arboreal bird of West Indian hardwood hammocks and pine and mangrove forests of southern Florida. It is most often seen flying swiftly overhead.

Description
12–14″ (30.5–35.5 cm). Adult dark slate-blue with immaculate white cap. Immature similar but paler; cap absent or indistinct.

Voice
Low-pitched *wof, wof, wo, co-woo.*

Similar Species
Rock Dove paler with white rump and 2 parallel black bars on wings; not generally found in same range.

Range
Southern tip of peninsular Florida and Florida Keys south throughout islands around Caribbean. Many winter in southern Florida and Keys, but majority move farther south.
Paul W. Sykes, Jr.

Red-billed Pigeon

Columba flavirostris
This shy and uncommon bird enters our range in southern Texas, where it is found in summer in dense woods along the Rio Grande.

Description
13–14″ (33–35.5 cm). Appears all-dark in field. Deep maroon-brown on head, neck, chest, upper back, and shoulders; elsewhere slate-gray. Throat pale. Bill red basally; tip yellow or whitish. Eyes, legs, and feet reddish.

Voice
Rich, cooing, *wooo, up-chuckapoo;* last 4 notes may be repeated.

Similar Species
No other Texas dove or pigeon is normally all dark. See Rock Dove, Band-tailed Pigeon.

Range
Local and uncommon in S. Texas (lower Rio Grande valley); mostly absent in winter. Resident from N. Mexico to Costa Rica.
Kenn Kaufman

Band-tailed Pigeon

Columba fasciata
The Band-tailed Pigeon occurs primarily in mountainous areas in the West. The inland race, *C. f. fasciata,* occurs in dry, pine-dominated forests; the coastal race, *C. f. monilis,* is found in moister forests and is particularly attracted to oaks. Both races are seasonally migratory and abundant. They are secretive nesters and therefore may be far more plentiful in an area than is commonly believed. They are attracted to feeders and may be semi-resident in some populous areas.

Description
13–15″ (35–38 cm). Band-tailed Pigeons look like Rock Doves, but their longer tails have a black bar and are tipped with a wide pale gray band. They appear gray to bluish-gray; adults have a conspicuous, iridescent nape and a white crescent above the nape on the lower back of the head; the head and upper breast vary from gray-brown in females to pink or purple in males. Both sexes have a yellow bill with a black tip and yellow feet with black claws. The

Adult
1. *White crown.*
2. *Dark body.*

   Large size.

Adult
1. *Dark maroon-brown foreparts.*
2. *Pale-tipped red bill.*

Adult
1. *Yellow bill with black tip.*
2. *White crescent on nape.*
3. *Yellow feet with black claws.*

color of the bill and feet in immatures varies from gray to yellow. Immatures remain gray with some buff to brown or russet edging on the wing coverts and primaries from fledging until at least 5 months.

Voice
Low-pitched, 2-toned cooing, *whoo-whoooo*, given several times in succession. A chirring or chirping call also given.

Similar Species
Rock Dove usually has white rump patch, red feet and bill; frequently multicolored. Mourning Dove smaller, brown to blue-gray, with pointed tail. White-winged Dove smaller with large white wing patches and white-tipped tail. All other doves in North America either smaller, browner, more scaled in appearance, or more noticeably white in flight. In Texas, see Red-billed Pigeon.

Range
Southeast Alaska, British Columbia, Washington, Oregon, and California primarily west of crest of Sierras into Baja California. Inland race occurs from Utah and Colorado south to Arizona, New Mexico, and central Mexico. Somewhat common in mountains of west Texas; accidental east of Rockies.   *Clait E. Braun*

Ringed Turtle-Dove

Streptopelia risoria
The Ringed Turtle-Dove occurs in several small populations in North America. It is maintained in part by human handouts.

Description
10½–13″ (27–33 cm). Pale overall; head and underparts whiter and upperparts slightly browner. In size and shape like a hefty Mourning Dove, but tail square-ended with white corners. Adults have narrow, black collar around back of neck.

Voice
Short note followed by soft, vibrating cooing, *coo-hr-r-r-rooh*.

Similar Species
See Mourning Dove and Spotted Dove.

Range
Introduced and escaped: occurs in Los Angeles, coastal southern California, southern Florida, Arizona, and suburban Alabama.
Louis R. Bevier

Spotted Dove

Streptopelia chinensis
This introduced bird prefers areas with large trees. In flight, it looks chunky, long-tailed, and short-winged.

Description
11–13½″ (28–34.5 cm). Body heavy; tail long, squared. Head and underparts pinkish-brown; central tail feathers, wings, and back brown. Outer tail feathers black with broad white tips. Wing linings dark blue-gray. Adults have broad black collar with fine white spotting; this briefly absent on juveniles. Legs and feet reddish.

Voice
A 3-part cooing with longer, rolling note in middle, *coo-coooo-coo*.

Similar Species
See White-winged and Mourning doves and Ringed Turtle-Dove.

Range
Coastal S. California from Santa Barbara to San Diego; some outlying populations. Native to S. Asia.   *Louis R. Bevier*

Adult in flight
1. *White crescent on nape.*
2. *Wide, pale gray band on tail.*

Adult
1. *Pale plumage.*
2. *Narrow black collar.*
3. *Long, narrow tail.*

Adult
1. *Brown plumage.*
2. *Black collar with white spots.*
3. *Long white-tipped tail.*

   Common in residential areas.

White-winged Dove

Zenaida asiatica
During the midday heat of long summer days in the southwestern desert, often the only sound heard is the monotonous, repetitious *who-cooks-for-you* of the White-winged Dove. In flight or perched, this big, heavy, grayish-brown dove clearly shows large, white areas on the wing and tail. This species is abundant in desert habitats including agricultural areas, riparian woodlands, residential areas, and canyons of lower mountain elevations. White-winged Doves frequently feed on the tops of flowering cacti. They are seen in large flocks in agricultural areas, often with Mourning Doves, from midsummer into fall. The flight is direct, with deep, consistent beats and occasional glides, with the wings often bent back at an angle.

Description
10–12½″ (25.5–32 cm). The overall body shape and coloration suggest a large, heavy Mourning Dove, but the White-winged Dove has white greater and median coverts that form conspicuous patches on the blackish wings. The broad, long, slightly fan-shaped tail has rectangular white patches on the end of the outer tail feathers. The rest of the body is grayish-brown to sandy-buff, paler on the lower belly and becoming darker on the upperparts. There is a small black spot on the side of the head, and a purplish sheen on the crown and nape. The iris is red.

Voice
A mournful, full *who-cooks-for-you* and *coo-uh-cuck-oo;* first 2 syllables separated from second 2 by slight pause. Also, mellower *hoo-hoot-who-who-hooo.* In general, first note somewhat rough.

Similar Species
Other pigeons and large doves lack black wings with bold white patches.

Range
Breeds from southeastern California through southern Nevada, western, central, and southern Arizona, southern New Mexico, and western and southern Texas, south into Mexico and Central America. Irregular and much less common during winter in southern portion of United States range, but locally abundant just south of border. Rare but regular in fall and winter in coastal California; casual elsewhere in fall.   *Scott B. Terrill*

Mourning Dove

Zenaida macroura
The Mourning Dove is one of the commonest and most widespread birds native to North America. It is found in almost every available habitat, except densely forested regions. Its mournful call is well known in most residential areas throughout its range. This species can often be seen in large flocks, especially in the south, in agricultural areas and near water in arid regions. The Mourning Dove calls before first light and flies directly and rapidly on stiff wingbeats well before dawn; it is often the first diurnal bird detected. The wingbeats make a considerable whistling noise upon takeoff that decreases but persists in flight. During the courtship display, the male performs a steep, climbing flight, which terminates in a series of circular glides on stiffly spread wings.

Description
11–13″ (28–33 cm). This rather elongated, soft brown dove has a rounded body topped by a slim neck and small head. The tail is long and tapered, narrowly bordered by white on the periphery. The

In flight
1. *Large white patch on black wing.*
2. *Long tail.*

Adult
1. *Sandy-brown plumage.*
2. *White wing patch.*
3. *Long tail with white outer corners.*

Adult
1. *Uniform gray-brown color.*
2. *Small head and thin neck.*
3. *Long, tapered tail with white feather tips.*

underparts are gray, washed with pinkish-buff to cinnamon. The upperparts are darker brown, and the wings are dark gray-brown, blackish at the tips, with indistinct blackish spotting on the scapulars and tertials. There is a blackish spot on the side of the head, and purplish iridescence, more noticeable on the male, on the nape and sides of the neck.

Voice
Who-ah, whoo-whoo-who with sharply rising, inflected second syllable; all other notes on same pitch, last 3 dropping slightly at end of each. Often only last 3–4 notes can be heard.

Similar Species
See Band-tailed Pigeon, White-winged and Inca doves. Ringed Turtle-Dove and Spotted Dove stouter, with square-tipped tail; Turtle-Dove has narrow black collar.

Range
Breeds from southeastern Alaska across southern Canada and throughout entire United States, Mexico (becoming local), and Panama. Many withdraw from northern areas in winter. *Scott B. Terrill*

Inca Dove

Columbina inca
A very small, light-colored dove, the Inca Dove superficially resembles a tiny, slim, scaly Mourning Dove. It is common to abundant in cities, towns, parks, farms, and feedlots in Arizona, New Mexico, and Texas. During lazy, hot summer afternoons, their mournful, monotonous *whirl-pool* call can be heard. Often seen in flocks on telephone wires, front lawns, roadsides, and empty lots, this little dove flushes with a quick flutter of the wings. After alighting and when alert, Inca Doves often jerk their heads sideways and forward—even more than other doves. Their flight is direct, with rapid wingbeats. Inca Doves walk around on short, rapidly moving little legs. Pairs can occasionally be seen lying on the ground, each dove alternately spreading a wing above the body to expose the rufous wing patches to the other. In colder months, Inca Doves often roost in large, tight clusters.

Description
7½–8½″ (19–21.5 cm). With its small head and thin, slender neck, this small, slender dove resembles a miniature Mourning Dove. The tail is long and narrow, and although it is actually square-tipped, when folded it often appears pointed. The bird is pale gray overall, with a scaly appearance that is bolder on the upperparts; the underparts are lighter. The tail is gray with white outer edges that widen toward tip; it is narrowly bordered by black. The primaries and wing linings are chestnut.

Voice
A mournful, hollow, repetitious *whirl-pool*, accent stronger on introduction to second syllable.

Similar Species
Mourning Dove larger, browner, not scaly, with pointed tail; has different calls. Common Ground-Dove rounder, stockier, darker; tail shorter with much more black on outer edges and white only on outer tips. White-tipped Dove much larger; dusty gray-brown above, paler below, with no dark scaling.

Range
Extreme southeastern California (Colorado River) through south and south-central Texas, south through Mexico into Central America. *Scott B. Terrill*

2

Immature
1. *Brownish plumage.*
2. *Scaly upperparts.*

Adult with wings spread
1. *Rufous patch on wing.*
2. *Long, narrow tail with white borders.*

Adult
1. *Grayish, scaled plumage.*
2. *Long, narrow tail with white borders.*

*Small size.
Mournful whirlpool call.*

Common Ground-Dove

Columbina passerina
The smallest North American dove, the Common Ground-Dove is
fairly abundant in areas of the Deep South and the Southwest and is
generally tolerant of man. It looks like a small Mourning Dove with
a short tail; like most other doves, it feeds on a variety of small
seeds. It prefers open, dry areas, where it nests on or close to the
ground; however, it is found in many different habitats, including
open woodlands, forest edges, orchards, fields, roadsides, sand
dunes, and gardens. The Common Ground-Dove nods its head as it
walks; when flushed, it flies with rapid wingbeats in a zigzag course
for a short distance before it drops to the ground or alights on a
branch.

Description
6½–7″ (16.5–18 cm). The Common Ground-Dove is light grayish-
brown with black spots on the back and upperwing coverts. The
outer half of the wings flash rufous in flight, and the short, rounded
tail is brown and black, with narrow, white corners.

Voice
A low, repetitious *woo-oo, woo-oo, woo-oo, woo-oo,* with rising
inflection at end of each syllable.

Similar Species
Inca Dove has scaly back and long gray tail with white margin.
White-tipped Dove much larger, lacks black spots on back and upper
wings.

Range
Resident from southern California, central Arizona, and Texas to
Florida, north to southeastern North Carolina; also south into South
America. *Paul W. Sykes, Jr.*

White-tipped Dove

Leptotila verreauxi
This inhabitant of brushy woods of southern Texas is very round-
bodied, shy, and never occurs in flocks.

Description
12″ (30.5 cm). Mostly dusty grayish-brown, darkest on back, wings,
and tail, fading to whitish on forehead, throat, lower breast, and
belly. Medium-long tail somewhat rounded with white-tipped outer
feathers. Rufous wing linings visible only in flight. Bill dark; legs
and feet dull pinkish.

Voice
A long, ghostly *oo-wooooo.*

Similar Species
See Common Ground-Dove and Mourning, Inca, and White-winged
doves.

Range
Locally common permanent resident in southern Texas. Widespread
in American tropics south to Argentina. *Kenn Kaufman*

Adult with wings spread
1. *Rufous patch on wing.*
2. *Short, dark, rounded tail.*

Adult
1. *Light grayish-brown plumage.*
2. *Black spots on back and wing coverts.*

   Small size.

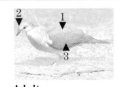

Adult
1. *Grayish-brown plumage.*
2. *Pale forehead.*
3. *No white on wing.*

   Shows white tail tip and rufous wing linings in flight.

Parrots

(Family Psittacidae)
Most members of this distinctive group are introduced in North
America. The Carolina Parakeet, once native to our range, is
extinct, and another native species, the Thick-billed Parrot, has not
occurred since the early part of this century. Red-crowned Parrots
are accidental in southern Texas; other members of the family from
northern Mexico may occur naturally along the border region.
Parrots have a large, heavy, short bill with a hinged, sharply
decurved upper mandible fitting down over a very deep, upcurved
lower mandible. The flight of members of this group is very direct,
with the wings remaining below the horizontal. The wingbeats are
very rapid and occasionally interrupted by gliding on stiffly held
wings. The legs and feet are thick and powerful, enabling these
birds to cling to and climb branches frequently. In flight, parrots
continuously give extremely raucous calls. Many species are highly
gregarious. (World: 340 species. North America: 4 species.)
Scott B. Terrill

Budgerigar

Melopsittacus undulatus
The Budgerigar is a small, common parrot native to Australia. In
North America, some of these popular caged pets have escaped or
been released and have become established in Florida.

Description
7″ (18 cm). Adult barred above with black and yellow; rump and
underparts green. Forehead, lores, and chin yellow; throat yellow
with dark spots. Wing linings green; tail greenish-blue. Immature
duller; throat spots vague or absent; has dark barring on forehead.

Voice
A pleasant warble, also subdued screech and chattering.

Similar Species
Canary-winged Parakeet slightly larger, plumage entirely green
except for yellow-and-white patches on wings; has much larger bill.

Range
Established along west-central coast of Florida; a few scattered
along southeast coast and elsewhere in state.   *Paul W. Sykes, Jr.*

Canary-winged Parakeet

Brotogeris versicolurus
These small South American parrots are most easily seen flying
overhead in groups of 2 to 15 individuals or at evening roosts.

Description
9″ (23 cm). Head and body green; secondary coverts yellow.
Secondaries and innermost primaries white; look like windows in
wings in flight. Tail long, pointed. Bill gray.

Voice
A rapidly repeated shrill metallic note when in flight or perched;
high-pitched chattering when feeding.

Similar Species
See Budgerigar.

Range
Introduced and established on southeastern coast of Florida
from West Palm Beach south to Homestead. Most abundant in
Miami-Coral Gables area. A few escaped birds elsewhere.
Paul W. Sykes, Jr.

Budgerigar
Thick-billed Parrot
Canary-winged Parakeet
Red-crowned Parrot

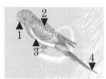

Adult
1. *Yellow face with tiny bill.*
2. *Black barring on yellow upperparts.*
3. *Green underparts.*
4. *Long, pointed tail.*

   Small size.

Adult
1. *Green unbarred plumage.*
2. *Long, pointed tail.*
3. *White windows on wings.*

   Small size.

Cuckoos

(Family Cuculidae)
This is a variable family of medium-size to large birds. They have
rather long bills with a curved culmen; many in the group have long
tails. Cuckoos are slender, sluggish birds and are often difficult to
see in dense foliage. They are therefore generally heard more often
than they are seen; each species has distinctive calls. Our cuckoos
are rather elongated birds with rounded wings; the long bills are
distinctly patterned. The rectrices are highly graduated. The
Roadrunner is a large terrestrial cuckoo with a bushy crest and a
long, wide tail. These birds are primarily southwestern in
distribution. They have long, powerful legs. The long, thick toes are
zygodactylous—2 face forward and 2 backward, as is the case with
all members of this family. Anis are blackish, medium-size, slender
birds with long, very rounded tails. The huge bills are very deep
with highly curved culmens. Anis are noisy and gregarious. (World:
129 species. North America: 8 species.)   *Scott B. Terrill*

Black-billed Cuckoo

Coccyzus erythropthalmus
This slender, long-tailed, common bird inhabits woodlands, forest
edges, orchards, and thickets.

Description
12″ (30.5 cm). Bill black and slightly decurved, sometimes with
dusky base. Brown above and white below; tail feathers graduated,
with small white tips; primaries have little or no rufous. Adults have
red eye-ring; that of immatures dull yellowish.

Voice
Fast, rhythmic groups of 3–4, *cucucu, cucucu, cucucu.*

Similar Species
See Yellow-billed and Mangrove cuckoos.

Range
S. Saskatchewan to Maritime Provinces, south to Se. Wyoming, N.
central Texas, Nw. Arkansas, S. Ohio, Maryland, and N. Alabama
and Georgia. Winters in South America.   *Paul W. Sykes, Jr.*

Yellow-billed Cuckoo

Coccyzus americanus
Found in woodlands, forest edges, thickets, orchards, and
farmlands, the widespread Yellow-billed Cuckoo is shy and quiet.

Description
11–13″ (28–33 cm). Bill slightly decurved; upper mandible black,
lower yellow. Brown above and white below; long black tail has 6
large spots visible from below at tips. Primaries above rufous.

Voice
Rapid, guttural *ka-ka-ka-ka-ka-ka-ka-ka-ka-kow-kow-kowlp-kowlp-
kowlp-kowlp,* slower at end; quite different from call of Black-billed.

Similar Species
See Black-billed and Mangrove cuckoos.

Range
Sw. British Columbia and W. Washington to California (locally),
east to S. Ontario and Maine and south into West Indies and Mexico.
Very rare to casual north of breeding range. Winters in South
America.   *Paul W. Sykes, Jr.*

Common Cuckoo
Oriental Cuckoo
Black-billed Cuckoo
Yellow-billed Cuckoo
Mangrove Cuckoo
Greater Roadrunner
Smooth-billed Ani
Groove-billed Ani

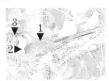

Adult
1. *Brown upperparts.*
2. *White underparts.*
3. *Black bill.*
4. *Small white spots on tail.*

   No rufous in wings.

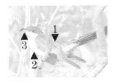

Adult
1. *Brown upperparts.*
2. *White underparts.*
3. *Yellow on lower mandible.*
4. *Large white spots on tail.*

   Rufous in wings.

Mangrove Cuckoo

Coccyzus minor
This shy species is locally common in coastal mangrove forests and upland West Indian hardwood hammocks.

Description
12″ (30.5 cm). Upper mandible black; lower yellow. Upperparts brown; chin, throat, and breast white. Belly and undertail coverts buff to cinnamon; wings show no rufous in flight. Tail long with 6 large white spots below. Adults have black ear patch.

Voice
A long, guttural series, *gawk-gawk-gawk-gawk-gaawk-gaawk.*

Similar Species
See Black-billed Cuckoo. Yellow-billed has rufous in primaries, lacks black ear patch.

Range
Breeds in Florida from Tampa Bay south through Keys, and from Mexico, Bahamas, and West Indies south into South America. A few winter in southern Florida.   *Paul W. Sykes, Jr.*

Greater Roadrunner

Geococcyx californianus
One of North America's most popular birds, the Greater Roadrunner is unique; it is a huge, ground-dwelling, crested cuckoo that escapes predation and pursues its prey of lizards, snakes, birds, and invertebrates by running very rapidly on long, sturdy legs. Typically associated with a desert landscape, the Greater Roadrunner is also found in chaparral, grasslands, open woodlands, agricultural areas, and even moist woodlands of eastern Texas. It is characteristically seen running swiftly with the neck outstretched and tail held parallel to the ground; it may stop suddenly, raise its neck, erect the bushy crest, and cock its head sideways; then it pumps its tail up, lets it fall slowly, and pumps it again. The Roadrunner usually holds its crest down while running; with each stop the bird appears to swell suddenly in size as it opens its wings slightly and erects its tail, crest, and body feathers. Occasionally, Roadrunners fly short distances on rounded wings, then glide into a landing.

Description
20–24″ (51–61 cm). The Greater Roadrunner is a large bird with a very long tail and neck, a large, long, pointed bill, and a bushy crest. At a distance, the Roadrunner appears mostly grayish, heavily streaked with dark on the neck, breast, back, and wings. Closer observation reveals iridescent blue-greens and bronze on the upperparts and on the long, white-tipped, otherwise dark tail. The rest of the underparts are off-white. There is a bright blue-and-red elongated patch behind the eye, lacking in young birds. Tracks left by the stout feet demonstrate that 2 toes face foward and 2 backward; the blue-gray legs are long and sturdy. In flight, the rounded wings display a white crescent.

Voice
A mournful, hollow *coo, coo, coo, ooh, ooh, oooh, ooooh, ooooh;* each note slurs downward and is slower and lower in pitch than the preceding note. Also a rapid, clacking noise made with bill.

Range
Northern California (local) east to southern Kansas, western Arkansas, and extreme northwestern Louisiana, and south into Mexico.   *Scott. B. Terrill*

Adult
1. *Black ear patch.*
2. *White breast.*
3. *Buff or cinnamon
   belly and undertail
   coverts.*
4. *Long tail with large
   white spots.*

Adult
1. *Bushy crest.*
2. *Blue-and-red patch
   behind eye.*
3. *Streaked plumage.*
4. *Long tail.*

   *Large size.
   Runs on ground.*

Immature
1. *Lacks blue-and-red
   patch behind eye.*

Smooth-billed Ani

Crotophaga ani
This long-tailed, heavy-billed, sociable bird occurs in southern
Florida where dense brush or hedgerows lie near fields or marshes.

Description
14″ (35.5 cm). Adult mostly dull black with bronze-brown edgings on
head and nape; scapulars, back, and lesser wing coverts have
crescents of iridescent green. Flight feathers of wings and tail
glossed with purple. Thick black bill has high, curved culmen.
Immatures slightly browner, especially on wings and tail.

Voice
Most typical call a rising *hoo-oo-eeek?* with whining, metallic quality.

Similar Species
See Groove-billed Ani and Boat-tailed Grackle.

Range
Resident in southern Florida; occasionally wanders to other
southeastern states. Also in West Indies and Central and South
America.   *Kenn Kaufman*

Groove-billed Ani

Crotophaga sulcirostris
Like the Smooth-billed Ani, this species is a sociable black cuckoo.
Anis feed mostly on the ground, hopping in a clumsy, loose-jointed
manner, and are often found with livestock, which stir insects from
the grass. The tails of perched anis often hang at odd angles. These
birds fly with several rapid flaps and then an unsteady, stiff-winged
glide. In Texas, the Groove-billed occupies semi-open country.

Description
12–13″ (30.5–33 cm). Long-tailed and with a puffin-shaped bill, this
species is mainly black, with a purplish gloss on the wings and tail
and greenish edgings on the head and upperparts. Young birds are
similar but browner. Most adults have long, parallel grooves on the
sides of the upper mandible, but these may be lacking in some adults
and many immatures.

Voice
A repeated *kee-wick* or *peek, kuwick;* also downward-slurred
whistles and short, clucking notes. Most calls slightly more
melodious or liquid than those of Smooth-billed Ani.

Similar Species
Smooth-billed Ani slightly larger, thicker-necked, seems to hold
head higher in flight; upper mandible usually has higher ridge
curving down to meet forehead, and lacks grooves (may show
crinkled area or partial groove at base of ridge); lower mandible
usually shows more pronounced angle in profile; feathers of nape
edged with bronze-brown, not greenish; seldom found in range of
Groove-billed, but both species wander widely. See Great-tailed
Grackle.

Range
Resident in southern Texas and uncommon summer resident in
western Texas; local in summer, fairly common in winter in southern
Louisiana. Wanders widely, as far as California, Arizona (almost
annual), Ontario, Virginia, and Florida. Also in Mexico, Central and
South America.   *Kenn Kaufman*

Adult
1. *High, curved ridge on upper mandible.*
2. *Black plumage with bronze-brown edgings on head and nape.*

   Long tail.
   Rising hoo-oo-eeek? *call.*

Adult
1. *Long parallel grooves on upper mandible.*

Adult
1. *Black plumage with glossy edgings on head and upperparts.*
2. *Long tail.*

   Repeated kee-wick *or* peek *calls.*

Barn-Owls

(Family Tytonidae)
In general, Barn-Owls are superficially similar to the typical Owls
(Strigidae), but the long face is accentuated by a heart-shaped set of
facial disks outlined by a thin dark line. The dark eyes are smaller
than the eyes of typical owls. The long, relatively slender legs are
covered with stubby, bristlelike feathering. In flight, Barn-Owls
appear very white from below. Their calls include raspy, screeching
noises and clicking sounds. (World: 11 species. North America:
1 species.)   *Scott B. Terrill*

Common Barn-Owl

Tyto alba
The distinctive Barn Owl is widespread and commonly found in open
habitats such as prairie, farmland, savannah, marshland, and desert;
it also occupies residential and urban areas. It is primarily
nocturnal, but can sometimes be observed at dawn, hunting with
low, quartering flight over an open field. It nests and roosts in tree
cavities, caves, and holes in the sides of arroyos, as well as in barns,
silos, and all sorts of unoccupied structures. During the breeding
season, the Barn Owl responds to recordings of its drawn-out song.
Although individuals or pairs generally live in isolation, a few
colonies have been found in desert habitat, with as many as 38 birds
sharing a group of abandoned buildings.

Description
14″ (35.5 cm). The Barn Owl has a large, distinctive, heart-shaped
facial disk, dark brown eyes, and a relatively long, narrow beak.
The underparts, including the wing linings, are white; the breast
and belly are sparsely sprinkled with small black spots. The
upperparts are light golden-brown with varying amounts of gray on
the central crown and across the mantle. The upperparts, except for
the flight feathers, are heavily sprinkled with small black and white
spots. The flight feathers are light golden-brown with narrow, dark
gray bars on the wings, and wide, irregular gray bars on the tail.
The legs appear long for the body; they have white feathers down to
the long, bristled toes.

Voice
Song a long, drawn-out, raspy screech, growing louder and harsher
toward end; seldom heard outside of breeding season (February–
August). Short, harsh hisses also given, especially during flight and
in nonbreeding season.

Similar Species
Snowy Owl much larger; facial disk small and rounded, not heart-
shaped; has yellow eyes and lacks golden-brown on upperparts.

Range
Breeds from British Columbia, North Dakota, southern Michigan,
and southern New England south through Central and South
America. Northern populations shift southward in winter. Nearly
cosmopolitan.   *Sadie Coats*

Common Barn-Owl

Adult in flight
1. *White underparts and wing linings.*

Adult
1. *Heart-shaped or round facial disk and dark eyes.*
2. *Golden-brown upperparts.*
3. *White underparts.*
4. *Long legs.*

Typical Owls

(Family Strigidae)
These birds are primarily nocturnal raptors. Their deeply hooked bills and sharp talons are similar to those of the diurnal birds of prey. However, owls differ from hawks and falcons in having a large head that is compressed, and the enormous frontally placed eyes are fixed in their sockets. This construction creates the need for extensive flexible head rotation. As is the case with most of the hawks and falcons, female owls are somewhat larger than males. The sexes have similar plumages. The very soft body feathers and the saw-toothed leading edge of the flight feathers allow for entirely silent flight. Many species have facial disks. Most owls are cryptically colored in complex patterns of brown, buff, and gray. Because most owls are nocturnal, they are often heard rather than seen. Fortunately, most have specific calls, but some species have extensive and variable repertoires. The easiest way to see owls is to attract them by imitating or playing recordings of the calls. (World: 135 species. North America: 19 species.)   *Scott B. Terrill*

Flammulated Owl

Otus flammeolus
The tiny Flammulated Owl is the smallest of the North American *Otus* species and the only one with dark eyes. It breeds in forests of the western mountains, especially ponderosa pine, where it may be rare to locally common. Flammulated Owls winter south of the United States, and occasional individuals are found in wooded lowland habitat during migration. This nocturnal owl responds to imitations and recordings of its song and is most easily found from May to July, when it may sing nonstop for several hours.

Description
6" (15 cm). The crown and back are basically variegated gray or gray-brown with irregular dark streaks, giving the appearance of furrowed tree bark. The wings and tail match the back, but are obscurely barred, with more pronounced barring only on the outermost primaries. Large white scapular spots heavily edged with rufous overlap to form paired white-and-rufous scapular stripes when the wings are folded. The ear tufts are very small and seldom seen. The dark brown eyes are narrowly rimmed all around with rufous; the eyebrows and lores are white. The pale facial disk is strongly outlined by a narrow black band and a wide rufous border. The breast and belly feathers are white with dark brown vertical streaks and narrow wavy crossbars. Many individuals have conspicuous rufous edging on feathers and feather markings. The legs are feathered, but the toes are bare. Juveniles are narrowly barred all over in gray and white and have rufous edging on the developing facial disk.

Voice
Song a cadenced series of mellow *hoop* or *hoo-hoop* notes at regular intervals of 3–4 seconds. Short clucks and barks also given.

Similar Species
Western Screech Owl and Whiskered Owl larger with yellow eyes; both lack rufous scapular stripe and rufous on facial disk.

Range
Breeds locally from southern British Columbia south along mountains into Mexico and through southern California (very local), Arizona, New Mexico, and western Texas. Winters in Mexico and Central America.   *Sadie Coats*

Adult, front view
1. *Small ear tufts.*
2. *Rufous-edged facial
   disks and dark eyes.*

   Small size.

Adult, rear view
1. *Rufous scapular
   stripe.*

Eastern Screech-Owl

Otus asio
The only small owl in eastern North America with erectile ear tufts,
the Eastern Screech-Owl is common in a variety of habitats,
including open woodlands, riparian groves, deciduous forests, farms,
and residential areas. Both red and gray-brown color morphs occur
together throughout the bird's range.

Description
7–10″ (18–25.5 cm). Gray-brown morph: crown, back, and wing
coverts variegated gray or grayish-brown with dark vertical streaks
and wavy crossbar markings. Large white spots on tips of scapulars
and greater coverts form 2 conspicuous lines of spots on wing.
Primaries barred gray and white; tail barred dark and light gray.
Underparts basically white with dark vertical streaks and wavy
crossbar markings; streaks especially heavy and regularly spaced on
throat and upper breast, less so on belly. Ear tufts conspicuous.
Eyes yellow; eyebrows and lores white; outer edge of whitish facial
disk has broad black stripe that continues onto throat. Toes
feathered. Red morph: deep cinnamon-rufous above with narrow
black streaks; underparts white with dark streaks and wide rufous
crossbar markings. Tail rufous, faintly barred with brown; wings
rufous or reddish-brown with 2 rows of white spots and some white
barring on primaries. Facial disk rufous, but otherwise like gray-
brown morph's. Juveniles of both morphs barred all over with brown
and white; red-morph young have rufous edging to bars.

Voice
Song a long "whinny," beginning on a rising pitch and quickly
descending with a pronounced waver. Also a rapid trill on 1 pitch,
variable in length, usually growing louder toward end. Short barks
or yelps also given.

Similar Species
Western Screech-Owl largely allopatric, has almost no red morphs.
In tiny zone of overlap (Texas), voice is only way to distinguish gray
forms of the 2 species.

Range
Southeastern Canada; widely distributed east of line from northern
Minnesota south through Texas to Gulf of Mexico, including Florida
Keys.   *Sadie Coats*

Western Screech-Owl

Otus kennicottii
This very common owl favors oak and riparian woodlands of the
West. The distinctive "bouncing ball" song is given by both sexes.

Description
7–11″ (18–28 cm). Nearly identical to Eastern Screech-Owl. Gray-
brown morph shows great variation: birds from dry southwestern
areas usually very pale gray; those from humid northeast browner.
Red morph very rare; occurs only in Pacific Northwest.

Breast feather

Voice
Song a series of 7–20 soft notes, all on same pitch; starts slowly and
speeds up. Also a short, slow trill and barks and yelps.

Similar Species
See Flammulated Owl, Eastern and Whiskered screech-owls.

Range
Se. Alaska along coast through British Columbia; widespread in
Rockies, W. Oklahoma, and Texas (east to Big Bend). Also Baja
California and Mexico.   *Sadie Coats*

Red morph
1. *Small ear tufts.*
2. *Cinnamon-rufous
   upperparts.*
3. *White underparts
   with rufous streaks
   and bars.*

Small size.

Gray-brown morph
1. *Small ear tufts.*
2. *Gray-brown
   upperparts with
   streaks.*
3. *White underparts
   with heavy streaks.*

*Small size.
Whinny and fast
trill calls.*

Adult
1. *Bars on breast finer
   than Whiskered
   Screech Owl's.*

*Distinguished from
Eastern Screech-Owl
by range and voice;
series of notes on
same pitch,
accelerating at end.*

Whiskered Screech-Owl

Otus trichopsis
The Whiskered Screech-Owl is a resident of dense oak groves in the pine-oak zone in the mountains of southeastern Arizona.

Description
6½″ (16.5 cm). Almost identical to gray morphs of the Western and Eastern screech-owls, but has more bristles around face, smaller ear tufts, and often slightly larger white scapular spots and heavier dark shaft streaks on breast and belly.

Breast feather

Voice
Song an unmistakable series of mellow, fairly evenly spaced single and double notes; resembles Morse code. Also a short series of single notes, with notes near end longer and spaced farther apart.

Similar Species
See Flammulated Owl. Western Screech-Owl has different voice.

Range
Southeastern Arizona south through Mexico to Nicaragua; red morph occurs in Central and South America.   *Sadie Coats*

Great Horned Owl

Bubo virginianus
The Great Horned Owl is easily the most powerful and aggressive of North American owls. Its diet includes animals as large as skunks, ducks, domestic cats and fowl, opossums, hawks, Great Blue Herons, and even porcupines, although encounters with the latter sometimes prove fatal to the owl. This highly adaptable species seems equally at home in deep forests, open country, or in city parks, where rats are its primary food. In the late afternoon or early evening, these birds often perch on telephone poles or atop dead tree snags, searching for prey. They are very early nesters, and females are occasionally found incubating eggs beneath a blanket of snow. This is the most widespread owl in the Western Hemisphere.

Description
18–25″ (45.5–63.5 cm). Great Horned Owls are very large and have prominent, widely spaced ear tufts, bright yellow eyes, and a conspicuous white throat that often forms a vertical blaze down the center of the breast. General color varies considerably from the pale white Arctic race to very dark Pacific forms, but most birds have dark gray-brown upperparts mottled whitish-gray. The underparts are buff with dark brown horizontal bars. The wings are uniformly dark above, and the wing linings are buff. The wings are long and broad; flight is usually rapid and direct.

Voice
Wide variety of sounds. Most frequent: low hoots, deeper and lower than Barred Owl's, *hoo-hoo-hoooo hoo-hoo*. Calls of male and female differ slightly in pitch. Also screams and gives catlike meows.

Similar Species
Barred, Spotted, Great Gray, and Snowy owls all lack ear tufts. Long-eared Owl much smaller; ear tufts set closer together, facial disks deep chestnut-orange; has more boldly patterned belly markings.

Range
Breeds from northern limit of tree line south throughout lower 48 states. Also throughout Central and South America. Generally nonmigratory. Restricted to Western Hemisphere.
Peter D. Vickery

Adult
1. *Small ear tufts.*
2. *Yellow eyes.*
3. *Bars on breast and belly heavier than Western Screech-Owl's.*

Small size. Mellow, Morse-code call.

Typical adult
1. *Large, widely spaced ear tufts.*
2. *White throat.*
3. *Barred underparts.*

Very large size.

Snowy Owl

Nyctea scandiaca
This large, white inhabitant of the tundra in northern Alaska and
Canada is a winter visitor to southern Canada and the northern
United States. The Snowy Owl is primarily a nocturnal predator of
open country, coastlines, and harbor areas. Pure white adults tend
to winter on their Arctic breeding grounds and are seldom seen;
most Snowies seen in the United States are lightly or heavily
barred, and may appear darker than their snow-white surroundings.
Many owls flying at night can appear white and be mistaken for the
Snowy when caught in a flashlight or headlight beam.

Description
20–27″ (51–68.5 cm). The Snowy is the only owl that is basically all-
white; it has yellow eyes and lacks ear tufts. Most Snowies are
moderately barred with dusky coloration, but a few may appear
pure white.

Voice
Usually silent, but can give a variety of croaks, growls, whistles, or
hoots, especially on breeding grounds.

Similar Species
White-phase Gyrfalcon slimmer, with longer tail and more pointed
wings. Barn-Owl almost pure white below but has heart-shaped
facial disk, mottled golden-brown upperparts. See Great Horned
Owl arctic race.

Range
Circumpolar. Breeds in tundra of northern Alaska and northern
Canada south to Hooper Bay, Alaska, and west coast of Hudson
Bay. Winters south to northern tier of states; south as far as central
states in years of periodic irruptions.   *Kim R. Eckert*

Northern Hawk-Owl

Surnia ulula
This bird of diurnal habits and open-country habitat has eluded most
birders because of its northern range. It perches conspicuously
along roadsides and in fields, often cocking its tail.

Description
14½–17½″ (37–44 cm). Grayish-brown with heavy barring from
breast to underside of tail. Bold black facial frames and black patch
under bill create square-headed, "fierce" look.

Voice
Usually silent. Occasionally a rapid, high, hawklike chatter: *kee-kee-
kee-kee*, often in series. Whistled trill on breeding grounds.

Similar Species
See Boreal Owl and Northern Goshawk.

Range
Resident from Alaska south to British Columbia and east to St.
Lawrence River, Labrador, and Newfoundland. Winters south to
northern tier of states. Also in Old World.   *Kim R. Eckert*

Adult

. *Overall white plumage with some dark bars or spots.*

. *No ear tufts.*

Large size.

Adult

. *Heavy black borders to facial disks.*

. *Barred underparts.*

. *Long tail.*

Active in broad daylight.
Hunts from exposed perches.

Northern Pygmy-Owl

Glaucidium gnoma
A tiny owl with a long tail and shrikelike flight, the Northern
Pygmy-Owl is often seen during daylight, especially near twilight.
These woodland owls are easily recognized by their small size, long
tails, and black nape patches. In western woodlands, their easily
imitated call will often attract numerous small, previously
undetected birds that mob Pygmy-Owls. Occasionally a Pygmy-Owl
will answer. If the observer continues the imitation, the bold little
owl may come out into the open and hoot back while fiercely glaring
down at the observer. Northern Pygmy-Owls are generally found in
coniferous forests and open pine-oak, oak, and riparian woodlands.

Description
6½–7½″ (16.5–19 cm). A small, grayish owl with a proportionately
small, round head. The upperparts are gray to gray-brown with
dense, light spotting on the crown and the nape and to a lesser
extent on the back and wings. There are 2 black patches on the
nape. The underparts are whitish, heavily streaked with black, and
there is a narrow dark collar on the whitish throat. The sides are
brownish-gray with dull white spotting. The tail is long, narrow,
rectangular, and dark with as many as 5 narrow white bars. The
eyes are yellow, the bill and cere dull yellowish.

Voice
Repetitious, low, whistled *hoot, hoot, hoot,* at 1- to 2-second
intervals; in central and southern Arizona, a disyllabic *hoot-hoot,
hoot-hoot, hoot-hoot,* sometimes repeated very rapidly.

Similar Species
See Ferruginous Pygmy-Owl. No other small "earless" yellow-eyed
owl has black nape patches, spotted upperparts, and long, white-
barred tail. Flammulated Owl has dark eyes, short tail. Elf Owl has
short tail, indistinct streaking on underparts; lacks black nape
patches. Screech-owls larger, stockier, short-tailed, and eared.

Range
Primarily resident from southeastern Alaska, British Columbia, and
western Alberta, and along Pacific Coast to southern California,
south in mountains and foothills throughout western United States;
east to Rockies, south to Guatemala.   *Scott B. Terrill*

Ferruginous Pygmy-Owl

Glaucidium brasilianum
This small owl is now very rare and local in the United States, but
remains common not far south of the Mexican border. It occurs
primarily in more densely vegetated desert areas with abundant
large cacti, but is also found, though perhaps less frequently, in
riparian woodlands. The call, a rapid *whoip* or *poip,* is usually the
first clue to the bird's presence. The call is easily imitated and will
often bring these little owls close to the observer in broad daylight.
Knowing the call is nearly indispensable for finding this bird in the
United States. Like the Northern Pygmy-Owl, the Ferruginous is
both nocturnal and diurnal. It flies low to the ground and directly
over short distances, with quick beats of the short wings. Upon
landing, the bird often cocks its tail.

Description
6½–7½″ (16.5–19 cm). The same size and shape as the Northern
Pygmy-Owl, the Ferruginous Pygmy-Owl has a different tail
pattern, usually barred rufous and brown or brownish and buff, but

Adult
1. *Black streaks on underparts.*
2. *Brownish-gray sides with white spotting.*

   Small size.
   Hoot, hoot, hoot call.
   Inhabits forests and woodlands.

Adult
1. *Gray-brown upperparts with white spots.*
2. *Narrow tail with white bars.*
3. *Two black patches on nape.*

Adult
1. *Rufous plumage.*
2. *Whitish spotting on forehead.*

   Small size.
   Rapid poik call.
   Inhabits desert areas.

occasionally solid colored. This species usually has dark streaking on the crown and nape, however it sometimes shows whitish spotting there instead. The sides are streaked rather than dark with light spots. The bird's overall color can range from very rufous to very gray; gray birds may more closely resemble the Northern Pygmy-Owl.

Voice
A rapid, popping *poik, poip, whoip,* or *wheit;* as many as several per second. Voice diagnostic.

Similar Species
Northern Pygmy-Owl has white lines on tail, white spotting on sides, different call; generally does not overlap in range; in Arizona, Northern Pygmy-Owl primarily in mountain forests, Ferruginous found in lowland desert. Elf Owl has short tail, lacks nape patches.

Range
Local in south-central Arizona and lower Rio Grande Valley of Texas; common south throughout lowland Mexico, Central and South America.   *Scott B. Terrill*

Elf Owl

Micrathene whitneyi
These widespread owls live in deserts, riparian areas, and oak and pine-oak woodlands near the Mexico border.

Description
5¾″ (14.5 cm). Tiny, "earless," with bright yellow eyes and short tail. Grayish-brown above with buff mottling; wings grayish-brown with buff spots. Scapulars form rows of large whitish spots. Whitish below with vague buff-brown streaking; facial disks pale reddish-brown or buff. White eyebrows extend to form whiskers.

Voice
Varied. Loud chirps and puppylike barks, often in rapid series.

Similar Species
See Northern and Ferruginous pygmy-owls, Saw-whet Owl, and screech-owls; Flammulated Owl has dark eyes.

Range
Se. California (very rare), central and S. Arizona, Sw. New Mexico, and S. Texas into Mexico. Winters in Mexico.   *Scott B. Terrill*

Burrowing Owl

Athene cunicularia
The diurnal, stilt-legged Burrowing Owl inhabits desert and open grasslands of western and midwestern North America and south-central Florida. Perhaps the easiest owl to identify, it commonly perches on fence posts or stands at the entrance to its nesting burrow. The long, exposed lower legs and the characteristic 'bowing' behavior that the bird displays when approached or otherwise disturbed quickly distinguish it. When approached or flushed, both sexes commonly give a sharp 'chatter' call. The Burrowing Owl is very active in the daytime. Burrowing Owls nest in abandoned rodent burrows; they modify these nests yearly by digging and scraping with the beak, wings, and feet. The burrow is often littered with scraps of paper and shredded dry manure.

Description
8–9″ (20.5–23 cm). Female Burrowing Owls are larger than the males. Both sexes are sandy-colored over the head, back, and wings, with barring on the breast and belly. The exposed, sparsely

Adult
1. *Streaked flanks.*
2. *Rufous or buff bars on tail.*

   Also shows black patches on nape, like Northern Pygmy-Owl.

Adult
1. *No ear tufts.*
2. *Yellow eyes.*
3. *Indistinct streaking on underparts.*

   Tiny size.

Adult with wings spread
1. *Rounded head without ear tufts.*
2. *Barring on breast and belly.*
3. *Long legs.*

feathered legs appear extremely long. The tail is very short; the head is rounded and lacks ear tufts. During the summer months, females usually appear darker than males.

Voice
Song a double-noted *Coo-coo*, given only by males during early stages of breeding season. Call notes a sharp *chuck* and a scream associated with a long series of chatter notes. Calls are often synchronized with bowing behavior. A rasping call, structurally similar to a rattlesnake's rattle, may be given from inside the burrow when bird is disturbed.

Range
Southern prairies of British Columbia, Alberta, Saskatchewan, and central Manitoba south through western and midwestern states into Central and South America. Also resident in central and southern Florida. Migrates from colder parts of range in winter.
Dennis J. Martin

Spotted Owl

Strix occidentalis
This medium-size, dark-eyed owl inhabits dense forests and rugged mountains of the West. Unlike most other large owls, it will usually allow humans to approach within a few feet.

Description
17–19″ (41.5–48.5 cm). Dark brown with creamy white spots; breast and belly have regular pattern of brown and white spots. Eyes very dark brown. Head round. Males slightly smaller than females.

Voice
A variety of hoots, barks, and whistles. Most common call a series of 4 hooting notes *hoo-hoo-hoo-hoo*. Female's call slightly higher.

Similar Species
See Barred Owl.

Range
Pacific Coast from Sw. British Columbia to S. California. Also in mountains of S. Colorado, extreme W. Texas, Utah, Arizona, and New Mexico; Mexico south to Michoacán.   *Eric D. Forsman*

Barred Owl

Strix varia
The Barred Owl or "Hoot Owl" is a particularly vocal species with a familiar, 9-note hoot: *Who-cooks-for-you, who-cooks-for-you-all?* Barred Owls prefer wooded swamps and deep forests; they are especially common along the lake shores and bottomland of the Southeast. They share this habitat with Red-shouldered Hawks, and it is not uncommon for nest sites to alternate between the 2 species on succeeding years, though Barred Owls generally prefer tree cavities. As its small, relatively weak talons indicate, the Barred Owl usually hunts small prey such as frogs, crayfish, small mammals, and birds, notably screech-owls. In recent years the Barred Owl's western range has been expanding south from British Columbia to Washington, Oregon, and northern California.

Description
17–24″ (43–61 cm). The Barred Owl is a large, big-headed woodland bird with no ear tufts. The body plumage is usually gray-brown mixed with buff-white edges and subterminal bars. Some individuals

Adult
1. No ear tufts.
2. Long legs.
3. Short tail.

   Active in daytime.
   Perches on ground
   or fence posts.
   "Bowing" behavior.

Adult
1. Rounded head.
2. Dark eyes.
3. Dark brown
   upperparts with
   creamy-white spots
   and blotches.
4. Entire underparts
   barred.

Adult
1. Large head without
   ear tufts.
2. Transverse barring
   on neck and upper
   breast.
3. Vertical brown
   streaks on belly.

are very pale and suggest immature Snowy Owls; however, Barred Owls have brown eyes. The transverse barring across the neck and upper breast contrasts with the vertical brown streaks of the belly. Barred Owls have short, broad wings and move easily through the forest on slow wingbeats.

Voice
Wide range of sounds. Most frequently heard 9 hoots: *Who-cooks-for-you, who-cooks-for-you-all?;* not as low as Great Horned Owl's call. Also screams, chuckling notes, and tremulous calls frequently ending with down-slurred *ooo-aaarrrr.*

Similar Species
Great Gray Owl larger, has yellow eyes and prominent white "mustache." Spotted Owl darker, richer brown, with spotted belly.

Range
Breeds from eastern British Columbia to Alberta, central Quebec, New Brunswick, and Nova Scotia, throughout eastern United States including Florida and Texas. Recent range expansion from British Columbia to Washington, Oregon, and northern California, where breeding is anticipated.   *Peter D. Vickery*

Great Gray Owl

Strix nebulosa
Although the "largest" of all owls, the Great Gray is all feathers and is easily outweighed by the Great Horned and Snowy owls. Like the other elusive northern owls, it is usually best looked for in winter when, in some years, it invades eastern Canada and the northern United States in large numbers. Despite its size, the Great Gray is difficult to spot because it is relatively silent, is usually nocturnal, and its dusky plumage blends in well with its dark forest surroundings. It will hunt in midday, especially in invasion years and on overcast days, but it is most often seen toward dusk on conspicuous perches along roadsides and in clearings in the boreal forest.

Description
24–33″ (61–84 cm). The Great Gray is large, brownish-gray, and "earless," with yellow eyes, a relatively long tail, and prominent circular facial disks. By far the most obvious and diagnostic field mark is the white "bow tie," a white patch on the throat that contrasts with the color of the underparts, and is visible from long distances.

Voice
A deliberate, lazy series of deep hoots, dropping in pitch and slowing in cadence at the end. Hoots only infrequently; low-pitched notes audible only at close range.

Similar Species
Barred and Spotted owls also large and "earless," but have dark eyes, are smaller; lack white "bow tie."

Range
Resident from central Alaska, Yukon, western Mackenzie, northern Saskatchewan, northern Manitoba, and northern Ontario south to central California (local), northern Idaho, central Saskatchewan, southern Manitoba, northern Minnesota, and east-central Ontario. Winters south to northern tier of states. Also in northern Europe and Asia.   *Kim R. Eckert*

Adult
1. *Brown eyes.*
2. *Gray-brown plumage with pale edges and bars.*

Adult
1. *Very large, round facial disks.*
2. *Yellow eyes.*
3. *White "bow tie" on throat.*

   Very large size.

Long-eared Owl

Asio otus
The medium-size Long-eared Owl, with its distinctive ear tufts, is
typically so nocturnal in its habits and so retiring during the day
it is rarely seen. Long-eared Owls are comparatively little known.
They seem to be more numerous in the West; however, it is likely
that appropriate roost sites in coniferous and riparian groves are
sufficiently limited in that part of the country, making it easier to
locate these birds. When disturbed, these owls may spread their
wings in a striking threat display.

Description
13–16″ (33–40.5 cm). The Long-eared Owl is a slim, medium-size
bird with obvious ear tufts set close together and long wings that
extend beyond the tail. The facial disk is typically bright orange-
chestnut, but is tawny brown on the pale western race, *A. o. tuftsi*.
Long-eared Owls lack a white throat patch; the breast is dark
brownish-gray with irregular white spots. The boldly patterned
belly feathers are crosshatched and have conspicuous, dark vertical
markings. The flanks and wing linings are tawny, as are the bases to
most feathers. The eyes are orange. The dark gray upper surface of
the wing has an orange base, less conspicuous than that of the
Short-eared Owl. Its buoyant, erratic flight is somewhat like that of
a moth or butterfly.

Voice
In breeding season, soft cooing, mellow, low-pitched hoots; also
shrieks, whines, meows, and *weck-weck-weck* alarm notes. At
winter roosts, soft twitters before dawn.

Similar Species
Great Horned Owl much larger with white throat patch, widely
spaced ear tufts. Screech-owls smaller and chunkier. In flight,
Short-eared Owl has pale band on trailing edge of flight feathers and
buff patch at base of primaries.

Range
Breeds from central British Columbia, southern Mackenzie, Ontario,
and southern Quebec to California, Texas, Arkansas, and Virginia;
also to northwestern Mexico. Some dispersal south in winter,
uncommonly to Mexico, Texas, and Florida. Holarctic distribution.
Peter D. Vickery

Short-eared Owl

Asio flammeus
Short-eared Owls occur exclusively in open areas, frequenting
tundra, moorlands, marshes, dunes, grasslands, and agricultural
fields. One of the most widespread owls in the world, the Short-
eared Owl occurs on every continent except Australia, and is known
from points as far removed as the Arctic and Antarctic circles. Its
crepuscular habits and preference for open habitat help make it one
of the most frequently observed owls. When hunting, Short-eared
Owls fly low, shifting back and forth on long wings with an easy,
irregular wingbeat that suggests that of a giant butterfly. Indeed,
its flight is so distinctive it is commonly known as the "Loper" in
some parts of Canada. Short-eared Owls prey primarily on small
rodents; 20 or more owls can sometimes be observed in areas of
especially high rodent concentrations. Insects and small birds are of
secondary importance as prey, though consumption of birds,
especially during migration, can be considerable. The male Short-
eared Owl is known to perform spectacular aerial courtship displays
that involve climbing to considerable heights, then making short

Threat display

1. *Upper surface of wing uniformly dark.*

   Frequently gives threat display with spread wings at nest or when disturbed.

Adult

1. *Long, closely set ear tufts.*
2. *Orange-chestnut facial disks.*
3. *Vertical markings on belly.*

   Medium size. Wings extend to or beyond tail.

Adult

1. *Rounded head.*
2. *Tawny belly with vertical streaks.*
3. *Wings extend to or beyond end of tail.*

   Frequents open areas.

dives and upward swoops while rapidly clapping its wings together beneath its body. The display concludes with the male tumbling to earth in a series of somersaults.

Description
13–17″ (33–43 cm). The Short-eared Owl is a medium-size bird with long wings that extend well beyond the tail. The tawny brown color can vary considerably and there seem to be 2 color phases, brown and gray. The relatively small facial disks and short, thick neck give this species a stout, blunt-headed look. The small ear tufts, set close together, are usually difficult to see. The dark brown upperparts are heavily mottled with buff spots and bars; the neck and upper breast are streaked with dark brown. The belly and flanks are buff with distinct, neat, dark stripes. The tawny facial disks have dark centers surrounding the bright yellow eyes. In its buoyant, loose flight, the Short-eared Owl bounds from side to side with frequent glides on wings angled forward, slightly ahead of the body. A prominent pale buff patch contrasts with the dark upperwing. The best character in flight is the pale band that extends along the trailing edge of all but the outermost flight feathers. The Long-eared Owl has a uniformly dark trailing edge in flight. The Short-eared Owl's tail is obviously barred with dark and light bands.

Voice
Generally silent except in breeding season: soft *toot-toot-toots*, barks, squeals, and hisses. In aerial courtship display, the wings clap together rapidly.

Similar Species
Barn-Owl paler, with unstreaked lower parts and white, heart-shaped face. Long-eared Owl in flight has dark, grayer upperwings that lack a pale trailing edge; the orangish patch at base of primaries is less conspicuous than in Short-eared Owl.

Range
Breeds on tundra from northwestern Alaska across Arctic Canada to Baffin Island and Newfoundland. Breeds locally on marshes, fields, and prairies south to central California, Utah, Kansas, Ohio, and New Jersey. Winters south to southern California, Texas, and Florida. Occurs in appropriate habitat on every continent except Australia.   *Peter D. Vickery*

Boreal Owl

Aegolius funereus
The Boreal Owl is probably the most sought-after of all 18 North American owls. Unlike the Snowy Owl and the Northern Hawk-Owl, it usually avoids open country and diurnal activity; unlike the Great Gray, it is small and can hide easily. A Boreal Owl may be seen roosting in a spruce tree, hunting at dusk along a roadside, or watching for shrews under a bird feeder. In contrast to the other northern winter owls, the Boreal Owl seldom reappears at the same location the day after it is discovered. Except for a remarkable invasion in 1978 in northern Minnesota, influxes of Boreal Owls are modest in size.

Description
8½–12″ (21.5–30.5 cm). This small brown owl, which may appear grayish in a headlight's beam, is best recognized by the prominent black facial frames which give this "earless" owl a square-headed profile and a "surprised" expression. The bill is yellowish. Juveniles are chocolate-brown with white eyebrows and cheek spots.

In flight, from below
1. *Long wings.*
2. *Dark wrist mark.*
3. *Pale buff area at base of primaries.*

In flight, from above
1. *Pale buff area at base of primaries.*
2. *Dark trailing edge of wing.*

Juvenile
1. *Chocolate-brown plumage.*
2. *White eyebrows.*
3. *White cheek spots.*

Small size.

Voice
A rapid series of about 10 hoots, lasting about 2 seconds, usually
rising in pitch at end. Very similar to winnowing of Common
Snipe. (There is no good evidence that this species gives a series of
notes like a high-pitched bell, as is often mentioned.)

Similar Species
Northern Saw-whet Owl somewhat smaller, lacks obvious facial
frames; has rounder head and darker bill. Screech-owls also have
black facial frames; with ear tufts flattened, resemble Boreal.
Northern Hawk-Owl has similar face pattern, but larger, with heavy
barring below.

Range
Resident from Alaska, Yukon, western Mackenzie, northern
Saskatchewan, northern Manitoba, northern Ontario, central
Quebec, and southern Labrador south to central British Columbia,
central Alberta, central Saskatchewan, northern Colorado (in Rocky
Mountains), southern Manitoba, northeastern Minnesota, and east-
central Ontario. Winters during invasions south to northern tier of
states. Also in northern Europe and Asia.   *Kim R. Eckert*

Northern Saw-whet Owl

Aegolius acadicus
The Saw-whet is the smallest of all the eastern owls. This tiny bird
has large, yellow eyes in flat facial disks; it is exceedingly tame—
often allowing itself to be picked from a tree and held without a
struggle—and it has aptly been described as "cute," even by
unsentimental ornithologists. A quite common resident of boreal and
montane forests, the Saw-whet is so small and so strictly nocturnal
that it remains a difficult owl to see. However, in winter it will roost
for days at a time at the same location, and in spring, on its breeding
grounds, the Saw-whet can be whistled into view by an imitation of
its song.

Description
7–8½″ (18–21.5 cm). Smaller than any other eastern owl, the Saw-
whet is also recognized by its round-headed profile, relatively large
eyes, head, and facial disks, and the lack of facial frames; all of these
characteristics give it a less "fierce" expression than that of most
owls. The bill is dark. Juveniles are colorful and unique with a
conspicuous buff belly and a white triangular patch on the forehead.

Voice
A very long series of toots or whistles, 2–3 notes given per second:
too-too-too-too . . . ; easily imitated. Sounds more like a high-pitched
bell or dripping water than does call of Boreal Owl. "Saw whetting"
call seldom given.

Similar Species
See Boreal Owl. Flammulated Owl has dark eyes. Elf Owl smaller.
Northern and Ferruginous pygmy-owls have longer tails and dark
eyespots on back of head. Elf Owl and both pygmy-owls also have
smaller heads and less obvious facial disks.

Range
Resident from southeastern Alaska, British Columbia, central
Alberta, central Saskatchewan, central Manitoba, central Ontario,
southern Quebec, New Brunswick, and Nova Scotia south to
southern California, Arizona, New Mexico, northern Minnesota,
Wisconsin, Michigan, Pennsylvania, and New England; rarely
breeds in New York. Winters south to Mexico, Arkansas, Tennessee,
and North Carolina.   *Kim R. Eckert*

Adult
1. *Black border on facial disks.*
2. *Fine spots on forehead.*
3. *White spots on scapulars.*
4. *Yellowish bill.*

Small size.

Adult
1. *Facial disks without black borders.*
2. *Streaked forehead.*
3. *Dark bill.*
4. *Short tail.*

Small size.
Too-too-too call.

Juvenile
1. *White triangle on forehead.*
2. *Bright buff belly.*
3. *Chocolate-brown upperparts.*

Small size.

Nightjars

(Family Caprimulgidae)
This is a widespread family of nocturnal and crepuscular insect-eaters. The birds have soft, cryptically colored plumage with elaborate blotching, barring, and streaking. There are often bold white patches on the wings, tail, or throat. Because these birds are highly vocal and their calls distinctive, many species have common names modeled after their vocalizations. Nightjars have enormous mouths with which they capture flying insects, either during flight or in fluttering leaps launched from a perch or from the ground. In general, they are compact birds with short, thick necks. The wings are relatively long, either pointed or rounded, and the tail is usually quite long. Nightjars often respond to imitations or recordings of their vocalizations. These birds have huge eyes that reflect light beams from a great distance; many individuals are seen in a headlight's beam in open country. During the day, these birds can be found with eyes squeezed tightly shut, resting motionless upon a limb or on the ground in leaf litter or rocky soil. (World: 77 species. North America: 9 species.)   *Scott B. Terrill*

Lesser Nighthawk

Chordeiles acutipennis
Although the Lesser Nighthawk overlaps locally with the very similar Common Nighthawk in distribution, the Lesser is associated with arid lowlands and southerly desert regions. With relatively large, very long wings and a rather long, fuselage-shaped body, the Lesser Nighthawk flies with deep wingbeats leading to a bounding flight that is suddenly checked by erratic fluttering. This low-flying aerial forager is most easily seen in the evenings and early mornings and less frequently during the day, especially during migration. Large numbers of these birds can often be found skimming very low just over riparian vegetation and adjacent water, where there is a high concentration of insects. Dispersed groups are found in desert and other open habitats in the Southwest.

Description
8–9″ (20.5–23 cm). Like the Common Nighthawk this species has long, pointed wings and a long, notched, rectangular tail. This species is mottled above and below with buff, brown, gray, and white; the undertail coverts are buff. The markings on the underparts are relatively pale. The throat is white. There is a whitish to buff patch two-thirds of the way between the bend of the wing and the wing tip; this patch is visible from below and when the wing is folded. The underside of the tail is barred and has a whitish subterminal band and a blackish tip, more distinct in the male. The bill is very short.

Voice
A low, soft, hollow trill, a louder whinny, and a low, soft *chuck* note.

Similar Species
Common Nighthawk has longer tail; flies with slower, deeper wingbeats, has less fluttery flight; wings longer in proportion and more sharply pointed; patch on primaries midway between bend of wing and tip; underparts show more contrast; undertail coverts white or whitish; call different. See Antillean Nighthawk.

Range
Breeds at lower elevations from north-central California south and east through southern Nevada and Utah, Arizona, and southern New Mexico and Texas, south into South America. Winters primarily south of United States.   *Scott B. Terrill*

Lesser Nighthawk
Common Nighthawk
Antillean Nighthawk
Common Pauraque
Common Poorwill
Chuck-will's-widow
Buff-collared Nightjar
Whip-poor-will
Jungle Nightjar

Adult in flight
1. *Long, pointed wings.*
2. *Pale wing patch close to wing tip.*
3. *Squared or notched tail.*

   Low, bounding flight. Soft chuck *call.*

On ground
1. *Mottled upperparts.*

Common Nighthawk

Chordeiles minor
Common Nighthawks are widespread and found in many habitats across North America, including forests, sagebrush plains, meadows, and cities. They feed primarily in the evening and at night, but can be seen airborne anytime of day, particularly during migration, when they congregate in flocks. After darkness sets in, the only clue to the presence of foraging birds high in the night sky is a buzzy, nasal *beerp* call. The birds can, however, be seen foraging near bright lights in residential areas. During most daylight hours, Common Nighthawks can be found perched motionless, lengthwise on tree limbs, fence posts, rocky outcroppings, or rooftops, with their eyes squeezed shut.

Description
8½–10″ (21.5–25.5 cm). The wings are long and pointed. The tail is long, notched at the tip and rectangular, except when fanned. Upperparts are blackish, mottled with grays, browns, buffs, and whites. Underparts are whitish, heavily barred with blackish-gray, most strongly on the breast. A white throat patch is conspicuous; there is a white spot on the wings, midway between the bend and tip, and a white subterminal band on the tail. Females look similar, but tend more toward brownish; the throat and wing patches can appear buff-white, and there is no white in the tail. The undertail coverts are white in both sexes. Juveniles are more nondescript and may nearly lack throat patch.

Voice
Abrupt, nasal, buzzy, insectlike, loud *beerp*, strongly accented at beginning and end of note; also described as *peent*.

Similar Species
See Lesser Nighthawk. Other nightjars have rounded, blunt-tipped wings and tail, and (except Pauraques) lack white wing patches and contrasting, even barring on underparts of nighthawk. Flight more mothlike, with foraging occurring nearer to or on ground.

Range
Breeds from southern Canada south throughout United States into Mexico, Panama, Caribbean Islands. Relatively local in some western states. Winters in American tropics and South America.
Scott B. Terrill

Antillean Nighthawk

Chordeiles gundlachii
Locally common in the Florida Keys and the Greater Antilles, this bird was formerly considered a race of the Common Nighthawk.

Description
9–9½″ (23–24 cm). Similar to Common Nighthawk but slightly smaller and paler. Upperparts are blackish, mottled with gray, brown, white, and buff. Whitish below, heavily barred with black. Tail long and slightly notched; wings long and pointed.

Voice
A 3-syllable *killy-ka-dick* or *pity-pit-pit*, often repeated.

Similar Species
See Lesser and Common nighthawks. Antillean Nighthawk reliably distinguished in field from Common only by voice.

Range
Florida Keys and possibly in S. Dade County; also in Bahamas and Greater Antilles. Wanders to S. peninsular Florida. Presumably winters in South America. *Paul W. Sykes, Jr.*

Adult in flight
1. *Long, pointed wings.*
2. *Wing patch close to bend of wing.*
3. *Squared or notched tail.*

   High, fluttery flight. Buzzy beerp *call.*

On ground
1. *Mottled upperparts.*
2. *Barred underparts.*

   Buzzy beerp *flight call.*

Adult
Distinguishable from smaller Common Nighthawk only by voice: killy-ka-dick, *often repeated.*
Florida only.

Common Pauraque

Nyctidromus albicollis
In brushy woods of southern Texas, the Common Pauraque is
numerous year-round, but it is most conspicuous in spring when it
calls most frequently. This large, long-tailed nightjar forages after
dark in openings in the woods or near the forest edge.

Description
11–12″ (28–30.5 cm). The Common Pauraque is finely patterned in
shades of brown and gray. In good light, the fairly plain, gray crown
(with a few darker streaks), chestnut ear patch, white area on the
lower throat, and large black spots on the scapulars are apparent.
The male's white bar across the primaries is conspicuous in flight;
when the tail is spread, a long, white stripe is visible near each
outer edge. In the female, the white is less extensive and may be
tinged with buff.

Voice
Hoarse whistle preceded by 1 or more low, hard notes: *go-weeeeeer*
or *guh, guh, guh, go-weeeeeer*. Various low throaty sounds when
disturbed or while foraging.

Similar Species
In flight, white bar across primaries rules out confusion with all
other rounded-winged nightjars; when Common Pauraque is
perched, tail looks proportionately much longer. Nighthawks also
have white in primaries but angular, pointed wings, less substantial
tails without longitudinal white stripes.

Range
Permanent resident in southern Texas, north along coast to
Aransas-Rockport area. Widespread in American tropics.
Kenn Kaufman

Common Poorwill

Phalaenoptilus nuttallii
The Common Poorwill is a common resident of dry, low, brushy
areas in western North America, where its characteristic namesake
call is heard at twilight and, less frequently, during the night.
Widely distributed from lowlands to mountain slopes, the Common
Poorwill inhabits a variety of arid upland areas. This species chases
insect prey by fluttering up from the ground like a big moth.
The migratory status of the Common Poorwill is not known.

Description
7–8½″ (18–21.5 cm). The Common Poorwill is smaller and shorter-
tailed than other nightjars. Seen in flight, it has white corners on
the tail and rounded wings. The upperparts are brown and velvety
silver-gray with fine black markings. A white band crossing the
throat is bordered by black on the breast and by the black face. The
rest of the underparts are black and gray, subtly barred. In
immature Poorwills, the tail corners and throat are less distinct and
are washed with buff.

Adult
1. *Chestnut ear patch.*
2. *Black spots on scapulars.*

   Goo-weeeeer *call.*

Adult in flight
1. *White bar in primaries.*
2. *Long white stripe near outer edge of tail.*

Adult in flight
1. *Rounded wings.*
2. *White corners on tail.*

Voice

Call (from which bird's name is derived) characteristically a *poor-will*, with long first syllable and accent on second. At close range, a third, soft note can be heard. When disturbed may give a *kweep-kweep* in flight.

Similar Species

Lesser Nighthawk forages in air; has long, pointed wings; female and juvenile Lesser Nighthawks lack white patch on wing or have only an inconspicuous one; they are frequently misidentified as Common Poorwills. Whip-poor-will has longer tail, generally darker coloration.

Range

From interior Washington to California, and in coastal foothills from central California south to tip of Baja; from southern interior British Columbia and southern Alberta, east along Great Plains to central Kansas, south to central Mexico. Winters at least from central California, southern Arizona, and southern Texas southward into Mexico.   *Louis R. Bevier*

Chuck-will's-widow

Caprimulgus carolinensis

The Chuck-will's-widow is a large, locally common goatsucker with rounded wings that inhabits pine and mixed forests, woodlands along river courses, and forest edges. Its flight is silent, alternating wingbeats with periods of sailing. It is strictly nocturnal and nests on the ground.

Description

11–12″ (28–30.5 cm). The Chuck-will's-widow has reddish-brown plumage mottled with black spots and streaks. The chin is brown, and the overall plumage has a brown tone. The male shows restricted areas of white on the outer tail feathers, and has a narrow white throat patch. The female has an entirely brown tail and a buff throat patch.

Voice

A loud, 4-syllable *chuck-will's-wid-ow*, repeated in long series, with accent on first and third syllables. Also utters a low, single note, *chuck*.

Similar Species

Whip-poor-will smaller, has blackish chin and overall gray tone to plumage; call quite different. Nighthawk has narrow, pointed wings with white on primaries; tail and underparts barred.

Tail of female

Range

Breeds from eastern Kansas to southern Ohio and southern New Jersey (sparingly north to southern Ontario, and southern New England), south to southern Florida, Gulf Coast, and central Texas. Winters from Texas, Louisiana, and Florida to northern South America.   *Paul W. Sykes, Jr.*

Adult
1. *Brown, finely marked upperparts.*
2. *Short tail.*

Small size.
Poor-will call.

Adult
1. *Mottled reddish-brown plumage.*
2. *Brown chin.*

Large size.
Chuck-will's-widow call.

Male in flight
1. *Rounded wings.*
2. *White on outer tail feathers.*

Female shows no white in tail.

Buff-collared Nightjar

Caprimulgus ridgwayi
This rare summer visitor to the Southwest has been found in arid
rocky washes and canyons; it occurs in varied habitats in Mexico.

Description
9″ (23 cm). Complete buff or rust collar diagnostic but hard to see.
Mottled dark gray and brown; paler below with fine barring. Flight
feathers have some rust or buff. Tail long, barred with buff and dark
gray; male's has white patches at outer corners.

Voice
Staccato notes, ascending and growing louder, dropping abruptly at
end: *cu-cu-cu-cuc-cuc-cuc-uh-chee-ah;* also a soft *chuck* or *quirk.*

Similar Species
Other nightjars lack full buff or rust collar, have different calls.

Range
Se. Arizona and Sw. New Mexico; more numerous in Mexico;
resident from Mexico to Honduras.   *Scott B. Terrill*

Whip-poor-will

Caprimulgus vociferus
Like the Chuck-will's-widow, the common, widespread Whip-poor-
will is nocturnal and feeds on flying insects that it captures on the
wing. This cryptically colored species inhabits deciduous woodlands
and forest edges, where it roosts during the day on the ground or
with the body positioned lengthwise on a horizontal limb.

Description
9–10″ (23–25.5 cm). The plumage is mottled grayish-brown with
black spots and streaks and a blackish chin; there is an overall
grayish tone to the plumage. The male has a narrow, white throat
patch and prominent white outer tail feathers; the female has a buff
throat patch and no white in the tail.

Voice
A loud, 3-syllable *whip-poor-will*, repeated in long series with accent
on first and last syllables, and with faster tempo than in call of
Chuck-will's-widow. Also, low, single, sharp *whip.*

Similar Species
See Chuck-will's-widow and Buff-collared Nightjar. Nighthawks
have barred tails and underparts, and narrow, pointed wings with
white bars across the primaries.

Tail of female

Range
Breeds from Saskatchewan, southern Ontario, and Maritime
Provinces south to eastern Kansas, northeastern Texas, northern
Louisiana, and northern Georgia; also from central Arizona, New
Mexico, and southwestern Texas south into Mexico. Winters from
North Carolina south to Florida, Gulf Coast, Central America, and
Cuba.   *Paul W. Sykes, Jr.*

Male
1. *Buff or rust collar.*
2. *White at tips of outer tail feathers.*

   Staccato song.
   Southwest only.

Adult
1. *Mottled gray-brown plumage.*
2. *Blackish chin.*

   Medium size.
   Whip-poor-will call.

Male in flight
1. *Rounded wings.*
2. *Narrow white throat patch.*
3. *White patches in tail.*

   Female lacks white tail patches, has buff throat.

Swifts

(Family Apodidae)
This is an extremely aerial group of birds with long, streamlined, compact bodies that taper at both ends and very long, pointed primaries that are often bowed. The secondaries are short. Most North American species have very short, stiff tails. Swifts are awkward when not airborne and must cling to a vertical surface rather than perch, as the similar but unrelated swallows do. Thus, swifts do almost everything in the air, even copulating on the wing. Their wingbeats are very rapid and stiff, producing a twinkling effect in smaller species; rapid gliding on stiffly-locked wings is frequent. North American swifts breed in dead trees and chimneys, and on steep cliffs and extensive rocky outcroppings. Most species are gregarious, and large flocks are often seen together in the air. Many species can be identified by their distinctive calls, which generally consist of twitters and chatters that carry a long distance. (World: 83 species. North America: 9 species.)   *Scott B. Terrill*

Black Swift

Cypseloides niger
The largest and least familiar of our North American swifts, the Black Swift is a widespread but patchily distributed summer resident in the western United States. Its larger size, uniform black color, and longer, slightly forked tail serve immediately to distinguish it from all other swifts. Foraging very high in the air, it ranges widely from its unique nest and roost sites behind mountain waterfalls and in seacoast caves. Black Swifts are most commonly seen in migration or during overcast weather, when flocks can be found foraging at low elevations, frequently over bodies of water or in company with other swifts or swallows.

Description
7–7½" (18–19 cm). Both sexes are nearly uniform sooty black with the exception of some frosted white edgings to the feathers of the forehead. White-edged belly feathers and undertail coverts occur in some individuals, usually females and juveniles.

Voice
A soft staccato *pic-pic-pic*, rarely heard away from nest or roost site.

Similar Species
Male Purple Martin has broader wings, slower flight, perches frequently; occurs away from Black Swift habitat and frequently in association with man.

Range
Summer breeding resident from southern Alaska, western Alberta, and Montana south to Colorado and southern California. Found near seacoast cliffs, particularly in Pacific Northwest, and in mountains elsewhere. Winters in Central America.   *Charles T. Collins*

Adult with young at nest
1. *Uniformly blackish plumage.*
2. *Narrow, swept-back wings.*

   Large size.

Chimney Swift

Chaetura pelagica
These gregarious birds fly rapidly on narrow, swept-back wings,
alternating bouts of shallow wingbeats with gliding.

Description
5½″ (14 cm). Nearly uniform brown, slightly darker above and on
wings; in fresh plumage, shows greenish gloss on wings and mantle.
Light below, palest on upper breast and throat. Tail stiff; slightly
rounded when fanned, with spines at tips of feathers.

Voice
A rapid, repeated series of staccato chips.

Similar Species
The narrow wings and rapid, erratic flight easily distinguish
Chimney Swift from any similar-size swallows. See Vaux's Swift.

Range
In summer from North Dakota to Maine, south to Gulf Coast.
Winters in South America. Recent record from southern
California.   *Charles T. Collins*

Vaux's Swift

Chaetura vauxi
The western equivalent of the Chimney Swift, Vaux's occurs more
frequently in forested areas, breeding in hollow trees or snags.

Description
4½″ (11.5 cm). Slim with narrow, swept-back wings; mostly dark
brown, paler below, particularly on throat and upper breast.

Voice
Similar to Chimney Swift's but slightly higher-pitched.

Similar Species
Chimney Swift slightly larger, usually more uniform brown; Vaux's
lighter grayish-brown on belly, distinctly paler on upper breast and
throat contrasting with darker crown. Identification of 2 species in
areas of sympatry should be made with care. Vocal and behavioral
differences may prove more reliable in field.

Range
British Columbia and W. Montana to central California. Winters in
Central America.   *Charles T. Collins*

White-throated Swift

Aeronautes saxatalis
This boldly patterned, black-and-white bird is familiar in the West,
where it frequents the rocky cliffs of mountain or desert canyons.

Description
6–7″ (15–18 cm). Prominent white throat and upper breast with
white midline streak extending to lower belly. Two bold white
patches on flanks and prominent broad white terminal edges on
secondaries. Tail long, slightly forked, with no terminal spines.

Voice
A drawn-out, descending twittering or *skee-e-e-e-e.*

Similar Species
Vaux's and Chimney swifts more uniformly colored and smaller.
Black Swift larger, blackish. See Violet-green Swallow.

Range
British Columbia south in mountains to Mexico. Winters from
central California and southwestern states south.
Charles T. Collins

Adult
1. Uniform brown
   upperparts.
2. Pale throat and
   upper breast.
3. Stiff tail with
   projecting spines.

   Highly social.
   Call a series of
   staccato chips.

Adult
1. Paler throat and
   upper breast than in
   Chimney Swift.

   Very similar to
   Chimney Swift; calls
   slightly higher-
   pitched.

Adult
1. White throat, upper
   breast, and midline.
2. White patches on
   flanks.
3. Slightly forked tail.

Hummingbirds

(Family Trochilidae)
These smallest of birds are incredibly versatile flyers, with
wingbeats so rapid that in most species single beats cannot be
detected and the wings are a blur. Hummingbirds are unique in
their ability to fly backwards as well as to hover and to fly vertically.
These birds have a very long, needle-shaped bill and an extrusible
tongue that they use to extract nectar from flowers, usually while
hovering. These birds have short secondaries and long pointed
primaries. Most North American hummingbirds are bright metallic
green on the upperparts, and the males have a patch of iridescent
feathers, called a gorget, on the throat. Females and immatures can
be very difficult to identify in the field; special attention must be
paid to things like call notes, patterns on the tail feathers, behavior,
and habitat. Many species perform spectacular courtship displays in
which the male dives down toward the female in steep arcs. Each
species has its own distinctive display. (World: 341 species. North
America: 21 species.)   *Scott B. Terrill*

Broad-billed Hummingbird

Cynanthus latirostris
The male Broad-billed Hummingbird often appears entirely black
except for a dark-tipped, bright orange-red bill, but in some lights,
it suddenly becomes a shimmering, iridescent deep blue and metallic
green. In very good light, these beautiful little hummers actually
seem irradiant, with even the bill glowing scarlet. Females have an
orange-red, dark-tipped, slightly decurved bill similar to the male's,
but lack the iridescence and forked tail. Broad-billed Hummingbirds
are common in desert mountain canyons, riparian woodlands, and
higher desert washes, especially where sycamore, cottonwood,
willow, and mesquite grow.

Description
3½–4″ (9–10 cm). The male is unmistakable, with an iridescent blue
throat that often extends onto the upper breast, where it blends
with the shimmering, metallic green that covers the rest of the
underparts. The undertail coverts are whitish or gray. The
upperparts are generally a dark, metallic, somewhat iridescent
green, with the forehead sometimes showing flashes of the brilliant
blue of the throat area. The forked tail is a dark, metallic indigo.
Both sexes have a dark-tipped red bill, but the female's is duller,
and the red is sometimes visible only on the lower mandible. The
upperparts of both sexes are a similar shade of green, but the
female's are duller. The underparts of the female are an even gray,
becoming whiter on the undertail coverts. The tail is slightly
rounded at the tip, green in the middle (the same shade as the back),
with blackish outer edges and white tips to the outer few feathers.

Voice
A dry, ventriloqual, low, tisking *jiit*, similar in quality to call of
Ruby-crowned Kinglet, but lower; often in rapid succession.

Similar Species
See White-eared Hummingbird.

Range
Breeds from south-central and southeastern Arizona, southwest
corner of New Mexico, and very locally in southwestern Texas south
through more arid regions of Mexico. Rare transient and winter
visitor outside breeding range in Arizona and to southern California.
Scott B. Terrill

Adult male
1. *Metallic green plumage.*
2. *Iridescent blue throat.*
3. *Red bill with dark tip.*
4. *Dark tail.*

Female
1. *Metallic green upperparts.*
2. *Gray underparts.*
3. *Red bill with dark tip.*

In flight, spread tail shows white tips on outer feathers.

White-eared Hummingbird

Hylocharis leucotis
Although abundant in the mountains of northern Mexico, the White-eared Hummingbird is scarce and erratic in its occurrence north of the border. Primarily a mountain species, this bird frequents wooded mountain canyons and is fond of hummingbird feeders.

Description
3½″ (9 cm). The male is metallic green with the crown, forehead, chin, and throat a deep iridescent purple to violet-blue; the purple is broken by a pure white line starting just above or behind the eye and curving steeply downward toward the shoulder. The lower belly and undertail coverts are whitish; the tail is dark with a squared tip. In both sexes, the bill is bright red with a dark tip. Females are green above like the male; this coloring continues onto the tail. The tail is broadly tipped with black, and there is white on the outer feathers. The female's underparts are whitish, heavily speckled or barred on the sides with green, and with green spotting on the throat; females may even appear solid green on the sides. The dark olive crown has a white eyeline curving downward posteriorly; it is bordered below by a parallel broad, black patch. First- and second-year males are intermediate between the adult female and male; they acquire more iridescence and more solid green below with age.

Voice
A saucy *stink* note. Sometimes in succession or in rapid pairs.

Similar Species
Female Broad-billed uniform grayish on underparts, with little or no green blotching and spotting; whitish ear patch bordered below by dark, but much less extensive, less well defined, and remains in straighter line, not sharply angled. Female Magnificent Hummingbird often confused with White-eared but much larger, with much longer, all-dark bill, and eye stripe poorly defined. White-eared's call note unique.

Range
Irregular but nearly annual summer visitor in small numbers to mountains of southeastern Arizona, most consistently at Ramsey and Cave Creek canyons. Rare in extreme southwestern New Mexico (Animas Mountains) and western Texas (Chisos Mountains). Through Mexican highlands south to Nicaragua.   *Scott B. Terrill*

Berylline Hummingbird

Amazilia beryllina
A recent addition to North American avifauna, the Berylline Hummingbird is quite common in northwestern Mexico. In Arizona, it is an erratic visitor to the Huachuca and Chiricahua mountains (with 1 breeding record for each spot), and the Santa Rita Mountains. This rather heavy hummer should be looked for in the mountain forests and moist canyons of southeastern Arizona.

Description
3½″ (9 cm). The Berylline Hummingbird is easily identified in the United States by its distinctly emerald-green underparts, although these appear dark in poor light; the lower belly and undertail coverts are grayish. The upperparts are dark green, and the wings and tail are a rich, dark rufous-purple. The tail is wide and slightly fan-shaped; the red bill has a dark tip. The relatively long wings occasionally beat with a discernible stroke. Females and immature birds look like males, but tend to be duller, with more extensively gray underparts.

Adult male
1. *White line behind eye.*
2. *Iridescent purple to violet-blue crown, forehead, and chin.*
3. *Red bill with dark tip.*

Adult female
1. *White line behind eye.*
2. *Green spotting on throat.*
3. *Barred sides.*
4. *Red bill with dark tip.*

Adult female
1. *Emerald-green underparts, with extensive gray on belly and undertail coverts.*
2. *Rufous-purple wings.*
3. *Rufous-purple tail.*

Similar Species
Buff-bellied Hummingbird pale buff rather than grayish below; tail noticeably forked.

Range
Erratic visitor to United States in Huachuca and Chiricahua mountains of Arizona, where has bred once. Also recorded from Santa Rita Mountains. Native to northwestern Mexico.
Scott B. Terrill

Buff-bellied Hummingbird

Amazilia yucatanensis
This species is an uncommon inhabitant of the undergrowth in the woodlands of southern Texas. In this genus, the sexes are alike.

Description
4½″ (11.5 cm). Head and upper chest emerald green; back and wings somewhat darker. Tail notched at tip; mostly rufous with some green on central feathers. Lower underparts very pale buff, slightly brighter on undertail coverts. Bill red with black tip.

Voice
High-pitched metallic notes.

Similar Species
In Arizona, see Berylline Hummingbird.

Range
Uncommon and local in summer in S. Texas; a few winter there or go north to upper Texas coast and S. Louisiana. Most common in W. Mexico and Guatemala.   *Kenn Kaufman*

Violet-crowned Hummingbird

Amazilia violiceps
This medium-size hummingbird, with its immaculate white underparts, bright red, black-tipped bill, and violet-purple or blue crown, is unmistakable. This species is known to breed in the United States only in the mountains of Arizona and New Mexico.

Description
4″ (10 cm). Olive-bronze above, slightly darker on wings and tail; crown is blue to purple and reaches to just below eye. Immaculate white below. Bill is red with dark tip. Sexes similar.

Voice
A dry, saucy *stick* note, often run together into chatter.

Range
Breeds in extreme Se. Arizona and Sw. New Mexico into Mexico. Casual throughout S. central and Se. Arizona in summer. One record from California. With a few exceptions, withdraws into Mexico in winter.   *Scott B. Terrill*

Adult male
1. *Emerald-green
   underparts, with
   less extensive gray
   on belly and
   undertail coverts
   than in female.*
2. *Rufous-purple
   wings.*
3. *Rufous-purple tail.*

Adult
1. *Emerald-green head
   and upperparts.*
2. *Pale buff
   underparts.*
3. *Rufous tail.*
4. *Red bill with black
   tip.*

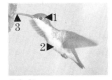

Adult
1. *Blue or purple
   crown.*
2. *White underparts.*
3. *Red bill .*

Blue-throated Hummingbird

Lampornis clemenciae
Found along the United States-Mexico border, this unmistakable
species is especially common at hummingbird feeders in the
Huachuca and Chiricahua mountains of Arizona. The bird's large
size and long wings make the wingbeats nearly discernible; the Blue-
throated often locks its wings stiffly and glides over short distances.
The loud, high, *seeep* song is diagnostic. This species inhabits
canyons of higher southwestern mountains, usually in the vicinity of
flowing water.

Description
5″ (12.5 cm). The Blue-throated Hummingbird is very large with
stout proportions and a very long bill. Males are a dark metallic
green on the upperparts with a dark tail and wings, and an
iridescent, powder-blue gorget. In both sexes, the tail is long and
very wide, with extensive white patches on the outer tail feathers.
A unique pair of whitish facial stripes, especially noticeable in males,
is present; the first is a narrow, decurving postocular stripe, the
second a whisker mark at the border between the dark metallic
olive-green sides of the face and the blue throat. The underparts are
generally dark gray, lighter on the undertail coverts, and washed
with greenish, especially on the sides and flanks. Females lack the
blue throat and show less definition in the whisker mark.

Voice
A high-pitched, loud *seeep* or *seeek*, often strongest at end of note,
given at intervals in flight. Same note given by males from
territorial perch, usually near running water. In this case, a
repetitious *seeek*, *seeek*, *seeek* at rapid intervals.

Tail

Similar Species
Magnificent Hummingbird only other large hummingbird in range;
tail more slender, with distinct, green tones and much less white;
lacks conspicuous whisker mark.

Range
Southeastern Arizona, southwestern New Mexico, western Texas,
and south into mountains of Mexico. Casual north to Colorado. One
record for California. Generally withdraws to Mexico in winter, but
occurs casually at Arizona feeders.   *Scott B. Terrill*

Magnificent Hummingbird

Eugenes fulgens
In southeastern Arizona, the big Magnificent Hummingbird shares
shady canyons with the Blue-throated Hummingbird but spreads out
into drier open pine forest, and reaches a little farther north. It is
generally less aggressive than other hummingbirds.

Tail   4

Description
4½–5″ (11.5–12.5 cm). This bird's head looks relatively narrow, with
a flat crown and a very long bill. The adult male is dark green on the
nape, back, wings, and tail; the underparts are black with a shining,
iridescent purple crown and a bright green throat. The bird's overall
dark look, which earns it the nickname "The Black Knight," is
broken only by pale undertail coverts and a small white spot behind
each eye. The female is green above and grayish below, lightly
spotted on the throat, and mottled with dull greenish on the sides.
The squarish tail is gray-green, with small, whitish outer corners;
the face is obscurely marked with a short, pale line behind the eye
and a slightly darker ear patch. Immatures resemble adult females.

Adult male
1. *Powder-blue throat.*
2. *Two white stripes on face.*
3. *Long blackish tail with large white patches on outer corners.*

   Large size.

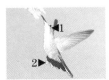

Female
1. *Two stripes on face.*
2. *Long blackish tail with large white patches on outer corners.*

   Large size.

Female
1. *Long bill and flat forehead.*
2. *No strong facial pattern.*
3. *Mottled throat and underparts.*
4. *Gray-green tail with gray corners.*

   Large size.

Voice
A sharp *schip*, shorter and slightly lower than call of Blue-throated.

Similar Species
Adult male unmistakable. Female Blue-throated has more substantial blue-black tail with large, white corners, more distinct striping on face, more smoothly gray underparts. Female Magnificent might also be confused with some other female hummingbirds, like Anna's, which is grayish below and moderately bulky. However, with good view Magnificent's larger size, flat forehead, and very long bill should be obvious. See also White-eared.

Range
Common summer resident in southeastern and central Arizona above 5000' in mountains; uncommon in New Mexico and western Texas. Wanders to Colorado. Normally leaves United States in winter, but a few remain at Arizona feeders. Resident from northern Mexico to Nicaragua; closely related form found in Costa Rica and Panama.   *Kenn Kaufman*

Lucifer Hummingbird

Calothorax lucifer
The Lucifer Hummingbird, which is scarce and local in North America, is closely associated with the century plant (agave) that is found in arid mesas and foothills in western Texas. The Lucifer's somewhat decurved bill sets it apart from other North American hummingbirds.

Tail   3

Description
3½" (9 cm). The male is iridescent bronze-green above and white below, with an elongated violet gorget. The sides of the neck are white, and there is a rich buff wash on the sides and flanks. The tail is long and narrow and rather deeply forked. The female lacks the iridescent gorget, has a more rounded tail, and is evenly washed with buff on the underparts. In both sexes, the bill is slightly but noticeably decurved.

Voice
Light, high-pitched chipping notes.

Similar Species
Male Costa's has violet on crown as well as gorget, lacks rich buff on sides. Other female hummers in range lack extensive buff across underparts; those that show much buff or rust on sides and flanks (*Selasphorus*) have shorter, straighter bills. Female Black-chinned has slight decurvature to bill, but buff is limited to inconspicuous spot on flanks.

Range
Breeds locally in Chisos Mountains of western Texas. Rare straggler west to southeastern Arizona in spring and summer. Also south to south-central Mexico.   *Kimball L. Garrett*

Adult male
1. *Purple crown.*
2. *Bright green throat.*
3. *Black underparts.*

Large size.
Looks very dark
overall.

Adult male
1. *Long violet gorget.*
2. *Rich buff wash on*
   sides.
3. *Deeply forked tail.*

Female
1. *Decurved bill.*
2. *Buff underparts.*
3. *Rounded tail.*

Ruby-throated Hummingbird

Display flight

Archilochus colubris
The only hummer occurring throughout most of eastern North
America, the Ruby-throated Hummingbird possesses the typical
hummingbird characteristics of small size, rapid wingbeats, and
nectar-feeding habits. It occupies woodlands, parks, and gardens
where flowers are plentiful.

Description
3¼–3½″ (8–9 cm). A small hummer, the Ruby-throat is
iridescent green above, including the crown, and mostly white
below. Adult males have a brilliant ruby-red gorget that is not
elongated on the sides; in poor light, the gorget may appear black.
The sides and flanks of the male are tinged with olive. Females lack
the ruby gorget and are unmarked whitish below, including the
throat. The deeply forked tail of the male is green in the center and
blackish on the sides. The female's tail is more rounded, with white
on the corners.

Voice
Thin, high *chick* call and other squeaky notes. Dull buzzing of wings
in flight.

Similar Species
Male of closely related Black-chinned Hummingbird has black-and-
purple gorget, more distinct white collar between gorget and olive
sides, less deeply forked tail. Female Black-chinned not safely
distinguished from female Ruby-throat in field. Rufous only other
likely hummer in East; shows extensive rufous or deep buff in all
plumages. Male Broad-tailed has rosier gorget, rufous edges to
rectrices, loud, musical wing trill in flight.

Range
Breeds in eastern North America from central Alberta east to Nova
Scotia and south through eastern Great Plains to south-central
Texas, east to southern Florida. Winters from Mexico south to
Costa Rica, rare north to Gulf States.   *Kimball L. Garrett*

Black-chinned Hummingbird

Archilochus alexandri
The Black-chinned Hummingbird, the western counterpart of the
Ruby-throated Hummingbird, commonly nests in the oak and
riparian woodlands of canyons and lowlands. There, females build
their nests in sycamores or other broadleaf trees. Flying males are
often located by the dry buzz made by their wings; they can be
observed in their woodland habitat performing shallow-arc
pendulum displays.

Description
3–3½″ (7.5–9 cm). Males have dark green upperparts and a black
chin bordered below by an iridescent purple-violet band. This dark
gorget, not elongated on the sides, is set off from the olive-tinged
underparts by a distinct white collar. The dark tail is shallowly
notched. Females are green above and whitish below, with an
immaculate throat and a slight tinge of buff on the flanks. The bill is
moderately long and very slightly decurved. Both sexes show a
small white spot behind the eye.

Adult male
1. *Ruby-red gorget.*
2. *Olive-tinged flanks.*
3. *Dark, forked tail.*

*Only hummingbird
in most of East.*

Female
1. *Green upperparts
   with no buff or
   rufous.*
2. *Plain whitish
   underparts.*
3. *Rounded tail with
   white feather tips.*

Female
*Not safely
distinguishable from
female Ruby-
throated.
Mainly western
distribution.*

Voice
Soft *chew* and various high, buzzy notes. Males give distinctive, dry
wing buzz in flight.

Similar Species
See Ruby-throated Hummingbird (females of the 2 not safely
distinguishable). Female Anna's slightly larger than female Black-
chinned; has grayer underparts and some red spotting on throat.
Female Costa's very similar to female Black-chinned but with
shorter bill, thin whitish line behind eye rather than white spot, no
buff on flanks, different voice.

Display flight

Range
Breeds in West from southwestern British Columbia and western
Montana south through southern California, Arizona, New Mexico,
and south-central Texas; also south to northern Mexico. Winters in
Mexico; casual north to south Texas, southern California.
Kimball L. Garrett

Anna's Hummingbird

Calypte anna
Slightly larger than other West Coast hummingbirds, Anna's
Hummingbird is an abundant resident of California parks, gardens,
chaparral, and woodlands; it is the only hummer to remain
commonly throughout most of the West Coast in winter. The rose
iridescence on both the throat and the crown of the male is unique.
Males are often spotted "singing" from a conspicuous perch, or
giving spectacular displays that combine a long, steep dive with a
loud, explosive popping sound given at the bottom.

Description
3¾–4″ (9.5–10 cm). Males are iridescent green above and duller
gray-green below with a brilliant rose gorget and crown; the gorget
is slightly elongated on the sides. Females lack the rose gorget and
crown, but have a variable amount of red spotting at the center of
the throat. The female's underparts are dingy gray, and the tail
corners white. Juveniles may show an immaculate throat.

Display flight

Voice
"Song" a patterned series of coarse, squeaky phrases given from
perch or in air at outset of display dive. Common calls include soft
chip and rapid, repeated *chee-chee-chee*.

Similar Species
No other hummer in North America shows rose-red on crown. Male
Costa's has blue-violet iridescence to crown and to elongated gorget.
Female Black-chinned and Costa's similar to female Anna's but
slightly smaller, whiter below, with unmarked or very finely spotted
throat. Juvenile Anna's with plain throat closely resembles Black-
chinned and Costa's, but grayer below, slightly larger; has different
calls. See Magnificent Hummingbird.

Range
Resident from northern California south on West Coast to Baja
California. Nonbreeders occur regularly north to southern British
Columbia (rarely to southeastern Alaska) and east to southern
Arizona (rarely to Texas coast).   *Kimball L. Garrett*

Adult male
1. *Black chin bordered below by purple band.*
2. *White collar between gorget and olive sides.*

Dry wing buzz.

Adult male
1. *Rose-red gorget, slightly elongated at sides.*
2. *Rose-red crown.*

Adult female
1. *Fine red spots on throat.*
2. *Dingy gray underparts.*

Slightly larger than other West Coast hummingbirds.

Costa's Hummingbird

Calypte costae

Costa's Hummingbird is a small hummer of the southwestern deserts that frequents arid washes and hillsides, dry chaparral, and suburban areas where exotic plants have been introduced. Territorial males often perch conspicuously on the stalks of yucca, ocotillo, and other shrubs, displaying a distinctive violet-blue crown and elongated gorget.

Display flight

Description
3–3¼" (7.5–8.5 cm). The male is green above and white below with an olive tinge to the sides. The crown and gorget of the male are iridescent violet to violet-blue; the gorget is greatly elongated on the sides. Females are gray-green on the upperparts and white on the underparts, including the unmarked throat. Females show a thin, white line behind the eye, and white spots on the tail corners. The bill is relatively short in both sexes.

Voice
Common calls include a light, high *pit*, given singly or run together into a rapid twitter; also a very high-pitched thin, whining whistle ascending, then descending in pitch, given by male while perched or in display flight.

Similar Species
See male Anna's and Lucifer hummingbirds. Female Anna's larger than female Costa's, with gray underparts and red spotting on throat. Female Black-chinned longer-billed than female Costa's, with buff spot on flanks, and very different vocalizations.

Range
Central California, southern Nevada, and southwestern Utah south through southern California and east to western and southern Arizona; also northwestern Mexico. Some winter withdrawal from northern parts of range. Vagrant north to Oregon and east to Texas.
Kimball L. Garrett

Calliope Hummingbird

Stellula calliope

The Calliope Hummingbird frequents meadows, riparian thickets, and other brushy areas within the coniferous forests of western mountains. Tiny even for a hummingbird, the Calliope is further distinguished by its relatively short bill; the male has a distinctive pattern of iridescent rays on the gorget. As in most hummers, this species' bill, forehead, and chin are often discolored by pollen.

Display flight

Description
2¾–3" (7–7.5 cm). The male is iridescent green above (tending toward blue-green rather than bronze- or golden-green) and generally white below. The gorget consists of a series of rose-purple rays on a white background; these rays are more elongated toward the sides of the throat. The female lacks the gorget rays and is washed with buff on the sides; the throat is finely spotted with dusky coloration. The tail of the female shows white corners and a small amount of rust near the base. In both sexes, the bill is straight and relatively short, and the tail is short, broad, and unforked.

Adult male
1. Violet-blue gorget, elongated at sides.
2. Violet-blue crown.

Female
1. Unmarked throat.
2. White underparts cleaner than in Anna's.
3. Thin white line behind eye.

Adult male
1. Rose-purple rays on gorget.
2. Short bill.

Very small size.

Voice
Very high-pitched *tsew* note and twittering calls; also a very high *zing* given by displaying males.

Similar Species
Female and especially juvenile Rufous and Allen's hummingbirds closely resemble female Calliope, but slightly larger and longer-billed, show darker and more extensive buff on sides, more rust in rectrices. Female Broad-tailed considerably larger and longer-billed.

Range
Breeds in higher mountains from southwestern Canada south through Pacific States, east to Utah and western Colorado. Winters in Mexico. Uncommon migrant through lowlands.
Kimball L. Garrett

Broad-tailed Hummingbird

Selasphorus platycercus
A montane hummingbird of the Rockies and the Great Basin, this species occurs commonly around meadows and patches of flowers within pine, fir, and aspen forests. Male Broad-tailed Hummingbirds are easily recognized by the loud, musical, cricketlike trilling produced by their wings in flight. These males are the only western hummers with a green crown and rose gorget.

Display flight

Description
3¾–4″ (9.5–10 cm). The male Broad-tailed is iridescent green above and mostly white below, with a bright rose-pink gorget that is not elongated on the sides. There are rufous edges to some of the rectrices, but these are inconspicuous. The female lacks the iridescent gorget, and has a wash of rich buff on the sides and some rufous near the base of the outer pairs of rectrices. The tail is relatively broad in both sexes.

Voice
Common call a sharp *tew*. Cricketlike wing trill given by adult males except when in molt.

Similar Species
Female Calliope Hummingbird smaller and shorter-billed than female Broad-tailed. Female and juvenile Rufous and Allen's Hummingbirds very similar to corresponding Broad-taileds but smaller with richer buff or rust wash on sides, more extensive rufous in tail, and more golden-green, less emerald, sheen to upperparts. See Ruby-throated Hummingbird.

Range
Breeds in mountains from eastern California east to northern Wyoming, south through Great Basin ranges and Rocky Mountains to southern Arizona and Western Texas; south to Guatemala. Winters in Mexico.   *Kimball L. Garrett*

Female
1. Dusky spots on throat.
2. Short bill.
3. Buff wash on sides.

Very small size.

Female
1. Bright buff sides.
2. Little rufous on tail.

Larger than Rufous and Allen's hummingbirds.

Adult male
1. Rose-red gorget, not elongated at sides.
2. Green crown.
3. Broad tail with little rufous.

Cricketlike trill in flight.

Rufous Hummingbird

Tail of female

Selasphorus rufus
This small, pugnacious western hummingbird differs from most
other North American hummers in having extensively orange-rufous
plumage. The buzzing of the males' wings may be heard in
northwestern gardens, parks, and woodlands during the breeding
season and through much of the Pacific lowlands in spring. Large
numbers occur around mountain meadows during the southward
migration. This species and Allen's are early migrants, moving north
as early as February and south by August.

Description
3¼–3½" (8–9 cm). Adult males are almost entirely orange-rufous
above and on the tail; they have an iridescent orange-red gorget
(appearing golden-green in some light) and an extensive orange-
rufous wash on the sides. Adult females lack the iridescent gorget;
instead they have small red to golden-green spots on the throat.
Their rufous coloration is confined to the rump, the basal half of
most of the rectrices, and a wash on the sides. Young males show
some red on the throat but have green backs.

Voice
Common calls a soft *tchup* and excited, buzzy squeal: *zeeee-chuppity-
chup*. Flying males produce high, trilling buzz with wings; this trill
quieter and less musical than that of Broad-tailed.

Similar Species
See female Calliope and Broad-tailed hummingbirds. Allen's almost
identical in all corresponding plumages and should be identified with
caution. Adult male Allen's has green crown and back, but otherwise
nearly identical; some male Rufous have complete or nearly
complete red gorgets but retain some green on back. Female Allen's
has outer rectrices comparatively narrower within each age class
(rarely useful distinction in field).

Display flight

Range
Breeds from southeastern Alaska and southern Yukon south
through Pacific States to southern Oregon, inland to southwestern
Alberta and western Montana. Winters in Mexico; in very small
numbers north to south-coastal California. Rare fall and winter
wanderer to Gulf Coast; vagrant elsewhere in East.
Kimball L. Garrett

Allen's Hummingbird

Tail of female

Selasphorus sasin
Nearly identical to the Rufous Hummingbird in appearance and
behavior, Allen's occurs in Pacific Coast parks and woods.

Description
3½" (8 cm). Adult male orange-rufous above with green on crown
and back. Females and immature males have narrower outer tail
feathers than the corresponding plumages of Rufous; otherwise
similar.

Voice
Nearly identical to calls of Rufous. Wing buzz of adult males also
similar, although may be slightly higher-pitched.

Similar Species
See Rufous Hummingbird.

Range
Along coast from Sw. Oregon to S. California. Winters in Nw.
Mexico. Resident on California Channel Islands and locally on
southern California coast.   *Kimball L. Garrett*

Female
1. *Rufous sides.*
2. *Much rufous in tail.*

Adult male
1. *Orange-red gorget.*
2. *Orange-rufous upperparts.*

   High-pitched wing trill in flight.

Adult male
1. *Orange-red gorget.*
2. *Metallic green crown and back.*
3. *Female has narrower outer tail feathers than female Rufous'.*

Trogons

(Family Trogonidae)
This is a unique group of long-tailed, medium-size, stocky-necked arboreal birds with broad, short bills. The colorful trogons are found primarily in tropical American, Asian, and African regions, with the greatest representation in the New World. In addition to the long, flashy tails, trogons generally have a strikingly contrasting breast and belly pattern, with metallic hues on the upperparts. In some species, the sexes are alike; in others, the female is similar to the male but duller. In general, trogons are rather elongated birds. They often sit upright with tails pointing downward, remaining nearly motionless for long periods of time on concealed perches in trees or shrubs. Owing to trogons' somewhat retiring nature, their far-carrying, often hoarse, barking calls are useful in locating and identifying them. The Elegant Trogon is the only member of this family that regularly occurs north of Mexico. (World: 37 species. North America: 2 species.)   *Scott B. Terrill*

Elegant Trogon

Trogon elegans
The Elegant Trogon is the only member of its family that regularly occurs north of Mexico. In southeastern Arizona, it is found on oak- or pine-oak-covered mountain canyons and in sycamore, walnut, and cottonwood trees along canyon streams.

Description
11–12½″ (28–32 cm). Males, with their distinctive Trogon shape, are metallic green above. The upperparts often have strong blue-green hues that extend onto the bronze-hued upper breast and onto the head. The forehead, cheeks, and throat are iridescent black or slate; the dark head contrasts sharply with the broad, bright yellow bill. The large eye is surrounded by a complete red eye-ring. The breast is separated from the bright geranium-red underparts by a white collar that widens toward the middle. The wings appear vermiculated with blackish and white; often there is a great deal of white, which is especially apparent in flight. The tail is long and squared, with graduated feathers; when closed, and in good light, the upper surface appears coppery-bronze with a black tip. The undersurface of the tail is strikingly different, with a series of thin black-and-white vermiculations broken by large whitish spots at the tip. Females are similar to males but have brownish upperparts; the pattern on the underparts is like the male's, but vague and washed. There is a conspicuous white spot behind and below the female's eye. First-winter males are duller than adult males; their plumage is somewhat intermediate between the male's and the female's.

Voice
A somewhat long, hoarse, carrying *co-ah*, *cu-way*, *co-wy*, or *cory*, repeated in series, usually in short bursts but occasionally extended.

Similar Species
Eared Trogon (extremely rare in Arizona) much larger, lacks white collar; underside of tail not vermiculated, mostly white.

Range
Locally, fairly common breeder in southeastern Arizona, primarily Huachuca, Chiricahua, and Santa Rita mountains. Very rare winter visitor and transient away from mountains in southeastern Arizona. Extremely rare in New Mexico and Texas. Mexico south to Costa Rica.   *Scott B. Terrill*

Elegant Trogon
Eared Trogon

Adult male
1. *Yellow bill.*
2. *Red eye-ring.*
3. *Metallic blue-green upperparts.*
4. *Red underparts with white collar.*
5. *Long, squared tail with black-and-white underside.*

Female
1. *Brownish upperparts.*
2. *Dull pink underparts.*
3. *Long, squared tail with black-and-white underside.*

Kingfishers

(Family Alcedinidae)
The kingfishers are small-footed, heavy-headed, long-billed birds
that perch above the water and dive headfirst to catch fish, insects,
and other aquatic life. For nesting, they dig burrows in vertical dirt
banks. Only 1 species is widespread in North America, but 2 more
occur near the Mexican border. Most of the world's kingfishers
inhabit the Old World tropics. (World: 91 species. North America: 3
species.)   *Kenn Kaufman*

Ringed Kingfisher

Ceryle torquata
A recent invader from Mexico, the large Ringed Kingfisher—or
"King Kongfisher"—is now locally common in southern Texas.

Description
16″ (40.5 cm). Large with bushy crest. Blue-gray above with broad
white collar. Small white spots above on tail and wings; in flight,
shows white patch on outer primaries. Rufous below; female has
rufous bordered by narrow white strip and blue-gray band across
chest. Undertail coverts white; tail barred black and white below.

Voice
A loud rough *ktick;* a clattering rattle like Belted Kingfisher's but
louder and wilder. In flight, repeated *tchack, tchack*.

Similar Species
See Belted Kingfisher.

Range
Recently resident along Rio Grande in S. Texas; widespread in
tropics from Mexico to Argentina.   *Kenn Kaufman*

Belted Kingfisher

Ceryle alcyon
Common and widespread, the Belted Kingfisher is a familiar bird
over much of North America. It frequents the vicinity of streams,
lakes, and even rocky seacoasts; it is solitary except when nesting.
Usually it perches conspicuously in the open. This bird may dive
from a branch to catch fish or hover above the water before
plunging. Its wingbeats are deep and rapid but irregular in pace,
giving it a distinctive flight style; often it gives an equally distinctive
harsh, rattling call either in flight or while perched.

Description
12–14″ (30.5–35.5 cm). The Belted Kingfisher is distinguished by its
blue-gray upperparts, mostly white underparts, large bill, and
bushy, double-peaked crest. It has a white throat and a broad white
collar around the neck; there are small white spots near the eye and
on the upper side of the wings and tail. The underside of the tail is
heavily barred with slate and white. In flight, a white patch on the
upper side of the blackish primaries is noticeable. Both sexes have a

Ringed Kingfisher
Belted Kingfisher
Green Kingfisher

Female
1. *Bushy crest.*
2. *Broad white collar.*
3. *Blue-gray*
   upperparts.
4. *Blue-gray chest*
   band.
5. *Rufous lower breast*
   and belly.

   Large size.

Male
1. *Stout bill.*
2. *Bushy crest.*
3. *Blue-gray*
   upperparts with
   white collar.
4. *Blue-gray band*
   across upper chest.

broad blue-gray band across the upper chest; the female has an
additional rufous band crossing at the midbreast and trailing down
the flanks.

Voice
A loud, clattering rattle, given from perch or in flight.

Similar Species
Near Mexican border, see Green Kingfisher. Ringed Kingfisher
much larger, mostly rufous below; shows more conspicuous white
collar.

Range
Breeds from Alaska east to Newfoundland, south to central
California, central Texas, and Gulf Coast states. Winters north to
southeastern Alaska, Great Lakes, and Maritime Provinces (in
interior, northern limits depend on open water) and south to
Panama, northern South America, and West Indies.
Kenn Kaufman

Green Kingfisher

Chloroceryle americana
Sparrow-sized, with a heronlike bill, the distinctive Green
Kingfisher is a fairly common but inconspicuous resident in southern
Texas. It favors small, shady streams, but may also be found at
larger bodies of water with heavy, low vegetation along the banks; it
perches low on overhanging branches, roots, or rocks, often just
inches above the water. When perched, this bird sometimes
twitches its tail up nervously. It flies low over the water, giving a
dry, ticking call and flashing its white outer tail feathers.

Description
7–8″ (18–20.5 cm). Unlike its larger relatives, the Green Kingfisher
shows only a hint of a crest. It is dark glossy green above with
extensive white spotting on the wings; the white outer tail feathers,
conspicuous in flight, are crossed by some dark spots. The throat
and narrow collar around the neck are white. The underparts
are basically white, but the male has a rufous chest band and heavy
dark green spotting on the lower breast, sides, and flanks. The
female lacks the rufous band and instead has heavy green spotting
that more or less coalesces into 2 bands across the breast.

Voice
Sharp metallic *tick*, repeated, sometimes run together in dry,
rattling series. Also a sharp squeak.

Similar Species
Belted Kingfisher larger, blue-gray above, conspicuously crested;
lacks flashing white outer tail feathers.

Range
Southern and south-central Texas, occurring up Rio Grande at least
as far as Del Rio and north onto Edwards Plateau to latitude of
Austin. Straggles into western Texas and southern Arizona.
Widespread in American tropics south to Argentina.
Kenn Kaufman

Female
1. *Stout bill.*
2. *Bushy crest.*
3. *Blue-gray band across upper chest.*
4. *Rufous band.*

Male
1. *Green upperparts with white collar.*
2. *Rufous chest band.*
3. *Dark green spotting on lower breast, sides, and flanks.*

Small size.
Female lacks rufous chest band.

Woodpeckers

(Family Picidae)
Woodpeckers are sturdy birds that use their strong toes to cling to
bark, which they hammer forcefully with a powerful, tapered,
chisel-like bill. This hammering, a foraging technique, can often be
heard over great distances. Territorial drumming is even louder and
is often distinctive for a species. Woodpeckers also have other
special adaptations for clinging to and hammering on trees; these
include a stiff, spiny tail, a very thick skull, short legs, and a very
long, protrusible tongue with a horny spear at the tip. In general,
woodpeckers have plumage of contrasting brown, black, and white,
frequently with barring and spotting. For the most part, the sexes
are similar, but females sometimes lack the red or yellow patches
apparent on the head of males. Woodpeckers often have distinctive
flight patterns, showing patches on the wings, the tail, or the rump.
Their calls are loud and generally easily identified. (World: 204
species. North America: 22 species.)   *Scott B. Terrill*

Lewis' Woodpecker

Melanerpes lewis
Lewis' Woodpecker is a rather large woodpecker of pine and other
forests, woodland edges, streamside trees, and recent forest
"burns." Its unwoodpeckerlike flight is direct rather than
undulating, and Lewis' frequently flycatches from a perch. Migrant
and wintering birds visit orchards and other trees around farms and
towns; they store acorns and other nuts in natural cavities and tree
bark and in the cracks of poles or posts.

Description
10–11″ (25.5–28 cm). Lewis' Woodpecker is greenish-black above
with a deep red face; it has a pearly or grayish breast patch that
extends as a collar around the neck and a pinkish-red belly and
lower breast. The sexes are alike. Immatures lack the collar and are
browner above, more whitish and less red below; the red on the face
is reduced, and bars and streaks are evident on the underparts.

Voice
Main call a harsh *churr* uttered in series of 3–8 notes. Drums weakly
in breeding season.

Similar Species
Adults unmistakable. Immature sapsuckers and Red-headed
Woodpeckers lack reddish coloring on belly; have white patches or
marks on upperparts and wings.

Range
Breeds from central British Columbia east to Montana and Black
Hills, south to central California, northern Arizona, northern New
Mexico, and Colorado. Winters south from Oregon and Colorado to
northern Mexico, sporadically north coastally; wanders east to Great
Plains in migration.   *Lester L. Short*

Adult
1. *Red face.*
2. *Gray collar.*
3. *Dark back, wings, and tail.*
4. *Pinkish-red belly.*

Churr, churr *call. Direct, not undulating, flight.*

Immature
1. *Little red on face.*
2. *No gray collar.*
3. *Brownish upperparts.*
4. *Streaks and bars on underparts.*

Red-headed Woodpecker

Melanerpes erythrocephalus
This woodpecker has a conspicuous red head, a black-and-white
body, and white wing patches that are very evident in flight. It
frequents woodland edges, farmlands, and dead trees standing in
the open. The Red-headed Woodpecker flycatches from posts or
trees, flies across open areas, and aggressively pursues other
woodpeckers. It stores nuts or acorns in tree crevices for winter
feeding. This species' numbers are subject to fluctuation; it may
disappear for some years, then reappear at the margins of its range.

Description
7½–8½″ (19–21.5 cm). As this bird's name indicates, the entire head
has a red hood; the breast, belly, and rump are white. The back and
most of the wings are blue-black, but there is a large white patch on
the secondaries, visible even when the bird is at rest. The tail is
blackish-brown. Males and females are colored alike. Immatures
have a dull brown head that extends to the upper breast, and dull
white, sometimes streaked underparts; the back is barred with
brown, and the wings and tail are brown. Immatures may show
some red on the head and have partly barred white wing patches.

Voice
Main call a loud *kweeer*, or *kwee-arr*, singly or in short series. Also
chattering notes, a *kerrr*, and rattling, aggressive calls. Drums
weakly in short bursts.

Similar Species
Adults unmistakable. Immatures resemble young sapsuckers, but
have white patch on rear of wings, and contrasting brown upper
breast and whitish lower breast.

Range
Breeds from southeastern Alberta across southern Canada to
southern Ontario, central New York, and southern New England
(irregular at northern margin); south through western Great Plains
to northeastern New Mexico, Texas, Gulf Coast, and Florida.
Winters irregularly north to Kansas, Ohio, and New Jersey.
Lester L. Short

Acorn Woodpecker

Melanerpes formicivorus
This medium-size, sociable bird of western and southwestern oak
and pine-oak woodlands also frequents parks and towns.

Description
8½″ (21.5 cm). Distinctive pattern formed by red cap (more
extensive in males), black facial area around white eye, white
forehead extending to yellowish-white throat, and black around base
of bill. Glossy greenish-black above with small white patch on
primaries and white rump. Black necklace breaks into streaks on
nape; streaks prominent on white sides and flanks, less so on belly.

Voice
Most commonly heard call an interactive *ya-cup, ya-cup, ya-cup*.
Also, chattering *aak-a-aak-a-ak*.

Range
Oregon through unforested California west of Sierras to N. Baja and
from N. central Arizona, New Mexico, and W. Texas in highlands to
Panama.   *Lester L. Short*

Adult
1. *Red head.*
2. *Black upperparts.*
3. *White patch on*
   secondaries.
4. *White underparts.*

   Loud kweer *call.*
   Shows white rump
   in flight.

Immature
1. *Brownish head.*
2. *Brown upperparts.*
3. *Two dark bars on*
   white secondaries.
4. *Whitish underparts.*

Adult male
1. *Red cap.*
2. *White forehead and*
   throat.
3. *Black face and*
   upperparts.
4. *Small white patch in*
   primaries.

   Shows white rump
   in flight.

Gila Woodpecker

Melanerpes uropygialis
The Gila Woodpecker is the southwestern counterpart of the very closely related Golden-fronted and Red-bellied woodpeckers. It is a medium-size, buff and black-and-white barred inhabitant of cactus deserts, streamside woodlands, and suburban desert towns and cities. It feeds in trees, cacti, and bushes, as well as on the ground and at feeders, eating all manner of insects, worms, and fruit; it will even feed on lizards and the eggs of other birds. This species excavates nesting and roosting holes in cacti and various trees. Vocal and conspicuous, Gila Woodpeckers are often seen in the open, perching on cacti and trees, or flying in the open with an undulating flight. This bird frequently gives a bowing display with accompanying calls.

Description
8–8½″ (20.5–21.5 cm). The larger, longer-billed male has a red patch on the crown that is lacking in the female. Both sexes have a pale forehead; the rest of the head and most of the underparts are an unpatterned gray-tan. The belly is golden-yellow, and the flanks are barred. The upperparts are barred with black and buff-white or white, including most of the wings and the center of the tail; the outer tail feathers and most of the primaries are black, with a small white wing patch visible in flight. Immatures are duller but recognizable as Gila Woodpeckers.

Voice
Distinctive *churr* or *dchurr* call, singly or in series. Also, rattly *kek-kek-kek*.

Similar Species
Ladder-backed Woodpecker has black-and-white striped face and streaky underparts. Flickers are brown- and black-barred above with spotted underparts and very different head pattern. Both lack Gila's wing patch. Ranges of Golden-fronted and Red-bellied do not overlap with Gila.

Range
Resident in southeastern California, southern Nevada, Arizona, and southwestern New Mexico; south to southern Baja California and Zacatecas, Aguascalientes, and Jalisco, western Mexico.
Lester L. Short

Golden-fronted Woodpecker

Melanerpes aurifrons
Restricted to Texas and Oklahoma in its North American range, the medium-size Golden-fronted Woodpecker is found in orchards, gardens, parks, and scrubby woodland. Conspicuous and vocal, it feeds on a great array of fruits, berries, seeds, corn, nuts (including acorns), and various insects that it sometimes takes by flycatching. Its other habits are very similar to those of the closely related Red-bellied and Gila woodpeckers.

Description
8–9″ (20.5–23 cm). Gold or orange on the nape with a gold nasal patch, the Golden-fronted Woodpecker is barred with black and white on the back, wings, and central tail. The face and underparts are tan-gray with a gold central belly and some barring on the flanks and belly. The rump and a small wing patch are white. Males have a rectangular red crown patch that is lacking in females. Immatures sufficiently resemble the adults to be recognizable as Golden-fronteds.

Male
1. *Tan head with red cap.*
2. *Grayish-tan underparts.*
3. *Black-and-white barred upperparts.*
4. *Golden-yellow belly.*

   Churr *call.*

Female
1. *Tan head with no red cap.*
2. *Grayish-tan underparts.*
3. *Black-and-white barred upperparts.*
4. *Golden-yellow belly.*

Male
1. *Red crown patch.*
2. *Golden-yellow nape.*
3. *Golden-yellow patch on forehead.*
4. *Barred upperparts.*
5. *Plain face and underparts.*

Voice
Main call a harsh *churr*, harsher than that of Red-bellied. Same array of other calls as Red-bellied. Drums in breeding period.

Similar Species
In Texas, Red-bellied Woodpecker distinguished by red nape; Golden-fronted's gold belly, if visible, is useful trait, as is gold nasal tuft. Ladder-backed Woodpecker has facial stripes, spotted underparts; lacks white rump and wing patches.

Range
Resident from central Texas and southwestern Oklahoma through eastern and central Mexico (where it occasionally hybridizes with Gila Woodpecker). Range borders that of Red-bellied Woodpecker in central Texas; where these meet, they hold territories against one another as if same species, but hybridize very rarely. Also from Central America to Honduras.   *Lester L. Short*

Red-bellied Woodpecker

Melanerpes carolinus
The Red-bellied Woodpecker is a vocal, conspicuous bird often seen at bird-feeding stations and in various wooded areas, especially wet woodlands, pinewoods, parks, orchards, and gardens. It is slightly migratory in the northern and northwestern parts of its range. It forages in a woodpeckerlike fashion on trees and branches but also gleans insects, flycatches, and takes various fruits, nuts, and berries, some of which it stores. This bird is more aggressive than the Downy and Red-cockaded woodpeckers, but gives way to Red-headed Woodpeckers and may be prevented by them from using more open habitats.

Description
8½–9½" (21.5–24 cm). This is a common woodpecker with a barred back. In the female, the nape, hindcrown, and nasal areas are red; in the male, red covers the entire top of the head. There is a red belly patch, often difficult to see, that varies in size and intensity of color. There may be some reddish on the gray face; most of the underparts are gray, and the flanks are barred. There is a small white patch, barred with black, on the primaries, and the rump is white. Males are larger than females.

Voice
Common calls include *churr* call in series or single notes, and long, rattling series, *cha-aa-aa*. Also *chip*, *chup*, *yuk*, and *ta-wik* calls in series. Drums in bursts to 1 second.

Similar Species
In most of range, barred back distinguishes Red-bellied. Red-cockaded and Ladder-backed woodpeckers have facial markings and side spotting; lack white rump, white wing patch, and red belly. Golden-fronted Woodpecker also in central Texas; has gold or orange nape and hindcrown, gold nasal tufts, and gold belly.

Range
Regularly breeds from central South Dakota, southern Minnesota, southern Ontario, western New York, and southwestern Connecticut south to central Texas and Gulf Coast. Irregularly north to Saskatchewan and Massachusetts. Migrates from northwestern part of range, especially in bad winters; southern populations resident.   *Lester L. Short*

Female
1. *Plain head with golden-yellow nape and forehead.*
2. *Barred upperparts.*
3. *Plain underparts.*

Female
1. *Plain head with red nape and forehead.*
2. *Barred upperparts.*
3. *Plain face and underparts.*

Male
1. *Red crown and nape.*
2. *Barred upperparts.*
3. *Plain face and underparts.*

Yellow-bellied Sapsucker

Sphyrapicus varius
Often noisy and conspicuous on its breeding grounds, the Yellow-bellied Sapsucker is quiet and secretive during migration and in winter. It drills a regular series of pitlike holes in trees, mainly in winter and spring, from which it feeds on sap and insects attracted to the sap pits. The pitted trees heal over, testifying to the presence of sapsuckers, even in such places as Hispaniola, where the birds occur only in winter. At other times, sapsuckers feed on insects and fruit, sometimes flycatching for insects. Mixed deciduous-coniferous forests, especially those with aspens, are this species' breeding habitat; in winter and migration it can be found in any woodland, forest, orchard, or park. The red-naped form from the Rocky Mountain and Great Basin region is often treated as a separate species (the "Red-naped" Sapsucker); both it and the Red-breasted Sapsucker hybridize locally with the Yellow-bellied Sapsucker.

Description
7–8″ (18–20.5 cm). This distinctive sapsucker has a pied black-and-white pattern, a striped face, a black patch on the breast, and black wedges on the sides and flanks. The upperparts are barred with black, white, and brown, and there are white patches on the black wings. The center of the belly is yellowish. Both sexes have a red forehead-crown patch; males have a red throat. Many female "Red-napeds" have a mostly red throat with a white chin; other females are white-throated. In the Yellow-bellied, there is an unbroken black "frame" to the red or white of the throat; in the "Red-naped," this frame is interrupted, and the red color of the throat spills out onto the lower cheek. Rocky Mountain birds have a red nape patch. The tail in all forms has black-and-white bars on the central feathers. Immature Yellow-bellieds are quite different—mottled and patterned with brown, black, and white; immature "Red-naped Sapsuckers" do not show brown, but are more black and white like adults. Immatures of both forms have a white mustache and eyebrows, and the same white rump and wing patches as adults.

Voice
Chur or *quarr* call given in series. Also *weep-weep* notes, *chee-aa* call, and others. Drumming usually 2–3 rapid beats followed by irregular series of double and triple beats, all within 2–4 seconds.

Similar Species
Other pied, striped-face woodpeckers lack black breast patch and red patch on forehead-crown. Closely related Red-breasted Sapsucker of West Coast has all-red hood broken by white malar stripe. Immature Red-headed Woodpecker similar to immature of this species, but dull white below; border of hood sharply defined on breast, and large white wing patch on secondaries; back usually barred, not mottled. Female Williamson's also resembles immature, but lacks white on face and is sharply barred on back and sides.

Range
Breeds from northeastern British Columbia across Canada to southern Labrador and Newfoundland, south through Rocky Mountains; also eastern Cascade Mountains of Oregon and eastern Sierra Nevada Mountains of California to central Arizona, southern New Mexico, and western Texas. East of Rockies, breeds south to southeastern Alberta, Black Hills of South Dakota, Missouri, Indiana, and Connecticut, and in Appalachian Mountains to northwestern Georgia. Winters from southern portion of breeding range south to Baja California, Central America as far as Panama, all of southern United States, and throughout West Indies.
Lester L. Short

Adult male
1. *Red forehead and crown.*
2. *Red throat.*
3. *Striped face.*
4. *White wing patch.*

   Shows white rump in flight.
   Chur or quarr *call.*

Female
1. *Red crown.*
2. *White throat.*
3. *Striped face.*
4. *White wing patch.*

Male "Red-naped" Sapsucker
1. *Red nape patch.*

Red-breasted Sapsucker

Sphyrapicus ruber
The Red-breasted Sapsucker is one of North America's most
brightly colored woodpeckers. Out of the breeding season, it has the
same quiet, secretive demeanor of its close relative, the Yellow-
bellied Sapsucker. Like the Yellow-bellied, the Red-breasted
regularly drills, maintaining rows of pits in certain trees from which
it feeds on sap. As far as is known, in most of its habits and behavior
it is very similar to the Yellow-bellied Sapsucker, with which it
hybridizes in California and British Columbia.

Description
7–8½″ (18–21.5 cm). The sexes of this species are alike; both have
nearly all-red hoods and a black-bordered whitish line extending
from the lores to above the bill. The black back is spotted, or has 2
lines of white marks; the rump and wing patches are white. The area
from the lower breast to the belly is yellow, and the sides are barred
and streaked with black. Immatures have a black crown and a
brown wash over the red on the head and breast. They molt into
adult plumage rapidly, compared with the "true" Yellow-bellied
Sapsucker. Birds in immature plumage are seen only in summer.

Voice
Drums and calls very similar to those of Yellow-bellied Sapsucker.
Chur call common, indistinguishable from Yellow-bellied's.

Similar Species
Nearly all-red hood diagnostic; Red-breasted's range does not
overlap that of Red-headed Woodpecker.

Range
Breeds from southern Alaska and all but far eastern British
Columbia south to southern California, west of Cascade-Sierra
Nevada mountains. Winters in much of breeding range, except
inland British Columbia and higher mountains; also south to Baja
California and occasionally Arizona.　　*Lester L. Short*

Williamson's Sapsucker

Sphyrapicus thyroideus
In most North American woodpecker species, there is little—if any
—difference in plumage between the male and the female. But the
sexes of the Williamson's Sapsucker are so different in pattern that
they were once described as separate species. This bird's habits are
very like those of the Yellow-bellied and Red-breasted sapsuckers;
however, its diet includes more ants. Williamson's Sapsucker
frequents spruce, fir, and pine forests, wintering more commonly in
pine and pine-oak woodlands adjacent to its breeding range.

Description
8–8½″ (20.5–22 cm). The male is mainly black with a red chin and 2
white facial stripes. The belly and lower breast are yellow, and the
sides are striped; the rump is white, and the wings and tail are black
with a white patch on the wing coverts. The female is mainly brown,
with black barring on the upperparts, on the sides, and on the
breast; there is variation from a barred breast in some birds to a full
black breast patch in others. The lower breast and belly are duller

Adult
1. *Red hood.*
2. *Black back with white spots.*
3. *White wing patch.*

   Shows white rump in flight.

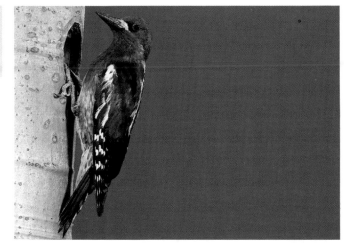

Immature
1. *Black crown.*
2. *Red hood and breast with brown wash.*
3. *White wing patch.*

Adult male
1. *Red chin.*
2. *White head stripes.*
3. *Black back.*
4. *White wing patch.*
5. *Yellow belly.*

   Shows white rump in flight.

yellow than in the male. The head is brown with black streaks on the crown, nape, and mustache. The rump is white, the tail barred, and there is a small white wing patch. Immatures generally resemble adults of their sex; however, immature males have a white throat, and immature females lack the breast patch that is sometimes seen in adults.

Voice
Main call a *chur-cheeur-cheeur* in single notes to series of up to 6, slower than those of Yellow-bellied. Other calls include *ch-ch-ch*, *wik-wik* series, and other similar noises. Drumming by both sexes like that of Yellow-bellied Sapsucker, but slower, more regular; roll followed by several short rolls or taps (*bddddr-rdddr-rddr-rd-ta-ta-ta*).

Similar Species
Red-throated males and white-throated immature males distinctive. Females on ground may resemble flickers, but have unspotted yellow belly and browner, less patterned head. Immature Yellow-bellied Sapsuckers can be differentiated from female Williamson's Sapsucker by mottling and less clear barring on and about sides; have facial stripes, show white wing patch when perched.

Range
Breeds from southern British Columbia south in Cascades, Sierra Nevada, and Rockies to southern California (locally), central Arizona, northern New Mexico. Winters adjacent to breeding range at lower elevations; south to Texas and central Mexico.
Lester L. Short

Ladder-backed Woodpecker

Picoides scalaris
Desert scrub and streamside trees are the habitat of this small woodpecker. This species feeds in trees, bushes, and yuccas, often wandering into parks and suburban gardens. Paired birds call frequently, and can be seen in undulating flight between trees or cacti.

Description
6½–7½″ (16.5–19 cm). As its name implies, the Ladder-backed Woodpecker is barred with black and white above, including the wings and outer tail feathers. Its underparts are buff-white with fine streaks on the sides and bars on the flanks. There is a black eye stripe connecting on the neck with a partial mustache—the mustache is checked with white near the bill. The nasal tufts are dusky. The larger, longer-billed males have red from the crown to the forehead and white spots on the forehead, but the red wears off the forehead by spring or summer in some individuals. Females have no red on the white-spotted black crown.

Female
1. *Brown head.*
2. *Barred brown body.*
3. *Yellow belly.*

   Chur-cheeur-cheeur
   call.
   Shows white rump
   in flight.

Immature male
1. *White chin.*
2. *White head stripes.*
3. *Black back.*
4. *White wing patch.*
5. *Yellow belly.*

Female
1. *Dusky nasal tufts.*
2. *Black facial stripes*
   not joined to black
   on back.
3. *Barred back.*

Voice

Call note a sharp *peek*, much like Hairy's. Rattle call longer, slower than Nuttall's rattle: *didididididididdt*. Also a faster, short rattle, a *kweek*, and other notes. Drums in short steady bursts, but infrequently.

Similar Species

Sympatric Gila Woodpeckers larger with white patch on rump and wings; lack facial stripes. Ladder-backed marginally overlaps with Hairy, Downy, Strickland's, and Nuttall's woodpeckers at edges of range; barred back distinguishes it from all but Nuttall's. Nuttall's less dingy, more sharply black-and-white, with outer tail less fully barred; black bars on back broader than white bars; face black-and-white striped, with more black in face; underparts whitish; call a double *pit-it*. The 2 species hybridize in southern California.

Range

Se. California, S. Nevada, Se. Colorado, and W. Oklahoma south through Mexico, including Baja California and central Texas, to Ne. Nicaragua.   *Lester L. Short*

Nuttall's Woodpecker

Picoides nuttallii

Nuttall's Woodpecker is a small, barred-backed species that lives in the chaparral, oakwoods, and streamside trees of the Far West. Only at the southern edge of its range does it meet another barred species, the closely related Ladder-backed Woodpecker. Nuttall's is often hidden in the foliage and may be heard before it is seen. It forages by gleaning, tapping, probing, and ocasionally flycatching, feeding mainly on insects. Sharply contrasting black-and-white markings make it a trim, "cleancut" woodpecker.

Description

7–7½" (18–19 cm). Black-and-white barred above, with a conspicuous unbarred black area on the upper back, Nuttall's Woodpeckers have mainly white outer tail feathers crossed with a few small bar marks. The face is black-and-white striped with a broad black eyeline and mustache extending to the black back and wings. The top of the head is black and variably spotted with white; males have a red nape patch, but this is lacking in females. The nasal tufts are white. The underparts are white with a slight grayish cast on the sides in fresh plumage. The sides are checked with black, and the flanks are barred.

Voice

Call note a double *pit-it* (like White-headed's); rattle call a *didididididi*, shorter, less strident than Ladder-backed's. Also *kweek* and other calls like Ladder-backed's. Drums in regular fashion.

Similar Species

Sympatric Downy and Hairy woodpeckers not barred on back. Ladder-backed not as black, with upper back barred rather than black and less sharply contrasting black-and-white markings; has dusky nasal tufts and white patch; mustache black to base of bill. Male Nuttall's has less red on head, but worn Ladder-backs may appear similar. Calls also differ. Immature Yellow-billed Sapsucker has mottled, not clearly barred back; also has mottled underparts and white wing patch.

Range

Resident from extreme northern California through western California to northern Baja California.   *Lester L. Short*

Male
1. *Red crown.*
2. *Dusky nasal tufts.*
3. *Black facial stripes not joined to black on back.*
4. *Barred back.*
5. *Barred outer tail feathers.*

Female
1. *White nasal tufts.*
2. *Black facial stripes connected to black patch on upper back.*
3. *Barred back.*

Unbarred outer tail feathers.

Male
1. *Red crown.*
2. *White nasal tufts.*
3. *Black facial stripes joined to black patch on upper back.*
4. *Barred back.*
5. *Unbarred outer tail feathers.*

Downy Woodpecker

Tail

Picoides pubescens
The most familiar of our woodpeckers, this small species frequents
urban and suburban parks, orchards, gardens, and various forests
and woodlands from pine woods to mixed deciduous-coniferous
forest. In the West, and to some degree in the South, it is primarily
associated with streamside trees. It allows closer approach than the
larger, very similar Hairy Woodpecker. It taps hard into bark less
often and less loudly than the Hairy. The Downy forages on the
trunks of trees and also hangs chickadeelike in the foliage. Smaller
trees than those used by the Hairy meet the Downy's needs.

Description
6–6½″ (15–16.5 cm). The Downy Woodpecker is patterned black-
and-white; some races have a gray or buff-gray tone, especially in
the West. Males have a narrow red patch on the upper nape that is
lacking in females. The black on top of the head is connected to a
black eye stripe; a fine black mustache connects with the back. The
eyebrow is white, and white also extends from the nasal tufts to
below the eye and to the sides of the neck. The back is white; the
underparts are white or gray-white and usually unmarked. The
white outer tail feathers have 2 or more black bars, and the wings
are barred black-and-white. Immatures of both sexes have red on
the center of the crown and streaking on the sides and flanks.

Voice
Call note a rather weak *pik*, uttered less often than Hairy's louder,
sharper *peek*. Other major call, rattling *ki-ki-ki-ki* series; resembles
call note, drops in pitch and speeds up through call. Various other
notes occur; young give chirping calls. Drums frequently in 1–1½
second bursts, like Hairy but softer.

Similar Species
Other small black-and-white woodpeckers do not have unbarred
white back. See Hairy Woodpecker.

Range

Generally resident from southeastern Alaska, southern Mackenzie,
James Bay, and Newfoundland south to southern California,
northern New Mexico, south-central Texas, Gulf Coast, and Florida.
Partly migratory in northern part of range and in high mountains.
Lester L. Short

Hairy Woodpecker

Tail

Picoides villosus
The medium-size, long-billed Hairy Woodpecker is often confused
with the smaller Downy Woodpecker, which shares most of its
range. The Hairy is a loud-tapping woodpecker; it inhabits large
trees in very diverse habitats, from coniferous forests to hardwood
forest swamps, and streamside woods to juniper-clad hillsides of
desert fringes. It is shyer than the Downy, and less often visits
feeders and suburban gardens. The Hairy usually flies ahead of one
when approached, while the tamer Downy will often remain, simply
moving upward in a tree. The Hairy's sharp calls draw attention, as
do its loud drumming signals. Territories of this woodpecker are
large, and an individual bird may range widely from day to day. This
species feeds almost exclusively on insects.

Description
7½–9½″ (19–24 cm). The Hairy Woodpecker is very similar to the
smaller Downy; it is pied black-and-white with a white back that is
sometimes partly barred or streaked, especially in races from the

Adult male
1. *Short bill.*
2. *Red nape patch.*
3. *Black bars on outer tail feathers.*
4. *Unmarked white underparts.*

Weak pik call.

Female
1. *Short bill.*
2. *No red patch on nape.*
3. *Unmarked white underparts.*

Female
1. *Long bill.*
2. *White back.*
3. *Unmarked white outer tail feathers.*
4. *Unmarked white underparts.*

Sharp peek call.

Queen Charlotte Islands and Newfoundland. Males have a narrow red nape patch that is lacking in females; males are also larger and longer-billed than females. The face is patterned with a black eye stripe and mustache, and a white eyebrow and line under the eye. The underparts vary from buff-gray or brownish to clear white, often with a few spots or streaks on the sides; some races regularly show bars and streaks on the flanks. The white outer tail feathers are usually unmarked. Immatures are usually streaked and barred below, and show red on the crown in both sexes.

Voice
Most frequent call a sharp, loud *peek* or *keek* call note. Half-second rattle call, *keek-ik-ik-ik* heard less frequently, 17–20 notes per second (faster than Downy's). Also *kweek*, *wick-a*, *tewk*, and other calls. Drums frequently but variably; indistinguishable from Downy's except at times by loudness.

Similar Species
Most black-and-white or brown-and-white woodpeckers (Strickland's, White-headed, Nuttall's, Red-cockaded) do not have unbarred white back; Strickland's and Nuttall's woodpeckers also spotted or barred below. Sapsuckers much less conspicuous; have patterned back and underparts. Female Black-backed and Three-toed have barred sides, black or barred back. Northern Flicker has barred outer tail. Hairy often confused with smaller Downy Woodpecker, but Downy has much shorter bill and white outer tail feathers with 2 or more black bars; calls differ, as does general behavior: Hairy shyer, flies more readily, taps more loudly and vigorously.

Range
Largely resident from tree line between southern Alaska and Quebec, also from Newfoundland south to Panama, Gulf Coast, Florida, and Bahamas. Some birds from high mountains or far North migrate downslope or southward.   *Lester L. Short*

Strickland's Woodpecker

Picoides stricklandi
Strickland's Woodpecker frequents oak and pine-oak woodland on the mountain slopes of southeastern Arizona. It works at the bark, excavating it with almost as much vigor and noise as the Hairy Woodpecker and using angled blows to strip the bark from dead trees to get at underlying insects. In Arizona, Strickland's is usually found below habitats occupied by the Hairy Woodpecker and above the desert scrub frequented by the Ladder-backed Woodpecker; however, it overlaps somewhat with both.

Description
7½–8½″ (19–21.5 cm). In its United States range, this bird is brown-backed with a brown eye stripe; blacker forms occur in Mexico. It is heavily spotted with brown below, and its white outer tail is barred. Males are heavier than females and have a narrow red patch on the upper nape; the top of the head is otherwise brown in males and all-brown in females. In both sexes, the tail and back of the neck are darker than the rest of the body. The rump is brown.

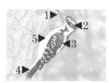

Adult male
1. *Long bill.*
2. *Red nape patch.*
3. *White back.*
4. *Unmarked white outer tail feathers.*
5. *Unmarked white underparts.*

Sharp peek *call.*

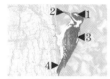

Juvenile male
1. *Red on crown.*
2. *Long bill.*
3. *White back.*
4. *Unmarked white outer tail feathers.*

Sharp peek *call.*

Female
1. *Brown crown.*
2. *Brown upperparts.*
3. *Heavy brown spotting on underparts.*

The wings are barred, but when the bird is perched, only a few bars in the primaries are evident on the brown wings. When apparent, the solid brown of the back, rump, and wing coverts is diagnostic. At a distance, heavy, dark ventral spots and spot bars are visible.

Voice
Main call a *peep*, very similar to that of Hairy Woodpecker. Also frequent, rattling *peep-eep-eep-ip* call, long (1–4 seconds), slow (7 notes per second), and of wavering quality (frequency modulated); notes longer than those of Hairy. Has other calls like Hairy's. Both sexes drum like Hairy Woodpecker, but usually faster.

Similar Species
Ladder-backed Woodpecker has barred back and spots on sides, but not on center of breast and throat. Hairy Woodpecker unmarked below, has clear white outer tail feathers. Other brownish woodpeckers show barring above and white rump.

Range
Resident from mountains of southeastern Arizona south through highlands of western to central Mexico.   *Lester L. Short*

Red-cockaded Woodpecker

Picoides borealis
This endangered bird largely occurs in forests where management practices do not require the cutting of pines before maturity.

Description
8½″ (21.5 cm). Black-and-white with barred back and wings and black tail with white on outer feathers. Black streaks and bars on flanks. Top of head black, with black mustache and white cheek. Males have a tiny area of red on side of nape. Immatures browner; may have red on center of crown.

Voice
Main call a wavering *shrrit*, longer than in any related species.

Similar Species
See Yellow-bellied Sapsucker, Downy and Hairy woodpeckers.

Range
Generally decreasing; disjunctly from Se. Oklahoma, Kentucky, S. Maryland, and S. Virginia to E. Texas, Gulf Coast, and central Florida.   *Lester L. Short*

White-headed Woodpecker

Picoides albolarvatus
The White-headed Woodpecker inhabits far-western pine forests, feeding on pine seeds and on insects obtained by probing and tapping in tree bark. It hangs on pine cones and branches and also forages on the tree trunks; most of its habits are similar to those of the Hairy Woodpecker. Of its relatives, only the Hairy, the Downy, and occasionally the Black-backed, Nuttall's, and Three-toed woodpeckers are likely to occur with it.

Description
7½–8½″ (19–21.5 cm). The throat, the face, and the area from crown to forehead are creamy white, sometimes showing a fine black eyebrow behind the eye; worn birds may be patchily blackish on the ear coverts. The rest of the body, the wings, and the tail are black except for a large white patch at the base of the primaries that is conspicuous in flight and partly visible on perched birds. Males are heavier and longer-billed than females and have a narrow red nape patch separating the white of the crown from the black of the lower

Adult male
1. *Brown crown and red nape patch.*
2. *Brown upperparts.*
3. *Heavy brown spotting on underparts.*
4. *Barred outer tail feathers.*

Adult
1. *Black cap.*
2. *White cheek.*
3. *Barred back.*
4. *Streaked flanks.*

Long, wavering shrrit *call.*

Adult male
1. *White crown, face, and throat.*
2. *Red nape patch.*
3. *Black body.*
4. *White patch on primaries.*

Peek-it *call.*

nape. Immatures are a duller, browner black; the wing patch is marked with bars or spots. Immatures of both sexes usually show red on the crown, but this may be lacking in a few females.

Voice
Main call usually a double-noted (sometimes 1 or 3 notes) *peek-it*, with quality of Hairy's call note and sharper and louder than the double note of Nuttall's Woodpecker. Also rattle calls, *di-di-di-di*, similar to those of Hairy; and other calls similar to Hairy's. Drums frequently with typical drum-roll.

Similar Species
Mainly white head and wing patches on black body very distinctive; not readily confused with other species.

Range
Largely resident from interior of southern British Columbia south through Washington and Idaho to southern California and western Nevada. Some downslope movement for winter.   *Lester L. Short*

Three-toed Woodpecker

Picoides tridactylus
This species inhabits coniferous forests, especially spruce and fir, and is attracted to burned areas and swampy forests with dead trees. It is broadly sympatric with the Black-backed Woodpecker, but one species is usually rare and the other more common in any given area. The Three-toed prefers denser conifers in mountains at higher elevations than the more southern Black-backed.

Description
8–9″ (20.5–23 cm). This species has a black eye stripe and mustache with a narrow white eyebrow and white line from the nasal tufts to the sides of the neck. The top of the head is black and flecked variably with white. Males have a yellow crown-forehead patch and are heavier and longer-billed than females. In both sexes the back is browner than the head and variably barred with white; eastern birds are blacker and may show very little white. The wings are barred with black and white, and the underparts are white with black bars on the sides and flanks. The black tail has white-and-black barred outer feathers. Immatures are duller and browner; all males and most females show yellowish in the center of the crown.

Voice
Often silent. Call note a *pik*, like that of Downy, but lower. Also a rattly *pik-ik-ik-ik*. Other calls resemble those of Hairy, Strickland's, and White-headed. Drums regularly in steady bursts.

Similar Species
Downy and Hairy have white back; buff to grayish-white or white below; males have red nape patch. Downy's flanks and sides unmarked. Hairy has little or no black barring on outer tail feathers. Black-backed lacks barring on back and outer tail feathers; even very black eastern Three-toeds usually show some white on back.

Eastern form

Range
Generally resident, but local from tree line in Alaska across to Quebec and south in mountains to southern Oregon, Idaho, Arizona, and New Mexico; in East, south to Minnesota, northern New York, and northern New England. Northern birds migrate irruptively southward during fall in some years. Also in Eurasia.
Lester L. Short

Female
1. *White crown, face, and throat.*
2. *Black body.*
3. *White patch on primaries.*

   Peek-it *call.*

Female
1. *Black crown.*
2. *Barred sides.*
3. *Barred back.*

   Low pik *call.*

Male
1. *Yellow crown patch.*
2. *Barred back (obscure in eastern race).*
3. *Barred sides.*

Black-backed Woodpecker

Picoides arcticus
The Black-backed Woodpecker occupies the northern and montane coniferous forests of the West, often sympatrically with the Three-toed. The 2 look very much alike, but their behavior and calls differ markedly and they rarely occur together. The Black-backed is vocally active and aggressive; it is often seen low in conifers or in the open in dead trees.

Description
8½–9½″ (21.5–24 cm). The Black-backed Woodpecker is glossy black above and white below, with regular black bars on the sides and flanks. The outer feathers of its black tail are white with no black bars. The wings are black with narrow white bars. The head is glossy black with a black mustache and a white line extending from the nasal tufts to the side of the neck; a very faint white eyebrow may be present. The throat is white. A yellow forehead-crown patch distinguishes the male from the lighter-colored, shorter-billed female. Immatures are dull and nonglossy; most have a yellow crown spot, but a few females may lack this.

Voice
Distinctive fast, sharp *kyik* call, very similar to Hairy Woodpecker's *peek* without its central *ee* part. Also a unique "scream-rattle-snarl," *wet-et-ddd-eee-yaaa*, uttered against other Black-backeds and other species. Variable drumming (fast or slow) in long, even rolls.

Similar Species
All-black back and barred sides of Black-backed diagnostic; yellow crown patch of males even more so; call also distinctive. Western Three-toed has barred back; blacker eastern form has barred outer tail feathers, dusky nasal tufts; always shows contrast between head and back and has some white on back. Female Hairy has white or buff-white back, paler face than female Black-backed.

Range
Generally resident from central Alaska, James Bay, and southern Labrador south through mountains to central California, western Nevada, Wyoming, the Black Hills of South Dakota, northern Minnesota, southern Ontario, northern New York, northern New England, and Newfoundland. Moves south irruptively in some years as far as Ohio and New Jersey.   *Lester L. Short*

Northern Flicker

Colaptes auratus
Unlike most North American woodpeckers, the Northern Flicker is basically a ground-feeding bird whose main diet consists of ants. It is widespread in all habitats that afford adequate nesting sites, preferring spruce forests, parks, suburban trees, and cactus deserts. This large species is vocal and conspicuous both in flight and as it hops along the ground. Several different populations, once considered to be different species, are now all treated as members of 1 species, the Northern Flicker. The eastern population was formerly called the "Yellow-shafted" Flicker, the western was known as the "Red-shafted" Flicker, and the southwestern was the "Gilded" Flicker. While they are variably colored, these populations share similar habits and vocalizations.

Description
11–14″ (28–35.5 cm). All forms of the Northern Flicker are barred black and brown above with a white rump patch. The underparts are buff-white with black spotting, and all have a broad black necklace.

Male
1. *Yellow crown patch.*
2. *Black back.*
3. *Barred sides.*

   Sharp kyik *call.*

Female
1. *Black crown.*
2. *Black back.*
3. *Barred sides.*

"Yellow-shafted" male
1. *Gray crown.*
2. *Red nape patch.*
3. *Black mustache.*
4. *Black-and-brown barred upperparts.*
5. *Yellow on wings.*

   Shows white rump in flight.

There are pinkish-orange to yellow wing linings and undertail
surfaces; the tail is black-tipped. Eastern birds have gray from the
forehead to the nape, with a red nape band that is lacking in all
other populations; the face and throat are tan, and the wing linings
and undertail coverts are yellow. Western flickers are brown on the
top of the head and gray on the face and throat, with pinkish-orange
or reddish-orange wing linings and undertail surfaces. The desert
Southwest is occupied by birds very like the western form but with
yellow on the undersides of the wings and tail. Males of the eastern
form have a black mustache; those of the western and southwestern
forms have a red mustache. Females of the eastern form are gray-
faced, including the mustache, while western and southwestern
females usually have a tan or cinnamon-colored mustache. Many
hybrids occur with mixed characteristics of these forms.

Voice
Territorial call (both sexes) a long, loud series, *wik-wik-wik-wik*,
faster and higher-pitched than similar call of Pileated Woodpecker.
Alarm call a sharp *peah*, given by adults or young. Also a conflict
call, *wik-a*, *wik-a*, and other calls. Drums rather weakly in regular
bursts.

Similar Species
Northern Flicker's brown color, barred back, white rump, and yellow
to orange wing linings and undertail surface all distinctive. Flicker is
only woodpecker apt to feed on open ground.

Range
Breeds from tree line in Alaska across to Quebec and south through
North America and Middle American highlands to Florida Keys.
Hybrids between eastern and western forms found from British
Columbia and Alberta through Great Plains to Texas. Hybrids of
western and southwestern forms occur in valleys of Arizona.
Migratory in north, birds wintering from edge of snow line
southward to California, Texas, and Gulf Coast. Southwestern
desert form resident, as are southern populations of eastern group.
A few eastern birds rare but regular in winter and migration in
West. Also resident in Nicaragua, Grand Cayman, and Cuba.
Lester L. Short

Pileated Woodpecker

Dryocopus pileatus
The Pileated Woodpecker is the big black woodpecker of our
continent. Crow-size, and with a bright, large red crest, it flies with
a heavy, undulating flight. Found in most forested areas, both
coniferous and deciduous, this species seems to have adapted to life
in some suburban areas, even nesting within sight of Manhattan.

Description
16½–19″ (42–48.5 cm). The Pileated Woodpecker is black-bodied,
occasionally with a few white bars on the sides; it has broad white
wing linings that are conspicuous in flight but barely visible at the
base of the primaries when the bird is at rest. The eyes are cream-
colored, and there is a black eyeline connecting to the nape; a broad
white stripe extends from the nostrils along the sides of the head
and neck, reaching the breast just under the wing. The rear of the
mustache is black, extending to the breast, and the chin is white,
gray, or streaked. Males are red from the forehead over the crown
to the crest; the front of the mustache is red. Females have a red

"Red-shafted" male
1. *Brown crown.*
2. *Gray face with red mustache.*
3. *Black-and-brown barred upperparts.*

   Pinkish-orange in wings.
   Shows white rump in flight.

"Gilded" male
1. *Brown crown.*
2. *Gray face with red mustache.*
3. *Black-and-brown barred upperparts.*
4. *Yellow on wings.*

   Shows white rump in flight.

Female
1. *Long red crest.*
2. *Black mustache.*

   Large size.
   Wuk-wuk-wuk *call.*

crest but are black or buff-colored on the forehead and forecrown and have an entirely black mustache. Immatures are grayer than adults and tend to be more streaked on the throat; the sexes show the same distinctions as adults but the red areas are orange.

Voice
Variable, long *wuk-wuk-wuk* series (slow, irregular, or fast, from *a-wik, a-wik* to *wok-wok-wok*), more "hollow" and slower than *wik* call of Northern Flicker; does not taper off at end. Also *waak, waaa, waan* and other calls, not nasal like Ivory-billed's. Steady drums louder and more resonant than those of smaller birds.

Similar Species
See Ivory-billed Woodpecker.

Range
Resident from northern British Columbia, southern Mackenzie, and southern Canada east to Nova Scotia, and south to northern California, Idaho, Montana, eastern Kansas, eastern Texas, Gulf Coast, and Florida.   *Lester L. Short*

Ivory-billed Woodpecker

Campephilus principalis
The large Ivory-billed Woodpecker is on the brink of extinction in eastern Cuba. Recent reports of sightings in the United States have not been substantiated, and the species must be presumed to be extinct on our continent. Formerly an inhabitant of North American forested swamps, this bird probably lived in and along the edges of pine forests; Cuban Ivory-billeds live in pines, as do the related Imperial Woodpeckers of Mexico. In such forests, the Ivory-billed finds stands of fire-killed trees, from which it strips the bark to obtain wood-boring insects for its young.

Description
19–21″ (48.5–53.5 cm). This huge black and white woodpecker has a crest that is red in males and black in females; both sexes have a black crown and forehead, and black around the ivory-colored bill and the throat. A white stripe on each side of the head extends from below the rear of the mustache area to the sides of the neck and onto the side of the back; these stripes connect midway down the back. There is a broad white patch on the rear of the upper wing. The eyes are yellowish; the tail, underparts, and the rest of the wing are black. Immatures are duller black with more restricted white and no red on the head.

Voice
Call a nuthatchlike, nasal *kent*, unlike any call of Pileated Woodpecker. Drum a double drum-tap, not a roll.

Similar Species
Pileated Woodpecker has dark bill, red or black mustache, white throat, white stripe from bill across cheek, and white patch only on forward two-thirds of wing lining. Call very different.

Range
Formerly resident from Missouri, southern Illinois, and North Carolina south to eastern Texas, Gulf Coast, southern Florida. Presently near extinction in Cuba.   *Lester L. Short*

Adult male
1. *Long red crest.*
2. *Red mustache.*

   Large size.

Adult male
1. *Ivory-colored bill.*
2. *Red crest.*
3. *No distinct mustache.*
4. *Large white patch on upperwing.*

   Huge size.
   Nasal kent *call.*

Adult female
1. *Ivory-colored bill.*
2. *Black crest.*
3. *Large white patch on upperwing.*

Tyrant-Flycatchers

(Family Tryannidae)
This is a large, diverse group found mainly in the American tropics.
In general, flycatchers perch upright, often on exposed perches from
which they launch insect-chasing sallies. While they can be quite
vigorous and erratic in their pursuit of prey, upon catching an insect
these birds snap their bills loudly and often glide evenly back to the
original perch. Most species have strong bristles at the base of the
wide bill, which is somewhat flattened and slightly hooked at the tip.
The pewees (*Contopus*) are drab, olive- to brownish-gray, somewhat
barrel-chested, with a head that shows a pronounced posterior peak.
They lack conspicuous eye-rings, but have varyingly conspicuous
wing bars. Pewees can be impossible to identify by plumage, and
thus, field identification is dependent upon vocalizations.
Empidonax flycatchers are small, erect, tail-flicking birds. All have
2 wing bars and nearly all a light eye-ring. Most "empids" are very
similar; the Dusky and Hammond's were once considered
indistinguishable. Songs and calls are diagnostic, and most habitats
have only one breeding empid. During migration, most species are
silent and may occur in a variety of habitats. Members of this genus
can be extremely difficult to identify, but by using a combination of
subtle and individually variable differences in appearance and
behavior, a careful, experienced observer can identify many
migrants. Phoebes (*Sayornis*) are medium-size flycatchers that sit
very upright, dipping and flipping their tails. They build nests of
mud on vertical faces such as cliffs, old buildings, and bridges. The
crested flycatchers (*Myiarchus*) are medium-size to large
flycatchers. In general, they have brownish to olive upperparts, a
grayish breast and throat, and a yellowish belly and undertail
coverts. Within this genus, special attention must be paid to calls
and subtle plumage characteristics; note especially the pattern on
the top surface of individual tail feathers and the shade and intensity
of color of various body feathers. The kingbirds (*Tyrannus*), are
large, barrel-chested, aggressive flycatchers with large, blunt heads
and large bills. Kingbirds are primarily found in quite open country,
where they perch conspicuously in exposed places. Several species
are quite difficult to identify. The Rose-throated Becard is a slow-
moving bird of riparian woodlands along the Mexican border. (World:
401 species. North America: 39 species.)   *Scott B. Terrill and
Richard Webster*

Northern Beardless-Tyrannulet

Camptostoma imberbe
Generally these vireolike birds are not conspicuous, remaining in
dense thickets of mesquite and hackberry and in riparian trees.

Description
4½″ (11.5 cm). Very small. Grayish-olive above, darker on crown
and nape. Wings blackish with 2 dull bars. Lores dull whitish.
Underparts dull whitish-gray, often washed with yellowish or
greenish. Bill small with pale lower mandible.

Voice
High, shrill, piercing, whining *pee-eee* or *pee-yeep*, strongest at
beginning of each syllable.

Similar Species
See immature Verdin, *Empidonax* flycatchers, and vireos.

Range
Se. Arizona and extreme Se. New Mexico; rarely to lower Rio
Grande valley of Texas. In winter, generally much more scarce.
Also Mexico south to Costa Rica.   *Scott B. Terrill*

Northern Beardless-Tyrannulet
Olive-sided Flycatcher
Greater Pewee
Western Wood-Pewee
Eastern Wood-Pewee
Yellow-bellied Flycatcher
Acadian Flycatcher
Alder Flycatcher
Willow Flycatcher
Least Flycatcher
Hammond's Flycatcher
Dusky Flycatcher
Gray Flycatcher
Western Flycatcher
Buff-breasted Flycatcher
Black Phoebe
Eastern Phoebe
Say's Phoebe
Vermilion Flycatcher
Dusky-capped Flycatcher
Ash-throated Flycatcher
Nutting's Flycatcher
Great Crested Flycatcher
Brown-crested Flycatcher
La Sagra's Flycatcher
Great Kiskadee
Sulphur-bellied Flycatcher
Variegated Flycatcher
Tropical Kingbird
Couch's Kingbird
Cassin's Kingbird
Thick-billed Kingbird
Western Kingbird
Eastern Kingbird
Gray Kingbird
Loggerhead Kingbird
Scissor-tailed Flycatcher
Fork-tailed Flycatcher
Rose-throated Becard

Adult
1. *Grayish-olive upperparts.*
2. *Dull buff wing bars.*
3. *Dull whitish lores.*

Very small size.
High, whining calls.

Olive-sided Flycatcher

Contopus borealis
A large, dark, "bullheaded" bird of northern and montane coniferous forests, the Olive-sided Flycatcher is almost always seen perched on high, conspicuous dead branches. Even in migration, it almost invariably chooses such perches, more so than any other flycatcher; a flycatcher seen high on a dead snag will often turn out to be an Olive-sided.

Description
7–8″ (18–20.5 cm). The Olive-sided Flycatcher has especially distinctive underparts with the dark sides separated by a white line down the center, giving the bird a "vested" appearance. Also diagnostic, if visible, are white tufts on the lower back, although these are usually hidden by the wings. Dark grayish-olive overall, this flycatcher has no eye-ring. Wing bars may be present, but these are indistinct.

Voice
A vigorous, 3-syllable whistle: *whip-wee-wheer* or *hic-three-beers*, first note short and abrupt and not audible from a distance; last note longer and slurred downward. Also a lower-pitched *pep-pep-pep*.

Similar Species
Greater Pewee same size, shape, and overall color, but lacks "vested" appearance. Wood-pewees can have similar underparts but smaller with more prominent wing bars.

Range
Breeds from central Alaska across north-central Canada to Newfoundland, south as far as Baja California, central Nevada, northeastern Arizona, New Mexico, and western Texas in West; in East, from central Saskatchewan, central Manitoba, northern area of Great Lakes States to northern New York, northern New England, New Brunswick, and Nova Scotia. Winters in South America.　*Kim R. Eckert*

Greater Pewee

Contopus pertinax
This rather large and stocky bird inhabits pine and pine-oak woodlands of the mountains near the Mexican border.

Description
7½″ (19 cm). Olive-gray above and slightly paler below, especially on belly, where tinged with yellow; no strongly contrasting areas below. Lower mandible and mouth lining orange. Thin, pointed crest distinctive.

Voice
Song a lazy, whistled *ho-say ma-ri-a*, with accent on second syllable. Call a repetitious *peep peep* or *pip pip*.

Similar Species
See Wood-pewees and Olive-sided Flycatcher.

Range
Mountains of central Arizona and Sw. New Mexico south. Winters mainly south of United States, rarely in S. Arizona and S. California.　*Kimball L. Garrett*

Adult
1. Dark flanks and white center on underparts.
2. Large head.

Often perches on tip of dead branch.

Adult
1. White tufts on lower back.

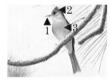

Adult
1. Bright orange lower mandible.
2. Thin, pointed crest.
3. Pale olive-gray underparts.

Larger than wood-pewee.
Hosay maria call.

Western Wood-Pewee

Contopus sordidulus
Both this species and the very similar Eastern Wood-Pewee flycatch
for insects, repeatedly returning to their perches after a sally. The
Western Wood-Pewee is virtually identical to its eastern
counterpart in general habits and appearance. The breeding ranges
of the 2 pewees overlap only marginally. The wood-pewees are only
reliably distinguished by voice.

Description
5–6″ (12.5–15 cm). This species is dark to grayish-olive above, with 2
prominent whitish wing bars; these bars are buff in first-winter
birds. There is no conspicuous eye-ring, though fall birds may have a
slight suggestion of one. The underparts are whitish, washed with
olive-gray on the sides of the breast; this wash may appear as a band
across the breast. The lower mandible is paler than the upper, and
the tail is uniformly dark.

Voice
Song (normally given at dawn or dusk, May through July) a long,
continuous sequence of emphatic *pheer-reet* call, alternated with less
harsh, somewhat rolling, 3-syllable *phee-rr-reet*, repeated without
interruption. Call a burry, slightly descending *pheeer*, or a more
emphatic *pheeer-reet*, given every 5–10 seconds, often with longer
pauses between phrases.

Similar Species
Eastern Wood-Pewee should be distinguished by voice. See Olive-
sided Flycatcher and Greater Pewee. Most *Empidonax* flycatchers
have prominent white eye-rings; Willow more brownish above, paler
below; lower mandible brighter orange-yellow.

Range
Breeds from Alaska and southwestern Canada south to Mexico, east
to central Manitoba, South Dakota, and central Texas; also in
mountains of Mexico and Central America. Winters from southern
Central America to northwestern South America.
Wesley E. Lanyon

Eastern Wood-Pewee

Contopus virens
Widespread in the East in deciduous and mixed woodlands and in
shade trees; arrives late in spring and forages high in the canopy.

Description
5–6″ (12.5–15 cm). Almost identical to Western, generally with no
eye-ring.

Voice
Song (normally given only at dawn or dusk, May through July) a
long sequence of daytime calls. Call a slow, plaintive whistle of 2–3
syllables: *pee-wee* (on 1 pitch) or *pee-a-wee* (second syllable lower),
alternated with *pee-a* (second syllable lower).

Similar Species
See Western Wood-Pewee, Olive-sided Flycatcher, Eastern Phoebe.

Range
S. central and Se. Canada to Gulf States, west to E. Kansas and
central Texas. Winters from S. Central America south.
Wesley E. Lanyon

First-winter bird
1. *Buff wing bars.*

Adult
1. *Pale lower mandible.*
2. *No eye-ring.*
3. *Olive-brown upperparts.*
4. *Whitish wing bars.*
5. *Whitish underparts.*

Pheer-reet, phee-rr-reet *song.*
Burry pheeer *call.*

Adult
Distinguishable from Western Wood-Pewee only by voice.
Pee-wee *or* pee-a-wee *calls.*

Yellow-bellied Flycatcher

Empidonax flaviventris
A relatively colorful flycatcher of spruce bogs and predominantly
coniferous forests, this species retains its yellow underparts in the
fall; consequently, it is one Empidonax that can often be identified
by sight.

Description
5–5¾″ (12.5–14.5 cm). The Yellow-bellied Flycatcher is extensively
yellowish below, with yellow on the throat and often on the eye-
ring. There is an olive wash on the breast, and the back is quite
green. The greater wing coverts and the bases of the flight feathers
are blackish.

Voice
Most common song on breeding grounds an abrupt, unmusical *killik*
or *chelink;* sounds somewhat metallic at close range. Less forceful
and less frequently given than Least Flycatcher's call. Also a
simple, whistled *chu-wee,* rising in pitch, given in migration as well.

Similar Species
Voice often most helpful feature in distinguishing among
Empidonax. In migration, Yellow-bellied can overlap Acadian
Flycatcher's range and habitat; in fall, immature Acadian also
yellowish below and greenish above, but tends to have whiter
throat. Yellow-bellied casual in West, so yellowish *Empidonax*
there is more likely to be Western or immature Hammond's.
Hammond's tends to be less yellow on throat. Western lacks olive
wash on breast; back not as bright; greater wing coverts and bases
of flight feathers not as dark; many Westerns lack bright yellow
underparts. Also, both flick wings and tail simultaneously, while
Yellow-bellied normally only flicks tail.

Range
Breeds in southwestern Mackenzie and northeastern British
Columbia, across northern Alberta and Saskatchewan east as far as
Newfoundland; south through northern Great Lakes States to
northern New York, New England, and Maritime Provinces.
Winters from Mexico to South America.   *Kim R. Eckert*

Acadian Flycatcher

Empidonax virescens
This is the only *Empidonax* that breeds in the southeastern United
States, where it is found in mature, extensive deciduous forests.
Except for the Yellow-bellied Flycatcher, the Acadian is also the
only eastern *Empidonax* that, as an immature, has largely yellowish
underparts.

Description
5½–6½″ (14–16.5 cm). The adult Acadian is forest green above. In
most adults, the underparts show only a pale yellowish tinge on the
flanks and lower belly. In fall, immatures and fresh-plumaged adults
are sometimes extensively yellow on the underparts, but tend to
have a white throat. All Acadian Flycatchers in the fall have buff
wing bars.

Voice
Song an explosive, forceful whistle: *peet-seet* or *peet-see-it,* second
syllable accented and higher in pitch. Call note a soft *peep* or a rapid
peep-peep-peep-peep.

Immature
1. *Buff wing bars.*

Adult
1. *Yellow underparts, including throat.*

Breeds in northern coniferous forest. Abrupt killick *song. Whistled* chu-wee *call.*

Adult
1. *Distinct eye-ring.*
2. *Greenish upperparts.*

Breeds in deciduous forests. Explosive peet-seet *song. Soft* peep *call.*

Similar Species
See Yellow-bellied Flycatcher. Willow Flycatcher has more
brownish-green back and no obvious eye-ring. Alder also has less
obvious eye-ring. Least Flycatcher sometimes shares same breeding
habitat; probably not distinguishable except by voice, but tends to
have more grayish-green back.

Range
Breeds from southeastern Minnesota, west-central Iowa, southern
Wisconsin, southern Michigan, southern New York, and western
Massachusetts south to eastern Texas, Gulf Coast, and central
Florida. Winters in Central and South America.   *Kim R. Eckert*

Alder Flycatcher

Empidonax alnorum
This flycatcher of northern alder swamps may also be found in a
variety of habitats, including thickets of aspen parklands.

Description
6½″ (16.5 cm). This *Empidonax* is atypical because its eye-ring is
very faint and ill-defined, often allowing sight identification.
Greenish above, but less so than Yellow-bellied or Acadian.

Voice
Song a burry, 3-syllable *way-bee-o;* accent on second syllable. Call a
buzzy, siskinlike *zshreer* and relatively loud, sharp, musical *peep*.

Similar Species
Least and Acadian flycatchers have more obvious eye-ring. See
Willow Flycatcher, Eastern Wood-Pewee.

Range
Central Alaska and British Columbia to S. Labrador and
Newfoundland, south to central parts of Minnesota, east to New
England. Winters in Central and South America.   *Kim R. Eckert*

Willow Flycatcher

Empidonax traillii
In North America, the Willow Flycatcher inhabits more southern
and western areas than its close relative, the Alder. It is found in a
wide variety of habitats ranging from brushy fields to willows,
thickets along streams, prairie woodlots, shrubby swales, and open
woodland edges. The Alder overlaps with the Willow Flycatcher in
the transition zone between prairie and boreal forest, but where
they meet the Willow prefers drier, smaller, more open groves.

Description
5¼–6½″ (13–16.5 cm). Like the Alder Flycatcher, the Willow lacks
an obvious, well-defined eye-ring, although the amount of color
around the eye is variable: in the West, birds tend to show no eye-
ring, but eastern birds sometimes have pale lores or a very thin eye-
ring. The bill is long and wide, with an orange lower mandible. Its
back is brownish-green, slightly browner than that of the Alder,
although this characteristic is often too subtle to provide reliable
distinction of the 2 species.

Immature
1. *Whitish throat.*
2. *Yellowish*
   underparts.

DAZ

Adult
1. *Faint eye-ring.*

Differs from Willow
Flycatcher in voice.
Way-bee-o *song.*
Musical peep *call.*

Adult
1. *Faint eye-ring.*

Differs from Alder
Flycatcher in voice.
Dry fitz-bew *song.*
Calls a dry sprrit
and whistled whit.

Voice
Song a sneezy, Eastern-Phoebelike *fitz-bew*, both syllables equally
accented; Alder's song accented on second syllable. Call note a dry,
burry *sprrit* or *fitz* and whistled *wheat* or *whit*, not as sharp as
Alder's *peep* note, mellower than Least's flat *wit* note.

Similar Species
All other *Empidonax* except Alder have obvious eye-rings. Alder
tends to have greener back; where 2 species breed together, Willow
usually prefers smaller, brushier, sometimes drier, more open
thickets; Alder usually prefers wet alder swamps or thickets among
larger trees like aspens. Willows and Alders best distinguished by
voice. See wood-pewees.

Range
Breeds from southern parts of British Columbia across to southern
Ontario, Great Lakes States, New York, and New England, south
to central California and Nevada, through Southwest to western
Texas, Oklahoma, Arkansas, Illinois, Indiana, Ohio, and North
Carolina. Winters from Mexico to South America.
Kim R. Eckert

Least Flycatcher

Empidonax minimus
The Least Flycatcher is widespread in deciduous forests, open
woodlands, farm groves, and towns. It is one of the most vocal
Empidonax flycatchers and it is smaller and stubbier-billed than
most other members of its genus. In the East, this is the empid
most often identified in migration, and is the only one likely to be
found anywhere except the Gulf Coast after early October.

Description
5–5¾″ (12.5–14.5 cm). The Least Flycatcher has a grayish-green
back; it may appear grayer above than most other *Empidonax*. Like
others of its genus, the Least may have a yellowish tinge on the
flanks and lower belly, but generally its underparts are quite pale.

Voice
Song a sharp, often-repeated *tibet* or *chebek*, with accent on second
syllable. Call note a flat *wit*. Sometimes also rapid chatter: *weep-
weep-weep-weep*.

Similar Species
Alder and Willow can share Least's breeding habitat, but lack
obvious eye-ring; Alder generally has greener back. Least is rare in
West during migration, but probably not separable from Dusky
Flycatcher there. Hammond's tends to be darker below, especially
on throat, with slight "vested" appearance; often flicks wings and
tail simultaneously (Least only flicks its tail upward). Fall birds
showing whitish outer web of outer rectrix most likely Dusky or
Hammond's. Gray Flycatcher paler gray above; flicks its tail
downward, not up. Acadian shares Least's habitat where ranges
overlap; probably only distinguishable by voice.

Range
Breeds from southern Yukon and southwestern Mackenzie east to
central Quebec, south to central Wyoming, South Dakota, northern
parts of Iowa, Indiana, Ohio, Pennsylvania, and New Jersey; south
in mountains to northern Georgia. Winters from Mexico to South
America.   *Kim R. Eckert*

Adult
1. *Slightly browner back than Alder Flycatcher's.*

Immature
1. *Distinct eye-ring.*
2. *Buff wing bars.*

Adult
1. *Distinct eye-ring.*
2. *Grayer upperparts than in Willow and Alder flycatchers.*

   Chebek *song.*
   Flat wit *call.*

Hammond's Flycatcher

Empidonax hammondii

Hammond's Flycatcher inhabits tall, moist, closed-canopy montane conifer forests, sometimes those with a broadleaf understory; in the far North, this species prefers deciduous forests. Hammond's forages among the branches, often high in the trees, in shade. Among western empids, it is distinguished by its small bill, proportionally long wings, short tail, and typically dusky or ashy coloration. Even while foraging, it characteristically flicks its wings and tail simultaneously in a nervous manner. This action often gives the impression that the long wing tips must flick out to make way for the tail.

Description

5–5½" (12.5–14 cm). This species' upperparts are a dull olive. There is usually an ashen wash across the breast that extends down the sides and blends into the flanks; this pattern may suggest a buttoned vest. A variable, yellowish wash (brightest in the fall) shades the belly and occasionally the throat, which is normally whitish-gray. The bill is narrow and short; the lower mandible is light at the base, blending into a dark tip that often covers most of the surface. The face, which is not noticeably paler than the crown, normally contrasts boldly with the narrow white eye-ring. The wing bars are white, becoming yellowish buff-white in fall; they contrast fairly strongly with the darker wings except when worn. In birds in fresh plumage, the narrow, outer web of the outermost tail feathers is pale gray, rather inconspicuously lighter than the rest of the tail. In this species, the combination of behavior and proportions is more distinctive than its plumage. Hammond's overall shortness is most marked at both ends: the small bill and tail accentuate the apparently plump body and large head. When combined with its habitual nervous wing-flicking, this species' long-winged, short-tailed look is very helpful in identification.

Underside of bill

Voice

Song very emphatic, most notes low and burry, without clear slides: *sebit! djurrp!, djurreet!* (sequence somewhat varied). Female's note a *heep!*, distinctively resembles note of Pygmy Nuthatch. Alarm call a *bick*, heavier than that of other *Empidonax* flycatchers.

Similar Species

Hammond's has burriest song of forest *Empidonax;* this feature very helpful in identification. Has limited breeding habitat overlap with Dusky and Western flycatchers, none with other empids. Dusky Flycatcher has longer tail, shorter wings; seldom wing-flicks when perched silently and undisturbed; tip of tail usually double-rounded. Dusky also longer-billed, appears to be smaller-headed; is paler, with less contrast, but these differences slight and overlapping. Least Flycatcher has lighter underparts, bill has obvious yellow-orange on lower mandible; Least usually shows greater degree of contrast in wing pattern; call different. See also Gray and Western flycatchers.

Range

Breeds from east-central and southeastern Alaska, central British Columbia, and southwestern Alberta south in coastal mountains to northwestern California; in Cascades and Sierra Nevada to central California; in Rockies to northeastern Nevada, northern Utah, and northern New Mexico. Winters from Mexico to Nicaragua, rarely in southeastern Arizona and perhaps casually in southern California. Migrant throughout West; fewer occurrences toward coast.

Stephen F. Bailey

Adult
1. *Large-looking head with bold white eye-ring.*
2. *Dull olive upperparts.*

   Plump build. Sebit!, djurrp!, djurreet! song. Sharp peek call.

Adult
1. *Dusky wash across breast.*
2. *Short, narrow, dusky-tipped bill.*
3. *Pale gray outer web of tail.*

Adult
1. *Short tail.*
2. *Long wings.*

   Nervously flicks wings and tail simultaneously.

Dusky Flycatcher

Empidonax oberholseri
The Dusky Flycatcher is slightly longer, slimmer, longer-tailed, longer-billed, and paler than Hammond's; in proportions, color, and habitat preference, it is intermediate between Hammond's and Gray flycatchers, although there is overlap in all of these characteristics. The Dusky's breeding habitat varies from montane chaparral to moderately dense lodgepole pine forest, including many montane conifer types and aspen. In general, the Dusky prefers drier, more open, or patchier forests; it finds a mixture or edge of small conifers and brush especially suitable. This flycatcher characteristically forages low over bushes and between small trees or shrubs. Unlike the very similar Hammond's, the Dusky seldom flicks its wings nervously, usually doing so only when singing, when agitated, or immediately after alighting. The Dusky also flicks its tail less consistently than Hammond's.

Description

5¼–5¾" (12.5–14.5 cm). The Dusky is colored like the Hammond's but typically is slightly paler with less contrast on the head, throat, and breast. The dusky wash on the breast tends to be slightly reduced, often allowing wider expression of the yellowish belly. The cheek is usually pale gray, providing only moderate to indistinct contrast with the narrow white or grayish-white eye-ring. In freshly plumaged birds, the long tail shows a more conspicuous grayish-white outer web. The second or third tail feather from the outermost is usually longest, making the tip double rounded when slightly spread. The short wings have wing bars of about the same contrast as on Hammond's, given the same degree of wear. The lower mandible is often a bit lighter but retains the dusky tip. The bill is as narrow as that of Hammond's but averages 1 mm longer; this tiny difference is sometimes apparent, making the head seem smaller. These subtleties, combined with the long tail, contribute to the longer, slimmer appearance of the Dusky.

Underside of bill

Voice

Song combines snappy, burry, and clear ascending notes: *sebit!*, *djuree!*, *pswee!* (sequence somewhat varied). Especially in late morning or late afternoon, mournful, sharp *deew, deew, deew-whip!* (number of both note types variable). Call a soft *wit.*

Similar Species

Dusky's song has some clearer notes than Hammond's; is burrier and more varied than Gray's. Breeding habitat and foraging style provide useful clues for distinction. Hammond's tends to migrate earlier in spring and later in fall; has relatively short tail and long wings that it usually flicks consistently; Hammond's also shorter, shorter-billed, chunkier, and ashier, with slightly more contrast in face, however these differences are slight and all overlap. Hammond's holds tail vertical more often; tail has little contrast to outer web; tip forked. Least Flycatcher whiter below, including throat; lacks distinctive pale outer edge to shorter tail; usually has shorter bill. See Willow and Gray flycatchers.

Range

Breeds from western British Columbia, southwestern Alberta, southwestern Saskatchewan, and western South Dakota south to higher mountains of southern California, southern Nevada, east-central Arizona, and northern New Mexico. Winters in Mexico; casual in southern California in winter, probably rare in southeastern Arizona. Migrant throughout West, scarce toward coast.   *Stephen F. Bailey*

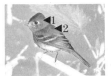

Adult
1. *Medium-size head; eye-ring seldom bold.*
2. *Dull olive upperparts.*

   Sebit!, djuree!, pswee! song. Deew, deew, deew-whip! call.

Adult
1. *Medium-length, narrow, dusky-tipped bill.*
2. *Grayish-white outer web of tail.*

Adult
1. *Long tail.*
2. *Short wings.*

   Seldom flicks wings except when singing or nervous.

Gray Flycatcher

Empidonax wrightii
The Gray Flycatcher is the breeding empid of the Great Basin tall sagebrush, piñon-juniper, and arid, very open pine woods; it sometimes overlaps with the Dusky Flycatcher in the latter habitat. The Gray Flycatcher does most of its foraging in the spaces between bushes and often flies to snatch insects from the ground. Of all empids it is the palest gray and has the longest, most slender proportions. Its tail movement is unique, consisting of a relatively slow wag downward and back up to the tail's original slant. Other empids jerk or quiver their tails very rapidly, with the initial motion upward (or backward if the tail is held vertically, as is common in Hammond's and Western). The Gray's usually slower tail movements, merely down and back, combined with wings that are usually held still, create a relatively placid appearance.

Description
5¼–6″ (13.5–15 cm). The Gray Flycatcher is colored like the Dusky, but is even paler and grayer, and shows still less contrast. The underparts are whitish, with a rather faint grayish wash on the sides and a very pale yellowish wash on the lower belly. The paler gray or brownish-gray upperparts provide only a weak contrast for the narrow white eye-ring and wing bars. The broad buff-white wing bars of fresh juveniles, however, may be quite bold. The Gray's wing tips appear medium-long. The tail is long, and in fresh-plumaged birds the narrow outer web is almost pure white and conspicuous. The lower mandible is bicolored, peach or whitish buff at the base with an abrupt, black tip. The head often looks small, perhaps because of the long, narrow, and very straight-sided bill; juveniles may have much shorter bills.

Underside of bill

Voice
Song relatively simple; first note full-voiced, second note thin: *chualup! seeal* (second note often omitted, first often doubled). Male gives aspirated whistle, *whea.* Call a *whit.*

Similar Species
All other empids flick tail rapidly upward. Gray Flycatcher's song less varied than Dusky or Hammond's, and without burry notes. Breeding habitat and foraging style provide helpful clues for identification. Dusky typically darker, with more pattern contrast, shorter wings and bill, and often plumper head and body; fresh edge of tail grayish-white, not pure white. Hammond's more often nervously flicks wings and tail; has darker, more contrasting plumage pattern, short bill, and short tail with pale gray edge; head and body plumper, tail often held vertically. Least Flycatcher lacks white edge to tail; has short bill and short tail; head proportionally larger; has more contrasting wing pattern and eye-ring. Willow Flycatcher much browner above; has wider bill, entirely light on lower mandible; tail lacks white edge; wing bars dull.

Range
Breeds from southern Washington, southern Idaho, and southwestern Wyoming south to eastern California, central Arizona, and central and western New Mexico. Winters mainly in Mexico, sparsely in southern California and southern Arizona. Accidental in East. Widespread migrant in interior West; very scarce toward coast. *Stephen F. Bailey*

Adult
1. *Small, rounded head.*
2. *Eye-ring not bold.*
3. *Pale, grayish plumage; little contrast with wing bars.*

   Chualup! seeal *song.*

Adult
1. *Long, slender bill, bicolored below.*

Juvenile
1. *Bold wing bars.*
2. *Long tail with white outer web.*
3. *Wings medium-long.*

   Slow, down-and-back tail movements.

Western Flycatcher

Empidonax difficilis
This most ubiquitous of western empids is relatively easy to
identify. Most individuals are yellower below and greener above
than other species in this group, except for the Yellow-bellied
Flycatcher. The Western's almond- or teardrop-shaped eye-ring is
diagnostic. Also distinctive is the large, peaked head with its broad,
convex-edged bill and the lower mandible that is entirely light to the
tip. This species prefers moist, shaded forest, either coastal or lower
montane, or higher in the Rockies and Great Basin ranges. Its most
typical habitats are canyon bottoms with conifers shading a
deciduous understory; however the breeding habitat may vary from
eucalyptus to tall riparian forest and firs on northern exposures.
Steep stream banks are favorite nest sites. Western Flycatchers
most commonly forage within shaded forest. They frequently flick
their wings and tails simultaneously, giving these birds a nervous
appearance like Hammond's.

Description

5¼–6″ (13.5–15 cm). The upperparts are olive-green, but worn
adults may appear very brownish. The wings are blacker, and the
browner tail has no pale edge unless it is worn. In fresh plumage,
the wing bars are prominent, ranging from white, pale yellow, or
pale buff to bright buff in immatures. Moderate to pale yellow
coloring extends from the throat to the undertail coverts, but in
faded individuals this tone may not be conspicuous. An olive wash on
the breast, flanks, and especially on the sides tends to highlight a
midventral yellow stripe. The bold eye-ring is almond-shaped, broad
and rounded in front, drawn out into a point in back, and usually
broken on top. The bill is wide, rather long, and convex-edged; the
lower mandible is entirely yellow-orange to pinkish-white. The head
usually looks large, partly because of the peak produced by partial
erection of the crown feathers. Other western empids show this
peak less often or in a less pronounced form. The body appears
plump, the tail is medium-length to short, and the wings are of
medium length.

Underside of bill

Voice

Song consists entirely of high, thin, squeaky whistles and snappy
notes: *pe-see! pit-tic, see* (*pit-tic* can only follow *pe-see!*, and is often
omitted in slow and halting song). High *see* note actually first, but
pe-see! is loudest and normally attracts initial attention. Male's call
note a rising whistle, *pawee!* (coastal) or *wee-eee!* (interior).
Female's note a very high and short *see*.

Similar Species

All other western empids have burry, rough, or lower notes in
songs. All lack almond-shaped eye-ring and strongly yellowish
throat; are never really greenish above. Hammond's, Dusky, and
Gray flycatchers have narrow bill with dark-tipped lower mandible.
Hammond's has most similar habitat, foraging and wing-flicking
behavior, tail coloration, and proportions of head, body, tail, and
wings; easily distinguishable, however, by song, bill, shape of eye-
ring, and whitish throat. See Yellow-bellied and Acadian
flycatchers.

Range

Breeds from southeastern Alaska, western and southern British
Columbia, southwestern Alberta, and western South Dakota south
along coast and mountains to southwestern California, southeastern
Nevada, southeastern Arizona, western Texas, and southern
Mexico. Winters in Mexico, rarely north to southwestern California.
Migrant throughout West.   *Stephen F. Bailey*

Adult
1. *Large, peaked head.*
2. *Almond-shaped eye-ring.*
3. *Olive-green upperparts.*

Pe-see!, pit-tic, see song.
Rising whistled calls.

Adult
1. *Wide, convex, longish bill, with lower mandible yellow-orange to tip.*
2. *Yellowish throat.*

Adult
1. *Tail lacks pale outer edge.*

Frequently flicks wings and tail simultaneously.

Buff-breasted Flycatcher

Empidonax fulvifrons
This small *Empidonax* flycatcher is scarce and extremely local in the United States. It is currently found consistently only in the Huachuca Mountains of Arizona and less consistently in the Chiricahua Mountains; within its limited range it establishes loose little breeding "colonies" in open, transition-zone pine and pine-oak woodlands. Its bright, cinnamon-buff underparts are seldom seen in the United States because this species molts only once a year in the later summer or early fall just prior to migration. The Buff-breasted has a very distinctive call note and song. The only other *Empidonax* regularly found in the same area during the summer is the larger, greenish-yellow Western Flycatcher, which has very different vocalizations. Buff-breasteds often forage from the low scrubby understory or close to the trunk, low or at midlevel in pines.

Description
4½–5″ (11.5–12.5 cm). The Buff-breasted Flycatcher molts primarily in August; in fresh plumage, it has brownish, olive-gray upperparts and a strong cinnamon wash on the underparts, especially on the breast. During most of its stay in Arizona, this species is mostly grayish, with a primarily buff wash on the middle of the breast; it presents a very drab, worn appearance during most of the breeding season. It can be identified at this time of year by its noticeably small size (for an *Empidonax*), its round head, and small, short tail.

Voice
Song quite musical but abrupt; a *pullick-chew* or *plitick-seeoo*, often repeated with little interruption. Call a dry, abrupt, short *pit* or *pt*.

Similar Species
Western Flycatcher larger, with very green upperparts and strongly yellow on underparts; has teardrop-shaped eye-ring; calls and sings with high, thin whistle, much different from Buff-breasted's calls. Other western *Empidonax* flycatchers usually have grayish or olive wash across breast, different call notes and songs.

Range
Breeds very locally in Huachuca and Chiricahua mountains of southeastern Arizona (formerly much more widespread); through highlands into central Mexico. Winters in Mexico.
Scott B. Terrill

Black Phoebe

Sayornis nigricans
These birds are almost always associated with water, especially in drier regions; they are common at moderate and lower elevations.

Description
6½–7¼″ (16.5–18.5 cm). Unmistakable; black with white belly, undertail coverts, and outer edge of outer tail feathers. Wing feathers also have lighter edgings. White belly extends up middle of breast, forming inverted V. Juveniles similar but browner.

Voice
Song a high-pitched, thin, somewhat buzzy *pi-tsee, pi-tsee,* usually in sets of 2. Also a soft single *tseee*. Call a loud, sharp *cheep* or *tsip*.

Range
Resident from N. California southwest of higher Sierra Nevada through W. and central California, S. Nevada, S. Utah, Arizona, New Mexico, and S. and W. Texas; south to Argentina.
Scott B. Terrill

Bird in worn plumage
1. *Round head.*
2. *Buff wash on breast.*
3. *Short tail.*

Small size.
Dry pit call.

Fresh-plumaged bird
1. *Brownish olive-gray upperparts.*
2. *Cinnamon wash on breast.*
3. *Short tail.*

Dry pit call.
Arizona only.

Adult
1. *Black head, back, and breast.*
2. *White belly and undertail coverts.*
3. *White outer edge of outer tail feather.*

Pumps tail.

Eastern Phoebe

Sayornis phoebe
This medium-size eastern flycatcher is easily identified by its persistent habit of tail-pumping. Almost always found near fresh running water, especially when breeding, the Eastern Phoebe is often detected year-round by its clear, sweet call note; in the breeding season its *fee-bee* song is distinctive. It is one of the earliest migrants to return to northern areas in the spring and lingers late into the fall. In its call note and behavior, it resembles the Black Phoebe.

Description
6½–7″ (16.5–18 cm). The Eastern Phoebe is grayish-black above; the head, wings, and tail are slightly darker than the back. This flycatcher has an all-black bill and no eye-ring. Adults lack distinct wing bars, however these are slightly more prominent in immatures. The underparts are whitish with a subtle, pale yellowish wash that is especially evident in immatures. The tail is rather long, giving the bird an elongated appearance.

Voice
Fee-bee, fee-bee, repeated over and over, alternately rising and falling. A distinctive, clear, sweet, weak *chip*, often best way to detect bird outside of breeding season along open, wooded streams, where it may not at first be easy to see.

Similar Species
Pewees and much smaller *Empidonax*es have wing bars, light-colored lower mandibles, and proportionately shorter tails. Most *Empidonax* flycatchers have eye-ring.

Range
Breeds from southern Mackenzie and northern Saskatchewan east to New Brunswick and south to central Texas, northern parts of Gulf States, Piedmont in Carolinas, southern Virginia, and Maryland. Winters from southern Oklahoma, northern Arkansas, southern Illinois, Tennessee and southern parts of Virginia, Maryland, and Delaware (uncommonly farther north) south to Mexico, Gulf of Mexico, and southern Florida.   *Henry T. Armistead*

Say's Phoebe

Sayornis saya
This highly migratory species is common in the open country of the West in areas with warm temperatures, a lack of dense vegetation, and little rain.

Description
8″ (20.5 cm). Brownish-gray above, darker and browner on head; tail blackish. Wings show very faint, narrow bars. Throat pale gray to whitish; breast gray; belly cinnamon to rufous.

Voice
Song a *pit-tsee-ar*. Call a whistled *pee-ur*.

Similar Species
See female Vermilion Flycatcher.

Range
Alaska to Saskatchewan, south between coastal ranges and central prairie states to central Mexico. Winters from central California, S. Utah, central New Mexico, and S. Texas to S. Mexico; local farther north.   *Richard Webster*

Immature
1. *Two wing bars.*
2. *Pale yellowish wash on underparts.*

Adult
1. *Black bill.*
2. *Dark head with no eye-ring.*
3. *Dark upperparts without wing bars.*
4. *Whitish underparts.*

Fee-bee *song. Habitually pumps tail.*

Adult
1. *Brownish-gray upperparts.*
2. *Brownish-gray breast.*
3. *Cinnamon belly.*
4. *Dark tail.*

Vermilion Flycatcher

Pyrocephalus rubinus
Vermilion Flycatchers are found almost exclusively near water, even such small amounts as stockyard puddles surrounded by scrubby mesquite. They are most abundant in wooded areas of cottonwood, willow, and mesquite bordering rivers, streams, and ponds, especially those near open brushy, grassy, or agricultural fields. As with many other flycatchers, the Vermilion forages from a conspicuous perch, often only a few feet above the ground or water, frequently fluttering to the ground and quickly back again. It frequently dips and spreads its tail in a phoebelike manner. In its remarkable courtship display, the unmistakable brilliant red male flutters upward on very fast, weak wingbeats with the breast and crown feathers fully erected, calling continuously, and finally reaching a height of 50 feet or more. Sometimes the bird drops back down immediately, or it may remain puffed up, hovering, calling constantly, or moving a short distance horizontally like a butterfly flying against the wind.

Description
5½–6½″ (14–16.5 cm). Males have a scarlet-vermilion crest that is often rounded; the scarlet underparts contrast sharply with the black bill, eye, eyeline, and upperparts. Females are somewhat phoebelike or pewee-shaped but much shorter-tailed and have a whitish breast; the belly, flanks, and undertail coverts are buff to salmon-pink, all overlayed with rows of dusky, broken streaks. Females often appear to have a blackish "mask" contrasting with the whitish throat and varyingly conspicuous light eyeline. First-winter males are similar to females but are deeper, brighter red on the belly. Second- and third-year males in breeding plumage closely resemble adult males, but are paler, often with yellowish tints to the feather edgings. Immature females are similar to adult females, but usually pale yellow to buff below, rather than pink or reddish. Juveniles may lack any reddish color on the whitish, streaked underparts.

Voice
Courtship song a constantly repeated, rapidly accelerating staccato, musical series: *pit-pit-pit-a-zeee, pit-pit-pit-a-zee-a,* or *pt-pt-pit-a-lee-zee.* Call note a sharp *pitsk.*

Similar Species
Immature Say's Phoebe may show relatively indistinct streaking and yellowish wash, but longer-tailed, larger, and never as white on breast as female and immature Vermilion Flycatchers.

Range
Breeds from southeastern California to southwestern Utah and central Texas, south to southern Argentina. Winters at lower elevations over much of winter range, but wanders widely, even regularly in winter, slightly north of breeding areas, west to southern California coast, and east through Gulf States. Also in Galapagos Islands.   *Scott B. Terrill*

Female
1. *Dark mask contrasting with whitish throat and eyeline.*
2. *Buff belly and undertail coverts.*

   Underparts distinctly streaked.

First-winter male
1. *Streaks on breast.*
2. *Red belly.*

Adult male
1. *Scarlet crown.*
2. *Scarlet underparts.*
3. *Blackish upperparts and eyeline.*

Dusky-capped Flycatcher

Myiarchus tuberculifer
From April into September, the Dusky-capped Flycatcher can be
found in pine-oak woodlands and along wooded stream sides in the
mountains of southeastern Arizona and southwestern New Mexico.
Though fairly common in suitable habitats, this bird is more often
heard than seen; in this respect it is like the more widespread Great
Crested Flycatcher of eastern woodlands, whose general habits it
shares.

Description
6–7″ (15–18 cm). The Dusky-capped Flycatcher is olive-brown
above, gray on the throat, and has a bright yellow belly and whitish
wing bars. The bill is long and black. The tail is dark, without any
rufous in the feathers.

Voice
Song (normally given only at dawn in breeding season) a prolonged
alternation of 2 calls, a single subdued *huit* and a longer, plaintive,
whistled *pee-ur*, rising slightly in pitch before falling. Call identical
to second part of song. Also a multi-syllable roll, usually introduced
by rasping note.

Similar Species
Great Crested, Brown-crested, and Ash-throated flycatchers larger
and have conspicuous cinnamon-rufous in tail; their calls also very
different.

Range
Breeds in southeastern Arizona and southwestern New Mexico; also
Central and South America. Winters north to northern Mexico.
Wesley E. Lanyon

Ash-throated Flycatcher

Myiarchus cinerascens
The widely distributed Ash-throated Flycatcher is a common
resident of open oak and juniper woodlands, streamside trees,
mesquite, and semiarid country in the West. The Ash-throated is
the only member of the genus *Myiarchus* likely to be found north of
southern Nevada and central Arizona, or in the southwestern states
during the winter months.

Description
7–8″ (18–20.5 cm). The Ash-throated Flycatcher has a gray-brown
back, a whitish throat, a pale gray breast, and a pale yellow belly.
The rufous on the tail does not extend to the tip of the tail feathers.
The bill is black.

Voice
Song (normally given only at dawn, April through June) a long,
rhythmic series of diagnostic daytime calls, *ha-wheer*. Call note a
subdued *ka-brick*, with emphasis on second syllable; also gives a *ha-
wheer*.

Adult
1. *Dark tail with no rufous.*
2. *Yellow belly.*

Adult
1. *Black bill.*
2. *Pale gray throat and breast.*
3. *Dark tail, with no rufous.*

   Whistled pee-ur *call.*

Adult
1. *Black bill.*
2. *Grayish-white throat and breast.*
3. *Yellowish-white belly.*
4. *Cinnamon-rufous in tail.*

   Ka-brick *and* ha-wheer *calls.*

Similar Species
Identification most reliable when based on voice. Great Crested
Flycatcher has substantially darker throat and breast, brighter
yellow belly, more olive back, and paler bill. Brown-crested slightly
larger, darker above and on throat; belly slightly brighter; rufous in
tail extends to tip. Dusky-capped slightly smaller, somewhat darker
throughout; lacks conspicuous rufous in tail.

Range
Breeds from Washington, Idaho, and Wyoming south through West
to Colorado and Texas; also south to central Mexico. Winters from
southern California (very rare) and Arizona south to Nicaragua and
Costa Rica; casual along Gulf Coast; accidental farther east in late
fall and winter.   *Wesley E. Lanyon*

Great Crested Flycatcher

Myiarchus crinitus
Although common in wooded residential areas, orchards, small
woodlots, and clearings in deciduous and mixed forest, the Great
Crested Flycatcher is more often heard than seen; fortunately its
calls are diagnostic. While searching for food, or in encounters with
other birds, the Great Crested typically erects its crown feathers,
peers about with outstretched head and neck, and slowly bobs its
head in a deliberate fashion.

Description
7–8″ (18–20.5 cm). This species is olive-brown above, with a darker
gray throat and breast, a bright yellow belly, and whitish wing
bars. The outer margins of the primaries and the inner portions of
the tail feathers are conspicuously marked with cinnamon-rufous
that is visible in flight. The lower mandible is horn-colored, at least
at the base.

Voice
Song normally given only at dawn, late April through June;
2 alternating phrases: *wheerrup* and *wheeer-rrr*. Call a harsh,
emphatic, ascending, far-carrying *wheeep.*

Similar Species
See Brown-crested and Ash-throated flycatchers.

Range
Breeds from south-central and southeastern Canada south through
East; west to North Dakota, Kansas, and Texas. Winters in
southern Florida; also Mexico and South America. Casual in fall in
California and Southwest.   *Wesley E. Lanyon*

Adult
1. *Pale yellowish belly.*
2. *Cinnamon-rufous in tail.*

Adult
1. *Cinnamon-rufous outer margins of primaries.*
2. *Cinnamon-rufous inner portions of tail feathers.*

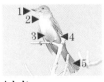

Adult
1. *Drab or horn-colored lower mandible.*
2. *Gray throat and breast.*
3. *Bright yellow belly.*
4. *Rufous in wings.*
5. *Rufous in tail.*

Harsh wheeep *call.*

Brown-crested Flycatcher

Myiarchus tyrannulus
A conspicuous and noisy summer resident of open cactus and
deciduous woodlands of the southwestern United States, the Brown-
crested Flycatcher shares its habitat with the very similar Ash-
throated Flycatcher. The Brown-crested is virtually identical in
general appearance and habits to the more widespread Great
Crested Flycatcher, which migrates through the Brown-crested's
range in southern Texas.

Description
7½–9″ (19–23 cm). This species is gray-brown above, with a gray
throat and breast, a yellow belly, and whitish wing bars. The
margins of the inner primaries and the inner portions of the tail
feathers are cinnamon-rufous. The bill is black.

Voice
Song normally given only at dawn, late April through June:
alternating isolated, sharp *huit* notes, soft *burr-r* notes, and longer
whee-rr, wheeer-burr-burg, or *whee-burr-burg*. Call a sharp *huit* at
infrequent intervals; also given in rapid series. Also disyllabic *whay-
burg*.

Similar Species
Age and seasonal variation make identification difficult without
recourse to voice. Great Crested olive-brown above, has slightly
darker throat and breast, somewhat brighter yellow belly, and paler
lower mandible. See Ash-throated and Dusky-capped flycatchers.

Range
Breeds from southern California, southern Nevada, central Arizona,
and southern Texas south to Costa Rica; also South America to
northern Argentina. United States populations winter in Mexico and
Central America; small numbers winter in southern Florida and
Keys.   *Wesley E. Lanyon*

Great Kiskadee

Pitangus sulphuratus
This noisy permanent resident of southern Texas usually perches
moderately high in trees with open foliage. Its bright color pattern
is diagnostic.

Description
9–10″ (23–25.5 cm). Heavy bill and bulky body create large
appearance. Strong head pattern with black crown, white forehead
and eyebrow, black face patch, and white throat; small yellow patch
on crown sometimes apparent. Warm olive-brown above, with
broad, bright rufous edgings on wings and tail; throat white; bright
yellow below.

Voice
Loud and far-carrying calls: clear *geeap;* repeated *fzzk, fzz-ker-
deear*, or *kis-ka-dee*.

Range
Southern Texas south to Argentina. Accidentals reported from
several southern states.   *Kenn Kaufman*

Adult
1. *Yellow belly.*
2. *Cinnamon-rufous outer margins of primaries.*
3. *Cinnamon-rufous inner portions of tail feathers.*

Adult
1. *Black bill.*
2. *Pale gray throat and breast.*
3. *Yellow belly.*
4. *Rufous in wings.*
5. *Rufous in tail.*

Huit *or* whay-burg *call notes.*

Adult
1. *Heavy bill.*
2. *Bold facial pattern.*
3. *Yellow underparts.*
4. *Rufous wings.*
5. *Rufous tail.*

Bulky build.
Fzz-ker-deear *call.*

Sulphur-bellied Flycatcher

Myiodynastes luteiventris
This large and boldly patterned bird is often heard giving its loud, unique call from sycamores in Arizona canyons.

Description
7½–9″ (19–23 cm). Large, somewhat stocky, and heavy-billed. Heavily streaked above with dark olive, brownish, and buff; rump and tail bright rufous. Sides of head patterned with whitish and dark gray; there is light eyebrow, dark mask, and light and dark whisker marks. Throat is whitish and narrowly streaked or thinly speckled with black. Pale to bright yellow below, heavily streaked with blackish-gray except on undertail coverts and center of lower belly.

Voice
High, loud, thin *squeez-zee* or *squeez-ea*, like squeeze toy; often in rapid series by 2 or more birds. Also lower, loud *squeel-ya*.

Range
Se. Arizona to Costa Rica. Rare in central Arizona and Sw. New Mexico. Winters in South America.   *Scott B. Terrill*

Tropical Kingbird

Tyrannus melancholicus
In North America, the Tropical Kingbird appears only as an uncommon and very local summer resident in southern Arizona. There it nests where groups of tall trees stand next to ponds or flowing streams at low elevations, sometimes near Western and Cassin's kingbirds. An odd reverse migration takes some individuals northwestward at the time they would be expected to move south; California birders now often find a few on the coast in fall.

Description
8–9″ (20.5–23 cm). This species has a longer and heavier bill than that of the Western or Cassin's kingbirds, but not heavy enough to rival the Thick-billed Kingbird's. The crown and nape are gray; there is a broad, slate-colored line through the eye. The throat is white; the upper chest is very pale gray, smudged with darker olive at the sides, blending at midbreast into a bright yellow that covers the remainder of the underparts. The back is gray green and the wings are dark brownish. The tail, notched at the tip, is dark dusty-brown with no white markings. Immatures resemble adults but have noticeable pale buff edgings to the wing coverts.

Voice
All calls consist of twittering trills; not especially loud, but with metallic quality that draws attention.

Similar Species
Couch's and Tropical kingbirds normally distinguished by U.S. range and by voice, but vagrant individuals seldom call. Any fall bird on Pacific Coast is probably Tropical. Farther east, wandering Couch's confirmed at least in western Texas and southern Louisiana, but Tropical could easily occur in these areas. Minor visual differences useless in sightings of lone wanderers. Immatures wander most often and may be unidentifiable even in hand. See Western, Cassin's, and immature Thick-billed kingbirds.

Range
Northern Mexico to Argentina. Breeds locally in southern Arizona. Wanderers appear every fall on California coast, casually farther north (even 1 Alaska sighting).   *Kenn Kaufman*

Adult
1. *Heavy bill.*
2. *Striped face.*
3. *Yellow, streaked underparts.*
4. *Streaked upperparts.*
5. *Rufous tail.*

Found in sycamores in Arizona canyons.

Adult
1. *Heavy bill.*
2. *Chest smudged with olive at sides.*
3. *Bright yellow underparts.*
4. *Dusky brown tail with notch at tip.*

Metallic, twittering calls.

Immature
1. *Pale buff edgings to wing coverts.*

Couch's Kingbird

Tyrannus couchii
In summer, Couch's may be fairly common in southern Texas, where it frequents the borders of woods and river-edge brush.

Description
8–9″ (20.5–23 cm). This species is almost identical to the Tropical Kingbird but has a slightly shorter bill, brighter greenish back, and paler brown wings and tail. It tends to be slightly larger than the Tropical and to have a shallower notch at the tail tip.

Voice
Song a series of *gweer* notes followed by *puwit, puwit-piweechew*, heard most often early in morning. Call note a short *kip* similar to that of Western Kingbird.

Similar Species
See Tropical and Western kingbirds and *Myiarchus* flycatchers.

Range
Resident in southern Texas; often less numerous in winter. Also in Mexico, Guatemala, and Belize.   *Kenn Kaufman*

Cassin's Kingbird

Tyrannus vociferans
Cassin's Kingbird breeds from desert riparian areas into the southwestern mountains, where it may be found in piñon-yucca, pine-oak, and even open pine forests; in western California, it inhabits open valley woodlands and foothill grassland communities. Although rare outside the breeding season, Cassin's is one of the most likely kingbirds to be encountered in late fall and winter in the Southwest.

Description
8–9″ (20.5–23 cm). Cassin's Kingbird has very dark gray upperparts and upper breast, becoming darkest on the mask area of the face; it is tinted with olive on the back. The chin and upper throat are white or grayish, contrasting boldly with the dark surrounding areas; the rest of the underparts are yellow, with varying tints of olive or gray-green, particularly on the sides and flanks. The tail and wings are dark brownish-black, the tail is unforked and usually lacks any white in the outer feathers; however birds in fresh plumage show a narrow pale tip and a less conspicuous pale outer edge.

Voice
Loud, nasal, rough *chic-queeer* or *chi-queer*, first note brief, saucy, second note accented sharply at onset, then rising slightly in volume and dropping at end. Often just *queeer;* also rapidly repeated staccato *ki-deer* or *ke-ke-ke-ki-dear*. Most calls variations of main vocalizations. Cassin's generally louder and much harsher than other kingbirds.

Similar Species
Worn or molting Western Kingbird occasionally shows little or no white on tail, but still appears much paler on upperparts and breast. Tropical and Couch's kingbirds very pale greenish-gray on upper breast; have larger, longer bill, green back, and brownish, deeply forked tail. Worn birds in early fall present greatest identification difficulty.

Range
Breeds from central California and southeastern Montana south to southern Utah, Colorado, southwestern Kansas, western Oklahoma, and western Texas; south into Mexico. Winters rarely in extreme Southwest; south to Central America.   *Scott B. Terrill*

Adult
1. *Large bill.*
2. *Yellow underparts.*
3. *Greenish back.*
4. *Notched tail.*

   *Southern Texas
   only.*
   Prreer *or* chigweer
   calls.

Adult
1. *Dark upperparts.*
2. *White chin.*
3. *Dark breast.*
4. *Yellow belly.*

Adult
1. *Dark upperparts.*
2. *Blackish tail with no
   white.*

Thick-billed Kingbird

Tyrannus crassirostris
Like many other riparian species of Arizona, the Thick-billed
Kingbird is often heard before it is seen; it calls from sycamore trees
in streamside areas dominated by cottonwood, willow, and
mesquite. Within its very limited North American range, this
species often frequents very large territories and commonly flies
great distances between perches. Early in the season, in May and
June, and early in the morning are the best times to locate this bird.

Description
9″ (23 cm). This flycatcher has a stocky neck and a large, black bill
that is especially thick at the base. The upperparts are dark brown,
darkest on the nape and the top and sides of the head, where a
nearly black mask can sometimes be seen. In good light, an olive tint
is visible on the upper back. The wings and the slightly notched tail
are dark brown or gray-brown. The underparts are generally
whitish with a bright to pale yellow wash across the lower
underparts that fades to whitish in worn plumage. Immatures have
brighter yellow underparts and rufous edgings to the wing coverts.
At a distance, these birds look bicolored, with the greatest contrast
between the dark head and white throat.

Voice
A very loud, often slightly burry, shrill *puareet;* very rapid and
rising sharply at end. Less commonly a loud *weerrr* or *kiterreer.*

Similar Species
Other North American kingbirds have more extensive yellow on
underparts; yellow or gray breast, gray or green upperparts.
Tropical similar to immature but has smaller bill, pale head, pale
edgings to wing coverts. *Myiarchus* flycatchers, in worn plumage,
especially Brown-crested, may look similar, but show reddish in tail
and wings; lack very dark head and white throat; bill less triangular.

Range
Local in southeastern Arizona from upper Santa Cruz River east
into New Mexico. May be increasing; has spread in distribution.
Very rare stray into Chisos Mountains of Texas and in winter and
migration in central Arizona and southern California.
Scott B. Terrill

Western Kingbird

Tyrannus verticalis
Throughout the western half of the United States, this kingbird is a
common breeder in almost any open habitat with scattered trees at
low to moderate elevations. Especially abundant in agricultural
regions, it often perches conspicuously on poles, fence posts, or tree
tops in open areas. It has conspicuous white outer edges to the
otherwise black tail; these are visible even at a distance. When the
tail is folded or worn, the very pale gray breast and head help to
distinguish the Western from other yellow-bellied kingbirds. Like all
other kingbirds, this species has an orange-red crown pattern that is
usually concealed.

Description
8–9½″ (20.5–24 cm). This species has the typical kingbird size and
shape—elongated but stout with a relatively heavy bill. The head,
nape, and breast are pale ashy gray, and the throat is grayish-white;
these areas contrast with the slightly darker lores and ear coverts,
which create a mask. The rest of the underparts are bright to pale

Adult
1. *Thick black bill.*
2. *Dark top and sides of head.*
3. *Dark brown upperparts.*

   Loud puareet *call.*

Adult
1. *Thick black bill.*
2. *Dark sides of head.*
3. *Whitish underparts with yellow tinge on belly.*

Adult, front view
1. *Grayish-white throat.*
2. *Ash-gray breast.*
3. *Yellow belly.*
4. *Black tail with white outer edges.*

   Often perches in full view on wires, posts, or bare branches.

yellow. The back is grayish with a greenish wash; the wings are dark brownish-gray. The relatively long, slightly fan-shaped tail is black with pure white outer webs on the outer tail feathers.

Voice
Call a loud, sharp *kit, whit,* or *pkit.* Flight song a *pkit-pkit-pkeetle-dot* or *pkit-pkit-deedle-ot,* with strong emphasis on initiation of *deedle-ot* or *pkeetle-dot,* which is highest pitched. Also various combinations of *pkit* call and several rapid, chattering notes.

Similar Species
See Cassin's Kingbird. Tropical and Couch's kingbirds have forked brown tail. Gray Kingbird larger, lacks yellow on underparts, has forked tail. Immature Scissor-tailed Flycatcher has whiter head and chest, orange-pink tinged underparts.

Range
Southern interior of British Columbia to southern Manitoba, south through western half of United States to southern Texas and northwestern Mexico. Rare but regular in fall on East Coast; winter visitor to Florida and Gulf Coast.   *Scott B. Terrill*

Eastern Kingbird

Tyrannus tyrannus
This conspicuous and widespread bird is familiar along rural roadsides, water courses, or woodland edges, and in almost any open environment with suitable perches for flycatching. It flies with shallow, quivering wingbeats and calls frequently.

Description
8½–9″ (21.5–23 cm). Unmistakable. Head and upperparts dark bluish-black with 2 indistinct whitish wing bars; white below with grayish wash on upper breast and sides. Tail has a broad white terminal band. Narrow red crown patch seldom visible.

Voice
A stuttering *kip-kip-kipper-kipper; dzee-dzee-dzee* and *dzeet.*

Range
Breeds from northern British Columbia east to northern Ontario and Maritime Provinces and south to northeastern California, central Texas, Gulf Coast, and southern Florida. Winters in South America. Very rare but regular in California.   *Wayne R. Petersen*

Gray Kingbird

Tyrannus dominicensis
This flycatcher is common to the coastal zone, primarily in Florida. It is found in mangroves, marsh edges, shrubs, and suburbs.

Description
8–9″ (20.5–23 cm). Bill heavy, black; upperparts gray; and ear patch black; mostly white below with gray wash across breast and sides. Black tail notched.

Voice
A loud, shrill, 3-syllable *pe-cheer-ry* or *pi-teer-rrry,* with accent on middle syllable; also a loud snapping noise made with bill.

Similar Species
See Eastern, Western, and Loggerhead * kingbirds.

Range
Breeds from southeastern South Carolina south along immediate coast through Florida Keys and along Gulf Coast to Louisiana; south to northern South America. Winters from Hispaniola south into northern South America.   *Paul W. Sykes, Jr.*

Adult, rear view
1. *Ash-gray head.*
2. *Black tail with white outer edges.*

Adult
1. *Blackish crown and sides of face.*
2. *Blackish upperparts.*
3. *Black tail with white tip.*
4. *White underparts.*

   Quivering display flight.

Adult
1. *Heavy black bill.*
2. *Black ear patch.*
3. *Gray upperparts.*
4. *Pale underparts.*

   Pe-cheer-ry *call.*

Scissor-tailed Flycatcher

Tyrannus forficatus
This graceful, long-tailed bird is a common summer resident of open
country in the southern Great Plains states. Not at all shy, it may be
approached rather closely as it perches on fences, wires, or exposed
branches. Quite similar to the Western Kingbird in voice and
behavior, it has hybridized with that species.

Description
12–15″ (30.5–38 cm). This species appears mostly pale, although the
wings are black (with narrow whitish edges), the uppertail coverts
and central tail feathers are black, and the very long outer pairs of
tail feathers are patterned with black and white. The back is pale
gray. The head and underparts are whitish to very pale gray,
suffused with pale pinkish-orange on the belly, flanks, and undertail
coverts; the wing linings and the sides near the base of the wing are
bright pinkish-orange. Females are slightly shorter-tailed and less
colorful than males; immatures are short-tailed, dull brownish on the
back, and even less colorful.

Voice
A hard *kip* and a variety of sputtering or "bickering" notes, quite
similar to notes of Western Kingbird.

Similar Species
Compare immature Scissor-tailed to Western Kingbird.

Range
Breeds from southern Nebraska and southeastern Colorado south to
western and southern Texas and western Louisiana; has nested
locally east to Indiana and Mississippi. Winters mostly in Mexico
and Central America; regular in southern Florida; occasional
elsewhere near Gulf Coast. Wanders widely east and west to both
coasts and north to Canada (many records outside normal range).
Kenn Kaufman

Fork-tailed Flycatcher

Tyrannus savana
Like our native tyrannids, this striking bird perches on low bushes,
fences, and wires, generally preferring open environments. Birds in
the United States often have tails of less than maximum length.

Immature

Description
Male 13–16″ (33–40.5 cm); female 11½–12½″ (29–32 cm).
Unmistakable. Head black with large, often concealed, bright yellow
crown patch. Back pale gray; wings darker grayish-brown. Tail very
long, forked, narrowly edged with white on upper half. White
below. Immatures have sooty brown cap without yellow on crown;
back dull gray; tail short.

Similar Species
See Scissor-tailed Flycatcher; Eastern Kingbird similar to
immature.

Range
Breeds in Central and South America; wanderers in September and
October to Atlantic and Gulf coasts.   *Wayne R. Petersen*

Immature
1. *Pinkish sides.*
2. *Dull brownish upperparts.*
3. *Short black tail with white outer edges.*

Adult
1. *Pale gray head.*
2. *Gray upperparts.*
3. *Pinkish sides.*
4. *Very long, forked tail.*

Often perches on wires, posts, or bare branches.

Adult
1. *Black crown and sides of head.*
2. *Gray back.*
3. *White underparts.*
4. *Long, forked tail.*
5. *Short tail in molting birds and immatures.*

Rose-throated Becard

Pachyramphus aglaiae
The sole North American representative of the widespread
neotropical subfamily Tityrinae, the Rose-throated Becard breeds in
the United States only in southeastern Arizona and, rarely, in the
extreme lower Rio Grande valley of Texas. This unmistakable
species is found in a limited number of mature groves situated near
flowing water; it usually prefers stands of sycamore, cottonwood,
and willow. Its unique nest—a construction of plant material woven
into a huge oblong closed mass with only a small hole in the side—is
hung, pendulumlike, by several small, thin attachments to a narrow
branch of a sycamore tree. This bird is relatively quiet and
inconspicuous, often remaining in one spot among dense foliage,
frequently near its nest, for long periods of time. It is rather
sluggish and moves slowly and deliberately; in many sightings the
first clue to its presence is a thin, high-pitched, wheezy chattering
that often becomes an excited onslaught when 2 or more birds are at
the nest site. Becards often sit upright like flycatchers, but usually
on interior branches instead of exposed perches. The status of this
species is unclear because its numbers and the extent of its breeding
areas seem to vary greatly from year to year. In addition, the
necessary riparian habitats of this and many other southwestern
species are now in danger of being destroyed.

Description
6½–6¾″ (16.5–17 cm). The Rose-throated Becard is a rather stocky
bird very similar to a flycatcher. It has a big-headed appearance
accentuated by a thick neck, a large, broad bill with a slightly
hooked upper mandible, and a bushy, erectile crest that is generally
not raised. The males are primarily dark gray on the upperparts and
lighter gray on the underparts. The crown, nape, and sides of the
head are blackish. The light gray of the underparts extends around
the lower nape to form a thin collar. Adult males also have a unique
rose or wine-colored throat patch. Females have a similar pattern,
but the dark and light grays are replaced with brown and buff; the
cap is black, and there is no rose on the throat. The female's buff
collar is wider than the light collar of the male. The immature male
appears intermediate in color between the female and the adult
male, often with a tint of pink on the throat. Males acquire full adult
plumage by their third breeding season.

Voice
A rambunctious chorus of rapid, high-pitched chattering and
twittering, often terminated with high, thin, rapidly descending
zeeeee or *zeeeoo;* this note sometimes given without twittering.

Range
Very local in southeastern Arizona from May to September,
breeding along Sonoita Creek and a few other isolated strips by
permanent streams. Rare breeder in lower Rio Grande valley in
Texas (primarily south of Falcon Dam) where there are also a very
few winter records.   *Scott B. Terrill*

Adult male
1. *Stout bill.*
2. *Dark on head.*
3. *Wine-colored throat.*
4. *Pale gray underparts.*
5. *Gray upperparts.*

Adult female
1. *Black cap.*
2. *Buff collar.*
3. *Buff underparts.*
4. *Brown upperparts.*

Larks

(Family Alaudidae)
Larks are cryptically colored brownish or grayish birds that often
have streaked plumage. Territorial birds that run rather than hop,
they are generally found in relatively open country. These birds
perform conspicuous display flights during which they deliver
complex musical songs. Larks have elongated hind toes and a
smoothly rounded posterior edge to the legs. The bill is rather stout,
but pointed. In general, the sexes are similar. Some species,
including the only native North American species, the Horned Lark,
are well known for their extensive geographical variation. During
most of the year, larks are generally gregarious; when flushed,
flocks often fly low over a short distance or whirl about in the air
before returning to the ground. (World: 78 species. North America:
2 species.)   *Scott B. Terrill*

Eurasian Skylark

Alauda arvensis
The Eurasian Skylark occurs in North America both as a rare
migrant and as a very local, introduced resident. Like other larks,
this species prefers open country, from Arctic tundra to grasslands
and cultivated fields. The exquisite song that is this bird's most
characteristic feature may be given from a perch, but reaches
perfection when given in flight. When threatened these birds tend to
crouch low to the ground, otherwise foraging with a deliberate
walking motion; their flight is undulating.

Description
6–8″ (15–20.5 cm). In general appearance, the Eurasian Skylark is
rather sparrowlike, but has a more slender bill. The upperparts are
brown with black streaking on the crown and back; the face has a
cream-buff eye-ring and eyebrow that extends narrowly to the bill.
The ear coverts are brownish-buff with streaks; the long crest
feathers may be raised, giving the crown a low, peaked appearance.
The wings are brown, and in flight show a whitish line along the
trailing edge. The outer tail feathers are white, the rest are
blackish. A necklace of dark streaks crosses the rich buff breast; the
flanks are also buff, and the rest of the underparts are white. The
legs are pink; the bill is horn-colored.

Voice
Song consists of pleasing, high-pitched trills and runs that may last
several minutes. Call a low, rough *trrit*.

Similar Species
Water Pipit long-tailed; bobs as it walks. Smith's Longspur buff
over entire underparts, has brown central tail feathers and deeper
bill. Vesper Sparrow has streaking onto flanks with whiter
background, deeper bill, chestnut lesser wing coverts (not always
visible). Sprague's Pipit shows plain buff face with beady, black eye.
None of these shows white trailing edge to wing.

Range
Rare migrant in western Aleutian Islands in summer and fall; casual
to Pribilof Islands. Accidental records from Point Reyes, California,
and Hawaiian Islands. Introduced and resident on southern
Vancouver Island and San Juan Islands. Native to Europe and Asia.
Introduced elsewhere in Pacific.   *Louis R. Bevier*

Eurasian Skylark
Horned Lark

Adult in flight
1. *Blackish tail with white outer feathers.*

Adult
1. *Slender bill.*
2. *Streaked crest.*
3. *Streaked upperparts.*
4. *Necklace of streaks on buff breast.*

Horned Lark

Eremophila alpestris
A black-tailed, stocky ground bird with a pinkish-brown back and a distinctive head pattern and voice, the Horned Lark occurs in a wide variety of open habitats, from coastal and alpine tundra to prairies, fields, and airports. The Horned Lark nests, migrates, and winters throughout much of North America, although its presence may be somewhat local.

Description
7–8″ (18–20.5 cm). The face is yellow, patterned with bold black mustaches and a black line across the forehead; these markings, combined with a black bar across the upper chest, are diagnostic. The amount and intensity of yellow in the face pattern varies geographically. There are distinctive, clear white outer tail feathers on an otherwise black tail; the underparts are pale. The "horns"— small, black feather tufts on the forward crown—are difficult to see at any distance. Juveniles are dark brown with spotting and scaling on the crown and upperparts; they do not show the adult's face pattern.

Voice
Song a high-pitched jumble of tinkling notes, characteristic of family; aerial and often long-sustained. Call note also distinctive, a clear *tsee-titi*, inflected on first syllable.

Range
In North America, breeds widely but often locally from mountains of northern Alaska and Canadian Arctic archipelago south to northern Mexico. Winters from southern Canada south. Also in much of Old World.   *Daniel D. Gibson*

Adult
1. *Striped facial pattern.*
2. *Black chest band.*
3. *Black tail with white outer tail feathers.*

   Tsee-titi *flight call. Prefers open areas.*

Juvenile
1. *Dark brown upperparts with spotting and scaling.*

Swallows

(Family Hirundinidae)
Swallows are slender, streamlined, aerially adept insect-hunters.
Small and short-necked with long pointed wings, these birds have
very short, broad, flattened bills but a very large gape. The legs and
feet are small, conspicuous, and weak. The outer tail feathers are
the longest, and quite pronounced in some species. The wingbeats
are not as stiff as those of swifts; swifts also have longer primaries
that can be bowed. Unlike the swifts, swallows often perch
conspicuously. Most swallows are relatively dark above and light
below; there are often metallic hues to the upperparts. In general,
species can be identified in the air by flight characteristics and calls,
as well as by plumage differences. Vocalizations consist of twitters,
chatters, and squeaks. Swallows are highly gregarious and many
species breed in colonies. They can be seen in huge, often mixed
flocks during the nonbreeding seasons, especially in migration.
Swallows nest in holes in trees, cliffs, or banks, as well as in
mud nests on the vertical surfaces of buildings and bridges.
(World: 80 species. North America: 13 species.)   *Scott B. Terrill*

Purple Martin

Progne subis
The Purple Martin is widespread but often curiously local. In the
East, it now breeds almost exclusively in man-made colonial martin
houses, but still uses tree cavities to a large extent in the West.
Martins prefer open agricultural areas, towns, or marsh edges,
especially those near open water. In the East, they form big, late-
summer roosts, often of many thousands. The Purple Martin is one
of the first spring songbirds to arrive and disappears in early fall.
Unlike most other swallows, Purple Martins often flap and sail
deliberately, and exhibit a circular, almost soaring, flight pattern.

Description
7–8¼″ (18–21 cm). This largest North American swallow has
somewhat triangular wings that are thicker and proportionately
shorter than those of other swallows. Unlike most of our swallows,
the Purple Martin exhibits marked sexual dimorphism. Adult males
are purplish-black, darker on the wings and tail. Females and
immatures have light bellies; otherwise their underparts are
grayish. The female often has a faint collar across the lower nape
and purplish-black upperparts, which are duller than the male's. The
tail in all plumages is rather long, broad, and forked.

Voice
Song complex, gurgling, liquid, and rich; rather long, beginning with
several clear, snappy, often descending notes and ending with
extended twitter something like Barn Swallow's. Call note a *swee-
swuh*, or *swee-swuh-swuh*, second and third notes lower. Also a rich,
descending, single (sometimes doubled) *tyu*, given in flight.

Similar Species
Nearly unmistakable. Starling has more obviously triangular wings.
Tree Swallow has bluish back; Violet-green Swallow has glossy
green back; both smaller, with clean white underparts.

Range
Breeds from southern and east-central British Columbia across to
southern parts of Ontario, Quebec, and New Brunswick, and central
Nova Scotia south to Texas, Gulf States, southern Florida, and
Mexico. Casual in Alaska. Local in Rockies. Avoids most other
mountainous areas; peculiarly local throughout much of range.
Winters in Brazil.   *Henry T. Armistead*

Adult male
1. *Purplish-black plumage.*
2. *Short, triangular wings.*
3. *Long, broad, forked tail.*

Flaps and sails more than other swallows.

Female
1. *Dull purplish-black upperparts.*
2. *Grayish collar.*
3. *Grayish underparts.*

Tree Swallow

Tachycineta bicolor
Conspicuous migrants, Tree Swallows are often seen in large
numbers in the fall in eastern North America; they are generally the
first swallows to return in spring when still susceptible to freezing
weather. At such times, they may feed on seeds and berries. Found
across North America, this large swallow usually forages near
bodies of brackish water such as ponds, small lakes, marshes, or wet
meadows. In flight, Tree Swallows climb with several rapid wing
strokes and make periodic glides. They nest in cavities.

Description
5–6″ (12.5–15 cm). A large, handsome swallow with wide-based
triangular wings and a slightly notched tail, the adult male is dark
greenish-blue above and pure white below. The head shows a clean,
sharp line from the white throat to the dark cap that extends just
below the eye; this pattern is seen in all plumages. The white of the
flanks often appears to extend to the sides of the rump, but is not as
extensive as the white rump patches of the Violet-green Swallow.
The adult female is duller than the male, almost brown; juveniles are
likewise brownish above and show a partial dusky breastband.
Young birds reach adult plumage by October.

Voice
A pleasing, liquid, twittering *klweet*.

Similar Species
Violet-green Swallow smaller, glides less, flaps more quickly; white
extends above eye, shows conspicuous white patches on sides of
rump. Bank and Northern Rough-winged like juvenile Tree but
smaller; Bank has distinct breastband; Rough-winged dusky on
throat; both lack clean-cut, capped look. See Purple Martin.

Range
Breeds to tree limit across North America from Alaska to Labrador
south along Pacific Coast to southern California, skirting Great
Basin and Great Plains to southeastern Wyoming and eastern
Nebraska, east to Maryland; rarely south to northern parts of Gulf
States. Winters from central and southern California (mainly near
Salton Sea and Colorado River), along Gulf of Mexico, and rarely
along Atlantic Coast (local); casually to New York area; south to
Central America.   *Louis R. Bevier*

Violet-green Swallow

Tachycineta thalassina
This bird of forests, woodlands, and steep-walled canyons forages at
great heights and sails twittering through the trees.

Description
5½″ (14 cm). Small with notched tail. White below, on face, and
sides of rump. Male intense green above, with purple or violet on
rump and wing coverts. Females usually browner above, especially
on head. Juveniles gray above; breast often washed with sooty
brown, and face shows dusky mottling.

Voice
High-pitched *tweet*, often in long series. Also a high *chip-chip*.

Similar Species
See Tree Swallow, White-throated Swift, and Purple Martin.

Range
Central Alaska to S. Mexico, east to South Dakota, Nw. Nebraska,
W. Texas. Winters from coastal California (very local) and rarely S.
Arizona to Central America.   *Louis R. Bevier*

Adult male
1. *Dark greenish-blue upperparts.*
2. *Dark crown extends to eye.*
3. *Pure white underparts.*
4. *Notched tail.*

   Usually forages over water.

Immature
1. *Brownish upperparts.*
2. *Whitish underparts.*

Adult
1. *Green upperparts.*
2. *White face.*
3. *White underparts.*
4. *White sides of rump.*
5. *Tail notched in flight.*

Northern Rough-winged Swallow

Stelgidopteryx serripennis
A light brown, rather solitary bird, the Northern Rough-winged
Swallow is widespread and fairly common, partial to stream banks,
road cuts, gravel pits, dams, and bridges. Its flight is a helpful aid to
identification; it is slower and more fluid than that of the smaller
Bank Swallow, and the wing tips appear to be pulled back after each
downstroke in a manner oddly evocative of the Solitary Sandpiper's
flight. This swallow arrives from its southern wintering grounds
very early in the spring, as soon as January in the Southwest and in
late March in many northern states. In fall, the last birds head south
by late October. Rough-wingeds nest in culverts, drainpipes, cracks in
bridges, tunnels, or old burrows. These birds typically breed in
isolated pairs or small groups.

Description
5–5¾″ (12.5–14.5 cm). The Northern Rough-winged Swallow is a
medium-size swallow with uniformly light brown upperparts; the
underparts are white except for the throat, which is suffused with a
brownish-gray wash. The tail is unremarkable, medium in length
and slightly notched.

Voice
A rough, rasping, rather harsh *brrrtt*, often repeated several times;
similar to Bank Swallow's but lower, more rasping and harsh.

Similar Species
Bank Swallow smaller and compact, with faster wingbeats and more
direct flight; has clear brown breastband (difficult to see at a
distance) contrasting with white throat and upper breast; slightly
darker brown above; breeds in colonies. Young Tree Swallows easily
confused with Rough-wingeds since they often have dull grayish
breasts, but usually have white throats and darker, grayer backs;
commonly seen with masses of other Tree Swallows. Calls of these 3
species subtly different.

Range
Southeastern Alaska and southern Canada to southern Quebec and
northern New England, south to Mexico, Gulf of Mexico, and south-
central Florida. Winters from southern California (rare), Arizona
(rare), and coastal Texas south into Mexico, along Gulf Coast, and in
southern Florida.   *Henry T. Armistead*

Bank Swallow

Riparia riparia
Quite common in much of the East, this small, compact swallow has
brown upperparts, white underparts, and a well-defined dark brown
band across the breast. Bank Swallows are gregarious and usually
nest in large colonies, peppering the sides of riverbanks, borrow
pits, and road cuts with their nesting burrows. They are local
breeders throughout much of their enormous range, owing to the
spotty distribution of suitable breeding sites. The mellifluous
scientific name, which is Latin for riverbank, aptly indicates the
bird's favorite habitat.

Description
4¾–5½″ (12–14 cm). The small, dark brown Bank Swallow is white
below, with a dark band that is prominent at close range running
across the upper breast and contrasting with the white throat. This
breastband can be difficult to see when the birds are darting around
in agile flight. The upperparts are brown; the plumage on the wings
and tail is darker than elsewhere.

Adult
1. *Brown upperparts.*
2. *Brownish-gray throat.*
3. *White lower breast and belly.*
4. *Notched tail.*

   Languid flight with deep wingbeats.

Adult at nest site
1. *Brown upperparts.*

   Nests in holes in banks or culverts.

Adult
1. *Brown upperparts.*
2. *White throat.*
3. *Brown breastband.*
4. *White belly and undertail coverts.*

   Small size.

Voice
A dry, grating, but rather weak chatter, twitter, or rattle, often first clue to bird's presence, especially during migration: *brrtt, brrtt, brrtt*. Also various similar single or double notes.

Similar Species
See Northern Rough-winged Swallow, Tree Swallow.

Range
Breeds in most of North America, from Alaska, Yukon, Mackenzie, northern Saskatchewan, Manitoba, and Ontario, central Quebec and southern Labrador south to northern California, western Nevada, Utah, northern New Mexico, western and central Texas, northern Arkansas, Kentucky, western Tennessee, northern Alabama, West Virginia, and Virginia; extremely local farther south. Winters in South America; casual in southeastern California. Also in Old World.
Henry T. Armistead

Cliff Swallow

Hirundo pyrrhonota
The Cliff Swallow is a chunky bird with a square-tipped tail that forages over water or open country, usually in flocks. It soars and circles on flattened wings, interspersing more and longer bursts of gliding into its normal foraging flight than do most swallows. Cliff Swallows nest colonially, building juglike mud nests against vertical or overhanging surfaces. At one time, this habit restricted these birds to the vicinity of cliffs and dirt banks; but today, nesting on buildings and under bridges, they are locally fairly common in the East and very common in the West.

Description
5–6″ (12.5–15 cm). The Cliff Swallow is strongly patterned; the blue-black of the upperparts is broken by a contrasting pale buff rump, narrow white stripes on the back, and a narrow pale collar across the nape. In most of North America, the forehead is white or pale buff, but in the Southwest, it may be chestnut or brown. The throat is dark rufous or chestnut, shading to black along the lower edge; otherwise, the underparts are dull white with a grayish wash along the sides. Juveniles resemble adults, but may have a darker or duller forehead and, often, white feathers mixed into the chestnut throat.

Voice
A low *chrrr* and nasal *nyew*. Song, often given in flight, a harsh series of squeaking and grating notes.

Similar Species
Juvenile Cliff Swallow might be confused with Cave Swallow, but Cave Swallow always has appearance of sharply defined black cap above pale throat; has medium rufous-buff rump, a shade darker than Cliff Swallow's. See Barn Swallow.

Range
Breeds from central Alaska east to Nova Scotia and south to central Mexico; not on most of southern Atlantic seaboard or in Gulf States, except very locally in Florida. Winters mainly in South America.
Kenn Kaufman

Adults at colony
*Nests in large
colonies, in burrows
in riverbanks.*

**Adults gathering
mud for nests**
1. *Pale forehead.*
2. *Buff rump.*

Adult at nest
1. *Pale forehead.*
2. *Dark rufous throat.*
3. *Blue-black back with
   white stripes.*
4. *Buff rump.*
5. *Dark, square-tipped
   tail.*

   Juglike mud nest.

Cave Swallow

Hirundo fulva
Having learned to nest in culverts and under bridges, this species is now a fairly common and increasing summer resident in west-central Texas, where it originally nested in caves.

Description
5–6″ (12.5–15 cm). Similar to Cliff Swallow in shape and color pattern, but forehead rufous-chestnut and throat pale buff, often forming collar around nape. Juveniles duller, sometimes with small dark spots on nape.

Voice
Clear *weet* or *pweet;* soft, low-pitched *prrt.*

Similar Species
See Cliff Swallow.

Range
Summer resident in south-central and western Texas and southeastern New Mexico; strays to Arizona and Florida. Breeds mainly in Mexico and West Indies.   *Kenn Kaufman*

Barn Swallow

Hirundo rustica
Common, gregarious, and extremely vocal, the very familiar Barn Swallow occurs almost worldwide. It is easily recognized by its deeply forked, long tail, blue-black upperparts, and rust or buff underparts. The Barn Swallow is a marvelous flyer, constantly swooping back and forth and making ceaseless turns and adjustments. Its flight is swift, with little gliding, and is characterized by a pronounced pulling back of the wing tips at the completion of each downstroke. Barn Swallows build their mud nests on any building offering overhead protection.

Description
5¾–7¾″ (14.5–19.5 cm). The Barn Swallow has a remarkable tail, long and deeply forked, with white spots. The upperparts are steely blue-black, showing more blue on the back and top of the head, blacker on the wings and tail. In males, the underparts are rust-colored or buff, there is a small chestnut patch above the bill, and the throat is chestnut; these areas are paler in females and immatures. Tails of recently fledged birds are deeply forked but shorter.

Voice
A complex, energetic series of emphatic, clear notes: *sip, sip, sip, sip,* interspersed with long, rather harsh, twittering rattle, often given incessantly. Call note a clear, excited *slip, slip* or *tsi, tsuh.* Also a softer *wit* or *wit, wit,* frequently given in flight.

Similar Species
Under normal conditions, Barn Swallow nearly unmistakable. Cliff Swallow has similar color pattern, but has pale rump, pale buff mark above bill, and square tail; call notes different, scratchy.

Range
Breeds from southern Alaska, Yukon, and Mackenzie, northern Saskatchewan and Manitoba, Ontario, southern Quebec, and Newfoundland south to southern California, Arizona, New Mexico (often local in these border states), Texas, Gulf States, and northern Florida. Absent from most southern inland parts of Gulf States, but expanding breeding range there. A few winter in extreme South, but majority go on to Central and South America. Also in Old World.   *Henry T. Armistead*

Adult
1. *Rufous-chestnut forehead.*
2. *Sharply defined blue-black cap.*
3. *Blue-black back with narrow white stripes.*
4. *Rufous-buff rump.*
5. *Square-tipped tail.*

Adult
1. *Chestnut throat.*
2. *Blue-black upperparts.*
3. *Buff or rust underparts.*
4. *Deeply forked tail.*

Slip, slip *call.*

Adult at nest
1. *Blue-black upperparts.*
2. *Deeply forked tail.*

Cup-shaped nest of mud and grass. Usually nests in buildings.

Jays and Crows

(Family Corvidae)
Members of this family are medium-size to large generalists found in
a wide variety of habitats. Most are noisy, gregarious, and
aggressive, and are therefore highly conspicuous. The bills of most
species are medium in length and rather sharply tapered but very
sturdy. In most species, the base of the bill is covered by a set of 4
pointed, bristlelike feathers. The legs and feet are longish and stout.
The sexes are similar, and young birds look like adults. The wings
are rather broad and rounded, as is the tail. Jays are medium-size
and often show conspicuous blue coloration. Magpies are relatively
large, boldly patterned with black and white, and have extremely
long tails. North American crows and ravens are large and entirely
black with massive bills. (World: 106 species. North America:
17 species.)   *Scott B. Terrill*

Gray Jay

Perisoreus canadensis
Gray Jays are tame, dusky-plumaged residents of montane and
boreal forests, well known for their habit of turning up at picnic
tables and campgrounds in their bold search for food. This jay has a
characteristic flight that is straight and direct, its rapid wingbeats
alternating with sustained glides. Because these jays are usually
silent, they can be difficult to spot even though they are relatively
common and widespread. Nonetheless, they are capable of a wide
variety of notes that can give pause to even an experienced birder.
One seldom finds a lone Gray Jay in the woods; these birds always
seem to wander in pairs or small groups.

Description
10–13″ (25.5–33 cm). The adult Gray Jay is uniformly gray on the
back, wings, and tail, and white on the crown, cheeks, and throat;
there is a distinct black patch on the nape that extends up to the
crown and into the eyes. Juveniles are distinct, with uniformly dark
gray, almost blackish, plumage; most also have a distinct white
whisker mark.

Voice
Usually silent, but gives wide variety of whistles and chattering
notes; these phrases usually short and soft.

Similar Species
See Clark's Nutcracker and Northern Shrike (only other gray,
black, and white birds in Gray Jay's range).

Range
Resident from tree line of Alaska, Yukon, Mackenzie, Manitoba,
Ontario, Quebec, Newfoundland, and Labrador south to northern
California, Arizona, northern New Mexico, Black Hills of South
Dakota, northern Minnesota, Wisconsin, and Michigan; also in
northern New York, Maine, New Brunswick, and Nova Scotia.
Kim R. Eckert

Juvenile
1. *Uniformly dark gray plumage.*
2. *White whisker mark.*

Adult
1. *White forehead.*
2. *Black nape patch.*
3. *Gray upperparts.*
4. *White cheeks.*
5. *Pale underparts.*

Bold and tame. Usually found in pairs or groups.

Steller's Jay

Cyanocitta stelleri
Closely related to the Blue Jay, Steller's Jay is the only crested jay
found in many areas west of the Rocky Mountains. This very dark
bird is common in coniferous forests. Like some other members of
its family, it is often very bold near human habitation and is thus
familiar throughout its range.

Description
13″ (33 cm). A very dark jay, Steller's is black on the head, breast,
and back and has a deep blue belly, tail, and wings. Most races show
no white or contrasting areas of lighter color in the plumage,
although inland races have a distinctive white eyebrow. This bird
has a prominent crest; the bill and legs are black.

Voice
Loud *shook-shook-shook* or *shack-shack-shack*.

Similar Species
Blue Jay, an eastern species, is paler blue, without black head,
breast, and back; has white spots in wings and tail and whitish
underparts with black breastband; crest shorter than in most
Steller's Jays. Scrub and Gray-breasted jays paler overall, lack
crest, rarely found in coniferous forest. Pinyon Jay stockier,
shorter-tailed, and longer-billed; lacks crest.

Range
Western North America. Largely resident from Kenai Peninsula,
Alaska, east to Rocky Mountains, south in montane and coastal
coniferous forests to Nicaragua.   *Daniel D. Gibson*

Blue Jay

Cyanocitta cristata
The noisy, flamboyant Blue Jay is common and widespread,
particularly where oak and pine forests are predominant. In flight,
its slow, shallow wingbeats alternate with swooping glides.

Description
11–12½″ (28–32 cm). Unmistakable. The head has a prominent blue
crest; the upperparts are blue with large white spots on the wings
and tail. The underparts are grayish-white with a black necklace.

Voice
Extremely varied. Common calls include a loud, emphatic *eeef eeef*
or *thieef thieef*, a whistled *too-weedle, too-weedle*, and a low,
mechanical, guttural, rattling *trrrrrrr*. Often mimics other birds.

Range
Central Alberta to Newfoundland, south to E. Colorado, E. New
Mexico, Se. Texas, Gulf Coast, and S. Florida. Rare but regular in
northwest. Often withdraws in winter from northern parts of
range.   *Wayne R. Petersen*

Inland race
1. *Long black crest.*
2. *White eyebrow.*
3. *Black breast.*
4. *Black back.*
5. *Deep blue wings, belly, and tail.*

   Shook-shook-shook call.

Coastal race
1. *No white eyebrow.*

Adult
1. *Blue crest.*
2. *Black necklace.*
3. *Blue upperparts.*
4. *White spots on wings.*
5. *Long blue tail with white tips.*

   Only jay in most of East.

Green Jay

Cyanocorax yncas
This flashy bird enters our range in southern Texas, where it is
fairly common. This species can be inconspicuous; some of its varied
calls are rather soft, and it often slips quietly through the trees.

Description
12″ (30.5 cm). Dark olive-green on back and wings; pale lime-green
below. Crown, nape, and patch below eye dull purplish-blue. Black
bib on throat and chest extends to side of neck, connecting with
black spot above eye. Tail dark blue-green with bright yellow outer
feathers, fairly long; rounded. Immature slightly duller.

Voice
Quite variable. Most calls involve repetition of a single element,
such as *chi-chi-chi-chi-chih* or *shink, shink, shink,* or double notes
such as *beedle-beedle.* Also dry rattles, and a short, low "snore."

Range
Widespread in tropics, extending north into southern Texas.
Kenn Kaufman

Brown Jay

Cyanocorax morio
Larger and louder than other North American jays, these birds live
in small flocks or family parties in the dense woods along the Rio
Grande. Often silent when foraging, flocks call in shrill, piercing
voices, pumping their tails as they fly with deep wingbeats.

Description
14–18″ (35.5–45.5 cm). Large, long-tailed, and heavy-billed; mostly
dusky brown, more blackish on head, paling to dull whitish on lower
breast and belly. Bill black in adults, yellow in immatures. This jay's
size and shape make it distinctive.

Voice
Common call a shrill, explosive *pow!* or *kreeow!*, higher than Blue
Jay's.

Range
In North America, found only in S. Texas, where recently resident
in limited area along Rio Grande below Falcon Dam. Also from Ne.
Mexico to Panama.   *Kenn Kaufman*

Scrub Jay

Aphelocoma coerulescens
Scrub Jays appear slimmer than most other jays and have long,
narrow tails. Their contrasting plumage pattern is distinctive. These
jays inhabit a variety of brushy areas from chaparral, open
woodlands, and residential areas in the Pacific States to piñon-
juniper and scrub-oak in the interior West and humid scrub-oak
communities in Florida. Scrub Jays often fly long distances from one
conspicuous perch to another. Their flight involves vigorous
flapping, frequently interrupted as the bird drops in a shallow arc on
stiffly spread wings and tail or on closed wings.

Description
11–13″ (28–33 cm). There is a fair amount of geographical variation
in this crestless species; differences in size and in the shade and
extent of blue occur on the upperparts and underparts. The
upperparts, including the wings and tail, are a rich, deep blue,
except for the back, which is a contrasting brown to gray-brown.
The throat and upper breast are whitish with narrow, bluish

Adult
1. Blue-and-black head pattern.
2. Olive-green upperparts.
3. Yellow outer tail feathers.
4. Black bib and pale green underparts.

South Texas only.

Adult
1. Blackish head.
2. Brown upperparts.
3. Whitish underparts.
4. Long tail.

South Texas only.
Kreeow *call.*

Dull-colored race
1. Blue upperparts.
2. Gray-brown back.
3. Whitish throat and upper breast with diffuse blue-gray necklace.
4. Gray underparts.

Harsh ike-ike-ike *call.*

streaking, boldly separated from the gray underparts by a jagged, blue to blue-gray necklace; this necklace may be diffuse and incomplete, depending on race. The undertail coverts are whitish to bluish, varying among the subspecies.

Voice
A very harsh, often-repeated *ike-ike-ike,* with slight upward inflection; longer, rough, slightly metallic, sharply rising *iennk;* rough, rapidly repeated *quick-quick-quick;* also several usually raucous variations.

Similar Species
Gray-breasted Jay stouter, usually shows less contrast and duller coloring; mask paler; lacks white eyebrow, white on throat, and bluish necklace. Immature Gray-breasted stouter, with shorter, less rounded tail. Calls and habitats different.

Range
Resident from southwestern Washington to southwestern Wyoming and Colorado, south to Baja California, central Texas, and into southern Mexico. Also isolated populations on Santa Cruz Island off California, and in central Florida.   *Scott B. Terrill*

Gray-breasted Jay

Aphelocoma ultramarina
This common, highly social jay is frequently found in evergreen oak woodlands, pine-oak, and adjacent riparian forest.

Description
11½–13″ (29–33 cm). Heavy, crestless, with strongly rounded tail. Deep blue above with dark lores and ear coverts. Back is grayish-brown. Gray below with whitish mid-belly and undertail coverts and grayish-white throat with narrow, indistinct gray streaking. Base of bill black. Immatures browner and grayer above, dingy below.

Voice
A varying *rink, wink, renk, drenk, yink, jink,* or *zink,* with slightly different inflections, usually ascending (*inks*) or flat in pitch (*drenk*).

Similar Species
See Scrub Jay.

Range
Resident from central and Se. Arizona, Sw. New Mexico, and S. trans-Pecos Texas through mountains to Mexico.   *Scott B. Terrill*

Pinyon Jay

Gymnorhinus cyanocephalus
This highly gregarious bird of piñon-juniper woodlands is also found in open forests of yellow pines in the interior mountains of the West.

Description
9–11½″ (23–29 cm). Stout, rounded, with short, rounded wings, short tail, and long, pointed bill. Dull blue to grayish-blue above and below, blue often deepest on head, paler on underparts; lores dark. Throat grayish-white, lightly streaked with blue.

Voice
Common call a high, descending, nasal, crowlike *caw-ah.* Other calls include various mewing, chattering, and cawing notes.

Similar Species
See Clark's Nutcracker.

Range
Resident from central Oregon and Montana to Baja California, central Arizona, New Mexico, and extreme Nw. Oklahoma. Erratic dispersal to outlying regions.   *Scott B. Terrill*

Brightly colored race
1. *Blue upperparts.*
2. *Gray back.*
3. *Whitish throat and upper breast with bold blue necklace.*
4. *Gray underparts.*

Adult
1. *Blue upperparts.*
2. *Gray underparts without necklace.*
3. *Dark ear coverts.*

Renk *or* wink *call.*

Adult
1. *Long, pointed bill.*
2. *Uniformly dull blue plumage.*
3. *Short, square tail.*

Usually travels in large, noisy flocks.

Clark's Nutcracker

Nucifraga columbiana
Clark's Nutcracker appears to be a sort of combination of
woodpecker and crow. Like a woodpecker, this species has a long,
stout, pointed bill that it uses to open pine seeds, its favorite food.
Like a crow, this bird is noisy, gregarious, bold, and intelligently
wary of man. Nutcrackers often walk like crows and are sometimes
seen pilfering food scraps at tourist overlooks in the high mountain
parks of the West. Commonly found near timberline along the crests
of higher mountains, these birds are often seen in small groups
perched on bare snags, breaking the silence with their harsh,
grating calls. Nutcrackers are residents of the mountains;
occasionally, in fall and winter, small bands or individuals move
away from the breeding grounds to the lowlands or lower
mountains, where they may sometimes remain until the following
summer.

Description
12–13″ (30.5–33 cm). Clark's Nutcracker is a stout, ash-gray bird
about the size and shape of a Common Flicker. The glossy black
wings show a large white patch in the secondaries; the tail is white
with black central feathers. The forehead, throat, and undertail
coverts are white. The bill is long, heavy, pointed, and black; the
eyes and legs are also black. Young birds are browner and duller
with brownish-tipped wing coverts.

Voice
A harsh, loud, throaty *kra-a-a.*

Similar Species
Gray Jay, Northern Mockingbird, and shrikes have similar
coloration, but are smaller, longer-tailed, shorter-billed. Pinyon Jay
very similar in shape, but smaller and essentially all blue.

Range
Mountains of southern Canada and western United States (central
British Columbia, western Colorado, and northern Baja California).
Occasional invasions during nonbreeding season to lower mountains
and lowlands beyond breeding range, into central Alaska, Pacific
Coast to southern California, western Great Lakes, and upper
Mississippi River valley.   *Louis R. Bevier*

Black-billed Magpie

Pica pica
These highly social birds are omnivorous scavengers; they are
common in open country over much of their range.

Description
18–22″ (45.5–56 cm). Black above and white below, with a white
wing patch and scapulars and grayish-white band on rump. Bill and
legs black (but much racial variation; some birds noted with
yellowish bill). Wings have blue gloss. Tail long; looks graduated
when fanned.

Voice
High, inquisitive *mahg?;* also *chek-chek-chek* or *wenk-wenk-wenk.*

Similar Species
See Yellow-billed Magpie.

Range
Resident from S. central Alaska and W. Canada to Ne. and extreme
E. central California, east to central Great Plains. Casual north and
east of range in fall and winter.   *Larry R. Ballard*

Adult
1. Long, pointed bill.
2. Ash-gray head and body.
3. Black wings.

Stout build.

Adult in flight
1. White patch on trailing edge of black wings.
2. White tail with black central feathers.

Harsh kra-a-a *call.*

Adult
1. Black bill.
2. Black head and breast.
3. White scapulars.
4. White belly.
5. Long black tail.
6. White patches in wings.

Large size.

Yellow-billed Magpie

Pica nuttalli
The conspicuous differences between the 2 magpies are the yellow
on the bill and the patch of bare, yellow skin below and just behind
the eyes of the Yellow-billed. This species is found only in
California, where it is a permanent resident.

Description
17–21″ (43–53.5 cm). Identical in plumage to the Black-billed but
generally smaller. The bill and a bare patch of skin below the back of
the eyes are yellow. Juveniles may show a grayish-yellow bill.

Voice
Identical to Black-billed Magpie's.

Range
Resident in Central Valley of California and adjacent foothills, also
inland valleys and foothills of Coast Ranges from Santa Clara
County south to northern Santa Barbara County. Local on coast,
casual north and south of range.   *Larry R. Ballard*

American Crow

Corvus brachyrhynchos
This distinctive, familiar, gregarious bird is most often found in open
and semi-open habitats. It is common in much of its range.

Description
17–21″ (43–53.5 cm). Entirely black, with a slight purplish gloss.
The tail is squared, and the large bill and the legs are black.

Voice
Call a distinctive *caw* or *cah*, given singly or in series. Young birds
often sound more nasal, more like Fish Crow.

Similar Species
See other crows; also Chihuahuan and Common ravens.

Range
Breeds from north-central British Columbia, central Quebec, and
Newfoundland south to Baja California, central Arizona, Colorado,
eastern Texas, and southern Florida. Winters north to southern
Canada. Rare or absent in parts of interior Southwest; more
widespread there in winter.   *Paul Lehman*

Northwestern Crow

Corvus caurinus
This is the common crow of the Northwest Coast; on the coast of
British Columbia and Alaska, it is the only crow one may expect to
see.

Description
17″ (43 cm). All-black, with a dull violet gloss above. Smaller and
slimmer than American Crow, with slim bill and small feet.

Voice
Common call a hoarse *caar*, and a series of 3–7 *cahs*. Also gurgling
and churring sounds and a rapid, low *cowp, cowp, cowp.*

Similar Species
American Crow larger, has slower wingbeat and different voice;
overlaps only in parts of lower Washington State and British
Columbia, mostly in late fall and winter.

Range
Pacific Coast from Puget Sound to S. Alaska.   *David Stirling*

Adult
1. *Yellow bill.*
2. *Black head and breast.*
3. *White scapulars.*
4. *White belly.*
5. *Long black tail.*

Large size. Shows white wing patches in flight.

Adult
1. *Wholly black plumage.*

Large size. Caw or cah call. Often seen in flocks.

Adult
1. *Wholly black plumage.*

Slender build. Hoarse caar call. Wingbeats faster than American Crow's.

Mexican Crow

Corvus imparatus
First recorded in the United States in 1968, this small, bass-voiced,
sociable crow now crosses the border regularly to visit the
Brownsville dump and other points in extreme southern Texas.

Description
14½–16″ (37–40.5 cm). Entirely black, with strong purple or
purplish-green reflections. Smaller than our other crows.

Voice
A croaking *urf* or *unk-unk*, much lower pitched and less nasal than
Fish Crow's call; quieter than most corvids in general.

Similar Species
American Crow accidental in range; has different voice. Chihuahuan
Raven larger, has heavier bill, more wedge-shaped tail, different
call. Compare adult male Great-tailed Grackle in molt.

Range
Visits S. Texas, mostly late August to March. Native to Ne.
Mexico.   *Kenn Kaufman*

Fish Crow

Corvus ossifragus
Usually associated with tidewater areas, the Fish Crow haunts
waterbird colonies, dumps, and islands as well as larger river
systems.

Description
16–20″ (40.5–51 cm). Nearly identical to American Crow; all-black
with a strong bill and feet; may appear glossy purplish-black.

Voice
Typical call a 2-toned, nasal *ca-hah*, second part lower and weaker.
Also a short, nasal *ca* or *car*, usually repeated 3–7 times.

Similar Species
American Crow only reliably distinguished by less nasal voice.

Range
S. New England to Florida, west to extreme E. Texas. Expanding
into interior. Also E. Oklahoma and along Mississippi River
drainage from S. Illinois south. Withdraws somewhat from
northern range in winter.   *Henry T. Armistead*

Chihuahuan Raven

Corvus cryptoleucus
This small raven lives in open, arid grasslands that are often
interspersed with yucca, mesquite, and cactus. The Chihuahuan is
difficult to distinguish from the larger Common Raven, and great
care is usually necessary to identify it. Chihuahuans are much more
gregarious than Common Ravens, often occurring in flocks of up to
hundreds of birds, primarily during the nonbreeding season. These
larger flocks frequently soar high into the air on thermals.
Chihuahuans prefer feed lots, agricultural areas, and areas with
water.

Description
19–21″ (48.5–53.5 cm). The Chihuahuan is a crow-size, all-black
raven with a slightly wedge-shaped tail; the large black bill has a
deep base and a curved culmen. The feathers on the neck and the
underparts are white at the base; this white feathering is diagnostic
but usually not visible. Occasionally the neck feathers are erected by
displaying birds, making the white obvious.

Adult
1. *Glossy purplish-black plumage.*

Small size.
Urf *or* unk-unk *call.*
Almost always in flocks.
South Texas only.

Adult
1. *Wholly black plumage.*

Small size.
Nasal ca-hah *call.*
Usually found in tidal areas or along rivers.
Often soars and glides in circles.

Adult
1. *Wholly black plumage.*
2. *Stout bill.*

Large size.
Flat kraaak *call.*
Often found in large flocks.
Prefers flat, open grasslands.

Voice
A hoarse, flat *kraaak* or *crack*, with most notes on same pitch.

Similar Species
Common Raven nearly identical; differences between 2 species
subtle and difficult to detect. In general, Common Raven larger;
lacks white feathers in neck; has larger bill and larger tail with more
clearly wedge-shaped outline. Common Raven also has slightly
longer wingspread relative to body length; flies with slightly slower
wingbeats. These birds best distinguished by calls: Common Raven's
a low, hoarse *crouk*, accompanied by other, higher pitched calls;
Chihuahuan's never as low, and lacks variation. Chihuahuan prefers
flatter more open, grassy areas; Common Raven more often in
rockier desert and mountain canyons. Common Crow square-tailed,
with thinner bill and different call; rarely overlaps in range.

Range
Southeastern Arizona, southern and eastern New Mexico,
southeastern Colorado, southern Nebraska, and western Kansas
south to central Mexico. Partly migratory in northern portion of
range.   *Scott B. Terrill*

Common Raven

Corvus corax
The Common Raven is a large, all-black bird similar to the Common
Crow. Though it is much larger and heavier than a crow, this
difference may be difficult to discern at a distance. The raven's
longer wings and long, wedge-shaped or rounded tail further
distinguish it from the crow, which has a shorter, more squared tail.
The bill of the Common Raven is huge, very deep at the base, and
relatively much larger than the crow's. The Raven's neck feathers
are pointed, giving it a distinctively shaggy appearance. Common
Ravens are amazing aerial acrobats, soaring, tumbling, rolling, and
even chasing hawks and eagles. These birds are omnivorous, and
seem to be especially fond of carrion; they are often seen over and
along highways searching for and feeding on road kills. This species
is found in a wide variety of habitats, including rocky seacoasts,
steep canyons, dense boreal forests, foothills, mountains (even at
altitudes above timberline), deserts, and Arctic tundra. Common
Ravens are usually seen singly, in pairs, or in small groups.

Description
21½–27″ (54.5–68.5 cm). This is a large black bird with a glossy,
metallic sheen to its plumage. It is stocky and rounded, with a thick
neck, a large head, and a large, very deep black bill. The legs are
thick, stocky, and black. The throat feathers are long and pointed,
creating a shaggy appearance. In flight, the wings appear long,
broad, and rounded at the tip rather than pointed; the large, wide
tail is long and wedge-shaped or rounded.

Voice
Very hoarse, low-pitched, croaking notes: *crock* and *quak*.

Similar Species
See Chihuahuan Raven. Common Crow much smaller, with
relatively smaller bill, shorter, squared tail, and very different call;
flies on rather continuous, relatively faster, rolling wingbeats.

Range
In New World, from Arctic Alaska across Canada to Greenland,
south through western United States and Mexico to Nicaragua; in
eastern United States, found in Maine, western Great Lakes region,
Adirondacks, and Appalachians. Also throughout Old World and
Southern Hemisphere.   *Scott B. Terrill*

Jays and Crows

  323

In flight
1. Black plumage.
2. Long, rounded wings.
3. Short, wedge-shaped or rounded tail.

Wingbeats faster than Common Raven's.

Adult in flight
1. Black plumage.
2. Long, rounded wings.
3. Long, wedge-shaped or rounded tail.

Wingbeats slower than Chihuahuan Raven's.

Adult
1. Wholly black plumage.
2. Very large bill.

Large size. Low crock call. Usually found singly or in pairs. Found in mountains, forests, or deserts.

Titmice

(Family Paridae)
Parids are small, very rotund birds with soft fluffy plumage and small, thin bills. They are extremely active, feeding and calling constantly, often in groups that move continuously through wooded areas. Members of this family are acrobatic generalists. The sexes and age classes are similar. Most have longish but not generous tails and very rounded wings. Their flight is often rather weak and jerky. Chickadees all have dark crowns and bibs that contrast sharply with white cheeks. Titmice are generally uniformly grayish birds with conspicuous crests. Most species appear relatively fearless to the presence of observers. In fact, they will react readily to spishing, squeaking, or owl calls, often approaching the source of the sound quite closely; they also often visit feeding stations. Titmice and chickadees have loud, similar, but specific vocalizations that they give frequently. Flocks of these birds form the nucleus of interspecific winter flocks. All titmice nest in cavities. (World: 47 species. North America: 10 species.)   *Scott B. Terrill*

Black-capped Chickadee

Parus atricapillus
This small, common songbird inhabits mixed and deciduous woodlands, thickets, and orchards.

Description
5¾" (14.5 cm). Cap and bib black; bib has ragged lower edge. Cheek large and white. Gray above and on long tail; whitish below with light rust or buff sides and flanks. White feather edges on middle portion of folded wing diagnostic but not always visible.

Voice
Song a clear whistle, *fee-bee-ee* or *fee-bee*, with first note higher. Call a clear *chick-a-dee-dee-dee* or *dee-dee-dee*.

Similar Species
See Carolina and Mountain chickadees.

Range
Largely resident from central Alaska to Newfoundland, south to N. central California, central Utah, N. New Mexico, N. Oklahoma, east to W. mid-Atlantic states.   *Paul W. Sykes, Jr.*

Carolina Chickadee

Parus carolinensis
Similar in appearance and habits to the Black-capped, this chickadee is a small, common, nonmigratory songbird of the Southeast, where it is found in most types of forest and woodland edges.

Description
4½" (11.5 cm). Cap and bib black; bib has sharply defined lower edge. Cheek large and white; upperparts and short tail gray. White below with pale buff sides and flanks. Gray feather edgings on middle of folded wing less well defined than in Black-capped.

Voice
Call a clear *chick-a-dee-dee-dee* or *dee-dee-dee*, higher and more rapid than the Black-capped's; song a *fee-bee, fee-bay*.

Similar Species
See Black-capped Chickadee.

Range
Resident from Se. Kansas to N. New Jersey, south to E. Texas, Gulf Coast, and central Florida.   *Paul W. Sykes, Jr.*

Black-capped Chickadee
Carolina Chickadee
Mexican Chickadee
Mountain Chickadee
Siberian Tit
Boreal Chickadee
Chestnut-backed Chickadee
Bridled Titmouse
Plain Titmouse
Tufted Titmouse

Adult
. *Black cap.*
. *Black bib.*
. *White cheeks.*
. *White edges on wing coverts.*
. *Buff flanks.*

Small size.

Adult
. *Black cap.*
. *Black bib.*
. *White cheeks.*
. *Gray edges on wing coverts.*
. *Buff flanks.*

Small size.

Mexican Chickadee

Parus sclateri
This is the only chickadee found within a very limited area of
Arizona and New Mexico. In the Chiricahua Mountains in Arizona,
this species can be found in almost any habitat with conifers, even
where these trees are sparse, such as in pine-oak areas. In the
summer, it is generally found in higher coniferous forests.

Description
5″ (12.5 cm). The Mexican Chickadee is predominantly very gray;
the black bib extends onto the upper breast, and the black cap
contrasts with the white cheeks and midbreast.

Voice
Highly variable, even for a chickadee. Most calls low, buzzy, and
nasal, including a *day-bree* and many wheezy scolds and chatters.

Range
Chiricahua Mountains of Arizona and Animas Mountains of New
Mexico; south in mountains to S. Mexico.   *Scott B. Terrill*

Mountain Chickadee

Parus gambeli
Mountain Chickadees are common in open, montane, coniferous
forests of the West. They are largely permanent residents.

Description
6″ (15 cm). Cap black, broken by thin white line extending from bill
over and behind eye. Throat black; cheeks and underparts white.
Back, sides, and flanks gray but show variation: birds of Great Basin
pale with more buff; birds from farther west grayer; birds of Rockies
have browner back, cinnamon sides and flanks.

Voice
A hoarse *chick-a-dee*, similar to Black-capped's. Also whistled *dee-
dee-dee*, with last 2 notes usually lower; varies over range.

Similar Species
Black-capped does not usually overlap; has back paler than sides.

Range
N. British Columbia to N. Baja California, S. Arizona, Colorado,
and Sw. Texas.   *Louis R. Bevier*

Siberian Tit

Parus cinctus
The Siberian Tit apparently breeds in riparian willow and spruce at
or near the tree line. In winter, it wanders widely through the river
valleys of western and central Alaska, but is never common.

Description
5½″ (14 cm). Quite pale and slightly long-tailed, this chickadee looks
like a hybrid of the Black-capped and the Boreal. It has a dusty
gray-brown cap, a dusty brown back, buff flanks, and white or light
gray edging on the tertials. The face and sides of the head are white.

Similar Species
Boreal Chickadee smaller, darker; side of head clean gray; bright
rufous flanks; found near conifers. See Black-capped Chickadee.

Range
Extreme northwestern Alaska, central Alaska Range and Brooks
Range; also in northern Yukon and northwestern Mackenzie
District. Native to northern Eurasia.   *Daniel D. Gibson*

Adult
1. *Black cap.*
2. *Black bib extending to upper breast.*
3. *White cheeks.*
4. *Gray flanks.*

Found only in southwestern mountains.

Adult
1. *Black cap and white eyebrow.*
2. *White cheeks.*
3. *Black bib.*

Small size. Prefers coniferous forests.

Adult
1. *Gray-brown cap.*
2. *White face.*
3. *Black bib.*
4. *Brownish back.*
5. *Buff flanks.*

Boreal Chickadee

Parus hudsonicus
A small, dark, brownish chickadee, this bird is a familiar sight in northern coniferous forests: it rarely occurs out of sight of conifers.

Description
5–5½″ (12.5–14 cm). The darkness of this species' plumage is relieved only by white lores, white on the forepart of the ear patches, and the dirty grayish-white center of the breast and belly. The cap and back are brown; the sides of the head are clean gray from the edge of the ear patch to the nape. The flanks are bright rufous and the wings and tail gray, with only slightly paler edging.

Voice
Wheezy, drawled notes, less distinct than those of Black-capped.

Similar Species
See Siberian Tit and Chestnut-backed Chickadee.

Range
Resident from tree line in W. and N. Alaska east, south to S. Canada and N. United States.   *Daniel D. Gibson*

Chestnut-backed Chickadee

Parus rufescens
This species prefers coniferous forests near the Pacific Coast, but it is also found in coastal riparian or eucalyptus groves of California.

Description
5″ (12.5 cm). Back rich reddish-brown or chestnut; cheeks white; cap brown with black lower edge. Flanks reddish-brown. White below with black throat. Wings and tail dark gray.

Voice
Call a harsh, sibilant *shik-zee-zee*, often just last 2 notes given; also lisping notes and characteristic *chek-chek*.

Similar Species
Boreal Chickadee has duller white cheek, duller back and flanks.

Range
Pacific Coast from Prince William Sound to W. Santa Barbara County in California; also interior S. British Columbia and Sw. Alberta to central Oregon. Inland locally in central California; at lower elevations to central Sierra Nevada.   *Louis R. Bevier*

Bridled Titmouse

Parus wollweberi
This smallest and most distinctively marked North American titmouse is common in riparian and oak woodlands of central Arizona.

Description
4½″ (11.5 cm). Dark gray above and pale gray below with a black throat and face markings, and a prominent gray-and-black crest.

Voice
Harsh, scolding contact call a series of many short notes, starting at high frequency, ending lower. Song a repetitive series of 1 syllable. Calls and songs like those of Plain Titmouse in areas of overlap.

Similar Species
Plain Titmouse larger, lacks black face pattern. Mountain Chickadee lacks crest.

Range
Resident from central Arizona and southwestern New Mexico south to central Mexico.   *Philip K. Gaddis*

Adult
1. *Brown cap.*
2. *White lores and face.*
3. *Gray ear coverts.*
4. *Brown back.*
5. *Bright rufous flanks.*

   Prefers conifers.

Adult
1. *Brown cap.*
2. *White cheeks.*
3. *Rich reddish-brown back.*
4. *Reddish-brown flanks.*

Adult
1. *Erect crest.*
2. *Black face markings.*
3. *Black bib.*

Plain Titmouse

Parus inornatus
Unsociable and taciturn, the Plain Titmouse inhabits western oaks
and piñon-juniper woodlands. It forages in typical titmouse style.

Description
5½" (14 cm). The Plain Titmouse is dark gray above, paler below,
with a prominent, erect gray crest.

Voice
California races give contact calls and songs like those of Tufted
Titmouse: a scolding *see-jert-jert;* song a repetitive series of 1
syllable. Scolding calls of Great Basin and Arizona forms a faster,
staccato series. Songs comparable throughout range.

Similar Species
See Bridled Titmouse, Hutton's and Gray vireos.

Range
Resident from extreme southern Oregon, Nevada, and Utah south
through California to Baja California and through Great Basin to
Mexican border.   *Philip K. Gaddis*

Tufted Titmouse

Parus bicolor
The Tufted Titmouse is a common and conspicuous resident of North
America's eastern forests. Outside the breeding season, it is
typically found in small flocks mixed with other species; like other
titmice, this bird forages actively and acrobatically at all levels of
coniferous or deciduous woods. It is exceptionally vocal, and its
harsh, scolding calls, as well as its songs, are unmistakable. During
the breeding season, it is found singly or in pairs and nests in tree-
holes.

Description
4½–5½" (11.5–14 cm). This titmouse is dark gray above, pale gray
below, with variably buff-colored flanks. In populations north and
east of central Texas, the conspicuous crest is dark gray; from
southern and western Texas to Veracruz, it is black. Gray-crested
birds have black foreheads, while black-crested birds have pale gray
or buff foreheads. The 2 forms intergrade where they meet in
central Texas.

Voice
Scolding calls, *seeja-wer* and *see-jert-jert*, are frequently heard
throughout the year. Loud, persistent song an unvarying series of
same phrase repeated 2–10 times; phrases typically of 2 notes: *peter.*

Range
Resident from Nebraska, southern Michigan, and southern New
England south to Veracruz, Mexico, and central Florida. Black-
crested forms occur from west and central Texas south.
Philip K. Gaddis

Adult
1. *Erect crest.*
2. *Uniformly gray plumage, with no pattern or markings.*

Gray-crested form
1. *Erect gray crest.*
2. *Black forehead.*
3. *Gray upperparts.*
4. *Buff flanks.*

Black-crested form
1. *Erect black crest.*
2. *Pale forehead.*
3. *Gray upperparts.*
4. *Buff flanks.*

Verdins

(Family Remizidae)
The Verdins are active little birds with small bodies, short wings, and relatively long tails; the bills are sharply pointed, with strongly but evenly tapered upper and lower mandibles. Most species are resident within their range, but there is some local dispersal and altitudinal migration. Verdins generally make large, elaborate, oblong nests with a small opening on the side near the top. Some observers have noted that mated pairs in this family often have helpers at the nest. (World: 10 species. North America: 1 species.)   *Scott B. Terrill*

Verdin

Auriparus flaviceps
Verdins are very small, round, mostly gray birds with yellow heads. They are surprisingly loud for such small birds, and are often heard before they are seen. Verdins are common in deserts at low elevations; they prefer areas with mesquite, palo verde, and other brushy thorn scrub as well as brushy riparian woodlands. Verdins are usually seen singly, but occur in pairs or small family groups around the breeding season. These birds have been seen roosting year-round in their bulky nests, sometimes even in small groups. Verdins are active birds, flitting constantly around bushes and flying jerkily for short distances with light, quick, erratic wingbeats.

Description
4–4½" (10–11.5 cm). This tiny gray bird, somewhat paler below than above, has a sharp, pointed, blackish bill and a longish tail. Adults have a bright yellow head and a somewhat obscure red shoulder patch. Immatures are entirely grayish, and also lighter on the underparts, but with more brownish tones. The immature's lower mandible is yellowish to pinkish at the base.

Voice
Calls a loud, sharp, emphatic *tszee* and *chip*. Songs are loud *tszee-tsee-tsee* to *tsee-tee-tee-tee*, with introductory note higher than those following, which are on same pitch. Notes often introduced with barely perceptible ringing tone.

Similar Species
Common Bushtit lives in higher-elevation oak woodlands, scrub oak, piñon-juniper, and chaparral; only rarely found in Verdin habitat. Bushtit longer-tailed than immature Verdins, with tiny, chickadee-shaped bill. Call notes much different. See Northern Beardless-Tyrannulet.

Range
Southeastern California, southern Nevada, and southwestern Utah to western and southern Texas; south to northern Mexico.
Scott B. Terrill

Adult
1. *Yellow head.*
2. *Gray upperparts.*
3. *Reddish shoulders.*
4. *Pale gray underparts.*

Immature
1. *Uniformly gray plumage.*
2. *Sharply pointed bill with pale base to lower mandible.*

Bushtits

(Family Aegithalidae)
Bushtits are tiny, rotund insect-eaters with very small bills and long, thin tails. Like the titmice, they are extremely active and acrobatic. The single North American representative, the Bushtit, travels in flocks during the nonbreeding season. These flocks can be quite large, the birds moving from vegetation clump to vegetation clump one after the other, calling constantly. Their calls consist of light, dry, single notes. The wings are small and rounded; the flight is weak, jerky, and of short duration. Although considered to be 1 species, Bushtits show marked geographical variation. Several rather different species occur in the Old World. (World: 7 species. North America: 1 species.)   *Scott B. Terrill*

Bushtit

Psaltriparus minimus
The Bushtit is a tiny, long-tailed, very sociable bird of scrub, oak woodland, and mixed deciduous habitats. Except in the breeding season, it travels in tight-knit flocks of 20 or more individuals, foraging actively in the outer branches of small trees or in understory vegetation. These flocks move along at a smart clip and give off a sparkling chatter of sharp but soft contact notes. The Bushtit is found singly or in pairs during the breeding season.

Description
3½″ (9 cm). The Bushtit is dull gray over the back and wings, with a geographically variable light brown cap and tail, and pale undersides. Races south of the Mexican border, formerly considered separate species, have black cheeks. "Black-eared" individuals may be found in populations near the border. Females have a pale yellow iris; the male's eye is dark brown.

Voice
Single or double, high, sharp *tseet* or *tsip* notes given frequently while foraging. Flocks crackle with combined calls; these notes strung together in trills when birds are alarmed or singing during breeding season.

Similar Species
Juvenile Verdin has much shorter tail; adult has yellow on head and shorter tail; rarely found in same habitat with Bushtit. Flocks of Bushtits may be accompanied by other small species: Ruby-crowned Kinglet has wing bars and eye-ring; Blue-gray and Black-tailed gnatcatchers have longer dark tails and eye-rings; *Vermivora* warblers have larger, longer bills.

Range
Resident from extreme southwestern British Columbia, southern Idaho, southwestern Wyoming, Oklahoma panhandle, and Trans-Pecos Texas south to Guatemala.   *Philip K. Gaddis*

Bushtit

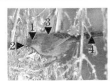

Female
1. *Pale yellow eyes.*
2. *Short bill.*
3. *Dull gray*
   upperparts.
4. *Long tail.*

   Males have dark
   eyes.
   Highly social.
   Inhabits woodlands.

"Black-eared" form
1. *Blackish ear coverts.*

Nuthatches

(Family Sittidae)
Nuthatches are small, stout birds with large heads and short necks.
Although their legs are short, the toes are so long that these birds
can forage on tree trunks, often heading straight down them. The
bill is rather long, straight, and slender, with the lower mandible
deflected upward at the tip. Nuthatches use this chisel-like bill to
forage in the bark, which they do as they move in short, somewhat
jerky hops over the trunk. The tail is very short and slightly
rounded or squared; the folded wings nearly cover the tail.
Nuthatches have loud, often repeated calls that sometimes develop
into excited chatters. Most vocalizations are composed of nasal or
piping notes. (World: 22 species. North America: 4 species.)
Scott B. Terrill

Red-breasted Nuthatch

Sitta canadensis
Nuthatches are small, short-tailed, tree-creeping birds that often
proceed head-downward as they seek food in the crevices of twigs,
branches, and tree trunks. This species is primarily a denizen of
coniferous forests, where it often gives calls that sound like a toy
horn as it forages high overhead. Its small size, stubby tail, and
jerky flight make it distinctive as it moves from tree to tree. In
winter, the Red-breasted Nuthatch is subject to periodic irruptions
that can substantially influence its winter abundance.

Description
4½–4¾″ (11.5–12 cm). The crown and nape are black in males,
grayish in females; both sexes are plain bluish-gray on the rest of
the upperparts. The underparts are largely rust-colored, paling to
buff-white on the throat, upper chest, and undertail coverts. These
birds have a prominent white eyebrow stripe and a black eyeline.

Voice
Most common call a slow, nasal *nyak nyak nyak;* also a more rapid
series of nasal notes when agitated.

Similar Species
Other nuthatches have white underparts, lack white eyebrow stripe.

Range
Breeds from southeastern Alaska east to Newfoundland and south in
mountains to southern California and Arizona; east to South Dakota,
northern Michigan, and south in Appalachians to western North
Carolina. Winters throughout most of breeding range, irregularly
south to Gulf Coast and northern Florida.
Wayne R. Petersen

Red-breasted Nuthatch
White-breasted Nuthatch
Pygmy Nuthatch
Brown-headed Nuthatch

Male
1. *Black crown.*
2. *White eyebrow.*
3. *Black line through eye.*
4. *Rust underparts.*

   High-pitched, nasal call.

Female
1. *Gray crown.*
2. *White eyebrow.*
3. *Black line through eye.*
4. *Rust underparts.*
5. *Stubby tail.*

   Creeps up and down tree trunks.

White-breasted Nuthatch

Sitta carolinensis
In flight, this common and widespread bird bounds along much like a
tiny woodpecker. It occurs in mixed hardwood and ponderosa pine.
Description
6″ (15 cm). Crown, nape, and extreme foreback black (grayer in
females); sharply defined against blue-gray back, rump, and
uppertail coverts. Sides of head and underparts white; undertail
coverts rust. Tail stubby with white corners visible in flight.
Voice
In spring, a series of low, rapid notes, *to-what what what what.*
Most common notes are a nasal *yank yank yank* and a soft *hit hit.*
Similar Species
See other nuthatches. Chickadees have black bibs.
Range
Breeds from S. British Columbia to N. New Brunswick and Cape
Breton Island, south to central Mexico and central Florida. Absent
from most of U.S. Great Plains.   *Wayne R. Petersen*

Pygmy Nuthatch

Sitta pygmaea
This species forages in loose flocks high in tall pines. Common where
it occurs, it has a patchy, mainly mountainous distribution.
Description
4½″ (11.5 cm). White to dull buff-white below, palest on throat and
lower ear patch; flanks blend into gray. Crown and nape brownish-
gray with dark line through eye. Vague whitish spot on hindneck.
Bluish-gray above; tail shows some white.
Voice
High-pitched, peeping *pee-di*, repeated rapidly and regularly.
Similar Species
Other nuthatches have different calls, lack pale nape patch, have
different face patterns, tend not to flock.
Range
S. central British Columbia to N. Baja and Mexico, east to Black
Hills (rare); also coast of central California.   *Louis R. Bevier*

Brown-headed Nuthatch

Sitta pusilla
The Brown-headed Nuthatch is a common and characteristic species
of pine woodlands along the coastal plain of the Southeast; it is
virtually never found outside this habitat and region.
Description
3¾–4¼″ (9.5–11 cm). Gray above, with brown crown and large
whitish nape spot; broad, dark brown eyeline often contrasts with
paler crown. Throat white, breast buff, belly and flanks grayish.
Voice
Most common call a peculiar, wheezy *vee-jah* or *vee-jah-jah.*
Similar Species
See Red-breasted, Pygmy, and White-breasted nuthatches.
Range
Resident from southeastern Oklahoma and eastern Texas east
across pine woods belt to central Florida and along Atlantic coastal
plain to southern Delaware.   *J. V. Remsen, Jr.*

Adult male
1. Black crown.
2. White sides of head.
3. Blue-gray back.
4. White underparts.
5. Stubby tail with white corners.

Creeps up and down tree trunks.

Adult
1. Brownish crown.
2. Blackish eyeline.
3. Blue-gray back.
4. Pale underparts.

Often in flocks. Forages in high branches, not on trunks. High pee-di call.

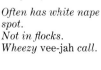

Adult
1. Brown crown.
2. Dark eyeline.
3. Blue-gray back.
4. Buff breast.
5. Grayish flanks.

Often has white nape spot. Not in flocks. Wheezy vee-jah call.

Creepers

(Family Certhiidae)
Like the nuthatches and woodpeckers, creepers cling to the vertical surfaces of tree trunks and limbs. Unlike nuthatches but like woodpeckers, they use their stiff, spiny, graduated tails to prop themselves against the trunk. Creepers differ from both groups in having long, slender, somewhat decurved bills that are used for probing rather than hammering. These birds are small and thin, cryptically colored above with a complex pattern of browns, buffs, black, and white; this patterning effectively conceals these birds against the bark. The underparts are light buff or white. The calls consist of very high, thin, piercing notes. Creepers characteristically feed by spiraling up treetrunks; upon reaching the top of the trunk, they often fly to the bottom of another nearby tree and begin their climb anew. (World: 6 species. North America: 1 species.)
Scott B. Terrill

Brown Creeper

Certhia americana
The Brown Creeper is a small, slim, inconspicuous woodland bird that is most often seen quietly spiraling its way up a tree trunk in a jerky fashion, using its stiff, longish tail as a prop and probing crevices in the bark as it ascends. As it flies from the top of one tree to the base of another, it displays a buff-colored wing patch. This species is the only representative of its family in North America.

Description
5–5¾" (12.5–14.5 cm). The Brown Creeper is unmistakable. The bill is thin and noticeably decurved. The crown and upperparts are brown, streaked with grayish-white. The underparts are whitish, tinged with some buff coloring on the flanks and on the undertail coverts.

Voice
Song, heard primarily in early spring, a short, thin, wiry *see-tee-wee-tu-wee;* has pitch and quality of Winter Wren's song. Common note a single, high, thin *seep;* less emphatic and more prolonged than similar note of Golden-crowned Kinglet.

Range
Breeds from southeastern Alaska east through central Canada to Newfoundland and south through western mountains to Nicaragua; southern Wisconsin east to New England, and in Appalachian mountains as far south as eastern Tennessee and western North Carolina. Winters to Gulf Coast and Florida.   *Wayne R. Petersen*

Brown Creeper

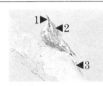

Adult
1. *Thin, decurved bill.*
2. *Brown crown and upperparts with grayish-white streaks.*
3. *Long, stiff tail.*

   Spirals up tree trunks.

Adult
1. *Whitish underparts.*
2. *Buff tinge on flanks and undertail.*

   High, thin seep call.

Bulbuls

(Family Pycnonotidae)
Bulbuls are a large Old World family; the members are primarily
tropical and relatively small. The bill is generally slender, of medium
length, and often noticeably decurved. The legs are short but
sturdy. The wings are short, broad, and rounded; the tail is also
rounded but relatively long. In general, these birds are rather drab,
however some species, like the introduced Red-Whiskered Bulbul,
have bright patches or prominent crests. The plumage is relatively
long and soft. The sexes are similar. Out of the breeding season,
many species are gregarious and noisy. The flight is usually low,
weak, and covers only short distances. (World: 123 species. North
America: 1 species.)   *Scott B. Terrill*

Red-whiskered Bulbul

Pycnonotus jocosus
The Red-whiskered Bulbul is a medium-size songbird native to the
Old World tropics. It was introduced or escaped and established in
southern Florida in the mid-1950s. It has adapted well to the array
of exotic plantings of suburbia. It primarily eats fruits but also takes
insects and other animal matter. This bird generally stays under
cover of vegetation, although it is not particularly shy and will on
occasion perch in the open on utility wires, branches, or foliage. The
flight is direct; when alighting, the bird often flares its long tail. This
highly gregarious species is usually seen in pairs or small groups,
and during the nonbreeding season uses established roost sites in
dense cover.

Description
7–7½″ (18–19 cm). The adult has a black cap with a large peaked
crest, red ear patch and undertail coverts, brown upperparts, and a
white lower cheek outlined with black; a black smudged line extends
from the nape onto the breast. The underparts are mostly white,
and the tail is blackish-brown with large white spots on the tips of
the feathers. The immature lacks the red ear patch and has pink
undertail coverts.

Voice
Song a loud, clear, musical, liquid whistle, notes rising and falling:
queep-kwil-ya and *queek-kay;* similar to song of American Robin.
Also gives various notes: *chur, chi-chur,* and chatters.

Range
Introduced and established south of Miami, Florida, in the Kendall
sector of Dade County. Native to Old World.   *Paul W. Sykes, Jr.*

Red-whiskered Bulbul

Adult
1. *Black cap with large, peaked crest.*
2. *Red ear patch.*
3. *Brown upperparts.*

Adult
1. *Dark smudge from nape to breast.*
2. *White underparts.*
3. *Red undertail coverts.*
4. *Long tail with white spots at tips of feathers.*

Wrens

(Family Troglodytidae)
Except for the Cactus Wren, these birds are small, rotund, stocky, and brownish. They all have slender, somewhat decurved bills and often carry the tail cocked over the back. North American wrens have conspicuous barring on the wings and tail. The legs and the toes are long; most wrens spend a lot of time on or near the ground. The majority have loud, musical songs. Their calls are sharp or chattering, and frequently given in response to spishing, squeaking, or imitations of owl calls. (World: 60 species. North America: 9 species.)   *Scott B. Terrill*

Cactus Wren

Campylorhynchus brunneicapillus
This very large wren is similar in size and shape to a small thrasher; it even feeds on the ground much of the time, in thrasher fashion. It is common in deserts at low elevations, notably where there is abundant cactus (especially large cholla), mesquite, palo verde, and other thorny trees. It is also fairly common in riparian brush and in desert residential areas, where nests have been found in street lamps. The Cactus Wren flies slowly on fast-beating wings; it covers short distances, moving jerkily from one perch to another. The bird's rough song is a characteristic sound of the desert; this wren often sings with its head up and tail pointed straight down from the top of a cactus.

Description
7–8¾″ (18–22 cm). The crown is a rich, often rust-colored brown, bordered by a conspicuous whitish eyebrow. The back is a similar rich brown, but often with less rust; it is marked with irregular, broken whitish streaks and blackish spots. The wings are heavily spotted with alternating rows of blackish and cinnamon-buff or white. The long, slightly rounded tail is heavily barred with blackish and light brown; black spotting is adjacent to and overlaps broad white areas (seen mostly in flight) on the outer feathers and on the bases of all but the central feathers. The underparts are whitish or light buff, heavily spotted with black, which becomes more concentrated on the upper breast, sometimes appearing as a solid, irregular black mass. The spotting decreases toward the rump, while the ground color becomes more tawny or rust.

Voice
Song a low, rough *choo-choo-choo-choo* to *chug-chug-chug-chug, cora-cora-cora-cora*, and other variations; all sound like a car refusing to start. Also various low, harsh scolds and mews.

Similar Species
Thrashers slightly larger; lack streaked upperparts, barred tail, and bold eyebrow.

Range
Resident in S. California, S. Nevada, Sw. Utah, W. and S. Arizona, S. New Mexico, and W. and S. Texas; south into central Mexican highlands.   *Scott B. Terrill*

Wrens

Adult at nest
1. *Rust-brown crown.*
2. *Whitish eyebrow.*
3. *Streaked back.*
4. *Barred outer tail feathers.*

Large size.
Builds conspicuous nests in cactus.

Adult
1. *Rust-brown crown.*
2. *Whitish eyebrow.*
3. *Spotted underparts.*

Choo-choo-choo
song.

Rock Wren

Salpinctes obsoletus

A stocky, terrestrial bird, the partially migratory Rock Wren lives in open, rocky, often arid regions of western North America; it shows no preference for areas with water. This bird is fairly common, rather tame, and extremely active. With its thin bill, it probes crevices and crannies for insects, bobbing and calling frequently, and making short, jerky flights from rock to rock, spreading its tail as it lands.

Description

5–6″ (12.5–15 cm). Rock Wrens are always pale, but the intensity of their coloring is variable. The upperparts are grayish-brown, very finely speckled with white and black; the rump is cinnamon. The rounded tail is brown above, barred with black, and tipped with buff on the corners; it has a black subterminal band. The eyebrow is whitish, but not sharply demarcated. The underparts are dull white, becoming buff to dull cinnamon on the flanks, lower belly, and undertail coverts. The breast has fine, dusky streaking. Immatures are very similar but lack the streaking on the breast and show faint barring above.

Voice

Song a mimidlike series of couplets, *kra-wee* or *tra-lee*, repeated 4 or more times and sometimes interspersed with tinkling notes. Call a *tick-ear* and a dry, fairly high trill on 1 pitch.

Similar Species

See Canyon Wren. Other wrens smaller or darker and more strikingly marked.

Range

Breeds from interior British Columbia to Saskatchewan, south to Central America; from Pacific Coast (generally within Coast Ranges) to western Great Plains and central Texas. Winters from California, southern Nevada and Utah, New Mexico, and central Texas south; migrants often reach coastal and lowland habitats not used in summer.   *Richard Webster*

Canyon Wren

Catherpes mexicanus

The Canyon Wren occurs over much of the same range and even frequents the same spots as the Rock Wren, however the Canyon's habits and haunts differ in several important aspects. The Canyon Wren is almost entirely resident over its range, although a few of the most northerly populations depart in winter, and some other birds perform altitudinal migrations to escape winter weather. The Canyon Wren is largely restricted to 2 major habitats: areas with water, such as boulder-strewn streams, rocky canyons, and river gorges; and major rock formations, such as tall cliffs, large caves, mesas, and buttes. This species is widespread and easily found, but its territories are large and the proper habitat is scattered. The Canyon Wren's beautiful song is often enhanced by the acoustical properties of rock formations.

Description

5½″ (14 cm). The bill is long and slender. The upperparts are generally a rich brown, grayer on the head and redder toward the

Adult
1. *Long, thin bill.*
2. *Gray-brown upperparts.*
3. *Buff tips on tail feathers.*

   Inhabits rocky places.

Adult
1. *Whitish underparts.*
2. *Buff flanks.*

   Tick-ear *call.*
   Stocky build.

Adult at nest
1. *Rich brown upperparts.*
2. *White throat and breast.*
3. *Rust belly.*
4. *Barred tail.*

   Builds twig nest in rocky canyon wall.

rump; they are dotted with dusky coloring and flecked with white. The wings and the very rusty tail are barred with black. The lower face, throat, and upper breast are bright white. The rest of the underparts are a dark rust, faintly speckled with black and white.

Voice
Song a series of about a dozen clear, descending, whistled notes—*tew* or *te-you;* carries well. Calls a metallic *tschee* and a harsh *nnrrr.*

Similar Species
Rock Wren has dull white throat and breast blending into cinnamon to buff belly, flanks, and undertail coverts rather than contrasting sharply. Most other wrens have eyebrows.

Range
Resident from southern British Columbia, Idaho, and Montana south to southern Mexico; west as far as Cascades and Coast Ranges of central and southern California; east to Rocky Mountains; east of Rockies only in southwestern South Dakota, western Oklahoma, and western and central Texas.   *Richard Webster*

Carolina Wren

Thryothorus ludovicianus
The largest eastern wren, this lively, loud, familiar bird is an habitué of undergrowth such as honeysuckle, greenbrier, and brush piles. Active and curious, it often scolds and bobs back and forth, cocking its tail, and investigating the birder as he spishes or does owl imitations.

Description
5½–6″ (14–15 cm). This stubby bird has bright rust-buff underparts, and rufous upperparts. There is a conspicuous, thick, long white eyebrow stripe, and a longish tail that is often cocked or switched back and forth. The rather long bill is somewhat decurved and there is some dark barring on the wings and tail. The flight is buzzy and jerking.

Voice
A clear, loud, ringing song, usually 3-syllabled, sometimes 2-syllabled, repeated 3–5 times or more: *tea-kettle, tea-kettle, tea-kettle, tea,* or *wheedle, wheedle, wheedle, wheedle;* myriad variations are readily recognizable. Call note a clear, descending *tiirrrr,* a little like noise made by running thumb down teeth of comb. Numerous buzzy, chattering scold notes and clear, nervous twitters. Songs and calls given all year.

Similar Species
Bewick's Wren lacks warm rufous coloring, is grayer above, dirty whitish below, and has white tail borders. Marsh Wren also has white eyebrow stripe but smaller, has small white stripes on back; appears less reddish-brown; rarely found in same habitat.

Range
Permanent resident from southern parts of Iowa, Wisconsin, and Michigan to southern New England, south to Texas, Gulf Coast, and southern Florida. Uncommon farther west (New Mexico) and north. Sensitive to extreme cold and subject to diebacks in North.
Henry T. Armistead

Adult
1. *Long, thin bill.*
2. *White throat and breast.*
3. *Rust belly.*

   Clear, whistled song.

Adult
1. *White eyebrow.*
2. *Long tail.*

   Clear, ringing, repetitious song.

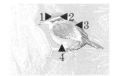

Adult
1. *Rufous crown.*
2. *White eyebrow.*
3. *Rufous back.*
4. *Rich buff underparts.*

   Large size. Clear, ringing, repetitious song.

Bewick's Wren

Thryomanes bewickii
Bewick's Wren is found in brushy clearings, thick undergrowth, suburban areas, and scrubby woods throughout much of the United States and in southwestern Canada. It often fans and flicks its tail sideways.

Description
5–5½″ (12.5–14 cm). This sparrow-size, slender wren has a conspicuous white eyebrow stripe, whitish underparts, and a long, limber tail with white outer tail feathers. It is the only wren with uniform whitish-gray underparts and white outer tail feathers, although the white on the tail can sometimes be difficult to see. The upperparts are brownish, and there is dark barring on the wings and on the tail.

Voice
A clear, complex, highly variable song very reminiscent of Song Sparrow's, but usually thinner, louder, and more musical. Call note a rather harsh, scratchy, grating *weed-it, weed-it*. Also various other notes.

Similar Species
See Carolina Wren.

Range
Breeds locally from southwestern British Columbia, southwestern Wyoming, southeastern Nebraska, southern Ontario, and southwestern Pennsylvania south to Mexico, northern Arkansas, and northern Gulf states. Resident in West; in East winters from Missouri, Ohio, and North Carolina south to Gulf of Mexico and northern Florida.   *Henry T. Armistead*

House Wren

Troglodytes aedon
This aggressive little wren can be heard singing its persistent, bubbling song in thickets, woodland openings, prairie coulees, canyons, and about human habitations over much of North America. As its name implies, it frequently nests in a variety of man-made locations. When singing, the House Wren often mounts a perch and points its usually cocked tail straight downward.

Description
4½–5¼″ (11.5–13.5 cm). The upperparts are dull, unstreaked grayish-brown with dusky bars on the wings and tail. There is a thin, light eye-ring and an indistinct, narrow grayish eyebrow stripe. The underparts are dull grayish white, lightest on the throat and breast, and like the sides and flanks have faint dusky barring and are tinged with buff-gray. The "Brown-throated" Wren (*T. a. brunneicollis*), a race of the mountains of northeastern Arizona, has rustier upperparts, a buff throat, breast, and eyebrow stripe, and more prominent barring on the sides and flanks.

Adult
1. *White eyebrow.*
2. *Brown upperparts.*

Adult
1. *Brown crown.*
2. *White eyebrow.*
3. *Whitish-gray
   underparts.*
4. *White tips on tail
   feathers.*

   Slender build.

**"Brown-throated"
form**
1. *Buff throat.*
2. *Buff eyebrow.*
3. *Rust back.*

*Found only in
mountains of
southern Arizona.*

Voice
Song a rapid, bubbling chatter that rises in pitch, then falls off
toward the end; given many times in succession. Scold note a rapid,
grating, sizzling sound; also gives a whining call.

Similar Species
Winter Wren smaller, darker, with shorter tail; has heavier barring
on flanks. Other wrens have either prominent eyebrow stripes, back
stripes, or tail spots.

Range
Breeds from central British Columbia east to central Ontario and
New Brunswick and south to southeastern Arizona, northern Texas,
Tennessee, and northern Georgia; also breeds in Mexico. Winters
from southern California, southern Arizona, and southern New
Mexico (rare) east to Virginia and Florida. Also in West Indies,
Central and South America.   *Wayne R. Petersen*

Winter Wren

Troglodytes troglodytes
This tiny wren flits and bobs among brush piles and along rocky
streams in coniferous forests, uttering its distinctive song.

Description
4¼″ (11.5 cm). Dark reddish-brown above, pale brownish below;
belly, flanks, and undertail coverts have dusky barring. Narrow buff
line present over eye.

Voice
Song a sustained, loud series of tinkling trills and tumbling warbles,
often ending on a high note or trill. Note a sharp *kip* or *kip-kip*.

Similar Species
See House Wren.

Range
S. Alaska to Newfoundland and south to central California, central
Idaho, Great Lakes area, and in Appalachians to N. Georgia.
Winters in S. California, Arizona, Gulf Coast, and Florida. Also in
Old World.   *Wayne R. Petersen*

Sedge Wren

Cistothorus platensis
Shunning the heavy cattails preferred by Marsh Wrens, Sedge
Wrens occupy wet meadows and the damp upper margins of
marshes and sphagnum bogs. Males can be heard singing their
distinctive songs from scattered low shrubs, but they are shy and
often difficult to observe. Sedge Wrens can be abundant in some
meadows but curiously scarce or absent in adjacent areas of
seemingly appropriate habitat. The species has declined markedly in
New England and has disappeared as a regular breeder in most
northeastern states.

Description
4–4½″ (10–11.5 cm). These dull, plain-faced birds are more
uniformly brown and smaller than Marsh Wrens; they lack the
obvious pale eye stripe so conspicuous in the Marsh Wren. The
crown is finely, somewhat obscurely, streaked with tan and dark
brown. The white stripes on the back are not as prominent as in the
Marsh Wren. The deep brown wing coverts are barred. The flanks

Typical form
1. *Indistinct eyebrow.*
2. *Grayish-brown back.*
3. *Grayish-white underparts.*
4. *Barred tail with no white spots.*

Adult
1. *Short tail.*
2. *Dark reddish-brown upperparts.*
3. *Pale brownish underparts.*
4. *Barred belly and flanks.*

Small size.
Bobbing behavior.

Adult
1. *Plain face.*
2. *Streaked crown.*
3. *Buff-orange flanks.*

Inhabits wet meadows and sedge marshes.

are buff-orange and the chin, throat, and center belly are dull white.
The undertail coverts are plain buff. The bill and tail are short.

Voice
Frequently sings at night. Deliberate opening notes with 2–3
(sometimes 5) sharp, distinctive *tsip-tsip-tsip*s, then changing into a
rapid, chattering trill that may descend at end. Typical song: *tsip-
tsip-tsip-trrrrrrrrrrrupp*. High, sharp call note a *tick* or *tsip*.

Similar Species
See Marsh Wren.

Range
Southern Saskatchewan east to southern Quebec, south to eastern
Kansas, northern Arkansas, northern Kentucky, and western
Pennsylvania; also Delmarva peninsula. Nearly absent from
Northeast; may breed irregularly in eastern New Brunswick.
Winters from northeastern Mexico, Texas, southern Illinois, along
Mississippi River, Gulf States, and from Virginia to Florida.
Widespread and variable from Mexico through South America.
Peter D. Vickery

Marsh Wren

Cistothorus palustris
This energetic wren is found in the tall, coarse cattails, tules, and
bulrushes that grow in marshes, along pond shores, in prairie
sloughs, and on the banks of tidal rivers. The male's vigorous
rasping trills can be heard throughout the breeding season. Males
arrive on breeding grounds to establish territories some 10 days
before the females and construct dummy nests whose practical value
is unknown. When the female arrives, she builds her own nest.

Description
4–5½″ (10–14 cm). This species appears drab at a distance, but is
actually fairly colorful and warm-toned, with a white chin, cinnamon
flanks, and a prominent white eyebrow; this stripe is the bird's most
obvious characteristic. The thin white streaks on the upper back
contrast with the unstreaked blackish-brown crown and the rust
lower back and scapulars. The warm cinnamon-orange flanks set off
the white chin and belly. The bill is long, thin, and decurved.
Juveniles are duller and less clearly marked; the white back streaks
are often faint or lacking, and the eyebrow may be so indistinct as to
suggest the Sedge Wren, but the Marsh Wren's crown is
unstreaked.

Voice
Song reedy, not musical: 1 or 2 low grinding, scraping, guttural
notes, followed by a squeak and then a rapid, rasping trill. Call note
a *tsuk-tsuk* or *chuk-chuk;* often 2 or 3 in succession.

Similar Species
Sedge Wren plain, lacking obvious white eye stripe; white back
stripes do not contrast with scapulars and lower back; crown
streaked, bill shorter. Carolina Wren larger with very conspicuous
white eye stripe and unmarked brown back.

Range
Southern British Columbia and Canadian prairies, to eastern New
Brunswick and Nova Scotia, and south to southern California, New
Mexico, Texas, and along Atlantic coast to Florida. Local in
Arizona. Apparently absent as breeder in interior Southeast.
Winters from Washington to California, Utah, and Mexico.
Sparingly from southern New England, Nova Scotia; regularly from
New Jersey south to Florida and Texas.   *Peter D. Vickery*

Adult
1. *Short bill.*
2. *Indistinct white streaks on back.*
3. *Barred wing coverts.*

Juvenile
1. *Duller brown plumage than adult's.*
2. *Indistinct streaks on back.*

Adult
1. *Bold white eyebrow.*
2. *Unstreaked crown.*
3. *White stripes on back.*
4. *Rust lower back and scapulars.*

   Inhabits marshes.

Dippers

(Family Cinclidae)
Dippers are highly aquatic passerines. They are plump and rotund with a shortish, laterally compressed bill and a stubby, squared, or slightly rounded tail that is held vertically, like that of a wren. With their dense plumage and specialized oil glands, Dippers actively plunge into raging torrents and forage for prey along stream and river bottoms. They are often seen perched on rocks in the middle of fast-flowing streams, vigorously bobbing up and down. The legs are very long and the feet are quite large. Dippers have a conspicuous silver nictating membrane, or inner lid, on the eye; this membrane causes a flash when the birds blink. These birds fly on short, pointed wings with stiff, rapid beats. The flight is often short and direct, usually just over the water's surface along a stream course. Although the Dipper's calls are loud and abrupt, the song, delivered year-round, is quite musical. The sexes are similar. The North American species is primarily gray. It is found in rapid streams in the West, primarily in areas of coniferous forests. (World: 5 species. North America: 1 species.)   *Scott B. Terrill*

American Dipper

Cinclus mexicanus
Closely tied to cold, rushing streams, the Dipper stands out in its habitat and unique behavior. These birds typically bob up and down on rocks, walk along streams, or disappear underwater, where they forage over pebbles for insect larvae or small fish. When flushed, they give a rapid *bzeet* call and fly low over the water, closely following the course of the stream. Dippers—known in Britain as Water Ouzels—become conspicuous residents at perennially cascading streams, building their mossy domelike nests near the water's edge or behind a waterfall. In 1894, John Muir wrote: "Among all the countless waterfalls I have met in the course of ten years' exploration in the Sierra, whether among icy peaks, or warm foothills . . . not one was found without its Ouzel . . . He is the mountain streams' own darling, the hummingbird of blooming waters, loving rocky-ripple slopes and sheets of foam as a bee loves flowers, as a lark loves sunshine and meadows."

Description
7–8½″ (18–21.5 cm). Dippers are stout, wrenlike birds about the size of a large bob-tailed thrush. They are almost entirely slate-gray except for a brown tinge on the head. Thin white crescents show above and below the eye and a pale membrane is often seen flashing over the eye. Winter adults and juveniles have pale-tipped feathers on the wings and underparts; juveniles are also tinged with rust and are quite pale on the underparts.

Voice
When flushed, a loud *dzeet* or *bzeet* given in flight; single or rapidly repeated, sometimes extended to *bz-ze-ze-ze-et*. Song given year-round, especially when streams fullest; rich, musical runs and trills, somewhat mimidlike but more subdued and higher pitched.

Range
Permanent resident of mountain streams from Pacific Coast to the Rockies; from northern Alaska and closer Aleutian Islands south along Coast Ranges and east to central Alberta, Black Hills of South Dakota, and eastern Rocky Mountains; reaches western Panama. Rarely found outside breeding range, but may move to lower streams at periphery, especially in fall and winter; some vagrants away from permanent streams.   *Louis R. Bevier*

American Dipper

Adult
1. Slate-gray plumage.
2. Brown tinge on head.
3. Short tail.

Stout build. Inhabits rushing streams.

Adult at nest
Builds domelike nest of moss at water's edge.

Part Three

Accidental Species

Accidental species are those that have strayed from their normal ranges and have been recorded only a handful of times on the North American continent.

Black-tailed Gull

Larus crassirostris. 18″ (45.5 cm). Medium-size, dark-mantled gull. Slightly larger than Ring-billed Gull, with proportionally longer, more narrow wings, and larger bill with black ring inside of red tip. Adult shows prominent black subterminal band on tail feathers; legs yellow. Usually lacks white spots on primary tips. Immatures rich dark brown with black primaries, black tail band, and pink-based, black-tipped bill; reminiscent of juvenile California Gull. Native to coastal Japan and Kurile Islands. Accidental in western Aleutian Islands, Alaska.   *Theodore G. Tobish Jr.*

Large-billed Tern

Phaetusa simplex. 15″ (38 cm). Large tern with stout yellow bill and black crown; in flight shows prominent white triangle in wings behind black primaries, reminiscent of Sabine's Gull. Native to South America. Two North American records.   *Thomas H. Davis*

Scaly-naped Pigeon

Columba squamosa. 15″ (38 cm). Uniformly dark slate-gray bird with metallic purple and chestnut hindneck. Feet and base of bill red. Eye-ring red in male, yellow in female. Native to West Indies. Accidental in Key West, Florida; old records only.
Scott B. Terrill

Zenaida Dove

Zenaida aurita. 11–12″ (28–30.5 cm). Chunky dove with brownish upperparts and metallic sheen on sides of neck. Head, neck, and underparts washed with cinnamon to cinnamon-pink; shows black spots on wings and 2 elongate dots on side of head. Tips of outer secondaries white (White-winged Dove has white on wing coverts); tail short, with white-tipped outer feathers. Native to West Indies. Casual in Florida, primarily in fall and winter.   *Scott B. Terrill*

Ruddy Ground-Dove

Columbina talpacoti. 7″ (18 cm). Size and shape similar to Common Ground-Dove. Male has rich cinnamon upperparts and similar, but paler, underparts with chestnut undertail coverts. Head pale bluish-gray. Central tail feathers cinnamon; outer tail feathers black. Underwing coverts show some black. Female much duller, more brownish-gray, with rust confined to wings. Common Ground-Dove has conspicuous spotting or scaling on breast; these markings entirely lacking in Ruddy Ground-Dove. Native to Neotropics. Straggler to southern Texas in winter and spring.
Scott B. Terrill

Key West Quail-Dove

Geotrygon chrysia. 11–12″ (28–30.5 cm). Plump dove with short tail and long legs. Has rich rufous upperparts with metallic sheen; sides of neck, nape, and upper back glossed with green and purple. Underparts whitish, washed with light purplish on breast. Shows very conspicuous white-dark-white horizontal striping on lower sides of head (white replaced by buff in similar Ruddy Quail-Dove). Bill and legs red. Native to West Indies. Four records from southern Florida in this century.   *Scott B. Terrill*

Ruddy Quail-Dove

Geotrygon montana. 10–12″ (25.5–30.5 cm). Chunky, round dove with short tail and long legs. Male has rich rust upperparts glossed with metallic purple; shows conspicuous buff-dark-buff horizontal

striping on face below eye; underparts purplish-buff. Females and immatures dark olive-brown above; head and underparts washed with cinnamon-buff; have suggestion of male's facial pattern. See Key West Quail-Dove. Native to Neotropics (including West Indies). Five records from Key West and Dry Tortugas, Florida.
Scott B. Terrill

Parrots

Thick-billed Parrot
Rhynchopsitta pachyrhyncha. 15″ (38 cm). Large green parrot with long, pointed tail and red forehead and bend of wing. In flight shows distinctive yellow stripe on underwing. Native to highland pine forests of northwestern Mexico. Formerly a winter vagrant to southeast Arizona, but unreported since 1938.   *Thomas H. Davis*

Red-crowned Parrot
Amazona viridigenalis. 12″ (30.5 cm). Stocky green parrot with short, relatively squared tail. Has entirely red crown, and red in secondaries. Flight direct with wingbeats below horizontal. Call a raucous, distinctive *creo crack crack crack*, frequently given in flight. Native to northeastern Mexico. Has strayed to lower Rio Grande Valley, Texas.   *Scott B. Terrill*

Cuckoos

Common Cuckoo
Cuculus canorus. 13″ (33 cm). Old World cuckoo dissimilar to North American cuckoos, shaped much like Merlin. Upperparts, head, and breast medium gray; underparts white and heavily barred with black. Hepatic-phase females have rich chestnut upperparts barred black on back and usually unmarked on lower back and uppertail coverts. Familiar *coo-coo* call, never heard in our area. Native to northern Eurasia. Casual spring and summer visitor to western Alaska; also 1 record from Massachusetts.
Theodore G. Tobish Jr.

Oriental Cuckoo
Cuculus saturatus. 13″ (33 cm). Very similar to Common Cuckoo. Although there is large overlap, Oriental may show broader black bars on upperparts than Common; 2 species best distinguished by different call (a booming, *hoo-hoo-hoo-hoo* on single scale) or in hand by unbarred white feathering at bend of wing under alula. Native to eastern Asia. Casual in western Alaska; old records only.
Theodore G. Tobish Jr.

Typical Owls

Oriental Scops-Owl
Otus sunia. 7½″ (19 cm). Tiny Old World eared Owl with gray-brown mottled plumage. Underparts less streaked and barred than North American screech-owls. Native to northern Eurasia. Two records from western Aleutian Islands, Alaska.
Theodore G. Tobish Jr.

Nightjars

Jungle Nightjar
Caprimulgus indicus. 11″ (28 cm). Large caprimulgid with overall gray tone to mottled plumage; distinctly grayer than any other North American nightjar or nighthawk. Males have 1 white primary bar, conspicuous white tail patches, black chin, and white throat; white areas on female duller and reduced. Native to central Asia (north as far as Kurile Islands). One record from western Aleutian Islands, Alaska.   *Theodore G. Tobish Jr.*

Swifts

White-collared Swift
Streptoprocne zonaris. 8″ (20.5 cm). Huge blackish swift with conspicuous white collar around neck; collar absent or reduced in juveniles. Tail long, wide, somewhat forked. May show white on forehead. Flight like that of swift, but wingbeats somewhat slowed by large size. Native to Neotropics (as far as northeastern Mexico and including West Indies). One record each from Florida and

California (both probably *S. z. mexicana*), and 1 from Rockport, Texas.   *Scott B. Terrill*

White-throated Needletail
Hirundapus caudacutus. 8″ (20.5 cm). Larger and longer-winged than North American swifts. Distinctly marked with white throat and forehead, soft grayish-white patch on lower back, and clean white undertail coverts and tertials. Native to northeastern Asia. Accidental in spring in western Aleutian Islands, Alaska.
Theodore G. Tobish Jr.

Common Swift
Apus apus. 6½″ (16.5 cm). Intermediate in size between Black Swift and Chimney Swift, with short, slightly forked tail and diffuse whitish chin and throat. Native to northern Eurasia; breeds in east-central Asia. Accidental in Alaska.   *Theodore G. Tobish Jr.*

Fork-tailed Swift
Apus pacificus. 7½″ (19 cm). Large blackish swift with distinct white rump, long rakish wings, and strongly forked tail. At close range, note diffuse white throat. Native to northeastern Asia. Casual in spring and fall in western Alaska but not north of Pribilof Islands.   *Theodore G. Tobish Jr.*

Antillean Palm-Swift
Tachornis phoenicobia. 4–4½″ (10–11.5 cm). Tiny blackish swift with boldly contrasting white rump. Underparts primarily white with conspicuous blackish chest band and sides of breast. White-throated Swift much larger; lacks breast band; white on breast tapers down in V. Eye in white part of face on White-throated; eye in black cap on Antillean Palm-Swift. Native to West Indies. Accidental in Key West, Florida; 2 summer records.
Scott B. Terrill

Green Violet-ear
Hummingbirds

Colibri thalassinus. 4½″ (11.5 cm). Entirely iridescent bronze-green hummingbird with large bluish-violet patches on lores, ear coverts, and center of breast. Undertail coverts dark gray; tail similar to upperparts but with dark subterminal band. Bill relatively short, slightly decurved. Females similar but slightly duller than males. Immature has feathers edged with gray. Native to Neotropics (as far as central Mexico). Casual in Texas.   *Scott B. Terrill*

Cuban Emerald
Chlorostilbon ricordii. 4–4½″ (10–11.5 cm). Male primarily bright green with white undertail coverts and deeply forked blackish tail; has pinkish lower mandible and small white spot behind eye. Female has duller green upperparts; underparts grayish, washed with greenish on sides; tail same shape as male's but rather bronze-colored. Female also has conspicuous white postocular stripe bordered below by dark stripe; lower mandible pinkish. Both sexes unique in North America. Native to West Indies (primarily Bahama Islands). Vagrant to southern Florida.   *Scott B. Terrill*

Plain-capped Starthroat
Heliomaster constantii. 4½″ (11.5 cm). Large hummingbird with very long bill. Upperparts bronze-green with conspicuous white stripe down rump; tail longish and full with white spots at tips of tail feathers. Bird has conspicuous white postocular and whisker stripes; throat flecked with blackish and iridescent red. Underparts grayish with white flank spots. Sexes similar; this species distinctive in North America. Native to Mexico. Strays to southeastern and central Arizona (approximately 7 records).   *Scott B. Terrill*

Bahama Woodstar
Calliphlox evelynae. 3½″ (9 cm). Male unique in North America,

with greenish upperparts and deeply forked tail; tail has black upper surface and rufous underside. Gorget (and, in some, forehead) red with metallic-violet hues. Breast shows white collar; rest of underparts rufous. Female similar but has rounded tail and lacks gorget. Both sexes have relatively short, slightly decurved bills and white postocular spots. Native to Bahama Islands. Vagrant to southern Florida (5 records). *Scott B. Terrill*

Bumblebee Hummingbird
Atthis heloisa. 2¾″ (7 cm). Tiny hummingbird with bill shorter than head; easily confused with Calliope Hummingbird. Male shows extensive rust at base of outer tail feathers which have black-and-white tips; in male Calliope, these feathers solid greenish-gray. Male Bumblebee's gorget solid, not striped as in Calliope. Females of 2 species not safely distinguishable in field, but female Bumblebee has buff tips to outer tail feathers as opposed to whitish in Calliope. Native to Mexico. One very old record from Huachuca Mountains, Arizona. *Scott B. Terrill*

Trogons

Eared Trogon
Euptilotis neoxenus. 13½″ (34.5 cm). Relatively small-headed and barrel-chested bird with long wings and long, very wide tail; has larger, longer, heavier build than Elegant Trogon. Sits with lower back and rump projected awkwardly outward. Male iridescent greenish-blue on back, head, and breast; rest of underparts brilliant scarlet. Tail largely white on underside, blue on upper surface. Females similar but much duller. Elegant Trogon has white collar, red underparts, yellow bill, and much different shape and posture. Eared has very untrogonlike vocalizations, including loud, squeaking *squeeel-chuck—squeeel* sharply inflected upward—and other whistling calls. Native to Mexico. Accidental in Chiricahua and Huachuca Mountains, southeastern Arizona. *Scott B. Terrill*

Hoopoes

Hoopoe
Upupa epops. 12″ (30.5 cm). Large, unmistakable Old World passerine with ground feeding habits. Upperparts show unique combination of buff-pink head and upper back and black-and-white wings and tail. Long, pale-based, decurved bill and shaggy, erectile crest also unique. Hoopoe only member of family Upupidae. Native to Eurasia. One fall record from mainland Alaska. *Theodore G. Tobish Jr.*

Woodpeckers

Eurasian Wryneck
Jynx torquilla. 7½″ (19 cm). Old World woodpecker with unusual shape and markings; thinner but similar in size to Hairy Woodpecker. Upperparts mottled soft gray and brown, with black stripe extending from crown to rump. Tail long; legs and bill pale. Native to northern Eurasia. One record from western mainland Alaska. *Theodore G. Tobish Jr.*

Tyrant-Flycatchers

Nutting's Flycatcher
Myiarchus nuttingi. 7″ (18 cm). Extremely similar to Ash-throated Flycatcher, but Nutting's mouth lining is bright orange, Ash-throated's flesh-colored. Nutting's has clear whistled notes lacking in Ash-throated; other notes more staccato, less rough than Ash-throated's. Unworn tail feathers in Nutting's have dark stripe on outer edge; do not curve inward to cover entire tip as in Ash-throated. Native to Mexico. One record (specimen) from central Arizona. *Scott B. Terrill*

La Sagra's Flycatcher
Myiarchus sagrae. 7½″ (19 cm). Similar to immature Ash-throated Flycatcher or those with worn plumage, but more olive on upperparts; underparts very pale, often entirely white, including belly. (Ash-throated has pale gray breast, pale to bright yellow

belly, and very brownish-gray upperparts.) Native to West Indies.
Two North American records.   *Scott B. Terrill*

Variegated Flycatcher
Empidonomus varius. 7½" (19 cm). Superficially resembles
Sulphur-bellied Flycatcher but smaller, slimmer, with much smaller
bill and boldly contrasting dark and light facial stripes. Variegated
has streaking on underparts much less distinct than in Sulphur-
bellied; lacks Sulphur-bellied's bold streaking on upperparts. Ground
color of underparts dull buffish in Variegated, lemon-yellow in
Sulphur-bellied. Native to South America. One record from Maine.
Scott B. Terrill

Loggerhead Kingbird
Tyrannus caudifasciatus. 9" (23 cm). Closely resembles Thick-billed
Kingbird, with brownish-gray upperparts and blackish sides of head
contrasting sharply with whitish throat. Loggerhead's lower
underparts yellowish; tail in most races has light tip (absent in
Thick-billed). Vocalizations of 2 species different; distributions very
widely separated. Loggerhead native to West Indies. Vagrant to
southern Florida (6 records).   *Scott B. Terrill*

Cuban Martin
Progne cryptoleuca. 7½" (19 cm). In the field, male appears nearly
identical to familiar Purple Martin. However, in hand, feathers on
anterior crissum can be seen to be dark at base and at tip, entirely
concealing pure white in middle. Females have extensive snowy-
white on lower abdomen (this area grayish in female Purple Martin).
The *Progne* complex to which Cuban and Purple martins belong is
exceedingly confusing; in most cases—especially where other
neotropical forms are concerned—field identification is usually
impossible. Cuban Martin native to West Indies. One record from
southern Florida.   *Scott B. Terrill*

Swallows

Gray-breasted Martin
Progne chalybea. 6½" (16.5 cm). Both sexes closely resemble female
Purple Martin, but smaller, with darker forehead and more distinct
white on belly; lack Purple's grayish collar around neck. Gray-
breasted native to Neotropics; migrant to northeastern Mexico.
Has strayed to southern Texas, however records in this century
undocumented.   *Scott B. Terrill*

Southern Martin
Progne elegans. 7–8" (18–20.5 cm). Adult male not separable from
Purple males in field, although tail more deeply forked in former.
Female and immature Southerns entirely dusky below (belly whitish
in corresponding Purple Martins). Southern is part of complex
Progne group, requiring a specimen for identification. Native to
South America. One very old record from Florida.
Scott B. Terrill

Bahama Swallow
Tachycineta cyaneoviridis. 6" (15 cm). Superficially resembles
Tree Swallow, with upperparts anteriorly iridescent green and
posteriorly violet-blue, and underparts immaculate white. However,
unlike Tree Swallow, Bahama has very deeply forked tail and flight
characteristics similar to Barn Swallow. Native to West Indies.
Casual in Florida.   *Scott B. Terrill*

Common House-Martin
Delichon urbica. 5¼" (13.5 cm). Similar to Tree Swallow, but
quickly distinguished by large white rump patch. While perched or
at close range, note fully feathered legs. Native to northern
Eurasia. Two records from western Alaska.
Theodore G. Tobish Jr.

Birding Equipment

In recent decades field ornithology has progressed greatly and birding equipment has followed suit, although the basic equipment still consists of a pair of binoculars, a field guide, a notebook, and a pen or pencil (preferably a fine pen with waterproof black ink). The following items are what many of today's best birders use during their field work.

Binoculars

The cornerstone of birding equipment is a pair of binoculars. A good pair, if handled properly, can last a lifetime. Binoculars probably represent the single most expensive item in the beginning birder's field kit and should be the finest he can possibly afford. The two most important considerations in selecting binoculars are magnification and light-gathering ability. Most birders choose $7 \times$, $8 \times$, $9 \times$, or $10 \times$ magnification; $10 \times$ binoculars might be difficult for some people to hold steady, but their strength makes them excellent for seeing pelagic birds, waterfowl, shorebirds, and birds of the forest canopy.

The light-gathering ability of binoculars is the amount of light that passes through the binoculars and enters the eye. This ability, known as the "exit pupil," should usually be 4 mm or 5 mm; the larger the exit pupil the better. This number can be determined by dividing the diameter of the objective lens (the larger end of the binoculars) by the magnification. Thus $8 \times$, 40 mm binoculars (otherwise known as an "8 by 40") has an exit pupil of 5 mm. In bright light the pupil of the human eye is closed by the iris to about 4 or 5 mm, but in dim light—at dawn or dusk, on a dark day, in shadows, or in a forest—it opens to about 7 mm. Thus binoculars that deliver an exit pupil of 7 mm (such as an $8 \times$, 56 mm pair) flood the retina with light and produce a very bright image. Of course the optical qualities vary with the cost of the binoculars; the most expensive brands have the highest clarity and overall quality of image and the least distortion and discoloration.

The standard offset-prism binoculars have largely been superseded by newer straight-prism types. These tend to be more resistant to penetration by dust and water, in addition to having superior optical qualities and exterior coating. Most straight-prism binoculars are available with rubber-armored casings that reduce the usual nicks and scratches and can often withstand a physical impact that can throw binoculars out of alignment. Some binoculars come from the factory pre-close-focused to about 15 feet, but most do not; in this case, it is a good idea to have this adjustment made by the importer, if possible. There is an additional charge for this service, but it is well worth it. Binoculars with central-focusing wheels focus very fast and are the most practical, but they are not as well sealed against water and dirt as binoculars with individual eyepiece focusing.

Binoculars and other optical instruments should be carefully cleaned after each day's use, especially after exposure to dust, rain, or salt water. A cleaning kit consisting of lens tissues, liquid lens cleaner, and a soft brush should always be carried along.

Telescopes

Sooner or later most serious birders find that they need increased magnification, especially for viewing waterfowl, shorebirds, and perched birds of prey. Most birders use a moderately priced telescope with a zoom-type eyepiece and magnification ranging from $20 \times$ to $45 \times$, but other combinations are possible. If a single eyepiece is selected, a wide-angle $25 \times$ lens is the best choice for all-around birding. A lightweight, sturdy tripod that easily extends to eye level and has channeled legs with "flip locks" is best. Also, make

certain that the extended legs remain spread apart when the tripod
is lifted. If they do collapse toward the center when lifted, this may
be corrected by simply adjusting a screw.
Much more costly are reflecting telescopes. They provide a superb
image, but because the image is reversed, these telescopes take a
little getting used to. Since you must look straight down into these
telescopes, a short and very sturdy tripod is required. However,
most birders find that once they have used these fine instruments,
no other type can satisfy them. Some lower-priced reflecting
telescopes are available; however, they are much inferior to more
costly instruments.

Field Guides, Notebooks, and Checklists

Even expert birders do not disdain field guides and although they
may not carry the books into the field, they often keep their guides
tucked away in the car. For those few experts who eschew the field
guides—and really for all birders—a pocket notebook is a must. A
notebook is essential for recording descriptions of rare or unfamiliar
birds, behavioral and distributional observations, population data,
journal or diary information regarding weather, vegetation,
companions, and even daily bird lists, although there exists a
plethora of small field checklists for virtually all of the popular
birding regions in the country. For economy of time in the field,
some birders have switched to small, lightweight pocket tape
recorders for note-taking; after the mini-tapes are transcribed into a
journal at a more convenient time, they may be saved or re-used.
Most experienced birders maintain an accurate journal that is
faithfully kept up to date and may prove an invaluable source of
recoverable data in the future.

Tape Recorders and Microphones

Solid-state technology, miniaturization, and the improved quality of
tape cassettes have allowed excellent, small, and relatively
lightweight field tape recorders to replace the larger, heavier, reel-
to-reel recorders. The finest of these small models can be modified to
increase their frequency range to levels high enough to record
almost any bird vocalization. If possible, they should have manual
volume controls for maximum playback efficiency; automatic volume
controls, found on most of these smaller models, do not serve as well
since they cannot record a distant bird at levels higher than normal.
The best-quality tapes should be used instead of bargain-priced
tapes, and they should be no longer than 90 minutes in length. By
punching out one of the tabs on the top of the cassette, you can
prevent accidental erasure.
The tape recorder is a versatile field tool, but it must not be abused
by playing back calls and songs to lure sensitive species away from
their nests or territories. Such recordings may even drive a less
aggressive male from its territory. Tape recorders must be used
with great care if your objective is to attract a species by a
recording of its voice. A few brief snatches of voice will often do
the job.
Recordings may be made as permanent records and as teaching
devices for oneself and others. Field notes may also be recorded and
transcribed later. The larger reel-to-reel recorders are still
employed by professional wildlife sound specialists, since the quality
of these machines can seldom be duplicated by the smaller recorders
and their cassette tapes. This heavy, elaborate equipment, however,
is not necessary for the simpler type of recording that most birders
wish to do.
It is usually best to select a good microphone first and then find a
suitable tape recorder, for even a modest, relatively inexpensive
machine can do wonders with a fine microphone. The best types are
those that capture the sound from a relatively small area so they can

pinpoint the singing bird and exclude extraneous sounds. The finest unidirectional microphones are often quite expensive but are relatively small (compared with parabolic reflectors) and lightweight, and can be easily carried through the brush or forest, preferably in some sort of carrying case. Since most of the small recorders operate on AA or C batteries, spares should always be carried; alkaline batteries are more expensive, but their life expectancy is longer and fewer need be stocked. The record and playback heads of your tape recorder should be cleaned regularly with cotton swabs dipped in rubbing alcohol or with special demagnetizing cleaning tapes.

Photographic Equipment

A rather recent development in field birding has been the growing popularity of bird photography, using small motorized cameras equipped with small, lightweight, powerful telephoto lenses. This fairly compact outfit, coupled with fast films, can be easily carried into the field to record birding activities. This type of shooting has the advantage of capturing a trophy while allowing the game to live on. It is doubly satisfying because others are able to view the results and share in the pleasure. There is a more practical side to this type of "collecting." Rare or extralimital species no longer need to be collected for accurate verification, as many of North America's most unusual foreign vagrants have been recorded on film. Additionally, collections of photographs or movies can be assembled for instructional purposes, for informative and entertaining programs at birders' meetings and gatherings, for publication in journals, magazines, and books, or just for the personal pleasure of assembling a "life list" of bird photographs.

Simple photographic techniques are involved in birding, requiring minimal photographic equipment. Stalking the quarry on foot or by boat or auto until one is close enough to photograph it with a hand-held camera and telephoto lens is the most popular method, but it is usually employed only for the larger, tamer species. Portraits of smaller and more timid birds require more complex and time-consuming techniques and other equipment; such photography is not usually compatible with simple field birding.

The most basic equipment for bird photography by stalking consists of a lightweight, motorized, 35 mm, single-lens reflex camera equipped with a 500 mm or 600 mm reflex lens with a fixed diaphragm of about f:8 and high-speed color or black-and-white film. A slow lens (such as f:8) requires the focusing screen in the camera to be of the simple ground glass type and not the usual split-field range finder (which goes black and is unusable at apertures smaller than f:5.6). Some single-lens reflex cameras have interchangeable viewfinder screen capability. Unlike an automatic film-advance system, a true motor allows the photographer to shoot up to 4 frames a second, which is an advantage with a flying or fast-moving bird. The advantages of reflex lenses are that they are small, lightweight, close-focusing, and moderately priced. Their disadvantages are that they are slow, tend to have a "hot" spot in the center and darkening of the image at the corners, are difficult to focus because of the darkened viewfinder, and out-of-focus highlights show up on the film as doughnuts or disturbing double images. Such a system can be hand held, but some sort of shoulder brace or pistol grip/gunstock device will produce sharper photos. Commercial types are available, but anyone with a little ingenuity can build a suitable brace. While a monopod is useful, a tripod is awkward, especially if one is photographing in dense cover or on a pitching boat. Such a hand-held system requires a fast shutter speed, which should be about equal to the focal length of the lens. Thus a 500 mm lens requires a shutter speed of 1/500th second, and obviously a very fast film.

To obtain portrait-quality images of smaller birds one needs lenses of 400 mm, 500 mm, or 600 mm focal length. For example, to acquire a portrait-type image of a 6-inch bird with a 500 mm lens, the photographer must be within 12 feet of the bird, and this usually entails the use of a blind and electronic flashes placed near a location frequented by the birds, such as a feeder, nest, perch, or pool of water. Stalking small land birds is very difficult because they are shy and tend to remain in dense cover where light is dim. For this type of photography, conventional refracting lenses of long focal length (such as 400 mm, f:3.5 or f:4.5; 500 mm, f:4.5; 600 mm, f:5.6) are required. These lenses are more expensive, larger, and heavier than the reflex lenses described above. The 400 mm and 500 mm lenses may be hand-held with a gunstock or shoulder brace, but the 600 mm lens requires a sturdy tripod. For close focusing with these lenses, an extension tube or bellows must be inserted between the camera body and the lens; this attachment eliminates infinity focusing until it is removed. Certain long telephoto lenses incorporate in a single unit the lens, extension bellows focusing mount, and pistol-grip/shoulder brace.

Some of the more expensive tele-extenders are quite good, increasing the effective focal length by a factor of $1.5\times$, $2\times$, or $3\times$, but the maximum lens aperture (speed) is reduced by a comparative factor. Thus a 500 mm, f:4.5 lens employed with a $2\times$ tele-extender (or doubler) becomes a 1000 mm, f:8 lens and requires extremely rigid mounting on a sturdy tripod to ensure crisp pictures at the slower shutter speed dictated by the f:8 aperture. Such a combination would not be suitable for use with slower films and fast-moving birds.

Some more experienced bird photographers ultimately build their photographic equipment collection around the types of film they use. Faster films (with ASA ratings of 200 or 400) are notoriously grainy, but the faster film speed provides a greater latitude of shutter speed and lens aperture. Slower films (with ASA speeds of 25 or 64) are virtually grainless and excellent for reproduction in books and magazines, but the photographer must compensate for the slow film by using expensive, fast, long telephoto lenses, or intense electronic flash illumination, or both. Bird photography thus becomes a compromise between shutter speed and aperture, which ultimately depends upon the film speed, the intensity of the lighting used, and the maximum aperture of the telephoto lens. For example, if one chooses to use a film of speed ASA 64 with a 500 mm lens, then the lens must have an aperture of f:4.5 to be used in sunlight at 1/500th second, whereas an f:8 lens under the same circumstances could only be used at 1/125th second, making photography of a flying bird impossible. Those photographers who choose to use slow color or black-and-white film are limited (with daylight) to expensive fast lenses. These conventional long telephoto lenses are equipped with iris diaphragms that can be adjusted to the shutter speed in use; the reflex lenses, however, have fixed apertures, so that the exposure is determined by the camera shutter. It is therefore best to choose a camera with an electronic shutter—providing essentially infinite shutter speeds within the ranges of the camera—for use with such fixed-aperture lenses.

Electronic Flash

For stalking small birds in dense cover, it is essential to use electronic flash for illumination. A small 500 mm reflex lens can be employed with a 35 mm single-lens reflex camera mounted with a medium-size "telephoto" electronic flash. One problem is that many single-lens reflex cameras are synchronized for electronic flash at 1/125th second or slower. This is acceptable if there is not much daylight, since it is the flash and not the shutter that makes the exposure. However, if there is enough ambient light for an exposure by the shutter as well, a double or "ghost" image will result. Also, the single on-camera flash yields very stark, unnaturally harsh lighting not suitable for portraiture. The intense black shadows may make for an unsatisfactory portrait, but may be perfectly acceptable in a photograph meant merely to verify a record.

Most serious bird photographers eventually realize that good bird portrait photography and field birding are seldom compatible. Time and patience, coupled with knowledge of the subject and the right equipment, make for the superb photographs achieved by the experts. Professional results require more elaborate equipment: blinds; long, fast lenses; several electronic flashes and slave units; tripods, clamps, ladders, platforms; and slow, fine-grained films. Infinite patience is also necessary.

The most powerful electronic flashes require nickel-cadmium batteries, which are rechargeable, or 510-volt dry battery packs, which are not. These flashes produce great light; recycling of the capacitors is almost instantaneous, providing immediate and almost consecutive exposures. These larger units are not very portable and should be used at a feeder or from a blind. Photographic and observation blinds enable the photographer to remain hidden while close to the subject. They may be constructed of natural materials, assembled from rods and cloth for portability, or even purchased commercially.

Valuable photographic equipment must be cleaned, maintained, and carefully handled. Spares of essential items should be carried along. A camera should be insured; when it is not in use, lock it away out of sight in a car or truck. For maximum traveling security, cameras are best transported in waterproof, dustproof, and shockproof aluminum carrying cases. It is a good idea to disguise the camera case to avoid obvious invitations to thieves. Padded backpacks are very useful for transporting photographic equipment far into the field.

"Owl Lights"

The location, observation, photography, and study of nocturnal birds requires powerful lights. Some units may be operated from a 12-volt auto battery by way of special clamps to the battery terminals or, more conveniently, by way of the cigarette lighter. However, their usefulness is limited by the length of the power cord. Spelunkers' head lamps are best because they are powerful and leave the hands free. Six-volt "hunter's lamps" can be set on the ground and the light beam aimed at a bird. A standard, six-volt flashlight may be powerful enough, but it is least useful since it must be hand-held and aimed at the subject, leaving only one hand free.

Traditionally, beginners commence with the basic "kit" and incorporate more elaborate equipment, depending upon their interests. Within the broad framework of their hobby, many birders ultimately specialize, devoting much of their time to sound recordings, painting, bird photography, censusing, life-listing, behavioral or distributional studies, writing, or a combination of these. Birding equipment may be as simple or complicated as a birder wishes, depending upon his aims and objectives.

Arnold Small

Reporting a Rarity

For the experienced birder as well as the novice, one of the greatest pleasures of birding is the sighting of a rare bird—a bird seen far from its normal range, a visitor from Mexico or Asia, or a species that for any other reason can be said to be "rare." Aside from the personal satisfaction, such sightings are of value to ornithology only when a complete report has been made and accepted.

Avian Records Committees

To facilitate making reports, certain guidelines have been established, and numerous committees have been formed in many states and provinces. These committees usually consist of five or six expert birders whose aggregate knowledge enables them to evaluate the reports of rare birds submitted to them. If the avian records committee decides that a particular report represents a bona fide record of a bird that is rare in the state or province, the record is accepted and becomes part of that area's published avifauna.

A bird may be considered rare because it has occurred at an unusual time of year or in an area where the species does not normally occur at all. All such records are suspect if not supported by a specimen. Since it is usually impossible to collect the bird, sight records should be accompanied by convincing and unimpeachable details.

Otherwise no avian records committee or regional editor of a local or national publication will accept a sight record. No one should consider this requirement an affront, and every birder, regardless of his level of expertise, should be willing to submit the specific details of his sighting to scrutiny by others. This is, quite simply, the only way to validate a record.

A birder who wishes his records to be of scientific value and his observations to be included as part of an area's written ornithological history should include meticulous details. These sightings and supporting documentation should also be submitted to the editors of state journals and *American Birds*.

Recording a Sighting

In the event of spotting a rarity, you should be equipped: The basic rule is never to go into the field without a notebook and pen or pencil. To prepare yourself, go into the field often and practice by scrutinizing any bird and writing down its characteristics as you look at it. Learn the external features of a bird so that you can pinpoint field marks with precision and speed. Try to standardize your note-taking in the field, always using essentially the same format and shorthand notations. Learn to make fast sketches in the field, indicating features with arrows. Always keep in mind that memory is not infallible: There is no substitute for a description and sketch made on the spot, with the bird in front of you.

When submitting a report to an avian records committee, be sure to indicate your distance from the bird, the exact location of the bird, as well as the date and time of the observation. Mention the duration of the bird's stay and details concerning any other species present for the purpose of size comparison. Include the names and addresses of other birders who saw the rare bird and indicate the type and power of optical equipment used by yourself and by them. Note the conditions of light, cloud cover, and weather at the time of the sighting. Include a description of the habitat in which the bird was seen.

Features to Note

A convincing description of the bird itself plays the most critical role in a report of a rarity. Include as much detail as possible on the bird's appearance, with emphasis on the color and pattern of plumage, size, shape, posture, behavior, voice, and any other pertinent data. If possible, describe the bird both at rest and in flight. Take note of the head and neck areas, mentioning the forehead, crown, ear coverts, and malar region; discuss the presence or absence of a median crown stripe. Describe the eyes and lores, noting eye-rings, eye stripes, and eyebrows. Note the color and shape of the upper and lower mandibles and the color of the legs and feet. The bird's upperparts (crown, nape, back, rump, and uppertail coverts) and underparts (chin, throat, breast, belly, side, flanks, and undertail coverts) should be fully detailed. The wing description should include notes on color, shape, relative length (comparison to tail length is often helpful), wing bars (if present), coverts, wing linings, and leading and trailing edges. When describing tail feathers, be sure to note the color, pattern, and shape of the innermost, middle, and outer feathers.

After you complete all of the above, add a final note on your previous experience and your familiarity with the reported species and those similar to it. State your reasons for the identification you have arrived at and how you eliminated similar species.

If possible use a camera or tape recorder to amplify and support your field description, but remember that a photograph or tape recording is no substitute for a written field description. These records are considered supplemental, not the basis for a submitted report.

Finally, encourage those who witnessed the rare bird with you to submit their own written reports to the committee. A report from an independent observer will greatly aid the committee in its deliberations.   *Susan Roney Drennan*

Rare Bird Alerts

Rare Bird Alerts are recorded telephone messages that announce recent occurrences of rare and unusual birds within the area covered by the sponsoring agency—usually a local Audubon chapter or ornithological society. The operation of a local Rare Bird Alert is largely a labor of love on the part of the volunteers responsible for the regular (usually weekly) updates of the recorded message. The messages vary from brief announcements to lengthy descriptions of the birds, complete with detailed directions to the places where the birds were last seen. Some Rare Bird Alerts cover only the immediate vicinity of a single city, while others cover an entire state or province. Sometimes the recorded message will refer you to another Rare Bird Alert telephone number for particularly noteworthy birds.

The following list of telephone numbers is the latest as of early 1983. The numbers occasionally change, and new Rare Bird Alerts are being added as birding becomes more popular. New Rare Bird Alert telephone numbers as well as changes in existing numbers are reported regularly in *Birding*, the bimonthly journal of the American Birding Association.   *James A. Tucker*

United States

Alaska (907) 274-9152—Anchorage

Arizona (602) 881-9464—Tucson

California (415) 843-2211—San Francisco
(213) 874-1318—Los Angeles

Colorado (303) 759-1060—Denver

Connecticut (203) 572-0012
see also New York City

Delaware *see* District of Columbia

District of Columbia (301) 652-1088

Florida (305) 644-0190

Illinois (312) 675-8466—Chicago
(217) 785-1083—Springfield

Iowa (319) 622-3353

Louisiana (504) 769-4190—Baton Rouge
(504) 246-2473—New Orleans

Maine (207) 781-2332

Maryland *see* District of Columbia

Massachusetts (617) 259-8805—Boston

Michigan (313) 592-1811—Detroit

Minnesota (612) 544-5016—Minneapolis
(218) 525-5952—Duluth

New Hampshire (603) 224-9900—After 5 p.m. E.S.T.

New Jersey (201) 766-2661
(609) 884-2626—Cape May

New York (212) 832-6523—New York City
(518) 377-9600—Albany/Schenectady
(716) 896-1271—Buffalo

Ohio (216) 696-8186—Cleveland
(614) 221-9736—Columbus
see also Detroit, Michigan

Oregon (503) 292-0661—Portland

Pennsylvania (215) 567-2473—Philadelphia
(412) 963-6104—Pittsburgh

Texas (713) 821-2846—Houston
(512) 565-6773—Rio Grande Valley

Vermont (802) 457-2779

Virginia *see* District of Columbia

Wisconsin (414) 352-3857—Milwaukee

Canada

British Columbia (604) 734-4554–Vancouver
(604) 478-8534—Victoria

Ontario (313) 592-1811—Windsor

Glossary

This glossary was prepared by Peter F. Cannell.

Accidental A species that has appeared in a given area a very few times only and whose normal range is in another area.

Allopatric Occupying separate, nonoverlapping geographic ranges. *Cf.* Sympatric.

Alula A small, feathered projection attached to a bird's wrist and extending outward along the leading edge of the wing; the alula can be moved independently and used to affect air flow over the wing during flight.

Anterior Toward the head.

Auriculars *See* Ear coverts.

Axillars The long, innermost feathers of the underwing, covering the area where the wing joins the body. *Cf.* Scapulars.

Back The portion of the upperparts located behind the nape and between the wings.

Barred Having stripes across the feathers.

Basal Toward or at the base of a structure. *Cf.* Distal.

Belly The portion of the underparts between the breast and the undertail coverts.

Bib An area of contrasting color on the chin, throat, upper breast, or all three of these.

Boreal Northern, specifically referring to the tundra and coniferous forest habitats.

Breast The area of the underparts between the foreneck and the belly.

Breastband A band of contrasting color that runs across the breast.

Breeding plumage A coat of feathers worn by an adult bird during the breeding season, usually acquired by partial spring molt, feather wear, or both; the male's breeding plumage is often more brightly colored than its winter plumage or than the adult female's breeding plumage.

Breeding range The geographic area in which a species nests.

Call A brief vocalization with a relatively simple acoustical structure, usually given year-round by both sexes. *Cf.* Song.

Cap An area of contrasting color on the top of the head.

Carpal joint *See* Wrist.

Casual Occurring infrequently in a given geographic area but more often than an accidental.

Cere A bare, fleshy area at the base of the upper mandible that surrounds the nostrils; swollen and distinctively colored in some birds.

Cheek The side of the face.

Chin The area immediately below the base of the lower mandible.

Collar A band of contrasting color that runs across the foreneck, hindneck, or both.

Colonial Nesting in groups or colonies rather than in isolated pairs.

Color morph or Color phase One of two or more distinct color types within a species, occurring independently of age, sex, or season.

Conspecific Belonging to the same species.

Cosmopolitan	Occurring on all continents except Antarctica; worldwide.
Coverts	Small feathers that cover the bases of other, usually larger, feathers and provide a smooth, aerodynamic surface.
Crepuscular	Active at twilight.
Crest	A group of elongated feathers on the top of a bird's head.
Crissum	The undertail coverts, especially when these are distinctively colored.
Crown	The upper surface of the head, between the eyebrows.
Cryptic	Serving to conceal by camouflage, either by coloring or by form.
Culmen	The midline ridge along the top of a bird's upper mandible.
Dimorphic	Having two distinct forms within a population, differing in size, form, or color.
Distal	Away from the center of the body. *Cf.* Proximal, Basal.
Diurnal	Active during the day.
Dorsal	Pertaining to the upper surface of the body.
Ear coverts	Small, loose-webbed feathers on the side of the face behind and below the eye, covering the ear region.
Ear patch	An area of contrasting color on the ear coverts.
Ear tuft	A group of elongated feathers above the eyes that resemble ears; characteristic of some owl and grebe species, and the Horned Lark.
Escape	A bird that has escaped from captivity rather than arriving in an area by natural means.
Exotic	Not native to an area, and coming from outside North America.
Eyebrow	A stripe on the side of the head immediately above the eye.
Eyeline	A straight, thin, horizontal stripe on the side of the face, running through the eye.
Eye plate	A small, horny plate adjacent to the eye.
Eye-ring	A fleshy or feathered ring around the eye, often distinctively colored.
Eye stripe	A stripe that runs horizontally from the base of the bill through the eye; usually broader than an eyeline.
Face	The front of the head, generally including the cheeks, forehead, and lores, and sometimes the chin or crown.
Facial disk	The feathers that encircle the eyes of some birds, especially owls.
Facial frame	A color pattern that borders or encircles the face, as in many owls.
Field mark	A characteristic of color, pattern, or structure useful in identifying a species in the field.
Filoplume	A hairlike or bristlelike feather that consists of a shaft, few side branches, and no vanes.
Flank	The rear portion of the side of a bird's body.
Flight feathers	The long, firm feathers of the wings and tail used during flight. The flight feathers of the wings are the primaries, secondaries, and tertials; those of the tail are called rectrices.
Forecrown	The portion of the crown just behind the forehead.
Forehead	The area of the head just above the base of the upper mandible.

Foreneck	The front or underside of the neck.
Frontal shield	A fleshy, featherless, and often brightly colored area on the forehead.
Gape	The angle between the upper and lower mandibles when the bill is open; the opening between the upper and lower mandibles.
Gonys	The prominent midline ridge along the lower surface of the lower mandible.
Gorget	In hummingbirds, a throat patch composed of iridescent feathers.
Greater wing coverts	A row of short feathers that covers the bases of the secondaries; also called greater secondary coverts.
Hallux	The innermost toe of a bird's foot; it usually extends backward, is sometimes reduced or absent, and sometimes raised above the level of other toes.
Hindcrown	The rear portion of the crown.
Hindneck	The rear or upper surface of the neck; the nape.
Hind toe	*See* Hallux.
Hood	A distinctively colored area usually covering most or all of the head.
Hybrid	The offspring of a pair made up of two different species. In certain cases (*e.g.*, Brewster's and Lawrence's warblers), hybrids may have their own names.
Immature	A bird that has not yet begun to breed, and often has not yet acquired adult plumage.
Inner wing	The part of the wing between the body and the wrist.
Introduced	Established by humans in an area outside the natural range.
Irruption	A large-scale movement into an area by a species that does not regularly occur there.
Juvenal plumage	The first covering of true feathers, usually of a somewhat looser texture than later plumages; the juvenal plumage, often brown and streaked, is usually replaced during the bird's first summer or fall.
Juvenile	A bird in juvenal plumage.
Lateral	Toward or at the side of the body.
Leading edge	The forward edge of the wing, composed of the lesser coverts, the alula, and the edge of the outermost primary; in flight, the surface that first meets the air.
Lesser wing coverts	The short feathers on the shoulder of the wing that are arranged in several irregular rows and cover the base of the median wing coverts.
Local	Of restricted occurrence within a larger, discontinuous range; birds with local distributions are often dependent on some uncommon habitat type.
Lore	The area between the eye and the base of the bill; sometimes distinctively colored.
Lower mandible	The lower of the two parts of a bird's bill.
Malar streak	*See* Mustache.
Mantle	The upper back and occasionally the scapulars and upperwing coverts when these are the same color as the upper back.
Mask	An area of contrasting color on the front of the face and around the eyes.

Maxilla	*See* Upper mandible.
Median	Situated in the middle or on the central axis.
Median crown stripe	A stripe of contrasting color along the center of the crown.
Median wing coverts	The row of short feathers that covers the bases of the greater wing coverts.
Melanistic	Having an excess of black pigment; melanistic birds are usually rare, but certain species have a high percentage of dark-phase individuals. *See* Color morph.
Migrant	A bird in the process of migrating between its breeding area and its winter range.
Migration	A regular, periodic movement between two regions, usually a breeding area and a wintering area.
Mirror	A translucent area on the extended wing of some birds, usually at the base of the primaries; in gulls, small white spots at or near the tips of the dark primaries.
Molt	The periodic loss and replacement of feathers; most species have regular patterns and schedules of molt.
Morph	*See* Color morph.
Morphology	The form and structure of an animal or plant.
Mustache	A colored streak running from the base of the bill back along the side of the throat.
Nape	The back of the head, including the hindneck.
Nares	The external nostrils; usually located near the base of the upper mandible; singular, naris.
Necklace	A band of spots or streaks across the breast or around the neck.
Neck ruff	Feathers of the neck that are enlarged or otherwise modified for display.
Nocturnal	Active during the night.
Outer wing	The part of the wing between the wrist and the tip.
Patagium	A membrane extending from the body to the wrist along the front of the wing, supporting many of the wing coverts.
Pectinate	Having short, narrow projections, like those of a comb.
Pelagic	Of or inhabiting the open ocean.
Permanent resident	A bird that remains in one area throughout the year; nonmigratory.
Phase	*See* Color morph.
Pinnae	*See* Ear tuft.
Plumage	Generally, the feathers worn by a bird at any given time. Specifically, all the feathers grown during a single molt; in this sense, a bird may have elements of more than one plumage at a time.
Plume	An elongated, ornamental feather, often used in displays.
Polyandrous	Mating with more than one male.
Polymorphic	Having two or more distinct types within a population, usually differing in size, form, or color.
Posterior	Toward the tail.
Postocular stripe	A stripe extending back from the eye, above the ear coverts and below the eyebrow.

Preen   To clean and smooth the plumage with the bill.

Primaries   The outermost and longest flight feathers on a bird's wing, forming the wing tip and part of the outer trailing edge; there are usually nine to twelve primaries on each wing, attached to the wing distal to the wrist.

Primary coverts   The small feathers of the wing that overlie the bases of the primaries.

Proximal   Toward the body. *Cf.* Distal.

Race   *See* Subspecies.

Rectrices   The long flight feathers of the tail; singular, rectrix.

Resident   Remaining in one place all year; nonmigratory.

Riparian   Pertaining to the banks of streams, rivers, ponds, lakes, or moist bottomlands.

Rump   The lower back just above the tail; may also include the uppertail coverts.

Scaly   Finely barred; the bars often formed by feather edgings of a different color.

Scapulars   The feathers of the upperparts at the side of the back that cover the area where the wing joins the body.

Secondaries   The large flight feathers of the inner wing, attached to the inner wing proximal to the wrist.

Sexual dimorphism   A difference between the sexes in size, form, or color.

Shaft   The stiff central axis of a feather.

Shoulder   The bend of the wing, or wrist, including the lesser wing coverts.

Side   The lateral part of the breast and belly.

Song   A specific and often complex pattern of notes, usually given only by the male during the breeding season. *Cf.* Call.

Spatulate   Spoon-shaped or shovel-shaped.

Spectacles   A color pattern formed by the lores and eye-rings.

Spishing   A squeaking or swishing noise made by some birders to attract birds into view.

Stray   A migrant found outside of its normal range.

Streaked   Having a pattern of vertical or longitudinal stripes, as opposed to horizontal bars; often formed by feather shafts that contrast with the rest of the feathers.

Subadult   A bird that has not yet acquired adult plumage.

Subspecies   A geographical subdivision of a species differing from other subdivisions in size, form, color, song, or several of these in combination; also called a race.

Subterminal   Before or short of the end or tip.

Summer resident   A bird that remains in an area during the summer but winters elsewhere.

Sympatric   Having overlapping ranges. *Cf.* Allopatric.

Talon   One of the long, sharp, curved claws of a bird of prey.

Tarsus   The lower, usually featherless, part of a bird's leg, often called simply the "leg."

Terminal   At the end or tip.

Territory	An area defended against other members of the same species, and usually containing a nest or food resource or both.
Tertials	The innermost secondaries (usually three), often with a different shape, pattern, and molt schedule from the other secondaries, and sometimes considered distinct from them; also called tertiaries.
Throat	The area of the underparts between the chin and the breast.
Trailing edge	The posterior edge of the extended wing, consisting of the tips of the primaries and secondaries.
Transient	A bird that occurs at a location only during migration between its winter and breeding ranges.
Underparts	The lower surface of the body, including the chin, throat, breast, belly, sides and flanks, and undertail coverts, and sometimes including the underwing surface and the under surface of the tail.
Undertail coverts	The small feathers that lie beneath and cover the bases of the tail feathers; sometimes referred to as the crissum.
Upper mandible	The uppermost of the two parts of a bird's bill; also called the maxilla.
Upperparts	The upper surface of the body, including the crown, nape, back, scapulars, rump, and uppertail coverts, and sometimes including the upperwing surface and the upper surface of the tail.
Uppertail coverts	The small feathers that lie over the bases of the tail feathers.
Vagrant	A bird occurring outside of its normal range, usually during or following migration.
Vane	One of the two broad, thin, flexible portions of a feather, separated by the shaft and composed of a row of barbs that are connected along the shaft; also called a web.
Ventral	Pertaining to the lower surface of the body.
Vermiculated	Marked by fine lines.
Web	The fleshy membrane that unites the toes of some water birds. *See also* Vane.
Window	A translucent area on the wing of certain birds that is visible from below on a bird in flight.
Wing bar	A stripe or bar of contrasting color on the upper surface of the wing, formed by the tips of one of the rows of wing coverts.
Wing lining	A collective term for the coverts of the underwing.
Wing stripe	A conspicuous lengthwise stripe on the upper surface of the extended wing, often formed by the pale bases of the primaries and secondaries.
Winter plumage	The plumage worn by a bird during the nonbreeding season; often duller than the breeding plumage and usually acquired by a complete molt in the fall.
Winter range	The geographic area occupied by a species during the winter or nonbreeding season.
Wrist	The forward-projecting angle or bend of the wing; also called the carpal joint.

The Authors

Davis W. Finch and Paul Lehman each reviewed some or all of the species accounts; Paul Lehman also read and commented on some of the special essays.

Henry T. Armistead,
a Philadelphia librarian, became interested in birds when he was nine years old. He is a regional editor of *American Birds*, book review editor of *Birding*, and compiles the Cape Charles, Virginia, Christmas bird count. His special interests include birds of the Delmarva Peninsula, colonial water birds of the Chesapeake Bay, mist-netting fall land birds, May birding marathons, and collecting books. On his family's farm in Bellevue, Maryland, Armistead has seen 240 species of birds.

Stephen F. Bailey
is on the curatorial staff of the Museum of Vertebrate Zoology at the University of California, Berkeley. An active bird tour leader, photographer, teacher, and consultant, his interests include the identification of such difficult groups as *Empidonax* flycatchers, gulls, hawks, and pelagics. Bailey has been a compiler for central California bird observations since 1978, and directs the Golden Gate Audubon Society's research projects.

Larry R. Ballard
has served as a consultant for a variety of publications, including *Birding* and *American Birds*, on the identification and distribution of western birds. He has also acted as consultant to the Santa Barbara Museum of Natural History, Santa Barbara City College, and the University of California. Currently working as a communications expediter in Santa Barbara, he spends about four hours a day in the field.

Louis R. Bevier
has been actively watching birds in California for 14 years. During the past five years, he has served as a field assistant and consultant for various research projects, environmental impact reports, and publications about birds. Currently, he is an undergraduate in environmental biology at the University of California at Santa Barbara.

Clait E. Braun
is a wildlife research leader for the Colorado Division of Wildlife and a faculty affiliate of the department of fishery and wildlife biology at Colorado State University at Fort Collins. He has 17 years of field experience in western North America with grouse and native columbids. Braun is an officer of the Wilson Ornithological Society and was editor of the *Journal of Wildlife Management* from 1981 to 1983. He is also a member of the American Ornithologists' Union, the Cooper Ornithological Society, and the American Association for the Advancement of Science.

Peter F. Cannell
graduated from Bowdoin College in 1977. After working at the Manomet Bird Observatory, he enrolled in a doctoral program at the American Museum of Natural History and the City University of New York. For his doctorate, he concentrated on the systematics of the "pre-passerines," based on the anatomy of the syrinx. During 1979 and 1980, he served as acting director of Bowdoin's Kent Island ornithological research station in the Bay of Fundy. Cannell's field research has included such topics as molt, migration, seabirds, and the genera *Corvus* and *Empidonax*.

Sadie Coats
received her training at the University of California, Berkeley, and conducted a large part of her graduate research at the American Museum of Natural History in New York City. Her major research interest is the phylogenetic relationship of the Strigiformes. A student of owls for many years, her field work has taken her on frequent trips to the southwestern United States, Mexico, and South America. Coats is a resident of Westchester County, New York, and Orinda, California.

Charles T. Collins
is a professor of biology at California State University in Long Beach, California. His special research interest is the breeding biology and ecology of swifts, which he has studied in many parts of the world, most recently in Venezuela. An elected member of the American Ornithologist's Union, Collins has served as president of the Western Bird Banding Association and as treasurer of the Cooper Ornithological Society.

Thomas H. Davis
is a lifelong resident of New York City. A telephone company technician and amateur ornithologist, he enjoys photographing, sound recording, and writing about birds. Davis's special interests are the field identification and distribution of the birds of New York State and the Neotropics. He has served as president and fellow of the Linnaean Society of New York. He is also an honorary associate of the Cornell University Laboratory of Ornithology, and a licensed bird bander.

Susan Roney Drennan
is author of *Where to Find Birds in New York State* (Syracuse University Press, 1981), as well as *The Birder's Field Notebook* and *The North American Birder's Library Lifelist*. She has written articles for both popular magazines and scientific journals, and is associate editor of *American Birds*, the ornithological field journal of the National Audubon Society. Drennan currently serves as president of the Linnaean Society of New York.

Kim R. Eckert
lives in Duluth, Minnesota, where he has done extensive field work. The author of numerous articles for *The Loon*, *Birding*, and *American Birds*, he has also written *A Birder's Guide to Minnesota*. Eckert has been a regional editor of *American Birds* magazine, and is currently a member of the Minnesota Ornithological Records Committee, and a naturalist of the Hawk Ridge Nature Reserve in Duluth. In addition, he has led bird tours in Minnesota and the Dakotas and taught bird identification classes.

John Farrand, Jr.,
is natural science editor at Chanticleer Press and associate in the department of ornithology at the American Museum of Natural History. Co-author of *The Audubon Society Field Guide to North American Birds (Eastern Region)* and a past president of the Linnaean Society of New York, he has watched birds in most of North America, as well as in Central and South America, Europe, and East Africa. Farrand lives in New York City, and makes natural-history forays into the surrounding countryside.

Davis W. Finch
lives in East Kingston, New Hampshire. Interested in birds since childhood, he has studied them in virtually all parts of North America including the Arctic, as well as in Europe and Central and South America. He is a founder and director of WINGS, Inc., a company that conducts bird-watching tours in many parts of the world.

Eric D. Forsman
is a wildlife biologist with the U.S. Fish and Wildlife Service. He
works for the service's Cooperative Wildlife Research Unit at
Oregon State University. For his master's and doctoral degrees, he
conducted research on the distribution, biology, and habitat of the
Spotted Owl in Oregon.

Philip K. Gaddis
is a native of Berkeley, California, and received his doctoral degree
in ornithology from the University of Florida in 1979. During 1981
and 1982, he held a Frank M. Chapman Memorial Fund Postdoctoral
Fellowship at the American Museum of Natural History in New
York City. He has made extensive field studies of the social systems
and vocalizations of the Tufted, Plain, and Bridled titmice.

Kimball L. Garrett
is currently an ornithologist with the Los Angeles County Museum
of Natural History. He has had extensive field experience
throughout western North America, and has led ornithological tours
in California, Arizona, Texas, and Mexico. In addition, he teaches
regular bird identification workshops for the extension program of
the University of California at Los Angeles. With Jon Dunn, he has
written numerous papers on bird identification for the Los Angeles
Audubon Society newsletter, *The Western Tanager*, as well as *Birds
of Southern California: Status and Distribution.*

Daniel D. Gibson
works at the University of Alaska Museum in Fairbanks, Alaska.
He has studied the status and distribution of Alaska's birds for
almost 20 years. Gibson's particular interests are the Palearctic and
Aleutian components of Alaska's avifauna, their routes of migration,
and their geographic variation.

Helen Hays
is chairman of the Great Gull Island Committee, and is a staff
member of the department of ornithology at the American Museum
of Natural History in New York City. She is currently directing a
long-term study on the reproductive success of Common Terns at
the museum's field station on Great Gull Island at the eastern end of
Long Island Sound.

Kenn Kaufman
spent his teens birding throughout North America and Mexico. Now
living in Tucson, Arizona, he continues to travel extensively as a
leader of birding tours. He has served as editor of *Continental
Birdlife*, and has been a regional editor for *American Birds* and a
field identification consultant for *Birding*.

Wesley E. Lanyon
has been on the staff of the American Museum of Natural History
for 26 years, where he is now Lamont Curator of Birds. He is a
recipient of the Brewster Memorial Award from the American
Ornithologists' Union and has served as president of that society.
He specializes in a museum and field approach to the identification
and specific limits of "problem birds," and his studies of
meadowlarks and tyrant-flycatchers have taken him throughout the
Americas.

Paul Lehman
is a resident of Santa Barbara, California. His major interests are
bird distribution and field identification. He received a master's
degree in physical geography in 1982, and is currently a part-time
instructor of geography and environmental studies. He also teaches
bird classes to adults. Lehman spends most of his time birding.

Dennis J. Martin

received his bachelor's degree from Illinois State University and did graduate research at the University of New Mexico before obtaining his doctorate from Utah State University. His early research concentrated on owl behavior; over the past decade he has studied general behavioral ecology and vocal behavior, focusing primarily on the Fox Sparrow. Martin recently retired as editor of *The Murrelet*. Currently he is an associate professor of biology at Pacific Lutheran University in Takoma, Washington.

Guy McCaskie

is a research associate for the San Diego Natural History Museum, and has been editor for the southern Pacific region of *American Birds* for over 20 years.

Ron Naveen

is editor of *Birding*, the journal of the American Birding Association, and the author of *Storm-Petrels of the World: An Introductory Guide to Their Field Identification*. Through his organization, Whales and Seabirds, he leads tours year-round to the outer continental shelf of the western North Atlantic and to the Galapagos Islands. He also leads Antarctic tour groups and lectures frequently about seabird identification and the conservation of whales, dolphins, and seals.

Wayne R. Petersen,

a resident of Massachusetts, has been an avid ornithologist for more than 25 years. His travels have taken him from Arctic Canada to South America and the West Indies. An active bird bander, Petersen is affiliated with the Manomet Bird Observatory and has worked in James Bay with the Canadian Wildlife Service, and as an Earthwatch investigator in Belize. In addition to his biology classes, he teaches bird identification courses, lectures extensively, and has published many papers on various aspects of ornithology. Petersen has served on the Council of the Northeastern Bird-Banding Association and as president of the Nuttall Ornithological Club.

J. V. Remsen, Jr.,

received his doctorate in zoology from the University of California, Berkeley, in 1978. Since that time, he has been employed at Louisiana State University as an associate professor of zoology and as curator of birds for its Museum of Zoology. Although his primary area of research is Neotropical ornithology, among his more than 40 publications are 9 that address field identification and distribution problems in North American birds.

Lester L. Short

is chairman and curator of the department of ornithology at the American Museum of Natural History in New York City. The author of 160 scientific publications and several books, including *Woodpeckers of the World*, he is also secretary of the A.O.U. committee producing the *Checklist of North American Birds*. Short has conducted field work on piciform birds and studied bird speciation and behavior in 70 countries throughout the world.

Arnold Small

is a professor of biology at Harbor College in Los Angeles, California and a senior extension lecturer at UCLA. For many years he was regional editor for the Southern California section of *American Birds;* he also coauthored the *Annotated Checklist of the Birds of Southern California* and *Birds of the West* and authored the two editions of *The Birds of California*. A former president of the Los Angeles Audubon Society and the American Birding Association, Small has been photographing birds for more than 20

years and has been a field ornithologist since 1942. He has led
natural history tours to many parts of the world, and during his
extensive travels has seen more than 5400 species of birds.

David Stirling
is a natural history specialist for the Parks of British Columbia, and
is interested in the identification, population dynamics, and
worldwide preservation problems of birds. An avid birder, he has
led nature tours and made bird-watching trips to 35 countries.
Recently, he has been involved in field work with the Northwestern
Crow and Crested Myna.

Paul W. Sykes, Jr.,
is a wildlife research biologist with the Patuxent Wildlife Research
Center of the U.S. Fish and Wildlife Service in Maryland. Involved
in various national and state ornithological societies, Sykes is a
regional Christmas count editor for *American Birds* and a member
of the American Birding Association checklist committee. He is also
cooperator on three U.S. Fish and Wildlife Service Cooperative
Breeding Bird Survey routes in Florida, and serves as a technical
and scientific consultant to federal agencies and several conservation
organizations. He has seen 746 species to date in North America
north of Mexico.

Scott B. Terrill
has been birding since he was ten years old. While working on his
bachelor's degree in zoology at Arizona State University, he, along
with others, pioneered systematic vagrant hunting and investigated
the distribution of the birds of Arizona. In addition, he became
involved in ecological research and environmental impact studies
while completing his master's degree in zoology. Currently, Terrill
is enrolled in the doctoral program at the State University of New
York at Albany. His research concerns the behavioral and ecological
factors involved in bird migration. He shares his birding enthusiasm
with his wife, Linda, with whom he has made birding trips as far
south as the Guatemalan border.

Theodore G. Tobish Jr.
was born and raised in eastern Pennsylvania. He has had a lifelong
interest in birds. Since 1973, he has lived in Alaska, where he
received a bachelor's degree in biology from the University of
Alaska. He has spent several field seasons in the Aleutian Islands
and throughout Alaska, working for the U.S. Fish and Wildlife
Service and leading bird tours. Tobish currently lives in Anchorage.

James A. Tucker
is the founder and executive director of the American Birding
Association. He has lectured from coast to coast and has authored
several books and numerous articles on birds. An educational
psychologist by profession, Tucker is president of Educational
Directions Incorporated, a consulting firm that serves school
systems throughout North America.

Peter D. Vickery
is on the staff of the Natural History Tour Services of the
Massachusetts Audubon Society, and has traveled extensively
throughout North America, Mexico, and Costa Rica. For six years,
he was a regional editor of the northeastern Maritime region for
American Birds. Vickery is the author of the *Annotated Checklist
of Maine Birds* and is now conducting further investigations into
Maine's avifauna.

Terence Wahl
is a research associate in biology at Western Washington University
in Bellingham, where he is studying the associations of seabirds with

oceanography in the North Pacific. He has served as a consultant on marine birds in Washington, and has led pelagic bird survey trips. His survey experience includes several research cruises in the Pacific and in the Bering Sea, where he has conducted thousands of seabird censuses by small boat, aircraft, and other means.

Richard Webster,
a lifelong resident of southern California, has been an avid birder since childhood. He has traveled extensively throughout the United States and has visited Mexico, Honduras, Colombia, Venezuela, Ecuador, Australia, and New Zealand on bird-watching and photography trips. A writer by trade, Webster is co-author of *The Birds of Santa Barbara and Ventura Counties, California.*

D. H. S. Wehle
received his master's and doctoral degrees in zoology from the University of Alaska at Fairbanks, where he studied the breeding biology and feeding ecology of Tufted and Horned puffins. While conducting his fieldwork, he also worked for the Bureau of Land Management collecting data on the ecology of Alaska's marine birds. He is currently a visiting professor at Cornell University's Shoals Marine Laboratory.

Claudia Wilds
is a research collaborator in the division of birds at the National Museum of Natural History; she is also the field identification editor of *Birding* magazine. Wilds lives in Washington, D.C., and has recently published a guide to finding birds in and around the nation's capital. Most of her field work during the past decade has been at Chincoteague National Wildlife Refuge on the Virginia coast, where she has made an intensive study of shorebird migration.

The Artists

As art editor, Al Gilbert selected the artists who were called upon to
provide color portraits and black-and-white illustrations. After
assigning the pictures, he supervised their accuracy and production
until completion.

Guy Tudor served as art consultant, making his knowledge of bird
art and photographic sources available to the artists.

James E. Coe

has exhibited his bird paintings at the Leigh Yawkey Woodson Art
Museum in Wausau, Wisconsin, and at the Cleveland Museum of
Natural History in Ohio. His drawings have appeared in *The Living
Bird* and *American Bird* magazines. Coe majored in biology at
Harvard University, and is currently a graduate student in painting
at Parsons School of Design in New York. His field work has been
concentrated in New York and southern New England, with
occasional forays into the Neotropics. Most recently, he completed
illustrations for a guide to the birds of New Guinea.

Michael DiGiorgio

is a freelance artist living in Potsdam, New York. He enjoys field
sketching and painting from life. His illustrations have been
published by the National Wildlife Federation, the New York State
Conservationist, the Cornell Laboratory of Ornithology, the
Massachusetts Audubon Society, and the Nature Conservancy. He
also illustrated the book *A Life Outdoors*.

Al Gilbert

began drawing birds and animals when he was a child. In his teens,
he received advice and guidance from George M. Sutton and Don
Eckelberry, who helped launch his career as a wildlife artist.
Working closely with Dean Amadon of the American Museum of
Natural History in New York City, he has illustrated many books,
among them *Eagles, Hawks and Falcons of the World* and
Currassows and Related Birds. His field work has taken him to
Africa, Madagascar, Mexico, and South America. In 1978, Gilbert
won the Federal Duck Stamp Competition. His paintings have been
exhibited in museums and galleries throughout the United States,
and he is currently president of the Society of Animal Artists.

Robert Gillmor

is a British freelance artist who received his training at the Fine Art
Department of Reading University in England. He is currently
chairman of the Society of Wildlife Artists, which he helped to
found. His illustrations have appeared in 70 books, as well as
numerous journals, and he has exhibited work in the United States,
Kenya, France, and the United Kingdom. Gillmor is art editor of
Birds of the Western Palaearctic, and a vice president of the British
Ornithologists' Union. His travels have taken him to Spitsbergen,
Iceland, the United States, and East Africa.

H. Jon Janosik

attended Oberlin College, where he studied zoology and anatomy.
His ornithological illustrations have appeared in such publications as
the *Encyclopaedia Britannica* and the *Florida Naturalist*. In
addition, he has worked for the National Geographic Society, the
Carnegie Museum in Pittsburgh, and the Saunders Company in
Philadelphia. Janosik's work has been exhibited at numerous
institutions, including the British Museum in London and the Los
Angeles County Museum. His special interests lie in North
American warblers and sea and shore birds.

Michel Kleinbaum

is an amateur illustrator who lives in New York City. His

illustrations have appeared in books on the birds of Venezuela, Colombia, and China. Kleinbaum has traveled to Mexico, Costa Rica, Panama, Guatemala, Venezuela, and Colombia; since 1978, he has helped in organizing bird tours to Senegal.

Lawrence B. McQueen
first became interested in birds in his native town in central Pennsylvania. He received his bachelor's degree in wildlife studies from Idaho State University in 1961, and went on to conduct field work on the birds of Idaho. He later attended art school at the University of Oregon, Eugene, where he now lives and specializes in ornithological paintings. His work has been exhibited at the Smithsonian Institution, and in England and Scotland. Currently he is doing field work in Peru.

John P. O'Neill
is a professional ornithologist and artist with a special interest in Neotropical birds. He served as the director of the Louisiana State University Museum of Natural Science from 1978 to 1982, and is currently acting as the university's coordinator of field studies. O'Neill lives in Baton Rouge, Louisiana, where he continues to research and paint birds.

Paul Singer
is a graphic designer who lives in Brooklyn. A graduate of the Philadelphia College of Art, he has designed exhibits for the Bronx Zoo, the New York Aquarium, the Franklin Park Zoo, the American Numismatic Society, and the Little League Baseball Museum. His work appears in more than 30 books, including the *Audubon Society Encyclopedia of North American Birds*.

Guy Tudor
is a resident of Forest Hills, New York, and has been a freelance wildlife illustrator for 25 years. With extensive field experience in 11 Neotropical countries, he has contributed illustrations to guides on the birds of Venezuela and Colombia. He is currently co-authoring a *Field Guide to South American Birds: Passerines*. His work has appeared in a variety of publications and has been exhibited at the Chicago Field Museum and the National Collection of Fine Arts. Tudor has co-authored articles for *American Birds*, *Birding*, and the *Wilson Bulletin*, and currently serves as a trustee of R.A.R.E., Inc., and as an elective member of the American Ornithologists' Union and the American Birding Association.

John C. Yrizarry
is a lifelong resident of Brooklyn, New York. He is a graduate of the Yale School of Fine Arts and a member of the Society of Animal Artists. His work appears in private collections and has been published in numerous books and magazines, including many nature guides. Yrizarry is an enthusiastic leader of birding tours in the United States, Central America, and the Caribbean.

Dale A. Zimmerman
teaches ornithology at Western New Mexico University in Silver City and serves as an elective member of the American Ornithologists' Union and as a fellow of the Explorers' Club. He travels frequently to his favorite African haunts, and has made birding visits to tropical Asia, Australasia, and the Neotropics. A former student of the late George M. Sutton, Zimmerman is chief artist and co-author of a forthcoming field guide to New Guinea birds. He is currently illustrating Ben King's comprehensive handbook to the birds of the Indian region.

Credits

Photo Credits
The letter immediately following each page number refers to the
position of the color photographs on the page; A represents the
picture at the top, B, the middle, and C, the bottom.

Alabama Ornithological Society: Charles W. Brasfield, 255C.
Ardea London: Jack A. Bailey, 47A.
Ron Austing: 169A, 205A, 355C.
Stephen F. Bailey: 99B, 101A, 105C, 139A, 177B, 261A, 265C, 267A,
267B, 267C, 285B, 341C.
William J. Bolte: 283A.
Fred Bruemmer: 41B, 83C.
P. A. and F. G. Buckley: 81B, 107C, 177C.
G. Vernon Byrd: 129B.
S. R. Cannings: 307B.
Ken Carmichael: 229B, 245A.
Robert P. Carr: 185A.
Herbert Clarke: 41A, 49C, 57A, 59B, 71C, 73B, 93C, 115C, 131C, 137B,
139C, 143C, 213C, 235A, 235B, 239B, 255B, 269A, 281B, 305C, 311B,
333B, 335B.
Bruce Coleman, Inc.: Fred J. Alsop, III, 171C; Bob and Clara
Calhoun, 351A.
Cornell Laboratory of Ornithology: J. H. Dick, 241B; Michael
Hopiak, 151B; William A. Paff, 289C; O. S. Pettingill, Jr., 253A; Gary
Shackelford, 257C, 307C, 331C; Perry D. Slocum, 187B; John Trott,
233C; Y. R. Tymbtra, 303A; K. Worden, 111B.
Kent and Donna Dannen: 211B, 311A, 339B, 347B.
Harry N. Darrow: 63C, 67A, 91A, 109C, 143A, 147C, 281C.
Thomas H. Davis: 47B, 75B, 83B, 85A, 95A, 301B.
R. H. Day: 67B, 73A, 129A.
Jack Dermid: 85C, 249A.
Larry R. Ditto: 155C, 175C, 285A, 289B, 323B.
Georges Dremeaux: 301A, 301C.
DRK Photo: Stephen J. Krasemann, 43C, 77C, 111A, 127B, 225A,
329A, 337C.
Lucy Duncan: 351B.
Harry Engels: 45C, 231C, 233A.
David L. Evans: 141B.
Kenneth W. Fink: 49A, 51C, 59C, 67C, 69A, 73C, 89C, 95B, 125C, 129C,
135B, 143B, 145B, 221C, 225B, 247B, 315C.
Jeff Foott: 87C, 305A, 317A, 317B, 357B.
Tom French: 113C.
John Gerlach: 171A.
Albert Ghiorso: 263B, 263C, 265B, 269B.
D. A. Gill: 63A, 81C.
James M. Greaves: 275C, 283B.
Joseph A. Grzybowski: 99A, 347C.
Velma Harris: 195C, 201A, 201B, 207B, 329C.
David F. Hatler: 119A, 123C.
Dale R. Herter: 95C.
F. Eugene Hester: 219A.
Sibley Higginbotham: 291C.
David Hunter: 351C.
Warren Jacobi: 107A, 163B.
Gord James: 245B.
Joseph R. Jehl, Jr.: 41C, 69B.
Isidor Jeklin: 175A, 189B.
Steven C. Kaufman: 37C.
G. C. Kelley: 133A, 153B, 167A, 225C, 227A, 273C, 287B, 287C, 313B,
313C, 331A.

Helen Kittinger: 137c, 339c.
E. F. Knights: 49b, 61c, 277c.
Dwight R. Kuhn: 135a.
Wayne Lankinen: 179a, 205b, 229a, 311c, 317c, 337b.
Tom and Pat Leeson: 229c.
Paul Lehman: 45b.
Linnea Associates: Bud Lehnhausen, 117b; Sue Quinlan, 117c.
Thomas W. Martin: 223b, 261c, 339a.
Virginia Mayfield: 227c.
Joe McDonald: 157c, 169c.
Anthony Mercieca: 55b, 107b, 141c, 187a, 195b, 201c, 203a, 205c, 207a, 221b, 223c, 231a, 241c, 247a, 275a, 285c, 303b, 305b, 315a, 327b, 345c.
Minnesota Ornithologists' Union: Marjorie M. Carr, 257b.
C. Allan Morgan: 209a.
National Audubon Society Collection/Photo Researchers, Inc.: Ron Austing, 157b; Tom Bledsoe, 357c; John Bova, 93b; W. V. Crich, 355a; John S. Dunning, 149c, 219b; Bill Dyer, 257a; Robert J. Erwin, 103b; Robert W. Hernandez, 63b; Russ Kinne, 91c, 153c, 349b; Stephen J. Krasemann, 323c; Tom and Pat Leeson, 297b; Thomas W. Martin, 151c; Tom McHugh, 131a; Anthony Mercieca, 165a, 347a; Leonard Lee Rue, III, 321c; Delbert Rust, 193a; Gregory K. Scott, 173a; Dan Sudia, 341b.
Naturfotograferna Bildbyra: Janos Jurka, 295c.
Blair Nikula: 83a.
J. Oldenettel: 111c, 181b.
Arthur Panzer: 175b, 179b, 203b, 273b.
Dennis R. Paulson: 39b, 61a, 147b, 155b, 319a, 343c.
Jan Erik Pierson: 79b, 97c, 153a.
Rod Planck: 179c, 237b, 259b.
Peter W. Post: 75c, 93a.
H. Douglas Pratt: 183c.
John T. Ratti: 245c, 303c.
C. Gable Ray: 299b, 299c.
J. V. Remsen, Jr. : 37a.
Laura Riley: 105a, 223a, 227b, 279c, 313a.
Don Roberson: 123a.
Root Resources: Ruth A. Cordner, 213a; Anthony Mercieca, 211a.
David G. Roseneau: 119b.
Leonard Lee Rue, III: 237a, 237c, 319b.
John Shaw: 321b, 325b.
Ervio Sian: 51b, 75a, 177a, 191b, 243b, 243c, 263a, 309b, 309c, 319c, 349a.
Perry D. Slocum: 199c, 211c.
Arnold Small: 43b, 51a, 53a, 53b, 53c, 55a, 57b, 59a, 61b, 79a, 97a, 109b, 123b, 145c, 169b, 181c, 209b, 209c, 243a, 265a, 269c, 289a, 345b.
Bruce A. Sorrie: 55c, 165c, 215b, 287a, 315b, 343b.
Barbara Spencer: 43a.
Alvin E. Staffan: 161a, 161b, 239a, 259c, 325c, 331b, 349c.
Lynn M. Stone: 77b.
Ian C. Tait: 183b, 217c, 329b, 353b.
Scott B. Terrill: 183a.
Frank S. Todd/Sea World, Inc.: 113b, 127a, 247c.
John Trott: 91b.
Rob Tucher: 199b, 291b.
R. Van Nostrand: 87b.
Peter D. Vickery: 173b.
VIREO (Academy of Natural Sciences of Philadelphia): P. Alden, 99c; Helen Cruickshank, 147a, 239c, 241a, 277b.
Terence Wahl: 79c, 81a.
Richard E. Webster: 57c, 71a, 71b, 85b, 89b, 121a, 159b.

Wardene Weisser: 87A, 213B, 271C.
Larry West: 353A.
Jack Wilburn: 39A, 69C, 89A, 163A, 167C, 207C, 215C, 235C, 353C.
Ron Willocks: 155A.
Bill Wilson: 37B.
Art Wolfe: 171B.
Michael Wotton: 39C.
Gary R. Zahm: 145A, 297A.
C. Fred Zeillemaker: 97B, 101B, 105B, 117A, 261B.
Dale and Marian Zimmerman: 161C, 253B.

Black-and-white Drawings

The letter immediately following each page number refers to the position of an illustration: A indicates the drawing at the top of a page, B, the second drawing, C, the third, and so forth.

James E. Coe: 42A, 42B, 42C, 56A, 58B, 58C, 86A, 86B, 90B, 92B, 96D, 96E, 98A, 102A, 102B, 102C, 110A, 112A, 150B, 150C, 152A, 236A, 236B, 242A, 318A.

Michael DiGiorgio: 140A, 142A, 144A, 146A, 204A, 206A, 206B, 208A, 208B, 210A, 212B, 296A, 298B, 300A, 300B, 302A, 302B, 304A, 306A, 306B, 316A.

Al Gilbert: 108B, 148B, 190B, 192A, 248A, 248B, 248C.

Robert Gillmor: 46A, 46B, 46C, 46D, 48A, 48B, 48C, 48D, 54A, 66A, 66B, 72B, 80A, 90A.

Lawrence B. McQueen: 114A, 114B, 116A, 116B, 120A, 120B, 122A, 186A, 188A.

Paul Singer: 34A, 108A, 136A, 148A, 150A, 156A, 158A, 180A, 190A, 194A, 214A, 216A, 220A, 250A, 294A, 298A, 308A, 324A, 332A, 334A, 336A, 340A, 342A, 344A, 356A.

John C. Yrizarry: 44A, 44B, 44C, 48E, 50A, 50B, 50C, 58A, 62A, 66C, 70A, 72A, 82A, 84A, 92A, 92C, 94A, 96A, 96B, 96C.

Dale A. Zimmerman: 148C, 160A, 162A, 200A, 200B, 202A, 212A, 212B, 262A, 262B, 264A, 264B, 266A, 266B, 268A, 268B, 290A.

Color Portraits

The letter following each page number refers to the position of the color portrait: A represents the portrait at the top of a page, B, the middle, and C, the bottom.

James E. Coe: 101C, 103A, 115A, 115B, 197B, 231B, 233B, 283C, 291A.

Al Gilbert: 193C, 197A, 217B, 249B, 249C, 323A.

Robert Gillmor: 47C, 65A, 65B, 65C, 77A, 113A, 133B, 133C.

H. Jon Janosik: 131B, 295B.

Michel Kleinbaum: 193B.

Lawrence B. McQueen: 45A, 103C, 119C, 121B, 121C, 125A, 125B, 127C, 135C, 185B, 185C, 187C, 189A, 189C, 255A, 307A, 355B.

John P. O'Neill: 139B, 141A, 327A, 327C, 333C, 335C.

John C. Yrizarry: 273A.

Dale A. Zimmerman: 149B, 159C, 167B, 197C, 199A, 203C, 251C, 253C, 259A, 271A, 271B, 275B, 277A, 279A, 279B, 281A, 293A, 293B, 321A.

Index

In this index, the names of orders are preceded by red dots; family names are preceded by blue dots.